Servants of the State

Servants of the State

MANAGING DIVERSITY
& DEMOCRACY IN THE
FEDERAL WORKFORCE,
1933–1953

Margaret C. Rung

The University of Georgia Press

ATHENS & LONDON

© 2002 by the University of Georgia Press

Athens, Georgia 30602

All rights reserved

Designed by Kathi Dailey Morgan

Set in 10 on 13 Electra with Syntax by Bookcomp, Inc.

Printed and bound by Thomson-Shore

The paper in this book meets the guidelines for

permanence and durability of the Committee on

Production Guidelines for Book Longevity of the

Council on Library Resources.

PRINTED IN THE UNITED STATES OF AMERICA

06 05 04 03 02 C 5 4 3 2 1

LIBRARY OF CONGRESS CATALOGING-IN-PUBLICATION DATA

Rung, Margaret C., 1963–

   Servants of the state : managing diversity and democracy

in the federal workforce, 1933–1953 / Margaret C. Rung.

      p. cm.

   Includes bibliographical references and index.

      ISBN 0-8203-2362-4 (hardcover : alk. paper)

   1. Civil service—United States—Personnel management.

2. Civil service reform—United States.   3. African Americans

in the civil service.   4. Women in the civil service—United

States.   5. United States—Politics and government—1933–

1953.   I. Title.

   JK765 .R86 2002

   352.6'0973—dc21   2001008552

BRITISH LIBRARY CATALOGING-IN-PUBLICATION DATA AVAILABLE

For

Elizabeth Coyne Rung

and

Donald Charles Rung Jr.

CONTENTS

A Note on Terminology *ix*

Acknowledgments *xiii*

Introduction *1*

1 Scientific Administration of the Civil Service

Prior to the New Deal *23*

2 Building the New Deal Civil Service *49*

3 Managing Human Relations in the Wartime

and Cold War Civil Service *76*

4 Unions and Federal Labor Policy *105*

5 Gender and the Civil Service *137*

6 Race and Merit *157*

Conclusion *184*

Notes *199*

Bibliography *245*

Index *257*

A NOTE ON TERMINOLOGY

Civil service remains an ill-defined term in the United States. Under the Pendleton Civil Service Act of 1883, the government created a category of jobs in which applicants had to take an exam as part of the application process. Not all jobs were placed in this category, and although Congress occasionally legislated on the issue, the president generally decided which positions would operate under the exam system. These jobs became part of the "classified" service while all other positions were categorized as "unclassified." Among unclassified workers were those paid by wage boards. Unlike for classified workers, whose salaries were set by a congressionally determined general pay schedule, these boards paid employees under a prevailing rate system whereby local wage rates for similar occupations were used to determine government workers' pay. The boards were often in effect for manual laborers, such as those at the Tennessee Valley Authority and navy shipyards. Finally, civil service rules at times differed for federal employees in the Washington, D.C., region, who were considered part of the "departmental service," as opposed to those employed outside the region, who constituted the "field service." In this study, I consider both classified and unclassified workers and both departmental and field employees to be part of the civil service.

Also, I have followed the practice of government officials, government publications, and other scholars in using the terms *agency* and *department* interchangeably.

Today, generally, five types of agencies comprise the federal government's executive branch: cabinet-level departments; independent regulatory commissions and boards; government corporations; entities of the executive office of the president; and other miscellaneous independent agencies. Cabinet-level departments, such as Treasury, Justice, State, Labor, and Agriculture, are the best known of executive branch agencies and are headed by secretaries appointed by the president with the advice and consent of the Senate. In the 1930s, people often referred to departments such as Justice, State, and the Post Office as "old-line agencies" due to their establishment in the earliest years of the republic. Moreover, at that time, people even referred to departments formed in the mid–nineteenth century, such as Interior and Agriculture, as old-line, to distinguish them from the slew of New Deal agencies created during Franklin Roosevelt's first two terms as president.

Indeed, the New Deal era witnessed a proliferation of independent regulatory boards and commissions, including the National Labor Relations Board and the Securities and Exchange Commission. These organizations, devoted to the regulation of various private-sector activities and industries, are often run by multiple people sitting on a board or commission rather than by a single secretary, as is the case with cabinet-level departments. In most instances, the president selects the members of the commission or board, again with Senate approval, although these members often serve for terms that extend beyond the tenure of the appointing president. In an effort to enhance the objectivity of these agencies, Congress generally removes itself from strict oversight of their activities, giving these agencies a measure of independence from political control. At times, however, efforts to expand the discretion of the agencies only further politicized them. During the 1930s, for instance, Congress exempted many of the New Deal independent boards and commissions from hiring employees through civil service exam registers, allowing for a greater degree of patronage hiring.

Government corporations, such as the Tennessee Valley Authority and the Federal Deposit Insurance Corporation, are run either by boards or by single directors but are often organized and operated much like private-sector corporations. Each one has a congressionally issued charter, giving these bodies more discretionary authority than an independent regulatory board. Many, for instance, have the ability to purchase, sell, and hold property in their own name rather than in the name of the federal government.

In 1939, President Roosevelt created an Executive Office of the President as a means of establishing a sub-branch of personal advisors and agencies. The president housed the Bureau of the Budget (now the Office of Management and Budget) in the executive office, and over time, the Council of Economic Advisors and the National Security Council, among other entities, have been added to the office.

Of course, the executive branch also consists of a number of miscellaneous agencies, such as the Civil Service Commission (now the Office of Personnel Management), that do not fit into any of these categories. During World War II, for example, President Roosevelt created a number of independent emergency war agencies, such as the Office of Price Administration and the

War Production Board, under authority accorded him by Congress. Many emergency war agencies were under war service regulations, which gave them greater latitude in hiring.

Constituency-oriented executive departments such as Interior, Agriculture, Commerce, and Labor began to appear in the mid–nineteenth century. The Interstate Commerce Commission, created in 1887 to administer the Interstate Commerce Act, became the first of many independent regulatory agencies.

ACKNOWLEDGMENTS

Over the years, pieces of this book have landed on the desks of friends, colleagues, mentors, and strangers. Each person who read and commented on it improved it, and I am indebted to all of them for their wisdom and encouragement. Of course, I accept full responsibility for any errors that may have crept in.

Richard Hewlett and Louis Galambos provided mentoring and sage advice at critical points in my career. Indeed, Louis Galambos shepherded me, and this book, through graduate school and beyond. Graduate school peers Christine Adams, Kathryn Fuller-Seeley, and Jonathan Zimmerman critiqued my work, but not me, and my housemates Colleen Ottoson and Jane McGough stepped in to proofread, inserting some much-needed humor into the process of dissertation writing. Excellent research, typing, and editing assistance from Julianne Rowen, Wendy Maier, and my sister, Anne Rung, helped me revise the dissertation into a book.

Research for this book took me all over the country, and I am grateful to the many dedicated archivists who helped me fish out dusty boxes. The staff at the National Archives and Records Administration, where I conducted the bulk of my work, deserve special recognition for their assistance; they represent the best of the American civil service. Travel grants from the Franklin and Eleanor Roosevelt Institute, Harry S. Truman Presidential Library, and Roosevelt University enabled me to complete necessary research for the project.

Colleagues at Mount Allison and Roosevelt universities graciously read numerous drafts of the manuscript, offering incisive commentary and much-needed moral support. A special thanks to David Torrance and Lynn Weiner for their comments and to Susan Weininger for creating an academic environment conducive to professional success. Lynn's contribution to this book stems not only from her keen historical insight but from her bottomless reservoir of faith in the merits of this work.

In the last stages of the process, my enthusiastic editor Alison Waldenberg demonstrated enormous patience, working with me electronically during my residence in Latvia. I thank her for making the book presentable and available to an audience beyond those people mentioned here.

Finally, I would like to acknowledge my family. My brothers and sisters have always supported me no matter what I do. The selflessness and democratic spirit of my Mom and Dad, to whom this book is dedicated, inspired my interest in the public service. They saw this project through from start to finish, never doubting me or my abilities. And for the last nine years, Andy Virkus has stood by me as well. His imprint is all over this book; to him, I offer a loving *paldies* (thank-you in Latvian) for sharing his intelligence, wisdom, and warmth with me.

Portions of chapter 2 appeared previously in a slightly different form in Margaret C. Rung, *American Review of Public Administration* 27, no. 4, pp. 307–23, copyright © Sage Publications, Inc. Reprinted by permission of Sage Publications.

Portions of the book have also appeared previously in *FDR and the Modern Presidency: Leadership and Legacy*, edited by Mark J. Rozell and William D. Pederson, copyright © 1997 by Praeger. Reproduced with permission of Greenwood Publishing Group, Inc., Westport, Conn.

Portions of the introduction and chapters 3 and 5 appeared previously in slightly different form in Margaret C. Rung, "Paternalism and Pink Collars: Gender and Federal Employee Relations, 1941–50," *Business History Review* 71 (autumn 1997), copyright © 1997 by the President and Fellows of Harvard College; all rights reserved. Excerpted by permission of *Business History Review*.

Servants of the State

Introduction

In 1938 personnel director Warner W. Stockberger retired from the Department of Agriculture after thirty-five years of service. During his tenure, Stockberger presided over the establishment of the government's first formal personnel office in 1925 and led the effort to systematize the civil service. He brought a professional perspective to his management duties, encouraging colleagues to develop an empirical, "scientific" approach to administrative tasks such as position classification, employee selection, and efficiency ratings. "The opportunity for a scientific approach," he asserted, "to [personnel] problems is no less in personnel work than in the physical and biological sciences." He later expanded his scientific methods to include studies of human nature, which he claimed would help supervisors understand the productivity problems of their subordinates. To promote worker morale, he orchestrated the creation of numerous employee services, including recreational leagues, housing assistance, and credit unions. Reviewing his accomplishments in 1935, Stockberger observed that these efforts "exerted a very wholesome influence upon the morale of employees" and infused the agency with a "more democratic spirit." It also, he added, made the Agriculture Department a "pleasanter place in which to live and work."[1] His position and long tenure put him in a unique position to witness, as well as shape, the process through which the civil service became more self-conscious about its "democratic" mission and its need to address the concerns of a diverse workforce. Particularly during World War II, the federal government led the way in providing new employment opportunities for women and African Americans.

In the 1930s and 1940s, civil service employment patterns both mirrored and fostered a national agenda aimed at promoting social justice. This period of intense economic and political crisis, at home and abroad, encouraged reform-oriented civil servants and elected officials to construct a national civic creed that addressed discrimination in a pluralistic society. As civil servants, elected officials and public administrators reoriented personnel practices to fit new liberal ideals. They rejected overt scientific racism; revisited their aversion to unionization and the hiring and promoting of women; and sought to elevate the prestige of civil service jobs. In this manner, they opened up a dialogue about diversity that included a discussion concerning merit: who, asked federal officials, was deserving of federal employment, who was not, and why? Others wondered about the role of federal agencies in pursuing workplace equity within the civil service. Soon after Franklin D. Roosevelt was elected president, for instance, members of the Colored National Democratic League wrote to him, asking him to investigate the dearth of promotions for African Americans in the Treasury Department. Although not fully committed to civil rights, Roosevelt responded to some of these entreaties, as he did when he asked his son to make inquiries into the proportion of blacks hired in the Government Printing Office (GPO), because he wanted to be certain that their numbers had not declined from previous years.[2] Politicians and administrators expressed similar concerns about women, and by the early 1940s, this focus on social justice combined with increasing prosperity enabled women to climb civil service ladders. Early in 1941, the progressive United Federal Workers of America (UFWA) within the Congress of Industrial Organizations (CIO) applauded the first four women to be promoted to accountants in the Federal Housing Administration. Two years later, with the war in full swing, personnel specialists argued that women could easily be retrained to take higher-paying jobs traditionally held by men, including those of typewriter repair person, map maker, and junior engineer. The Department of Agriculture's personnel director claimed that "despite conventional prejudices [concerning the employment and training of women], adequately trained women are well qualified to handle the duties of many lines of work."[3] The dialogue on diversity, combined with unionization and economic pressures associated with the war, translated into new employment opportunities for women and African Americans in the 1940s.

At the same time, however, many government officials also continued to discriminate against women and African Americans. While this oppression reflected prevailing attitudes regarding the inferiority of these groups, it also reinforced discrimination in the larger society. Because the government was a national employer, its personnel activities affected small towns and big cities throughout the country, and its policies lent symbolic legitimation to racism and sexism. In some instances, the government's personnel policies were copied by large corporations, and during the Second World War, the federal government devised personnel standards for contracting firms. Consequently, federal labor practices had relevance outside the walls of government offices. Despite declining unemployment rates in 1941, one young woman learned that although she scored well on her civil service examination, the office to which she applied hired men only. In 1939, government administrators put out a call for male stenographers, whom they needed for posts abroad because women were not "tough enough" to cope with "harsh climates." Climatic concerns may explain statistics from 1942, which revealed that 849 men and 7 women served as foreign service officers.[4] Hence problems with labor segmentation and discrimination remained through the 1930s, 1940s, and 1950s, reconfiguring themselves within new intellectual and structural contexts. This study of governmental labor relations explains how and why a new acknowledgment and discussion of workplace diversity, while instilling a "democratic spirit," failed to install a democratic structure within the federal service.

In this book I examine federal labor relations policies, practices, and ideology from the perspective of managers. Their ideas and behavior, as revealed in oral histories, correspondence, personnel manuals, professional journal articles, meeting minutes, and newspaper articles, shaped the hiring, firing, and evaluation process in the federal government. Through their activities, we see how they structured working life and opportunities for ordinary workers, particularly women and African Americans, in this era of rapid state expansion. We see how, during the 1930s and 1940s, elected officials, government administrators, and federal employees built the foundations of the modern American bureaucracy. Growing employee unionization and a heightened attention to administrative management make this period critical in the history of federal labor relations.

A study of managerial policies and practices illuminates both the flaws in the reform agenda and the obstacles faced by those advocating change. While administrative reformers confronted racial and sexual discrimination, they often perceived racial and gender distinctions within a social scientific framework that reified these categories. By the late 1930s, public-sector management discourse, including its rhetoric and practices, was tightly bound to psychology and sociology. Although this was a potentially liberating connection, it also served to reinforce a sex- and race-based division of labor. Meanwhile, the imposition of a rather rigid, ostensibly merit-based hierarchy encouraged individual advancement but did not resolve institutional racism or sexism. And finally, in the postwar era when radical unions lost power in the wake of anticommunist purges, fewer and fewer reformers tied civil rights issues to class inequities, making it difficult to diagnose and cure the economic consequences of discrimination. At midcentury, the majority of women and African Americans in the service still found themselves concentrated in the lowest-paying, lowest prestige positions.

The wide-ranging influence of the twentieth-century public-sector workforce on American society makes the study of this institution vital to understanding the experience of millions of employees who labor in large bureaucracies. Between 1871 and 1961, civilian employment in the federal government rose from 51,020 to 2,435,804.[5] Even at the turn of the century, in the age of giant corporate entities, a new cadre of public administrators like Stockberger recognized that the federal government was one of the largest employers in the country.

An examination of public-sector employment, furthermore, illuminates key differences from the private sector. On the one hand, the federal government's own labor relations policies in the 1930s and 1940s appeared decidedly less progressive than those constructed for the private sector. Although the federal government began its historic support of private-sector unions with the passage of the National Labor Relations Act in 1935, it did not have a parallel law offering bargaining rights to federal civil servants. On the other hand, New Deal liberalism and World War II established the government's rhetorical commitment to workplace equity. More so than the private sector, the federal government publicly addressed the question of diversity in the workforce. Significantly, the Fair Employment Practices Committee (FEPC), which began to investigate employment discrimination in 1941, had jurisdiction over federal agencies as well as government contractors. Even today, the federal government remains both a conservative and enlightened employer: it still does not recognize the collective bargaining rights of its employees, but it has been more aggressive than many private firms in hiring and promoting women and minorities.

Most Americans have a fairly negative image of this public-sector employment engine. Some perceive the bureaucracy as antithetical to American traditions of democratic individualism; critics see it as bloated and inefficient as well as full of red tape and faceless bureaucrats. The 1995 bombing of Oklahoma City's federal building reveals the extreme and tragic consequences of such beliefs. Yet, historically, federal workers have often struggled to maintain individualism in the form of a meritocracy, even as they organized to promote collective concerns. The clash between individualism, in the form of workplace evaluation, and collective rights shaped the management of diversity in the federal civil service.

Other Americans complain about federal employees who frequently "go postal." One expert, commenting on the rash of violence during the 1980s and 1990s at the post office, remarked that public employees "are low down on the totem pole when it comes to prestige. We make them the butt of our jokes. They're a caricature on TV shows like *Cheers*."[6] As employee violence suggests, we need a better understanding of working life in government agencies. Just as Stockberger tried to boost morale by establishing recreation leagues, postal service officials in 1991 tried to alleviate stress by creating a hot line for worker complaints and conducting a survey of workers' "hopes, fears and views on job fulfillment."[7] But like Stockberger, they did not address what union leaders charged was the real cause of worker problems: a rigidly structured hierarchy and increasing automation. A former postmaster general regretted that he was unable to alter the service's corporate culture, in which supervisors felt that "I ate dirt for 20 years, now it's your turn to eat dirt."[8] An analysis of the historical development of institutional culture within the federal bureaucracy as a whole demonstrates the crucial interplay between political crises, labor force demographics, ideology, and institutional relationships in creating divergent perceptions of workplace problems and their solutions.

Stockberger's views contributed to an emerging managerial ethos that sought not only to balance the often competing desires for efficient and democratic government but also to define the relationship between gender or race and federal employment. At the end of his career in the 1930s, a faith in pluralism and merit appeared to be key to that relationship. On the one hand, pluralism seemed to conflict with President Franklin D. Roosevelt's desire to expand national authority at the expense of local power and loyalties. Through arts projects, economic recovery efforts, and relief programs, New Deal politicians and public administrators strove to create a national culture and symbols that would transcend parochial identities and concerns. But, paradoxically, the administration also recognized the existence of diverse subcultures within the United States and sought to provide disempowered groups, such as farmers and industrial workers, access to governmental resources. Party realignment and the formation of the New Deal coalition within the Democratic Party graphically illustrated the success of this campaign to align national institutions with the needs of a more diverse society.

In order to reconcile their aspiration for a cohesive and homogeneous national identity with the promotion of pluralism, New Deal liberals such as Eleanor Roosevelt, Rexford Tugwell, Harold Ickes, Clark Foreman, and Robert Weaver, among others, emphasized inclusion through the creation of common political and class values that would mute the divisive cultural conflicts of the 1920s.[9] By the 1940s, their liberalism became more focused on rights, which included a faith in merit, as they strove to heighten awareness of the discrimination faced by different groups. A wartime federal personnel report, for example, listed the "appearance" of "partiality or discrimination" as a significant cause of employee "unrest."[10] To address discrimination and to calm unrest, government reformers encouraged an assimilation of subcultures under the rubric of a common civic creed centered upon a commitment to governmental activism, democratic participation, and individual merit. Any individual with ability, they maintained, had the right to pursue "happiness" in American society.

In the 1930s and 1940s the notion that everyone, regardless of sex and/or race, had the right to compete for a federal job was neither fully accepted nor historically supported. Through much of the nineteenth and twentieth centuries, Americans and Europeans referred to "meritorious" individuals as those who deserved some kind of reward for their talents. Because the word *meritocracy* to describe a system of rule by those with talent and ability was not coined until 1958 in an essay by British author Michael Young, Americans in the 1930s and 1940s referred to a "merit system" within the civil service. As we shall see, government officials often disagreed on the talents constituting merit.[11] Hence, while the term *merit* has always suggested worth, especially when applied to employment or education, it does not convey a fixed idea of the characteristics defining worth. The perception of who constituted a meritorious individual and how to assess his or her merit changed over time. Consequently, the definition of merit has to be evaluated in both a temporal and cultural context, and the mechanisms for evaluating merit should be scrutinized and understood historically. Merit's ingredients shifted significantly across time and place.

In the nineteenth century and the twentieth, a merit system with reference to government was, and is, contrasted to a highly personal, exceedingly arbitrary system of evaluation, such as patronage. Late-nineteenth-century American reformers constantly stressed this distinction, calling for a civil service system that used impersonal, objective criteria to hire people. Many of these reformers associated patronage with monarchical rather than democratic principles of government, which they argued supported a merit system. Yet, as Jay M. Smith observes in his study of merit among the French nobility in the seventeenth and eighteenth centuries, the term *merit* also had wide currency among the aristocracy prior to the Enlightenment. Nobles eager to serve the king sought to demonstrate their worth through displays of liberality or magnanimity, honor, and bravery and by pointing to those qualities among their ancestors. To a certain extent, they also attached worth to a form of education, arguing that their aristocratic upbringing made them more astute, moral, and selfless than those who were raised among the lower classes.[12] Critically, of course, in dispensing public offices and favor, the king had the ultimate responsibility for assessing merit, and as Smith points out, he did so "through personal and subjective judgments, not through abstract standards." But at the end of the seventeenth century, the crown began to introduce a more impersonal means of assessing worth and concomitantly a more utilitarian notion of merit. With the introduction of training schools, the monarchy paid more attention to performance, as reflected in an increasing tendency to count "services performed, battles attended, [and] wounds suffered" among those interested in military careers. For Smith, a new understanding of merit based upon universal standards of assessment, tied to talent rather than birth, arose not out of the Enlightenment but out of a late-seventeenth-century absolute monarchy struggling to expand its authority.[13]

For most of Europe and in North America, however, support for a systematic means of evaluating merit for government service grew out of Enlightenment ideals that encouraged a belief in individual rights. As one scholar noted, while an adherence to the ideals of liberty, equality, and fraternity encouraged the French to devise an educational system accessible to those outside the old aristocracy, each individual nevertheless had to pursue his or her potential through specialized, professional training controlled by the state. The French government, for instance, established a system of specialized *grandes écoles*, designed to train individuals for service to the state. Admission to one of these schools of higher education required passing a competitive exam, the *concours*, consisting of an oral and a written component. Individual performance on the exam was ranked and used to determine one's eligibility for further education. Entrance into government service consequently required passing the concours and successfully completing schooling at one of the state-run grandes écoles. The state therefore sought to establish greater equality among citizens by instituting a distinctly hierarchical educational structure.[14] While government employment was theoretically opened up to all social classes, thus advancing the ideal of equality, the new educational system itself created new forms of systematized inequality.

The relationship between Great Britain's administrative state and its educational system was less formal, although typically the highest public servants possessed either Cambridge or Oxford University pedigrees. The British government began experimenting with noncompetitive exams (a small number of nominees were allowed to take the exam or incumbents took an exam of competence) in the Indian Civil Service and other departments between 1833 and 1870. In 1870, the British government adopted a formal competitive exam system for bureaucratic posts.[15] The Americans followed in 1883 with the Pendleton Civil Service Act, which required exams for some civil service jobs.[16]

But the implementation of exams did not in itself mean that the system of selection was more open and democratic or more completely impersonal than a system that privileged birth. First of all, in countries in which government service was closely tied to the education system, the training of civil servants focused on a knowledge of classical subjects. British civil service exams, which included questions on Latin and Greek, emphasized general rather than specialized knowledge. School curricula likewise promoted the idea that the mastery of critical reasoning skills rather than specific theories or practical trades was the best preparation for service in the highest levels of government administration. Although the French civil service exams tended to be specific to a particular corps or ministry, the French concours, as one author noted, tested a "broad range of theoretical and cultural knowledge."[17] In some countries, schools and the possibility of taking exams were not limited by law to specific groups of people, but clearly the time and expense required to prepare children for exams and to provide a prolonged classical education would privilege families with wealth.

Further, exams that tested intellect were not the only criterion for entrance into government service. British Lord Thomas Macaulay, who in the 1830s advocated the exam system for the Indian Civil Service, believed that intellect and superior character were very closely related qualities. Consequently when the British established a competitive examination system in 1870, they also included strict guidelines for the physical health, morality, character, and in certain instances age of candidates for government service.[18] For the most part, the upper classes more often possessed these subjective requirements concerning proper appearance and character, making it difficult for members of the lower classes to obtain high-status government posts.

Late-eighteenth- and nineteenth-century Americans also associated meritorious individuals with more than simply an ability to master exam subjects, demonstrate critical faculties, and perform a job adequately. In judging fitness for a position, President George Washington, for instance, also considered geographical representation, previous experience, reputation, and support for the Constitution. In his famous reference to a "natural aristocracy," Thomas Jefferson called for the creation of an elite judged not on family genealogy but on ability. Importantly, however, he perceived virtue as an equally significant quality.[19] In 1848, Ralph Waldo Emerson extolled the benefits of "aristocracy," claiming that some people were "naturally" superior to others. As he claimed, "the existence of an upper class is not injurious as long as it is dependent on merit." In defining the qualities of merit, however, Emerson extended his discussion beyond the possession of intellect and a "commanding talent," emphasizing physical well-being and character. Men who were smart, he claimed, also needed physical strength: "it is certain that a sound body must be at the root of any excellence in manners and actions. . . . When Nature goes to create a national man, she puts symmetry between the physical and intellectual powers. She moulds a large brain, and joins to it a great trunk to supply it."[20] His aristocrat was a well-balanced person, not only in terms of mental and physical capabilities but also in temperament. Other qualities would have sounded familiar to seventeenth-century aristocrats. According to Emerson, leaders needed a will and commitment to public service, eloquence, "refining and inspiring manners," generosity, loyalty, nobility, and self-reliance, all of which reflected a superior character. Emerson rejected the idea that family name and birth made one fit for leadership, even though he maintained that the qualities one had for leadership were present at birth: "an aristocracy would not exist unless it were organic. Men are born to command," he wrote.[21] Ultimately the question for men like Emerson concerned the qualities and criteria that should be privileged in selecting meritorious men, rather than the righteousness of a hierarchical system in which some commanded and some served.

Establishing procedures to find and evaluate those men who were born "to command" remained at the root of the argument over merit. Seventeenth-century French aristocrats may have accepted the right of the king to determine worth, but nineteenth-century Americans like Emerson overtly spurned the notion that one ruler determined fitness. While Emerson longed for a machine, an "anthropometer," to assess each adult and place him or her in the proper place, he instead settled for a community decision. "Each community," he observed, "is the best judge of its citizens." Town meetings and congressional service, for example, would identify the best legislators, while brilliant doctors and lawyers would rise to prominence based on their performance.[22]

America's "natural aristocracy" included not only government men but also businessmen. Nineteenth-century Americans frequently pondered the traits needed for success in the private sector. The popularity of Benjamin Franklin's autobiography, Frederick Douglass's slave narrative, and later Horatio Alger's fictional stories of Ragged Dick attested to the importance of the self-made man theme in American culture. With its stress on individual achievement, this theme meshed comfortably with a modern, utilitarian conception of merit. In attempting to describe the characteristics necessary for business success, writers highlighted ambition, shrewdness, practical skills, dedication, discipline, and determination—but not formal education. Instead, self-education either on the job or through private learning typified the self-made man. Academic credentials mattered little. In the business world, merit could be quantitatively measured by the amount of wealth produced.[23] This division between formal education and financial success contrasted with ideals promoted in places such as Great Britain, where education, superior character, and wealth were often bound together.

The rise of higher education, introduction of the social sciences, and implementation of the merit system in the American civil service at the end of the nineteenth century helped transform the characteristics connected with merit and the way in which it was measured. While some of the traits associated with the successful entrepreneur and with Emerson's aristocracy (such as character) would continue to inform the evaluation of merit, the increasing stress on examinations and academic degrees clearly altered how Americans defined and assessed the "meritorious" individual in the twentieth century.

Complicating the determination of merit was the tendency to see merit in layered terms. On one level, Americans perceived merit in a collective sense. In the nineteenth century and early in the twentieth, Americans had separate sets of expectations with respect to the abilities of various groups of people, such as white men, white women, black men, and black women. Generally, given the racial and gender ideologies of the era, all white men, regardless of their credentials, appeared to be superior to white women and African Americans. Sex and race, therefore, helped determine membership in America's natural aristocracy. Importantly, these perceptions of collective worth were neither accepted passively nor fixed. The period from 1865 to 1900, for instance, marked an era of fluid race relations and the perception of African-American merit underwent significant and continual renegotiation. Conversely, cultural assumptions concerning collective worth both created and reinforced divisions of labor based on sex and race in the private and public sectors. In turn, defenders of the status quo used these divisions to legitimate a belief in the natural hierarchy of groups or cultures.

Encompassed within this collective perception of merit was an individual understanding of merit. Within each group, some individuals would be worthier than others, and the introduction of civil service exams was designed to discover these people. Written and oral examinations obviously reflected the biases of those who constructed them and in this sense disadvantaged the groups that may have had different cultural experiences.[24] Nevertheless, these tests narrowed the array of excuses that appointing officials could use to pass over women and African Americans in hiring and promotion decisions. High exam scores and demonstrated performance on the job also gave individuals in socially disadvantaged groups the opportunity to disrupt perceptions of deficient group capabilities. In this manner, the individual definition and evaluation of merit became a potentially powerful weapon for African Americans and women who fought for equal treatment in the federal civil service. By the 1930s some progressive administrators began to reevaluate perceptions of group inferiority, privileging instead an individualist merit system that they believed would eliminate discrimination in a pluralist society.

Stockberger, like many other public administration specialists, union members, and low-level workers, was deeply committed to the individualist merit system. Indeed, his rise through the ranks underscored the degree to which the merit system, instituted under the Pendleton Civil Service Act of 1883, helped individuals with talent to succeed. Although it initially removed only a small number of positions from the patronage system, by 1932 80 percent of all government positions had been placed under the merit system.[25] This system reinforced the pursuit of individual achievement. As Cindy Sondik Aron has illustrated in her study of government workers, middle-class values such as competitiveness and individualism were transforming the civil service system at the end of the nineteenth century.[26] A desire among public servants to retain those values remained strong through the 1930s and 1940s. In 1939, one reporter noted that federal personnel directors appeared to be "lukewarm" toward the issue of automatic pay raises, fearing that these would create a "psychological hazard" because they would diminish worker ambition. According to directors, the "rugged individualism" that drove employees "to get ahead on [their] own merit and footing" would vanish.[27]

Merit reformers remained wedded to a Jeffersonian faith in a natural aristocracy who were rewarded for talent and ambition with wealth and power. While social scientists vigorously debated whether talent and intellect were innate attributes or determined by environment, most agreed that they could scientifically measure each individual's mental capacity and hence worthiness. Psychologists, in particular, perfected the "science" of psychometrics. Accordingly, they proclaimed that standardized intelligence tests could ascertain the "right" person for the "right" job. Government administrators eagerly put these tests to use, drawing up registers of eligible applicants based upon civil service test scores.

Once the administrators began to push for a single merit system used to evaluate all employees, they faced the difficult task of implementing and operating a color- and gender-blind system. Although many in the 1930s argued that impartial entrance exams and efficiency ratings would produce a bias-free system, these assessments remained only one criterion government administrators used in making personnel decisions. From the 1880s through the 1950s, government personnel policy and practice supported a wide variety of preferential programs (now labeled "affirmative action"), including bonus points for veterans, noncompetitive exams for employees hired as temporary workers, and geographical quotas.[28] For instance, congressional implementation of veterans preference affirmed a relationship between patriotism, masculinity, militarism, public service, and merit. While clearly aimed at rewarding men willing to sacrifice their lives for their country, this preferential program signified a critical way in which merit was defined outside the boundaries of talent or job performance. Moreover, extensive personal and professional networks associated with academic programs, family, and state and local government employment helped decide who was fit for federal work and who was not. Finally, the introduction of human relations techniques at the end of the 1930s heightened attention to an individual's personality as a critical factor in personnel determinations. In practice, the operation of the merit system retained some striking similarities to the personal patronage system.[29] Accordingly, as one scholar noted, managers often relied upon "faceless" rules to hide the "nature and origin of power." Although individuals may have perceived the bureaucracy as a pluralistic structure that did not favor any particular group, it actually functioned to protect the interests of the few, not the many.[30]

Individuality, as expressed through personality, became an especially crucial component of the evaluation process if job productivity was not easily quantified. Max Weber's seminal work on bureaucracy claimed that in its ideal form, an organization was defined by its universal rules, including those governing the acquisition and duties of a job. But these rules remained open to interpretation. Rules used to assess employee performance or capabilities, for example, reflected a masculine culture that devalued women's labor.[31] When bureaucratic mechanics set out to "fix" bureaucratic inefficiencies, they adopted schemes that fortified, rather than altered, a male-centered power structure and a sexual division of labor. In the 1940s, for instance, use of the human relations school of management served to entrench cultural perceptions of female nature as well as black culture within the administrative apparatus of the federal bureaucracy. Work standards based on personality incorporated contemporary gender and racial distinctions, coding behavior in "masculine" and "feminine" as well as "black" and "white" terms. These practices reified stereotypes and fortified a rather rigid sexual and racial division of labor within the service. Hence, Weber's "ideal" bureaucracy needs to be perceived in historical and cultural terms.

A number of scholars including Kathy E. Ferguson have investigated the dialectic between bureaucratic norms and culture. Ferguson conceives of bureaucracy as both a structure and a process that "must be located within its social context." A bureaucracy therefore mediates existing sex-, race-, and class-based inequalities, "projecting them into an institutional arena that both rationalizes and maintains them." Applied to the American administrative state, this theory illustrates how the state reproduces, reinforces, and formalizes patriarchal and racial domination. For Ferguson, bureaucratic structure and discourse are clearly gendered in male terms. Hierarchy, she notes, reflects a male form of organization and model of decision making in opposition to a more collective female approach. Because bureaucratic rules and structure reflect the cultural sensibilities of the white men who devised them, rules and organizational structure will likely devalue the contributions of people who bring different social and cultural perspectives to the organization.[32]

Examining bureaucracies in this manner has significantly enriched our understanding of organizational culture and power relations within the administrative state. This approach encourages an examination of the assumptions held by the individual administrators who devised and implemented universal personnel rules in the early-twentieth-century federal bureaucracy. It asks how the state as an institution created different opportunities for men and women, blacks and whites. Nevertheless, while the public-sector labor market clearly replicated, reinforced, and in some instances created new social and cultural inequalities, public-sector employment was itself the site of an ongoing struggle over the gendered and racial terms of work. Toward the end of the nineteenth century, for instance, male civil servants struggled to reconcile manliness and white-collar civil service work. In part because clerical work was also performed by women and in part because it did not involve strenuous physical activity, many Americans stigmatized federal workers as weak and effeminate.[33] Similarly, supporters of political machines and patronage reviled merit reformers and tenured civil servants as "political hermaphrodites." At times, this resulted in an effort to make the state even more "manly," but it also reflected the constant struggle among civil servants over the equation of masculinity and whiteness with cultural, political, and economic supremacy.[34] Although largely controlled by men, the administrative arm of government was not the sole preserve of men. Women and African Americans also received paychecks from the executive branch and at various locales and points in time shared office space with white men. While working in a largely patriarchal and racist environment, some women and African Americans sought to undermine the more egregious aspects of discrimination, and at certain intervals they made progress in this direction. Hence, the administrative state did not retain a consistent patriarchal or racist agenda, and this study examines how, when, and to what extent that agenda changed at specific historical moments.

For African Americans and second and third generation Americans, working for the federal government provided an opportunity to prove one's employment ability and one's worth as an American. Federal employment encouraged the construction of identifications that cut across racial and even gender boundaries, particularly as it linked workers to powerful national institutions, providing them with the symbolism of patriotic service and political participation and thus with a distinctly "American" identity. One study of blacks in Washington, D.C., noted that in the early twentieth century, black Americans labored to protect their access to federal jobs because these posts promised both "security" and "dignity." One civil servant, in turn, used his elevated position in the patent office to demonstrate the ingenuity of black Americans by conducting a study of patents extended to them. Over a thousand, he proudly noted, had been granted by the late nineteenth century.[35] Frederick Douglass also extolled the importance of black participation in all aspects of governance. In an 1883 address to the Kentucky "Convention of Colored Men," he told the crowd that there would be little opportunity to overcome racism and discrimination "while we are known to be excluded by our color from all important positions under the Government." He also warned against black withdrawal from candidacy for office, noting that apathy would only "be taken as a proof of [black] unfitness for American citizenship."[36]

Nineteenth-century African Americans fully embraced the ideal of individual merit, believing that it would help dispel myths of racial inferiority. A notable example was John Lynch, son of a Mississippi slaveowner and a female slave. Lynch rose to political prominence after the Civil War, becoming a Republican congressman from Mississippi in 1873. After losing his seat during the era of redemption when southern Democrats regained control of state politics, he became the fourth auditor in the Treasury Department under President Benjamin Harrison and an informal advocate for black employees during the change from Harrison's to Democrat Grover Cleveland's administration. In advocating for the jobs of a white lawyer and black physician, he urged the secretary of the interior to focus on the credentials and efficient performance of these appointees, rather than on the fact that both belonged to racially mixed marriages. Lynch defended the lawyer as an "able and brilliant" man who did not deserve to be punished for having the courage to marry the woman he loved. When President Cleveland asked to see Lynch early in his administration, he inquired about Lynch's ability to supervise white women in his department. Assuring the president that he and his employees accorded one another mutual respect, he also reassured him that his "contact with the clerks and other officials in the office was official, not social." He then encouraged the president to have little anxiety about "the appointment of a colored man of intelligence, good judgment and wise discretion as head of any bureau in which white women were employed."[37] But despite this faith in merit, African Americans would face a substantial challenge to merit-based promotional practices in the early twentieth century.

Unfortunately, racial segregation asserted itself in the civil service in the early twentieth century, beginning, it appears, under the administration of President Theodore Roosevelt, when the Treasury Department's Bureau of Engraving and Printing physically separated some black and white workers. By 1909, other divisions in the departments of Treasury and Interior established separate wash and locker rooms for black and white employees.[38] Physical segregation and a racial division of labor spread under President Woodrow Wilson, with appointing officials more frequently using the "rule of three" to avoid hiring African Americans. The rule of three allowed department appointment officials the discretion of choosing from among the top three performers on civil service exams. Because applicants after 1914 were required to furnish photographs and often to attend interviews, it became fairly simple to identify "unqualified" candidates. In this sense, as scholar Desmond King has demonstrated, the federal government's segregation policies "operationalized the assumption of racial inferiority."[39] African Americans, especially in Washington, D.C., remained devastated by the loss of these "dignified" jobs. Hence when the civil service system became more open in the 1940s, African Americans eagerly sought new white-collar positions that would give them a chance to integrate economically within the middle class.

Civil service employment also reflected and encouraged the process of acculturation. Office workers had to demonstrate proficiency in English and a willingness to wear American office attire and adhere to office etiquette. Their employment signaled some familiarity with large bureaucratic environments, which by the 1930s had become part of the mainstream work experience. The assimilative function of the federal civil service facilitated an acceptance of pluralism as a positive value and worthwhile employment policy. As sociologist J. Milton Yinger has asserted, "pluralism as a value and as a policy is unlikely to appear until some assimilation occurs."[40]

In the 1930s and 1940s, support for assimilation and an acceptance of pluralism did not mean that managers perceived all subcultures as equal. Although pluralism suggests the "recognition of the legitimacy and even the value of some cultural and associational variation," in this era, federal officials assumed that cultures outside the white, male mainstream were basically flawed.[41] To assimilate, individuals had to shed their inferior identities and customs, at least at work. According to one administrator at the Government Printing Office, the first woman to finish a four-year printer apprenticeship "went through the course here just like a boy."[42] And yet, administrators did not always reward these attempts to fit in with the boys. Individuals who crossed cultural boundaries found themselves disadvantaged in the government labor market. Women who displayed traits categorized as "masculine" (such as aggression) were deemed maladjusted. African Americans who demonstrated too much interest in race-related issues were not "white" enough to occupy positions of authority. A number of civil servants found themselves trapped in this paradox. Even among liberal administrators, a hierarchy of cultures continued to exist.

Despite these drawbacks, the culture of pluralism that began to infuse the civil service in the late 1930s and 1940s destabilized preexisting patterns of discrimination, forcing administrators to produce new justifications for occupational compartmentalization based upon gender and race. The rejection of scientific racism and substitution of social forces for biological ones to explain racial hierarchies made racial categories more fluid and open to change. It was not as easy to jettison the biological basis for gender differences, but social scientists stressed socialization as a critical element of these differences. The liberal feminism of the Progressive era and the 1920s, which maintained that women deserved an equal opportunity to demonstrate their worth, led to a reconsideration of their segregation within certain positions. By addressing questions regarding diversity and assimilation, liberal reformers introduced pluralism as a positive value and a policy more appropriate for the federal government than the earlier emphasis on a conformist, homogeneous civil service workforce in which only white males had the opportunity to succeed. Some women and African Americans used these wedges to defy stereotypes and acquire prestigious and lucrative positions. The GPO employee who finished her printer course "just like a boy" also became the first woman ever to qualify for the position of master printer in that agency.[43] Eventually, more would follow.

In detailing the rise and fall of various corporate managerial languages such as scientific management, welfare capitalism, and human relations, labor historians have presented personnel management as an ongoing struggle of managers to "control" employees and, at various times, resurgent union movements.[44] These factors likewise figured prominently in governmental personnel administration. But in examining how and why personnel specialists adopted specific managerial philosophies for the American civil service, we should place more emphasis on the managers themselves: how did they perceive their world and how did they seek to alter their environment? How did gender and race inform management ideologies as well as management decisions? How and why did public personnel administrators integrate a hierarchically oriented bureaucracy into a decentralized American democracy? As Stephen Waring noted in his intellectual history of business management, studies of management "can reveal managers making history, not just responding to it, and help show how they developed and legitimated governmental methods."[45]

Government administrators in the 1930s were remarkably self-conscious about their methods. Although Stockberger was careful to disassociate his programs from "paternalism," his notion that the department was a place to "live" as well as "work" conveyed his sense that the department should be a metaphorical home, and its employees a family. His attention to the "democratic spirit" among workers spoke as well to a growing concern in the 1930s that the civil service system promote American political values. And his calls for "scientific" administration point to a desire to present personnel decisions as objective. While Stockberger's rhetoric hides the cultural conflicts that often threatened to disrupt his harmonious home, it reveals that managers hoped to use what they perceived to be "objective" scientific techniques to establish familial bonds and promote democratic values among civil servants.

Ideological as well as structural forces vitiated the more egalitarian aspects of pluralism. At the turn of the century, when Stockberger entered the civil service, it was becoming more corporate in its orientation. Corporate structures associated with the rapid industrial expansion of the late Gilded Age and Progressive era profoundly influenced architects of the administrative state. President Theodore Roosevelt's New Nationalism laid the foundation for a professionally based civil service organized around business principles. In the early twentieth century, administrative reformers therefore frequently legitimated their "governmental methods" by likening government to corporations. They borrowed corporate values (such as efficiency), corporate forms (like hierarchy), and managerial practices (such as Taylorism and later the human relations school of management), in an effort to make the federal personnel system appear more businesslike and sophisticated.

By the 1930s, public-sector managers, like their private-sector counterparts, were arguing that labor-management conflict was inefficient and should be avoided at all costs. Public managers eagerly pursued strategies that would harmonize the interests of agency elites with those of the rank and file. Human relations experts in business had championed the need for workers to participate in management through employee councils and individual consultations. Public administrators heralded this practice, calling it a democratic approach consistent with American political traditions.[46] But again, like private-sector managers, they pursued these aims in a hierarchical framework that contradicted their own emphasis on employee participation. These contradictions heightened class friction within the service.

Public managers did not transmit private-sector management theories and practices into the federal service without some modification. Neither the existing structure nor the traditions of the federal bureaucracy would permit New Deal managers to make government a corporation. The federal bureaucracy's sprawling organizational form and its nonprofit, political character thwarted such attempts. A desire to win worker loyalty was also a key feature of human relations and one that public managers joined to a concept of political allegiance to the United States government. "Company" loyalty and patriotism thus became fused in the federal service. This process of modification created hybrid forms of the human relations ideology in government agencies. American business culture, with its emphasis on productivity and its adulation of managers and management theory, thus deeply influenced, but did not solely define, the outlook of public-sector managers.

Among the ideological and structural forces that weakened pluralism in the public sector were powerful concerns regarding the place of executive branch employees in the political system. An important element in public management ideology, not evident in the private sector, was a nineteenth-century concept of civic responsibility or public accountability—that is, the idea that government employees were servants to the general public. Under the nineteenth-century spoils system, public officials assumed that patronage restricted the autonomy of government employees and made them accountable to elected officials and, by extension, to the voting public. After the introduction of the merit system and formal personnel rules, this idea was applied in a new bureaucratic setting. Throughout the early twentieth century, administrators, particularly those dealing with employee relations, struggled to reconcile traditional concepts of popular sovereignty with the emergence of a strong bureaucracy and potentially autonomous bureaucrats. Professionals who claimed allegiance to a specific, nonpartisan body of knowledge were one threat to the concept of civic responsibility. Struggles over employee unionization also brought this tension to the fore, prompting various groups to debate the meaning of civic responsibility. Could government employees organize, strike, and/or bargain with agency administrators? Could they then still remain accountable to public taxpayers?[47] Unclear lines of authority and questions of responsibility manifested themselves in frequent conflicts between low-level employees and agency administrators.

While Theodore Roosevelt's New Nationalism established a foundation for a more corporate and class-conflicted state, it was President Franklin D. Roosevelt's New Deal that ultimately gave the state a "personal" orientation. To characterize the state at midcentury as "personal" may seem incompatible with Weber's vision of an ideal bureaucracy. Weber theorized that as "civilizations" became more "complex," rational organizations based upon "legal authority" developed. Formal rules, a division of labor, and special-ized functions characterized these modern bureaucracies. Workers laboring within these hierarchical structures were atomized and their work routinized. "Bureaucracy," he maintained, "develops the more perfectly, the more it is 'dehumanized,' the more completely it succeeds in eliminating from official business love, hatred, and all purely personal, irrational, and emotional el-ements which escape calculation." In contrast to the preindustrial artisanal workshop, bureaucracies left workers fewer opportunities to exercise auton-omy under the formal rules now governing the workplace. In this sense, the federal government's adoption of the merit system in 1883 and the elab-oration of workplace rules that followed made the twentieth-century state "impersonal" in comparison to a nineteenth-century bureaucracy oriented around the traditional personal authority associated with the spoils system.[48]

Weber's theories and the sharp distinction often made between a "per-sonal" patronage system and an "impersonal" merit system obscure the sub-stantial efforts made by federal administrators like Stockberger to produce a "wholesome," homelike workplace in which supervisors recognized the hu-manity of their subordinates. As Stockberger implied, personality did not have to be obliterated by the existence of large-scale organizations. His hu-man relations approach used psychological, anthropological, and sociological models to explain worker behavior. He stressed the need for supervisors to attend to the personal problems of their employees in an effort to promote worker morale and productivity. Just as welfare programs opened the private lives of recipients to public scrutiny, so too did human relations make the personal lives of civil servants matters of public concern. Just as corporations became intertwined with public agencies, obscuring the boundaries between the public and private sectors, so too did human relations blur the bound-aries between the personal and the political. In placing the merit system in the hands of the Civil Service Commission and agency appointing officials, the government transferred the personal authority associated with patronage from the president and Congress to executive branch bureaucrats. Tellingly, British clerks in the 1780s resisted a ministerial effort to promote employees on the basis of knowledge and hard work, rather than seniority, because they perceived this merit system as too arbitrary.[49]

In Stockberger's home, the Department of Agriculture, each worker was to have a role best suited to his or her perceived capabilities. Gender and race often conditioned the appraisal agency administrators made of those capabilities. Weber's analysis of bureaucratic forms of authority failed to integrate the cultural biases that inevitably informed the evaluation process in the "ideal" bureaucracy. For example, the Department of Agriculture, which had strong ties to southern Democrats and planters, hired blacks only in messenger or custodial positions, if at all. Similarly, managers generally placed female employees, regardless of performance, experience, or education, in subservient positions. Yet this attention to gender and racial distinctions directly conflicted with an individualist merit system.

In addition to cultural images and ideology, institutional relationships also shaped the struggle for control of the federal workplace. While legislators established the broad parameters of the civil service system, they paid less attention to the management of the daily operations of government offices. Personnel managers did not complain. A desire for administrative authority motivated them to minimize their contact with Congress. They were relatively successful, as the evidence suggests that they wielded significant discretionary power to shape agency employee relations statements. Managers also remained somewhat aloof from the president. Despite President Franklin Roosevelt's efforts to strengthen executive control over the bureaucracy and to reinforce New Deal liberalism within the institution, he found it difficult to oversee the execution of personnel policies. Presidential control efforts and various statutes certainly constrained personnel managers, but these same managers devised many of the personnel laws, making them flexible enough to support a range of interpretations at the agency level. Neither Congress nor the president demonstrated much interest in micromanaging agencies. Legislators retained the power to set salary schedules, hours, and employee evaluation procedures, but they made frequent exceptions to the rules and rarely investigated the manner in which the laws were applied. As managerial experts, personnel officials mediated employee-labor relations within government agencies. Because the service remained difficult to control from one central source, administrators often took the initiative in attempting to develop and unify government labor policies.

Public-sector personnel specialists at times deliberately and at times inadvertently became active participants in the conversation over diversity in the federal workforce. Although rarely proactive, especially during the 1930s, federal administrators had significant power to influence race relations on the office floor. During the 1930s and 1940s, as a new generation of managers entered the service, they acted within a set of inherited institutional boundaries that served to guide and set limits on their behavior. While some managers in the New Deal and World War II civil service pursued efficiency and merit, others articulated new managerial ideologies to fit the changing gender and racial makeup of the workforce, shifting party alignments, and growing concerns about the viability of democracy. By the end of the 1940s with the advent of anticommunism, the government's reform project with respect to labor relations waned. In 1953, when Republican Dwight D. Eisenhower entered the White House, his administration weakened fair employment regulations and ended agency efforts to create uniform personnel rules for the entire government. Through the 1950s, elected officials and government administrators demonstrated little interest in a progressive employment agenda; few officials voiced support for either the construction of a diverse workforce or the establishment of formal bargaining rights for unions. As the country grapples with affirmative action programs, it is wise to deliberate on the federal government's historical struggle to reconcile democratic ideals with the existence of large bureaucratic organizations. The federal government's personnel policies and practices as an employer demonstrated the possibilities and limitations of a campaign to create a democratic bureaucracy befitting a democratic nation.

1 Scientific Administration of the Civil Service Prior to the New Deal

In the late nineteenth century, good government advocates across the political spectrum chanted a similar mantra: party machines that were dependent upon patronage had allowed the "lower element" (usually immigrants) to "infiltrate" and "corrupt" the political system. As one author noted, the reform "crusade aimed to replace the 'scum' . . . of Washington with properly educated men of intelligence, principle, and genuine loyalty to the republic." Reformers hoped to distance the public and "coarse, selfish, unprincipled" politicians (and political machines) from "issues of state."[1]

In its earliest post–Civil War manifestation, the merit reform movement had associated immorality and corruption with patronage and had sought to substitute it with a merit-based personnel system that would return government institutions to virtuous citizens. These reformers—known variously as independents, mugwumps, and (to their opponents) "snivel service" reformers—battled political machines at the local, state, and national levels. President James Garfield's death at the hands of an unbalanced office seeker confirmed the mugwump perception of the evil and immoral nature of the spoils system. Editors such as E. L. Godkin of the *Nation*, William Curtis of *Harper's Weekly*, and Carl Schurz of the *New York Evening Post* used the assassination along with various political corruption cases to rally widespread public support for a national civil service law. Congress relented to the pressure in 1883 and passed the Pendleton Civil Service Act.

Under the law, applicants for clerical positions in Washington, D.C. (with some exceptions), and positions in post offices and customs houses with more than fifty employees were to be subject to entrance exams. This placed only about 10 percent of the entire service under the merit system, although the president had the authority to extend entrance exams to other positions through executive order. The act also protected employees in these "classified positions" from dismissal on political grounds and prohibited government officials from attempting to pressure them into political action. Congress created a Civil Service Commission to administer the act.[2]

Having codified their program into law, merit reformers moved their struggle to new terrain. On the new battlefront, administrative interest groups, including the National Civil Service Reform League and Bureau for Municipal Research, appropriated organizational models from the corporate and military world and technical language from emerging scientific disciplines to argue for structural changes in the administration of government personnel. This new discourse enabled reformers to cloak themselves in an aura of professional impartiality and masculine authority, thus shielding themselves from challenges by lower-level civil servants. Reformers compared the executive branch to a large business corporation with a multitude of functions. Their job was to build agencies capable of developing and coordinating new personnel functions, to establish divisions between line and staff, and to create position and salary "schedules" and more effective exam and efficiency rating procedures. Although increasing federal responsibilities—exemplified by the Interstate Commerce Act of 1887 and Sherman Anti-trust Act of 1890—and a larger federal workforce partially accounted for these structural alterations, a number of other cultural and political factors shaped administrative reform as well. These reform efforts took shape within a Progressive cultural matrix that not only deified efficiency, scientific method, and technological innovation but also associated these concepts with a higher civilization consisting of white, Anglo-Saxon manliness.[3]

Women and men tiptoed around the problematic association of women with a wide variety of Progressive causes and the new professionalism and bureaucratization that accompanied Progressive reform. Eager to participate in the public sphere of business, academics, and politics, women often jumped into the public sphere, much to the concern of some male reformers, who felt that female participation would weaken their cause. The rise of the social sciences reflected these tensions. Increasingly, disciplines began to split between one camp that engaged in scientific study, investigation, and theorization within the academy and another that applied social science knowledge to social ills. As the prestige of the former rose, women came to dominate the latter. Hence, men tended to take positions in universities, while women rushed to the front line as social workers. In the field of public administration, experts attempted to bolster their discipline by coding efficiency, discipline, the standardization of rules, and use of business methods in government as a particularly male approach.[4]

Equally prevalent in this era was the tendency to perceive civilization in racial terms. The intimate tie forged between culture and biology during the Victorian era persisted into the Progressive era, as Progressives often touted the "organic inevitability of progress." Because adherents of Darwinian evolution believed that whites monopolized the last and most advanced stage of civilization, it became difficult for them to perceive how blacks could compete as equals. President Theodore Roosevelt espoused an evolutionary view of civilization in which whites remained superior. Conceding that African Americans were a permanent fixture in American society, he deplored what he saw as the inevitable violent (and barbaric) conflict that would erupt between the races. Consequently, he employed the individualist conception of merit, suggesting that if a black were able to prove his "merits as a man," he should be accorded "no more and no less than he shows himself worthy to have." Even so, Roosevelt continued to believe that it would take centuries for African Americans to achieve the highest plateau of civilization.[5]

White feminist Progressives echoed these views. Jane Addams, who supported the National Association for the Advancement of Colored People and complained about D. W. Griffith's racist film *Birth of a Nation*, nevertheless offered only tepid support for integration. Like many white Progressives, she remained patently opposed to social equality between blacks and whites.[6] Demonstrating a less ambivalent approach to race, Charlotte Perkins Gilman advocated for an equality between the sexes that was based upon an inequality between black and white Americans. To prove the worth of women, she denigrated African Americans. Like Roosevelt, she acknowledged that a few individual African Americans might be able to advance but otherwise expected that the process would be slow and not at all inevitable. At one point, in a plan reminiscent of Edward Bellamy's national trust, she suggested that those African Americans incapable of productive lives be consigned to a nationally run army of menial laborers. Tellingly, she did not propose that they be provided white-collar government jobs, suggesting that she perceived whites as more innately capable of the rationality and efficiency necessary to perform clerical duties. On the whole, Progressives failed to assault America's racial caste system, and race riots punctuated the era. As one author noted, Progressives continued to perceive African Americans as people outside the boundaries of citizenship and more generally as a people outside the nation.[7]

Merit reform therefore generally expressed conformist characteristics, as some activists worked to promote cultural uniformity or a brand of 100 percent Americanism that trumpeted the superiority of white, native-born,

Protestant society.[8] For many, the construction of the civil service offered an opportunity to define Americanism in an increasingly diverse society. Immigration heightened the connections made between ethnicity, nation, and citizenship, and the Progressive era consequently revealed a preoccupation with hyphenated Americans. Reformers such as Addams, who clearly felt that immigrants could be absorbed into mainstream American society, opted for a benevolent approach to immigration, seeking assimilation through settlement houses. The popularity of the home missionary movement also highlighted the Progressives' desire to build loyalty among the newcomers and to assert a single national identity. At the same time, Progressives also gave strength to nativist sentiments. President Roosevelt, for example, strongly opposed Japanese immigration, contending that it would lead to a "race problem and invite and insure a race contest." He also worried that a declining birth rate among native-born Americans would lead to "race suicide." The rise of eugenics and the 100 percent Americanism campaign associated with World War I extended beyond the boundaries of mainstream progressivism but testified to the strength of the conformist campaign in the early twentieth century.[9] A debate over government work intersected with this campaign. Whereas party machines routinely rewarded recent immigrants for their political loyalty with government jobs, the merit civil service would elevate the "best men"—white males with character, education, and social status—to government posts.

Second generation administrative reformers supported recruitment of the best men into government service and labored to implement changes on two levels; on one level, they extended merit systems to new government posts and agencies, and on another level, they developed management programs. Both were to be based upon scientific principles. As it turned out, scientific reform concepts encouraged but ironically had difficulty accommodating civil service unionization. Organizations such as the National Civil Service Reform League, which lobbied for the expansion of the merit system, and the Institute for Government Research (IGR), which advocated for modernized personnel systems, opposed an autonomous union movement. Merit reform and the subsequent attempts through World War I to create a more systematic personnel structure proved problematic because they relied on simplistic concepts of bureaucratic organization and worker behavior. Because reformers conceptualized the executive branch as a single institution capable of direction from one source of authority, they concentrated on reform from the top down. This approach obscured from view the complex problem of occupational stratification and class conflict within agencies. No doubt reformers believed that the job security and promotional opportunities afforded by a merit system, along with pay standardization, would mute labor strife within the civil service. But they had little conception of how working conditions and power relations within agencies created discontent among civil servants. Not surprisingly, unions emerged to protect the interests of career employees, a development reformers found difficult to address, because in their view workers had to be subservient to the public interest and to congressional, presidential, and Civil Service Commission regulations.

Diversity offered another challenge to scientific reform efforts. The presence of women and African Americans created schisms within the bureaucracy. On the one hand, the vocabulary and structural alterations of administrative reform served to anchor caste divisions within the service. On the other hand, gender and race discrimination posed a potential threat to the reformers' claim that judgments based on merit reflected an individual employee's performance and ability. In the early twentieth century, nonetheless, middle- and upper-class Americans widely accepted ideologies that justified the subordination of African Americans and women on the basis of biological or genetic inferiority. Importantly, therefore, administrative elites did not perceive racial and gender occupational barriers and segregation either as immoral or as a challenge to the individualist merit system but rather as the consequence of natural, scientific factors associated with group worth.

Reform and the Science of Administration

Toward the end of the nineteenth century, a group of social scientists devoted to the study of the political system began developing new theories of civil administration modeled on emerging corporate structures. Woodrow Wilson's 1887 essay "The Study of Administration" called upon reformers to recognize merit reform "as but a prelude to a fuller administrative reform." Administration, explained Wilson, was a "science" and a "business" lying "outside the proper sphere of *politics*." Thirteen years later, Frederick Goodnow, an administrative law professor at Columbia, published his treatise *Politics and Administration*, in which he drew a clear distinction between political decision making and administrative implementation and enforcement.[10]

By drawing this distinction, technical reformers conceptualized the federal bureaucracy as a single business enterprise. According to Goodnow, the executive branch needed to be reorganized in conformity with business principles.

Increasingly, the business principles to which reformers looked were those of the new corporate structure with its emphasis on centralization, hierarchy, and standardization.[11] These principles, Goodnow said, would enable administrators in the executive branch to implement public law more effectively. But administrators, he emphasized, should be responsible for executing the will of elected officials. In this sense, a dual and somewhat contradictory concept of public accountability existed within his analysis. On the one hand, he wanted administrators to be responsive to officials elected by the public. On the other hand, he argued that expert administrators, rather than party hacks beholden to elected officials, were most fit to discern the public interest. The tension between democratic accountability and professional autonomy lay unresolved in his treatises.[12]

To effect the Pendleton Civil Service Act, for example, a centralized Civil Service Commission was to be responsible for generating and overseeing the implementation of standardized regulations regarding hiring and dismissal procedures, a single system of performance ratings for the entire service, and a comprehensive division of labor that would enable the government to standardize salaries across departmental lines. In its 1897 report to Congress, the Civil Service Commission's chief examiner maintained that the government's employee selection procedures were designed to imitate those of the "most successful business concerns."[13] In the abstract, many people, including congressional representatives and senators, agreed with these ideals. They did so even though they understood that in practice, as historian Cindy Sondik Aron has pointed out, business firms themselves still "relied upon less than 'rational' criteria in recruiting employees," including kin and friendship networks. Standardization in government was even more difficult. Not only was congressional oversight of executive branch agencies divided among committees, but institutional battles between the legislative and executive branches also made an overall management scheme virtually impossible to effect. The fragmented condition of the bureaucracy—with its overlapping functions, contradictory missions, and wide variation in personnel policies and practices—was itself a reflection of a system structured around a separation of powers.[14]

Nevertheless, once civic-minded writers articulated a separation between politics and administration, and once they had made it seem a feasible theory, they began to treat the executive branch as a corporate body. Goodnow believed that executive branch administrators should pursue their scientific, judicial, and business activities within an "efficient" organization.[15]

During the 1910s, the academic and political interest in administrative reform spawned new quasi-public institutions. In 1906, a group of New York academics formed the Bureau of Municipal Research and devoted themselves to studies of governmental fiscal and personnel administration. Organized by a network of individuals active in administrative politics, the bureau provided local and national government with a pool of expert consultants. Many offered their services to elected officials interested in administrative reform. Several, for example, became members of President William Howard Taft's 1910 Economy and Efficiency Commission, designed to review and reform the government's fiscal and personnel functions. Despite their political agenda, bureau members shielded the political nature of their work behind a mask of "scientific" administration. Their emphasis on public service tended to obscure their professional networks of power, including their heavy reliance upon philanthropic funding. Although the bureau's funding source—the Rockefeller Foundation—did not dictate the content of studies, it certainly strengthened the bureau's corporate orientation.[16]

The bureau provided a model for social scientists interested in the study of public institutions. Several years later, a group of university academicians and other interested citizens joined together to form the IGR (later the Brookings Institution), patterned on the Bureau of Municipal Research. In one of its founding documents, the IGR justified its existence by noting that the United States government was "one of the largest and technically one of the most complicated business undertakings in the world." With expenditures already topping $1 billion a year and employees numbering in the hundreds of thousands, the government, IGR's founders said, would inevitably extend its activities, thus requiring the development and implementation of new administrative procedures.[17] Institute researchers hoped to train men in this administrative science for government careers. The institute fielded requests from university professors who wanted to construct courses on the "art" of government; these courses were to offer such "practical instruction in government as the law schools now afford to men about to enter upon the practice of law."[18]

Both traditional civil service reformers and "modern" social scientists favored a government served by an elite class of virtuous and capable citizens. Their respective conceptions of a virtuous and competent public service were, however, distinctive. Whereas the original movement was rooted in notions of noblesse oblige and the rule of an old patrician elite, new reformers drew on concepts of public service emanating from the country's emerging scientific and professional ideologies. Individuals trained in new educational institutions and subjects and who had strong and virtuous characters had an obligation, these "modern" reformers argued, to serve the public. Richard Ely, an economist, spoke of a "natural" aristocracy that reached its position by virtue of natural abilities and special training.[19]

After the turn of the century, Goodnow and other bureau members therefore helped redefine the assessment of "merit." Nineteenth-century Americans, as Warren Susman has argued, frequently employed the term *character* to connote a person with self-discipline and a sense of "duty, honor, and integrity." In political terms, this notion was closely akin to the republican concept of civic virtue in which individuals, when necessary, sacrificed their own self-interest for some larger public good. As Susman pointed out, "citizenship" was closely associated with the term *character*. Mugwumps believed that public service was itself an act of citizenship, requiring meritorious individuals willing to sacrifice personal gain for the public welfare.[20]

Administrative reformers who pushed for a closer alliance with academic, business, and engineering professions placed less emphasis on character. Instead, following a general movement toward a heightened twentieth-century focus on "personality," reformers gradually entered a new stage in assessing candidates for public service. Reformers began to examine not only academic credentials but also the aptitudes of candidates in an effort to place them in a job suitable for their respective dispositions.[21] Character did not disappear from the government's personnel selection and employee evaluation process; rather it became something acquired as a result of public employment. William F. Willoughby, a student of the political system and one-time statistician in the Labor Department, maintained that a "political education is primarily and essentially one of training rather than education, of character building rather than scholastic instruction." For him character meant more than the possession of a sense of duty and honor. He imbued character with traits associated with bureaucratic life. To build character and become politically educated, he noted, individuals should engage in "efficient, disinterested and impartial administration."[22]

Willoughby's reservations about scholastic instruction notwithstanding, he and other first generation public administrators supported the use of exams to measure and scientifically assess job candidates. As devised under the auspices of the Pendleton Act, entrance exams tested an applicant's basic skills in penmanship, spelling, letter writing, copying, and arithmetic. Early reformers had boasted that in contrast to British exams, which had been based upon a classical education, they designed American exams to measure practical, job-related skills. Accordingly, American merit supporters maintained, the federal civil service represented a democratic institution, open to anyone with ability. In reality, the absence of a classical emphasis within the exams did not mean that academic training was irrelevant. Federal civil service exams disadvantaged a number of Americans, who because of cultural biases and structural obstacles lacked the proper training to score well on these tests. Moreover, appointing officials used other criteria, including citizenship, character references, place of residence, and physical exams to determine fitness for federal work.[23]

Concomitant with the rise of professions and occupational specialization in the late nineteenth century, the Civil Service Commission began to develop supplemental exams in areas such as history, geography, physics, and chemistry to augment the basic skills test. Examiners used these when applicants sought jobs requiring specific skills. One contemporary observer applauded this trend, noting a new emphasis on determining "a man's fitness for a particular job." Examinations that tested aptitude "succeeded in putting round men and women snugly into round holes."[24] These ideals coincided with the views of intellectuals such as Herbert Croly, who believed that people became personally fulfilled and contributing members of society when they engaged in work best suited to their abilities.[25]

Government officials also aimed to gauge employee performance. Departments had experimented with promotional exams during the Gilded Age, measuring skills such as penmanship, arithmetic, English grammar, and efficiency (the most heavily weighted element), but by the late 1880s, the tests had fallen into disuse. Modern reformers revived the concept of performance measurement under Presidents Roosevelt and Taft and gave it new credibility by devising numerical rating schemes based upon the quantity and quality of work completed by individual employees. By 1913, the government had created legislation and an institution, the Division of Efficiency, to implement a formal rating system.[26]

World War I reinforced the government's commitment to entrance as well as promotional exams and encouraged the marriage between the social sciences and workplace management. During the war, elected officials appointed business leaders, engineers, and social workers to develop new methods of mobilizing personnel. Business administrators and Taylor Society members Mary van Kleeck and Morris Cooke worked for the Ordnance Department to help recruit industrial workers for war production. Using their positions as officials of the United States government, they spread their management philosophy to a larger sphere of business than had been previously possible through professional associations.[27] Psychologists Robert Yerkes, Lewis Thurman, and Henry H. Goddard, among others, joined a special psychology committee under the National Research Council. Their well-known research into intelligence testing for the military established new standards for employment examinations. Not coincidentally, a number of testing supporters, including Goddard, were also advocates of eugenics. As historian JoAnne Brown pointed out, psychologists could not offer a definitive description of intelligence, but they contended that as a "natural property," it was nevertheless still measurable. As they discovered its myriad properties, they would refine their tests accordingly.[28]

Another group of exam experts led by psychologists Walter Dill Scott, Edward L. Thorndike, and L. L. Thurstone formed the Committee on the Classification of Personnel to assist the army in employee placement. They developed vocational aptitude tests, thus emphasizing the necessity and capability of finding the "right" person for a particular position. These studies in employee selection and placement resulted in the development of personnel rating systems, which were then adopted by the United States Rubber Company, the Metropolitan Life Insurance Company, the Winchester Repeating Arms Company, and several other large corporations. In addition, the government sponsored personnel courses at several major universities and colleges. At the end of the course, instructors directed students to a government placement service that located jobs for them in the private sector.[29]

The informality and variety of federal management practices encouraged administrative reformers to experiment in the new field of psychometrics. These personnel selection and placement tests, maintained psychologists, were objective measurements designed to eliminate any "personal" or subjective judgment from the evaluation process. Simultaneously, however, these experts also asserted that psychometrics could determine vocational aptitude by revealing personality traits. In essence, experts argued that they could use impersonal objective tests to measure personal characteristics.[30] This technical framework especially appealed to government officials who assumed that proper personnel allocation would make the administrative state more efficient and thus make democratic government more effective. Psychometrics allowed personnel officials to introduce personal factors into the evaluation process while cloaking that process in an aura of impartiality. It also enabled them to retain sexual and racial divisions of labor while continuing to champion the merit system.

In the first two decades of the century, government departments primarily relied upon outside experts to modernize personnel techniques. On occasion, as with Yerkes and Scott, the government funded research, but federal agencies did not train their own experts. According to public administration specialist Leonard White, few of the Civil Service Commission's employees had been trained in the "principles underlying classification and compensation work, principles of test construction and statistical evaluation of test results." White did not believe that civil service commissions and their expert employees should have the authority to discipline and remove civil servants. Instead he wanted commission employees to perfect the "techniques" of exam construction and evaluation; to classify positions and salaries; and to develop uniform efficiency rating systems. In the 1910s and early 1920s, many of the U.S. Civil Service Commission's employees were former teachers, engineers, or politicians. Not until the late 1920s, observed White, was there a "marked tendency toward increasing the size of the technical staff as compared with the clerical staff."[31]

Bureau of Efficiency employees, who often conducted investigations of executive branch personnel practices, also lacked formal qualifications as "experts" in administration. The bureau's efficiency ratings chief, William McReynolds, had entered government service as a postal clerk in 1906 (as had the bureau's 1922 assistant chief, Malcolm Kerlin). Harold Graves, who joined the civil service as a teacher in the Philippines in 1908, returned to the United States in 1917 to serve as assistant chief of the bureau.[32] In these key personnel agencies, however, each of these self-made experts pushed for broader control over agency personnel practices.

The Taft Commission on Economy and Efficiency, organized in 1910 to study administrative practices, had envisioned such a role for personnel agencies. Commission members suggested that the Civil Service Commission be placed within the executive office and vested with the authority to oversee promotional examinations, arbitrate labor-management disputes, regulate working conditions, and implement a uniform efficiency rating system. To facilitate standardization, member Frederick Cleveland suggested that the Civil Service Commission develop a comprehensive occupation and salary classification system for the bureaucracy. This centralized system would eliminate the congressional practice of appropriating a lump sum to departments for salaries, a custom that had offered departmental administrators substantial discretion. Fearing that many of the Taft Commission's recommendations would expand presidential power over the executive branch, Congress largely rejected them.[33] Neither the Civil Service Commission nor the Bureau of Efficiency, which was created as a result of the Taft Commission, had sufficient power to standardize or centralize management structures. Both the foreign service and the public health service, for example, had the authority to administer their own entrance exams.[34]

Consequently, personnel practices varied significantly at the agency level. Most agencies had chief clerks (some also had appointment clerks) who, at the bidding of department secretaries and bureau chiefs, obtained job registers from the Civil Service Commission. Clerks also maintained personnel records, but they had no control over the allocation of pay, employee evaluation, or dismissal actions. Even when positions were classified under civil service rules and subject to examination, bureau and division chiefs retained substantial control over hiring. As noted, under the rule of three, exam registers provided by the Civil Service Commission listed the three candidates with the highest scores, any one of whom could be chosen by department officials. Although chief and appointment clerks served as departmental contacts with the Civil Service Commission, personnel administration was highly decentralized within agencies.[35]

Some agencies had formal hierarchies that vested most administrative authority in an assistant secretary. A single assistant postmaster, for example, oversaw general management issues throughout the Post Office Department. In the Department of Agriculture, on the other hand, an ideology of professionalism and strong bureau autonomy had led to the development of a less formal hierarchy. In 1905 Secretary of Agriculture James Wilson had created a personnel committee, consisting of the solicitor, assistant secretary, and chief clerk, to investigate employees charged with "dereliction of duties and actions prejudicial to the interests of the Department." Generally, however, secretaries had spread personnel duties among the chief clerk, solicitor, and assistant secretary until 1925, when the department consolidated personnel administration in a single division.[36]

Federal Labor-Management Relations

Although fragmented power, especially as it was divided between the president and Congress, thwarted the centralization of authority over the executive branch, President Theodore Roosevelt used an executive order in 1902 to assert control over one aspect of civil administration—labor relations. Before the first general union, the National Federation of Federal Employees, was officially founded in 1917, the only organized government workers were craft workers (usually in the Navy and War departments), belonging to private-sector unions, and Post Office employees.[37] Displeased with the efforts of these postal employees to join unions and lobby for salary revisions, Roosevelt issued a "gag" order forbidding all executive department employees—either individually or in association with others—from soliciting pay raises or other legislation in their interest from Congress. Any issues they wished to raise before legislators had to be fed through department heads. By so doing, the president severely limited the ability of employees to use Congress as protection against the arbitrary authority of departmental administrators. A few years later, Roosevelt altered the civil service rules to enable either the president or a department head to dismiss employees without notice (previous rules required written notification). Two months after that, he added employees of independent agencies to his gag order.[38] Roosevelt's actions toward labor highlighted the challenge autonomous unions presented to Goodnow's assertion that executive branch employees should remain accountable only to elected officials and the general public.

Although scientific reformers remained convinced that the corporate model would improve executive branch operations, they were unsettled by the labor strife that accompanied the creation of hierarchical structures and economy drives in the government. In 1909 Taft extended Roosevelt's 1902 gag order by forbidding bureau, office, and division chiefs, subordinates in any department, and naval, army and marine corps officers stationed in Washington, D.C., from petitioning Congress for legislation, for appropriations, "or for congressional action of any kind, except with the consent and knowledge of the head of the department."[39] Administrative reformers such as finance professor Frederick Cleveland exacerbated labor tension by emphasizing the need for frugal government operations. Labor agitation among government employees began to increase, as workers complained about deteriorating work conditions, an increased workload caused by agency cutbacks, and low pay. Perhaps emulating French postal workers who had gone on strike in 1909, ten American railway mail workers in the Midwest refused to do extra work when the department failed to fill a vacancy in 1911. Meanwhile two hundred sympathetic South Dakota postal clerks not only resisted the department's suggestion that they replace the protesting railway workers but also threatened to resign unless vacancies were filled or extra compensation provided. Departmental authorities demoted and dismissed numerous employees for their role in this mini-insurrection.[40]

Arsenal and navy yard workers expressed similar discontent with the initiatives of the president and the administrative reformers. Organized under the National League of Government Employment, they vigorously opposed attempts by department officials to implement scientific management plans. Joseph Cain, head of the league, considered scientific management "synonymous with a degrading, slave-driving, sweating and humiliating process." He asked that the War and Navy Department substitute scientific management with a "more common sense method" of labor relations. "The Government should be a leader, or in other words," he stated, "*the Government should be a model employer.*" In a letter to the secretary of war, the War Department's ordnance chief Brigadier General William Crozier disputed Cain's complaints point by point, noting that "the mutual pulling and hauling of employer and employee to secure a greater share of the profit of enterprises undertaken has no place in a government establishment where there are no profits to divide, and where the employing officers have no motive for depressing wages." Congress, however, was more responsive to Cain's concerns, particularly because workers at the Watertown arsenal in Massachusetts had walked off the job in protest against the Taylor system. A congressional committee conducted hearings in 1911 on the conflict; legislators later resolved the controversy by passing appropriation bills with riders forbidding the use of time and motion studies (even prohibiting the use of stopwatches) in government agencies and installations.[41]

Occasionally government employees benefited from the struggle between the president and the legislators to control administrative practices. In revolt against repeated attempts by Roosevelt and then Taft to increase presidential prerogatives, Congress passed the Lloyd-LaFollette Act in 1912, repealing Roosevelt's and Taft's gag orders and preventing employee dismissals without just cause. Nevertheless, the law also explicitly prevented postal unions from striking. Thus, although Congress weakened the control of executive and departmental authorities over employees, it failed to recognize employee unions as anything more than lobbying organizations.[42]

Reform advocates either brushed the union issue aside or argued that as a model employer, the government should improve work conditions, compensation, and discipline procedures in partnership with employees. If it did so, government unions, they claimed, would weaken and disappear.[43] National Civil Service Reform League officials remained uncomfortable with the politicized activity of employee unions; they hoped that this activity could be "curtailed without completely depriving the [employee] organizations of some legitimate method of expressing their demands through official channels." Petitions, they noted, should go through departmental authorities and not directly to Congress. Under no circumstance, asserted league members, should employees be allowed to dictate the terms of employment. As one said, "it ought to be the rule in the government that the employees were the servants of the nation and not the master."[44] In matters of unionization, the league conveyed a business-style aversion to collective employee action but defended it as an issue of political accountability.

Gender, Race, and the Civil Service

The few women and African Americans who worked in the civil service in the early twentieth century served the nation at the lowest echelons of the bureaucratic hierarchy. Labor segmentation reflected just one of the ways in which contemporary gender and racial ideologies informed the administrative reform process. Turn-of-the-century public administration scientists, for instance, sought to masculinize their subject matter within the context of late Victorian ideals concerning separate spheres. Party supporters had attacked early civil service reformers by referring to them as "Miss Nancys," "goody-goodies," "political hermaphrodites," and "the eunuchs and sissiri of American politics." This highly charged sexual imagery suggested that the merit reform movement had "effeminate" characteristics quite unlike those assigned to the "manly" party system.[45]

According to Camilla Stivers, nineteenth-century civil service reformers and early-twentieth-century public administrators became increasingly defensive about the association of virtue and morality with women, maternalism, and the domestic sphere. In an effort to make merit and administrative reform appear more "muscular," Progressives attempted to "purge reform of any taint of sentimentality—of femininity—by making sure that it was seen as tough-minded, rational, effective, and businesslike."[46]

Thus, public administrators, like business managers, increasingly adopted the engineering rhetoric of efficiency, in effect gendering their field in masculine terms. Executive management, quantitative analysis of work rates, development of hierarchical structures, and classification of occupations and salaries attached personnel administration to the masculine worlds of business, science, engineering, and the military. Afraid that the "taint of sentimentality" would undermine their professional status and hence their ability to effect structural change within the civil service, public administrators emphasized the need to discover universal "scientific" principles of organizational behavior. This, they believed, would accord their field of study professional authority and would infuse their efforts with an aura of scientific objectivity; as a result their new rhetoric glossed their organizational plans with a sense of evolutionary inevitability.[47]

Evolutionary models also affected the employment prospects of both women and African Americans in the federal government. Their service to the nation proved problematic for administrative reformers who sought to equate the classified service with citizenship and democracy. Although issues concerning the rights of women and African Americans had been hotly contested in the nineteenth century and early in the twentieth, most Americans continued to reserve the rights of full citizenship for white males. By segmenting women and African Americans into low-paying and low-status jobs, government officials avoided a substantive discussion of the citizenship rights of female and African-American federal employees, thus legitimating inequality and underscoring the distinction officials made between group and individual merit.

Women had occupied civil service positions since 1861 when the Treasury Department hired female clerks in a "bold experiment." As Cindy Sondik Aron has demonstrated, the federal bureaucracy became one of the few places in which the nineteenth-century concept of separate spheres broke down. Yet, the "bold experiment" in a sex-integrated workforce did not mean that women competed on equal footing with men. The experiment was not that bold. The Agriculture Department, for example, discouraged the appointment of married women and expected any woman who married a federal employee to resign her position so as to make the position available for another "worthy" individual.[48] Wage scales were divided on the basis of gender; in 1864 Congress established $600 as the wage ceiling for female clerks, a figure half that accorded to men. In later years officials maintained that women "would consider themselves well paid at $1,000 a year," even though men in comparable positions earned $1,200 to $1,800. And once a woman occupied a position, the job tended to be assigned a lower salary, ironically making it more difficult for any man who subsequently held the position to increase his salary.[49]

Even after passage of the Pendleton Act, government officials continued to deprive women of appointments and promotions to high-status, high-paying jobs.[50] One fourteen-year female veteran of the civil service remarked in 1893 that "so frequently have I seen young men pushed over me that I feel disheartened." She also recalled that one young man, who was several years her junior and who had ten years less experience in the service, had recently earned a promotion that gave him $200 more a year in salary than she received.[51] These experiences were commonplace. They reflected popular perceptions concerning the worth of female labor and the potential capabilities of women. Accordingly, men held a monopoly on the position of bureau chief until 1912, when Julia Lathrop became the head of the Children's Bureau.[52]

By that time, lower-level female workers were attempting to use the personnel system to improve their status within the bureaucracy. Gertrude McNally, a worker in the Bureau of Engraving and Printing, helped organize a small union in 1909 to protest unsanitary lunchroom conditions and inadequate pay. Aided by a similar women's union in the Government Printing Office, McNally and her fellow union members earned the right to a minimum wage; they achieved their victory despite the opposition of the bureau's all-male plate printers' union. Four years later, the union successfully blocked departmental efforts to implement a piece-rate system. By 1917, McNally's union had become one of two charter locals in the American Federation of Labor's National Federation of Federal Employees (NFFE). The engraving and printing lodge remained active, holding group meetings to gather occupational and salary information for a Joint Congressional Commission on Reclassification. It also convinced national headquarters to protest an executive order that had abolished twenty-eight merit-based positions within the bureau. Calling this an "affront" to the merit system, the union halted this "spoils raid" and forced the department to reinstate the dismissed employees.[53]

The World War I labor shortage aided women, as did the fact that they often interpreted aspects of the new technical orientation toward personnel administration in gender-blind terms. Prior to the war, women had constituted between 5 and 10 percent of all government workers. That percentage rose to 20 percent during the war, and was even higher in Washington, D.C., where women made up 75 percent of all new appointments.[54] Many of these politically active women and female civil servants expected the merit system to ignore gender differences with regard to appointment and promotion.

Professional women, many of whom were trained for careers in social work, found in the government an outlet for their professional aspirations. Management specialist Mary van Kleeck, for instance, worked for the army during the war. She promoted new personnel management schemes in the munitions industry and encouraged women to pursue careers as employment managers so that they could ease other women into new war industry posts. Mary Anderson, like van Kleeck, entered government during the war to aid with the mobilization of labor. She then became the first head of the Women's Bureau in the Department of Labor, joining Lathrop at the Children's Bureau as another female bureau chief.[55] Although she well understood the barriers to women working in the civil service and the failure of the classification system to provide equal pay for equal work, Anderson found much to praise about the federal service. "Nowhere perhaps has the advance of women with any employer been more dramatic than with Uncle Sam," she concluded.[56]

Pressure by professional and unionized women combined with the wartime labor shortage to eliminate some explicitly gender-biased regulations. A study by the Women's Bureau revealed that women were prohibited from taking more than 64 percent of scientific and professional exams and 87 percent of exams under the mechanical and manufacturing trades. Overall, some 60 percent of civil service exams were not open to women. All clerical exams, on the other hand, were open to women. Salary levels reflected these prohibitions. Eighty-six percent of women earned salaries ranging from $900 to $1,299, whereas only 36 percent of the men in the service fell under that salary bracket. As a result of the bureau's extensive study, the Civil Service Commission lifted gender restrictions on tests in 1919. In that same year legislators forbade appointment officers from stipulating gender in their requests to the Civil Service Commission for certifications, unless "sex is a physical barrier to the proper performance of duties of the position to be filled."[57] Finally, under the Classification Act of 1923, Congress provided for equal pay for equal work, "irrespective of sex."[58] Agency officials, however, frequently circumvented these regulations simply by specifying why a position required the employment of a man or woman or by changing job titles to obscure unequal pay schemes. In addition, enforcement of equal opportunity statutes was essentially nonexistent. At the end of the 1920s, women held 40 percent of the positions in the departmental service but only a total of 166 served in supervisory or executive positions that paid more than $4,000 a year.[59]

African Americans had a more difficult relationship to the new technical school of personnel administration than did women. Initially, the Pendleton Act seemed to improve the employment prospects of African Americans. At the time the Pendleton Act was passed in 1883, approximately 620 African Americans held jobs with the federal government. Eight years later approximately 10 percent of the federal workforce in Washington, D.C., was black. The Civil Service Commission supported this trend, noting in a section of its annual report the merit system's "benefit to the colored race," which gave African Americans "the chance to enter the Government service on their own merits in fair competition with white and colored alike." Although the report also reflected stereotypes concerning the competence of black politicians, it generally heralded the opportunity of educated blacks to join public service. These benefits were short-lived. A general deterioration of race relations through the 1890s harmed employment prospects for blacks in the federal service.[60] The return of Grover Cleveland and the Democrats to power in 1893 combined with the depression and Jim Crow laws in the 1890s resulted in a steady decline in the percentage of African Americans in the civil service. According to one scholar, the Civil Service Commission counted 2,400 blacks in the departmental service in 1891. The following year the number declined to 1,532.[61]

For much of the first decade of the twentieth century, the percentage of African Americans in the civil service hovered between 4.5 and 6 percent. In 1907, the Census Bureau reported that people of color constituted 6.1 percent of the civil service. Of these 11,328 employees, 8,352 were African American. In the nation's capital, one federal employee in ten, said the bureau, was black. Scholar Samuel Krislov argued that the percentages inadequately describe the increasing race prejudice experienced by African-American public servants in the early 1900s.[62] President Theodore Roosevelt gave an early assurance to Booker T. Washington that he would appoint black Americans to government posts, but Roosevelt actually did little to see that this promise was carried out. The African-American newspaper in the capital, the *Bee*, actually complained about Washington's control over appointments and his unwillingness to challenge Roosevelt's poor record with respect to African-American federal employment. During the early 1900s, promotions for African Americans holding clerical, messenger, and laboring positions became a rarity. According to one study, by 1908 only three to four black men in the entire service had been elevated to supervisory positions; in the State Department no blacks served above the rank of messenger. In 1909 department officials appointed a black man who was a personal friend of the secretary of state to the position of clerk.[63] President William Howard Taft made only a perfunctory effort to remedy this discrimination. His appointment of nine blacks to high-level posts appeared to signal an enlightened attitude toward race; but then he explained that he thought it better to appoint a few blacks to prominent positions rather than spread "a lot of petty [appointments] among the mass of their race."[64]

The merit system of the technical reformers had proven to be anything but color-blind. Department officials used the discretion accorded them under the rule of three to eliminate black applicants from consideration. Elected officials also sanctioned race discrimination, as they began to review Jim Crow bills for Washington, D.C., in 1907. At least one congressman introduced a bill to bar all African Americans from federal jobs.[65]

While the introduction of merit and vocational aptitude tests, along with efficiency ratings, offered a potential challenge to nativist claims that African Americans were genetically less intelligent, government officials often reasoned that as a "race," African Americans were not equipped to assume the full duties of citizenship. Civil service reform advocate President Roosevelt demonstrated some inclination to perceive merit in color-blind terms, as he explicitly insisted that government appointments go to the "best men" irrespective of race, color, or creed. As an adherent to contemporary social and physical science theories, however, Roosevelt linked genetics and environment to the development of races. One historian has explained that "Roosevelt's opinions about the extent of participation of any race in American politics rested primarily on his conviction that centuries of evolutionary development preceded attainment of the level requisite for participation in affairs of state." A few individual blacks, Roosevelt conceded, may have reached that level, but the vast majority "would have to wait until the interacting forces of racial inheritance and environment prepared them to assume more responsible roles."[66] Many psychometricians shared these views, suggesting that only some groups could be educated into citizenship. According to historian JoAnne Brown, exams became necessary in order to ascertain the " 'mental levels' of these prospective outcasts and citizens, in order to tell them apart."[67] Neither Roosevelt nor psychometricians offered a pure form of biological determinism, but their reliance upon scientific— including biological—methods, models, and metaphors continued to reify racial categories.

Roosevelt's successor, President Taft, perceived a direct correlation between merit and race. In comparing blacks to people who had physical disabilities, he stipulated that "there is no constitutional right in anyone to hold office. The question is fitness. A one-legged man would hardly be selected for mail carrier, and although we would deplore his misfortune, nevertheless we would not seek to neutralize it by giving him a place that he could not fill." The president also sanctioned segregation in the Census Bureau, initiating a pattern that would be copied in numerous agencies over the next several decades.[68]

A race-based merit system became more entrenched in the years surrounding World War I. Democrat Woodrow Wilson's New Freedom program promised an opportunity to all citizens to compete for wealth and status. But once in office, the president dismissed all but two of Taft's high-level black appointments; he gave the position of Washington, D.C., Recorder of the Deeds, a post that had gone to black men since 1881, to a white; and he failed to object to an intense lobbying effort by white supremacists either to remove all blacks from public service occupations or to restrict them to menial jobs— or at the very least to segregate them in the workplace. His private screening of *Birth of a Nation* further demoralized African Americans. Three of Wilson's southern-born cabinet members, Postmaster General Albert Burleson, Secretary of the Treasury William McAdoo, and Secretary of the Navy Josephus Daniels, supported segregationist policies in their respective departments. By the fall of 1913, McAdoo had agreed to a policy that segregated workers by room and forbade blacks from eating at lunch tables as well as from using certain toilet facilities.[69] Congress followed suit. The House Committee on Civil Service Reform held hearings in March 1914 on two bills that would have required racial separation in all agency work spaces and would have prevented the appointment of any black to be a supervisor of a white. In the words of the bill's sponsor, "the Almighty by the stamp of color decreed that the Caucasian race should occupy positions of authority and control the destinies of this country. . . . It is unjust to a member of [the] inferior race to put him in positions of authority . . . even over his own race."[70]

Restrictive measures under the Wilson administration tended to mitigate the slight benefit blacks derived from their increased federal employment during the wartime labor shortage. Even then, many agency officials continued to refuse appointments to black applicants and created a strict division of labor that relegated most blacks to messenger or custodial positions.

Meanwhile, rising living costs and static government salaries undermined the advantage that job security offered these black civil servants, members of the city's middle class. The resurgence of antiradicalism and race riots of 1919, along with the depression in 1920–21, further narrowed the opportunities of African Americans in the public service. Throughout the war years, federal administrators failed to perceive the contradictions between race discrimination and technical reform policies. In a telling example of the extent to which administrators ignored these contradictions, Navy Department officials required black civil servants to do their work behind screens. In a literal as well as figurative sense, the screens shielded these employees from public view and power.[71]

Postwar Administration

In 1919, the government began a crackdown on labor radicalism, the Chicago race riot erupted, and Congress appointed IGR staffers Lewis Meriam and Frederick Cleveland as administrative experts on a commission to consider a new position and salary classification system. Efforts to centralize and standardize operations paralleled nativist attempts to impose cultural uniformity upon American society. Passage of a Budget and Accounting Act in 1921 with its emphasis on careful calculation of personnel costs paved the way for a comprehensive bill to standardize and unify government salaries. Reformers took advantage of congressional support for standardized personnel policies to impose a more rigid career grid on the federal service. In its final form, the Classification Act of 1923 created five services: professional and scientific; subprofessional; clerical administrative and fiscal (CAF); custodial (CU, later subsumed into the crafts, protective and custodial service or CPC); and clerical-mechanical. Within each service, the law subdivided positions of the same character into "classes" and created "grades" that carried a specified salary range at each level.[72] Proponents asserted that the act presented "not only a scientific attack on the problem of salary equalization and standardization . . . but also provided machinery through which other phases of personnel administration might be facilitated."[73]

The political struggles that had taken place over the classification legislation and that would later erupt over the administration of the act suggested that a personnel "science" was a fiction. Legislators, Civil Service Commission representatives, and the employees themselves highlighted the subjectivity involved in dividing positions and occupations into categories such as "professional," "clerical," and "administrative." During one hearing on salary reclassification, a representative from the Civil Service Commission lectured lawmakers on the difference between a "calling" and a profession. Too many callings and tasks, he complained, had been included in the scientific and professional service; thus the schedule had been "diluted to the point of absurdity." One legislator defended the inclusion of callings such as translators, civil service examiners, economists, and historians in this schedule by quoting the *Century Dictionary* definition of a profession.[74]

Initially, government unions, especially NFFE, provided support for scientific administration, although they had reservations about its application. They believed it would solidify the merit system, thus expanding career opportunities within the bureaucracy.[75] Union members also actively campaigned for a classification system but differed with IGR experts and league members over the allocation of positions and salaries. These differences notwithstanding, administrative reformers and government employees agreed on the advantage of uniform personnel procedures over arbitrary patronage practices, thus muting conflicts within the personnel movement for much of the 1920s.[76]

Women likewise supported technical reform, believing that impersonal regulations and standards would give them a chance to advance up the career ladder. In the 1920s, the League of Women Voters, for instance, acted as a vigorous proponent of the extension of the merit system, and the Women's Bureau in the Department of Labor became a significant source of information on the advancement of women in the civil service. Yet few officials— either female or male—offered a critique of the essentialist categories undergirding a sexual division of labor. In a commencement address to Mount Holyoke college graduates, public administration specialist Frederick Davenport claimed that government needed the "moral guidance of women." Modern political systems, he said, needed the "maternal" instinct of women to guide policies concerning education, public health, race, housing, juvenile courts, and prohibition. Because women were far superior to men in benevolence, nobility, and sacrifice, he claimed, they could make significant contributions to social work and reform. He emphasized that he was not suggesting that women make a career out of politics but only that they take government employment as an opportunity to perform human service.[77] One public personnel specialist had a more pointed perception of female labor. He reminded "extreme feminists" who advocated strict statutory prohibitions against sex discrimination "that the experience of all large personnel systems is that it is better . . . to confine the force entrusted with a given class of work entirely to one sex," even if both men and women were qualified to do the work.[78]

Another personnel expert, Herman Feldman, who was more sympathetic to women's concerns, argued that the government should provide women with equal opportunities and dispel "erroneous" notions that women were less qualified, on the basis of hereditary and socialization patterns, for many high-level posts. Even so, he said, one could not always "make light" of this opinion, "because some of those who hold this view have gone out of their way to make new places for women and they relate their experiences with chagrin." Feldman claimed that he had no intention of settling this controversial issue and instead offered a vague suggestion that a central personnel agency work to clear up "misunderstandings" among both men and women regarding discrimination. If necessary, he said, the agency should implement a broad educational program based upon the agency's findings and experience.[79] Like Feldman, most administrative reformers could not disentangle themselves from this gender quagmire. While they believed in principle that a merit-based system was gender-blind, they operated within a culture that accepted certain limitations upon women as "natural" and universal.

Racial diversity also continued to shape the new technical orientation toward personnel administration. Although the percentage of African Americans in the federal service rose steadily in the 1920s, reaching approximately 9.6 percent in 1928, most occupations above the level of messenger and custodian remained off-limits to people of color.[80] In the federal government, where success was not measured by profits generated, job titles provided an important mark of success. An employee's place in the job hierarchy often determined his or her status. One black messenger hired by the War Finance Corporation in 1920 recalled that at the end of his five-year tenure with the agency, he was making more than the lowest grade of clerk but was still classified as a messenger. Even after he began assisting another clerk with filing, he kept his messenger title. Whenever he requested a promotion, department officials raised his salary by $5—but never his job classification. Another African-American messenger remembered that the appointment clerk in his agency remarked that blacks would be hired as clerks "only over his dead body." The only black employee promoted from messenger to clerk prior to World War II in that agency was a worker who had been with the agency for sixty years. Very late in his life, his boss recognized his expertise with a promotion. Agency administrators rewarded him with a higher rating and more pay but refused to give him all of the duties or status of a clerk.[81]

Scientific administration thus skirted the knotty questions posed by unionization and the employment of women and African Americans. Passage of the Pendleton Civil Service Act had only initiated the construction of a merit-based career service. The act had merely started a process of administrative reform. Administration reformers, many associated with the Bureau of Municipal Research, IGR, Taylor Society, and other quasi-public organizations molded that movement to suit their own vision of an American civil service epitomizing scientific social progress. That vision included the construction of a hierarchical structure that did not accommodate a diverse workforce. In the 1930s, government administrators would find it necessary to deal with the tensions that class, gender, and racial differences were producing within the federal bureaucracy.

In the late 1920s, two organizations devoted to governmental personnel issues—the Civil Service Assembly of the United States and Canada and the National Civil Service Reform League—negotiated a division of the "field" of public personnel administration. Under their informal agreement, the assembly was to research personnel problems in an effort to "work out the answers to technical problems." It would issue "authoritative statements" on personnel matters. The league, on the other hand, was to be responsible for generating publicity and support for new personnel programs. This, said one expert in public personnel administration, would free personnel operators from the "disagreeable necessity" of engaging in publicity work, "which often subjects them to embarrassment." This same author celebrated the new technical and scientific focus of personnel operators and lauded the fact that young men and women with college course work in the functions, organization, and administration of government, in the "principles" of job classification, test construction, and statistical evaluation, and in a general "scientific approach to personnel problems" were now being recruited by public personnel agencies like the United States Civil Service Commission. These staff members, familiar with the "methods and tools" of science, were helping government agencies conduct new research on personnel problems.[82]

This acknowledgment of a split between "scientific" and "propaganda" activities reflected the degree to which a major shift had occurred in the sixty-year history of the merit reform movement. By 1930 the technical, scientific school of public personnel reform had become the dominant tradition, fully replacing an earlier tradition of moral reform, which opponents had labeled "soft" and "effeminate" in an effort to discredit it.

Turn-of-the-century architects of the administrative state perceived a larger regulatory role for government in the American economy, although they strongly opposed socialism and remained suspicious of mass democracy. Instead they envisioned a corporatist administrative arm that would promote national power without dampening an individualistic, capitalist spirit, and that would define Americanism without succumbing to a plural definition of citizenship.[83]

As Cecelia Tichi and JoAnne Brown have observed, elements of Edward Bellamy's popular novel *Looking Backward* stood as both a reflection and prototype for the new American state. Although American organizational builders rejected Bellamy's extreme nationalism and his socialist proclivities, they, like Bellamy, admired efficiency and strove to harness individual talents.[84] Just as Bellamy's utopia described how efficiency and happiness resulted from slotting individuals into the occupations best suited to their abilities, Progressive era reformers turned to vocational aptitude tests to fit "round men and women into round holes." But defining *round* proved to be highly dependent upon social and cultural forces. Although new management practices and the use of exams had the potential to disrupt preexisting gender and racial employment patterns, in the 1910s and 1920s, they accommodated and perpetuated gender and racial stereotypes. Like Bellamy's utopia, the federal civil service downplayed pluralism, instead opting to present a vision of America as a land of white, middle-class citizens whose speech, customs, and values blended together in a harmonious whole. The New Deal and World War II would introduce new visions of the civil service and suggest new managerial techniques designed to recognize pluralism.

2 Building the New Deal Civil Service

Long after the Progressive era ended, the National Civil Service Reform League continued to proselytize for its cause. As late as 1935, the league's executive officers were encouraging civics instructors to "teach [students] a vivid picture of a system of [civil service career] ladders leading from the lowest to the highest positions in the public service." In this manner, league officials commented, "Jefferson's aristocracy of virtue and talent may be drawn into the public service early and stay in it."[1] Under this system, government employees could begin their careers as messengers and end them as bureau chiefs. Wall Street financier Russell Leffingwell, former assistant secretary of treasury (under Woodrow Wilson), endorsed a more elitist approach to civil service staffing: "The Government ought to be out for the triple A men," he stated, and should recruit these "triple A men out of the graduating classes of our great universities, as they do in England and in France."[2] Leffingwell's concerns parroted those of various public officials. Two years earlier, in 1934, Secretary of Treasury Henry Morgenthau, commenting on the creation of the Social Science Research Council's Commission of Inquiry on the Public Service (approved by President Franklin D. Roosevelt), noted that the expansion of government activities would make the public more interested in the sources from which the government recruited its workforce. One civil service commissioner, in supporting the creation of a distinguished career service, told Roosevelt that he objected to the practice of giving relief workers jobs similar to those of regular career civil servants. This, he claimed, would denigrate the work done by civil servants and make the service a "haven" for the unemployed.[3]

Although reformers offered different prescriptions for the ills of the civil service, they all agreed that the qualifications and placement of government workers was a problem worthy of discussion. The creation of Roosevelt's "brain trust" and the administration's interest in creating an elite corps of administrators sparked a venomous discussion among federal civil servants.[4] During the 1930s they bitterly debated the advantages and disadvantages of hiring "triple A men" out of "great universities." One reporter warned that the government was establishing a "caste system," in which favored individuals from "favored schools" were "hand-picked" to take jobs at the top that might have gone to employees who through years of effort had prepared themselves for a promotion.[5] A union leader claimed that there was "a total absence of any system of promotion in the Federal civil service" and that those few who did manage to rise from rags to riches did so with "considerable" political aid.[6]

The Great Depression and Franklin D. Roosevelt's inauguration in 1933 transformed the terms of debate regarding the construction of the American civil service. As the president and Congress quickly implemented new programs, Roosevelt began to recruit intellectuals from America's elite universities to staff new agencies. To facilitate hiring, Congress exempted many of these emergency agencies from civil service rules.

At the same time, the administration trumpeted the cause of the "forgotten man," providing ordinary citizens public employment on projects such as the Civilian Conservation Corps and the Works Progress Administration as well as offering appointments in New Deal agencies to members of previously excluded groups.[7] As one historian commented: "Roosevelt's all-embracing strategy was to appear as the patron of the average American, commanding attention not merely because he was the nation's leader, blessed with a benignly superior, cultivated background, but also by suggesting that he could help define the true average."[8] The contradiction between the New Deal's mission to employ "average" Americans in government posts and its efforts to attract a new cadre of intellectual aristocrats into the civil service caused significant class tension within the federal bureaucracy.

Hence while the conflict between supporters of the merit and patronage systems continued to fester during the New Deal era, a more contentious discussion concerning the merit system took shape. Among administrative reformers, it was not clear whether the Roosevelt Administration should recruit a more professional workforce or whether, as some argued, the civil service was to be a democratic institution, used as a means of upward mobility for ordinary Americans. A number of Roosevelt's advisors, for instance, revealed a strong desire to develop an administrative aristocracy by recruiting highly educated individuals into the career service.[9] This issue was especially problematic during the Great Depression as the crisis encouraged Americans to reexamine how issues of class and capitalism related to the meaning and workings of democracy.

In 1938, Roosevelt issued Executive Order 7916 extending the merit system to a variety of occupations, while exempting some professional positions. To address the status of these positions, he established a special Committee on Civil Service Improvement in 1939, chaired by Supreme Court Justice Stanley Reed. The committee was to create a "blueprint of principles and methods to be followed in procuring the highest type of men and women for the Government service." [10] While the president and his close advisors continued to link the improvement of the civil service to the implementation of a merit system, they did not always feel that the Civil Service Commission was capable of recruiting the most talented Americans. Hence the Reed committee considered creating a new "elite" service alongside the regular classified civil service and outside the jurisdiction of the Civil Service Commission. [11]

But creating parallel recruiting systems threatened to establish a two-tier career service: a classified service of clerks to be funneled through the Civil Service Commission and an elite group of professionals selected under a separate system of rules. To those who entered the civil service as messengers or low-level clerks, these reforms promised to create a stratified career service of favored recruits and struggling staffers with severely limited promotional possibilities.

Long-time civil service workers as well as the chair of the Civil Service Commission, Harry Mitchell, pointed to organizations such as the National Institute of Public Affairs (NIPA) as evidence of this trend. Founded by civic activist Frederick Davenport and funded by a grant from the Rockefeller Foundation, NIPA began recruiting young college students in 1935 as interns in various federal agencies. Mentors in the service were to groom these educated interns for professional careers in government. [12] Helen Miller, representing United Federal Workers of America (UFWA) Local 12, concluded in 1940 that NIPA and similar programs gave "special privileges to a favored few in disregard of the interests of the thousands of government employees now in the service who are qualified for promotion." Indeed, she charged, the method of selection was "undemocratic and noncompetitive." Only those with money, she said, could afford to work without pay. Black interns and students from free metropolitan universities were noticeably absent from NIPA intern registers. Consequently, Miller claimed, the program was susceptible to "favoritism, intrigue and politics—the very evils which the merit system was designed to eliminate." On behalf of union members, she requested that the Labor Department cease its participation in the program. Two southern congressmen had expressed similar concerns earlier, urging government recruiters to select those with proven ability and the "necessary character qualifications" even if they had been "denied a college education."[13]

Reporter Scott Hart, author of the *Washington Post*'s "Federal Diary," also revealed a bias toward experience over education in building a civil service career system. He commended personnel director Thomas McNamara's commonsense approach to management at the Railroad Retirement Board and his deep commitment to a government service "wherein practical and competent men can demonstrate what they've got on the ball, and having demonstrated it, move up." In Hart's view, McNamara vocalized the necessity of retaining opportunities for low-level civil servants by favoring a system of career development that would be free of "red tapes of technicality and theory." This approach, Hart believed, would appeal to those upset about the federal government's trend toward hiring bureaucrats "with pockets full of college degrees."[14] Although many ambitious civil servants sought educational credentials themselves by attending a number of the night, or "sun down," schools speckled throughout Washington, D.C.—including the government's own Department of Agriculture Graduate School—they did not want the service reserved only for those who had already acquired elite educations. Employees with talent and initiative were to rise through the ranks to positions of prominence, for as Charles Piozet, personnel director at the Navy Department, remarked, it was "un-American that an individual in the Government service could not advance."[15]

Deeply embedded in the concept of an American merit civil service was the notion that applicants would qualify for appointment on the basis of an examination *and* that once in, civil servants with talent would have an opportunity to climb the ladder leading to success. To believers, the fusion of merit and upward mobility made the civil service system democratic, for any worthy person could rise, regardless of "class" or "status." Those advocating for a different system preferred an English model that created two general tiers: an elite administrative class recruited from the best universities and a lower clerical class that had little chance of promotion into the senior civil service. Although mobility occurred within each class, American proponents of a democratic merit system preferred an open system of promotion that gave low-level clerks with talent the opportunity to rise to senior positions.[16] Yet even these American champions of the merit system ignored two critical issues: first, that *merit* was a loosely defined and highly contested term and, second, that ladders suggested hierarchy and thus signified inequity. These administrators failed to specify the criteria that would be used to evaluate candidates for higher posts. Moreover, their belief in upward mobility implied a desire to have elite positions vested with authority to control the behavior and activities of those occupying lower positions. Even those favoring social mobility were not criticizing the existence of a hierarchy but the means by which people obtained top positions.

In this debate, "caste" referred to occupational barriers created by academic credentials, but other caste systems operated in the federal government. In fact, the debate over education—and class mobility—broadened into a discussion about other hurdles to advancement. When Helen Miller criticized the NIPA in 1940 for failing to recruit black interns, she touched on the existence of the deeply rooted caste system based upon skin color. Gender likewise acted as a barrier to advancement for women. Many women, for instance, earned a place on NIPA registers only after World War II removed many male candidates.[17] Similarly, the increasing emphasis placed upon education and experience in filling professional posts, observed officials in the Women's Bureau, disadvantaged women. One official noted that more women than men tended to pass entrance exams and thus, in previous years when exams weighed more heavily in the application process, women had had more of an opportunity to secure a position.[18] During the Great Depression, racial and gender barriers often became more pronounced as many Americans felt white males to be most deserving of scarce jobs. In the federal bureaucracy, however, challenges to these barriers eventually opened up a new dialogue concerning the rights of women and African Americans in the federal workplace. A fight over the employment of married women and the efforts of civil rights activists to fight inequality forced federal administrators to confront issues of sex and race discrimination. Unions often provided lower-level employees with the vocabulary, organizational power, and procedural mechanisms with which they could combat these inequities. Depression and New Deal politics encouraged a new discussion about pluralism in America, even if the discussion did not result in an immediate shift in power relations.

Federal Employee Unions and an "Old" Deal

As a cornerstone of New Deal efforts to empower ordinary working Americans and create a more inclusive society, federal support for unions became a symbol of New Deal opposition to America's aristocracy, the corporate elite. Promulgation of section 7(a) of the National Industrial Recovery Act (NIRA) and its successor, the National Labor Relations Act of 1935, encouraged American workers to organize and to exercise their right to bargain collectively. These laws, however, did not extend to federal civil servants, who occupied a nebulous position in the world of union labor. Over time, small groups of militant civil servants challenged their exclusion from New Deal labor laws, thus creating a more adversarial relationship between agency administrators and staff. For these activists, support for the merit system and promotional opportunities constituted part of a larger movement to secure bargaining rights and control over the office floor.

Due to the dearth of civil service unions prior to the 1910s, government officials developed few policies with regard to unionization.[19] The 1912 Lloyd-LaFollette Act recognized the right of postal workers to join employee organizations and petition Congress on their own behalf. Federal employees outside the Post Office simply assumed that they were covered by the act. Hence, prior to the 1930s, union-government relations were defined by a mutual, but essentially unwritten, understanding that Congress had the right to determine the terms of employment for the federal government.[20] The constitution for the oldest general civil service union, the National Federation of Federal Employees (NFFE), for example, stated that it was organized in order to petition Congress and that its members would not engage in strikes.[21] The union acted as an organized interest group. Under long-time president Luther Steward, NFFE engaged in a tireless battle against political patronage by allying closely with the National Civil Service Reform League and pressing Congress to eliminate occupational exemptions to civil service laws.

NFFE's separation from the American Federation of Labor (AFL) in 1932, the creation of a new AFL union, the American Federation of Government Employees (AFGE), and the advent of the New Deal signaled a new and more turbulent period in government labor relations.[22] This was true even though leadership in the AFGE was actually relatively conservative, with strong links to supervisory officials and administrators in the Civil Service Commission. Like the NFFE, the new union emphasized lobbying, denounced strikes, and fought against patronage.

But the New Deal changed the demographics of the federal workforce, and a number of new union members challenged this conservatism. Many of the men and women migrating from northeastern industrial cities into Washington's civil service during the 1930s actively supported the administration's industrial labor policies, and they hoped these would be applied to the federal civil service.[23] This small group of committed union members also became increasingly vocal about the needs of clerks and other low-level staffers in federal agencies, many of whom were female and/or African American. By the end of the decade, they had become strong civil rights advocates. Overall, they fought hard to protect promotional possibilities and the right of employees to engage in negotiations involving grievances.[24]

Civil servant militancy was fueled when newly elected President Franklin D. Roosevelt signed into law the Economy Act. Passed during the first one hundred days, the legislation was designed to fulfill Roosevelt's promise to maintain a balanced budget and to economize on government operations. It expanded on a similar measure passed in the waning days of Herbert Hoover's administration; that act had cut the salaries of government workers and furloughed them without pay.

Union reaction to Roosevelt's Economy Act was swift, strong, and unanimously negative. Although NFFE prefaced its opposition by noting that federal employees were eager to do their patriotic duty to spur economic growth, it also noted that pay cuts would hinder consumption, a necessary precursor to recovery. Steward evoked Progressive Party reform rhetoric, claiming that the cuts were an attempt by the "powerful . . . to stamp out services that the people rightly have demanded of a civilized Government." The American people would not fail, he said, to take a "united, decisive stand against a Bourbon policy based on long out-moded principles of laissez-faire." A few months later, he pledged to fight the shortsighted "wage reductionists . . . who seem unable to think of any other solution of an economic depression than to diminish the earning and spending power of the wage earner."[25]

Other unions raised similar objections. Both Edward Gainer, president of the National Association of Letter Carriers (NALC), and E. Claude Babcock, president of the AFGE, pointed to the National Recovery Administration's (NRA) aim to raise the wages, and hence the consumption, of working men and women. Why, they wondered, would the government pursue the opposite policy with respect to its own workforce?[26] By citing the NIRA, union leaders drew attention to the comparison between industrial and civil service labor. This inevitably raised the expectations of some rank-and-file members that the new industrial labor relations policies articulated under section 7(a) of the NIRA would be introduced in government work.

Some government administrators of course resented union demands. One AFGE lodge in the Bureau of Internal Revenue, for instance, circulated a

"Memorial to Congress" calling for a restoration of the wage cuts instituted under the Economy Act. William McReynolds, assistant to the treasury secretary and later Roosevelt's personal advisor on personnel issues, informed Babcock that government departments could not ethically "sanction participation of Federal employees in opposition to the President's desire."[27]

A local AFGE lodge in the NRA became the first to test the administration's commitment to the rights of civil service labor. John Donovan, a civil servant representative of many of the young people coming to Washington, D.C., in the 1930s to help the government set up its "New Deal," served as the first president of AFGE lodge 91. Donovan had received his bachelor's and master's degrees from Columbia. There, he had engaged in political activism, joining the Social Problems Club, created to work on behalf of radical instructors who were being harassed. He was in the midst of pursuing more graduate work in economics and economic history when he left to take a job at the NRA in Washington, D.C. Not surprisingly, he took a position in the Labor Advisory Board, because as he later noted, he was interested in the conditions of labor everywhere, including his own agency. Lodge 91 attracted other members committed to union principles; it counted among its ranks Henry Rhine, who would later become the chief organizer for the UFWA-CIO in the late 1930s. NRA's AFGE lodge, established in November 1933 after frequent complaints by the clerical and stenographic staff of forced overtime (employees often worked twelve- to eighteen-hour days), immediately became active on behalf of the agency's staff employees.[28]

An objection from an employee about the agency's promotion policy precipitated the most significant controversy surrounding the NRA union. Demonstrating her concern with upward mobility, stencil cutter Nancy Luke asked her supervisor for a clear statement regarding pay raises and promotions. After she and another employee continued to press the issue, their supervisor circulated a petition proclaiming the pair a nuisance and recommending that they be reprimanded. When the two appealed to a higher-level executive, Heath Onthank, they received little satisfaction. In the meantime, Luke joined the union lodge, which agreed to look into the problem. When Luke's supervisor issued her a pink slip, union president Donovan sought an audience with NRA head Hugh Johnson. He visited Johnson's office on several occasions, usually with a small delegation, but had little success—despite Johnson's "open door" policy—in securing a meeting with him. At one point, Johnson did agree to see Donovan, but only Donovan, and in his capacity as an "employee" rather than as a union member.[29]

On the morning of June 18, 1934, Donovan tried to see Johnson once again. This time, the receptionist informed Donovan and his thirteen-member delegation that the director would not be able to see them and that they would have to depart the office. Undeterred, Donovan's group waited until 1:00 P.M., at which time Donovan wrote a note stating that the union had been waiting for an appointment for a month and would wait only twenty-four hours more. At 5:00 P.M., Johnson summoned Donovan to his office and dismissed him for "inefficiency, inattention to duty, unauthorized absence from duty, and insubordination."[30]

The next day, Johnson granted the union's initial request and reinstated Nancy Luke to a position in the agency, but a subsequent investigation revealed that the NRA's administrators had long disapproved of the union and its president. For example, Donovan had been in frequent conflict with his boss at the Labor Advisory Board, Gustav Peck. Peck, in fact, had accused Donovan of sending NRA employees to lobby senators against Peck's plan to curtail the activities of the Labor Advisory Board. Peck also had been perturbed by the AFGE's tactics and had accused Donovan of harassing Johnson on government time.[31]

In dismissing Donovan, Johnson tried to cover his anti-union bias. Rather than draw attention to Donovan's union activities, Johnson inquired about Donovan's efficiency as a worker and then called AFGE president E. Claude Babcock. He told Babcock that Donovan was mismanaging union activities and that he was dismissing Donovan not because he belonged to a union but because Donovan was inhibiting the work of the agency and bothering him excessively about the Luke matter. In fact, Johnson said, as a demonstration of his own pro-union stance, he would be willing to help build up the union lodge after Donovan's departure. But Johnson's assurances rang hollow. According to several NRA employees, Donovan was an effective and efficient worker who had contributed much to the development of the labor codes. Certainly, Donovan's sudden dismissal was based on his "radical" approach to labor-management relations.[32]

Civil servants and private-sector union members immediately rallied to Donovan's side. Rank-and-file union members and local activists set up pickets outside the Commerce Department to protest the dismissal. Rhine then wrote to the president requesting a hearing before the National Labor Board (NLB) or a special board of appeals under section 7(a) of the NIRA. Johnson appeared cooperative, suggesting that the case be reviewed by the Federal Trade Commission, the Civil Service Commission, or the NLB.[33] In early August, after the NLB had been transformed into the National Labor Relations Board (NLRB), the board honored the AFGE's request to rule on Donovan's dismissal.[34]

The case revealed much about prevailing attitudes among federal administrators concerning the administrative hierarchy and its channels of communication. Johnson's concept of an open door policy, for instance, emerges as merely a lingering vestige of paternalism and personal authority in government agencies. As Johnson himself later argued, his days simply were not long enough to accommodate all who wished to see him. Thus, in reality, his door was only open when he said it was.[35] Peck, similarly, was annoyed by Donovan's opposition to his labor policies and thought it highly inappropriate that Donovan, a subordinate, would voice those objections to congressional members. To Peck, the lines of authority ran from the top of the agency pyramid down; for an employee to bypass a superior and articulate displeasure with his policies to legislators was grounds for dismissal. To make matters more difficult for aggrieved employees, the agency failed to provide a formal means for employees to appeal administrative decisions. It was highly unusual (in fact unprecedented and not repeated) that the NLRB would rule on such a case. At this time, the government had no in-house tribunals or appeal boards for its employees.

Donovan's case demonstrated the fragility of the government's policy regarding unionization in federal agencies. Johnson and his supervisory staff obviously opposed the presence of the union. Union members alleged that on the evening before their first meeting, Johnson called a member of his staff and asked him to dismiss Donovan and co-worker and union member Margaret Stabler from the Labor Advisory Board.[36] Although Johnson, like many other agency heads, publicly claimed that he approved of the right of NRA employees to organize, he privately worked to minimize the impact of the union and to channel its activities along nonconfrontational paths. If he had to fire a union member to achieve that objective, Johnson had no hesitancy in doing so.

The specific complaints against Donovan also indicate what government administrators considered proper employee behavior. Johnson complained that Donovan and his representatives were attempting to undermine the efficacy of the agency by urging striking workers across the country to ignore the NRA chief's edicts.[37] Not surprisingly, Johnson also objected to Donovan supporters' picketing of government buildings and their use of "insulting" placards, including one proclaiming Johnson to be "Chiseler No. 1." To Johnson, "this type of conduct" established Donovan's unfitness "to assume the oath of office" and was "utterly inconsistent with continued employment or reemployment of any employee in any position of public trust." Roosevelt supported his NRA chief, noting in one letter about the Donovan case that the "mere circumstance that a government employee is an official of a local union cannot be permitted to interfere with his work as a government employee." Civil servants were to keep their opinions and politics to themselves and to voice their complaints in a manner prescribed by their supervisors and hallowed by tradition.[38]

This case revealed the reluctance of many civil servants to accept quietly the government's ambivalence toward unionization. As with the Economy Act, civil servants were vocal and swift in their denunciation of a governmental decision that they found contrary to their best interests. This incident also demonstrated the willingness of civil servants to appropriate the language and techniques of the private-sector labor movement. Admittedly Donovan's case was somewhat unusual in that he actually worked with labor issues and section 7(a); thus his commitment to workers' rights in his own agency was to be expected. But he was not alone. Other departments, like Agriculture, harbored vocal and active union members who began in the 1930s to demand rights consonant with those accorded private-sector unions.

Public-sector unions and their members—like millions of other American workers—were becoming impatient. Union lodges were no longer content to act merely as social and recreational bodies while their national organizations lobbied Congress for civil service legislation. During the New Deal era, union members attempted to negotiate *at the agency level* on such issues as administrative pay raises, grievance procedures, and promotions. Overall, the activism displayed by several of AFGE's lodges in Washington, D.C., was critical to the establishment of the UFWA within the Congress of Industrial Organizations (CIO) in 1937. By the end of the 1930s the UFWA would perfect and expand the use of administrative bargaining as a means of achieving job security, pay raises, and promotions for civil servants.

Rank-and-file activists were much more willing than union leaders to push the private-sector analogy to full expression. For instance, while AFGE's president, E. Claude Babcock, a former secretary of the Civil Service Commission, formally supported the reinstatement of Donovan, he voiced that support along narrow lines. AFGE's official newspaper, the *Government Standard*, called for an investigation of the dismissal but reminded all that there was "no question as to the complete loyalty of the union and its members to the NRA." Babcock further stated that Congress had already confirmed the right of employees to join unions and thus could take no disciplinary action, *unless* an employee became "unreasonable." In the end, he noted, the public interest (not the employee) was the ultimate concern of the union.[39]

National union leaders did not use the Donovan case to broaden their power. To the AFGE elite, the mere fact that the NLRB agreed to hear the case was a victory. They believed it ended their search for an appeal board for government employees.[40] After the case was over and Donovan had been reinstated, the NLRB asserted that it had no jurisdiction over federal employees and never ruled on another civil service case. But AFGE leaders failed to protest this decision. Likewise, Babcock pushed through an amendment to the union's constitution stating that the AFGE was "unequivocally opposed to and will not tolerate strikes, picketing or other public acts against governmental authority which have the effect of embarrassing the Government." Delegations to visit administrators were thereafter limited to five.[41] By 1937, AFGE leadership had lost all tolerance for "militant" activism on the part of its members; it would not hesitate to expel several lodges for "communistic" activity. Consequently, rather than resolving questions concerning the boundaries of civil service unionization, the Donovan case brought them into sharper relief as many more civil servants began to assume that the government's protection of private-sector labor rights also applied to them.

AFGE lodges continued to cause problems for the administration and for management-oriented union leaders in the AFGE and NFFE.[42] An economic downturn in 1937 and congressional efforts to "economize" on government operations brought back memories of the 1933 Economy Act. This time, AFGE members formed a Committee Against False Economy to prevent such a recurrence, but AFGE's new president, former congressman Charles Stengle, refused to recognize the organization. The committee, made up of lodges in the Labor and Agriculture departments, Interstate Commerce Commission, Works Progress Administration, Resettlement Administration, and General Accounting Office, responded with a threat to take independent action. Stengle first issued a "cease-and-desist" order and then suspended them from the AFGE. Five of the targeted lodges challenged the move, claiming that they were the objects of a "vicious red scare" by leaders who wanted to get rid of "progressive elements who opposed them." A few months later seven former AFGE lodges joined the UFWA-CIO then being organized by Denny Lewis, brother of the CIO's founder, John Lewis.[43]

As the UFWA emerged, it became clear that its members believed they had the power to negotiate with agency administrators. Although the UFWA officially denied its members the right to strike, its member lodges pushed the boundaries of collective bargaining. Renegade AFGE Lodge 31, which would join the UFWA in the summer of 1937, claimed that the Agriculture Department had accorded them that right. When department officials unilaterally set policies on reemployment and promotions, the lodge complained bitterly, calling it an infringement on "the basic rights of collective bargaining." The lodge even labeled its grievance work a form of collective bargaining, prompting Secretary Henry Wallace to ask the White House for clarification on its union policy. Presidential aides responded to his requests by noting that they could find only two cases of agreements made between agencies and civil servants.[44]

While the leadership of NFFE and AFGE distanced themselves from the provisions of the National Labor Relations Act, they still modeled their general aims on those of the private-sector union movement. Both the AFGE and NFFE wanted to make the wage system more just and humane. Lee Somers of the AFGE put it most succinctly: "Any so-called white collar worker who today will not admit that unionization is the answer to the salary and wage and condition of labor problems, is simply refusing to think." But he added, "no revolution is necessary . . . the AF of L represents Evolution."[45] *Evolution* was a code word for lobbying; as one AFGE vice president noted, Congress would ignore the needs of civil servants unless they had an organized voice. Power could be achieved through collective action, but only Congress could remedy their problems.[46]

Race relations also contributed to the rifts occurring within the public-sector labor movement. When the UFWA-CIO emerged, the fight for racial justice became part of a larger ideological disagreement with the NFFE and AFGE over the nature of power relations in the federal government. Traditionally, the leadership of the AFL supported the right of its affiliates either to exclude or to segregate black workers if they desired to do so. Hence, AFL President William Green was not necessarily thinking of black employees when he noted in 1934 that it was "no less necessary for Government employees to organize than for other groups. In a way, it is more important for them to organize than for anyone else, for Government employment tends to set labor standards."[47] Two years later, the AFGE did consider creating a "colored lodge," but there is no evidence that such a lodge surfaced. The organization of the UFWA that same year likely siphoned potential black members away from the AFGE because the UFWA, as a CIO union, followed a policy of racial inclusion. Other AFL public service unions either excluded or segregated black employees. As of 1931, for instance, the AFL's Railway Mail Association explicitly forbade black membership, while its National Rural Letter Carriers Association and National Association of Letter Carriers enforced segregated locals. Not surprisingly, black postal employees therefore formed the independent National Alliance of Postal Employees, which over the years worked closely with the National Association for. the Advancement of Colored People (NAACP) to eradicate race discrimination in the Post Office.[48]

In the minds of NFFE and AFGE leaders, unionization was not designed to challenge office hierarchies, administrative paternalism, or the racial caste system. While they recognized that control continued to rest at the top of the organizations, they were satisfied insofar as bosses recognized that they had responsibilities toward employees as well as authority over them. Government officials and their servants had a mutually beneficial covenant. Comparing the relationship to that between lords and vassals, Somers noted that in return for the complete loyalty of employees, government supervisors protected them from undue demands on their health and strength and from arbitrary discharge, unsuitable working conditions, and inadequate pay.[49]

The confrontational approach and progressive demands of some agency lodges threatened to break this social covenant. These techniques offended the more traditional union leadership of the AFGE and NFFE. In an open letter to members of the NFFE, President Luther Steward and Secretary-Treasurer Gertrude McNally condemned militant activity. They scolded AFGE lodges for engaging in sit-down demonstrations and strikes, claiming that the actions brought "shame on all federal employees" and threatened the goodwill NFFE had so carefully nurtured between government administrators and employees. Strikes would not be tolerated in the public service, they informed members, because workers were always able to approach Congress with grievances. Striking, they added, would only alienate the public and Congress from civil service unions.[50] AFGE leaders also rejected these tactics, as they demonstrated when they expelled those union lodges that had publicly criticized the president's economy measures after the 1936 election.

In an effort to marginalize the UFWA and undercut its strength, the AFGE and NFFE emphasized the difference between private- and public-sector labor. Henry Iler, national organizer for the AFGE, for instance, explained to his superiors how the AFGE lost its lodge in the Tennessee Valley Authority

(TVA) to the UFWA. Many in the union, said Iler, were under the mistaken impression that they were protected by the National Labor Relations Act. When Iler informed them that they had been misled, seventy-five members decided to rejoin the AFGE. Iler claimed to have undermined the credibility of the UFWA-CIO.[51]

Apparently, the damage was minimal as the UFWA-CIO continued to grow and challenge the boundaries of labor-management relations. Within a year of its founding, President Roosevelt felt compelled to clarify the proper relationship of unions to the federal government. In addition, his Executive Order 7916, issued in 1938, created a Council of Personnel Administration consisting of agency personnel directors. These directors sought to develop and administer labor relations policies across agencies. They confronted the union issue directly and developed a complex series of administrative procedures that in the 1940s effectively thwarted the most radical aspects of the union movement.

Government Women and the Great Depression

During the Great Depression, class and caste divisions operated on other levels as well. For one, government officials did not conceal their prejudice against women, particularly married women. In fact, they used state power to disadvantage women in the labor market. They routinely laid them off during reductions-in-force and blocked their upward occupational mobility, claiming that women did not need to work. A labor surplus and pervasive patriarchal values combined to provide personnel managers with a convenient rationalization for various forms of sex discrimination in the civil service.

As jobs became scarce, government statutes and popular opinion conspired to keep married women out of the workforce. Such obvious forms of discrimination, however, offered women one benefit. Even if they could not always alter employment practices, women could at least object to sex discrimination openly.

Women in the New Deal civil service did just that. They were highly organized and sophisticated political actors, as evidenced by the proliferation of women's groups debating protective labor legislation and an equal rights amendment.[52] As their participation in Progressive era and New Deal reform movements demonstrated, women eagerly wielded government power when given the chance. And in a civil service system that claimed to be merit based, women had developed expectations that they would move up career ladders.[53] When officials responded to the Depression era labor surplus with laws banning married women from the federal service, women used their power to dispute these policies.

Discriminatory legislation enacted under the Hoover Administration reflected the persistence of patriarchal values among government officials. In 1932, legislators passed a comprehensive appropriations act designed to economize on government operations. Encapsulated within the law was section 213, the "married persons clause," which legislators hoped would spread coveted civil service jobs among as many families as possible. It stipulated that in any reduction of executive branch personnel, "married persons (living with husband or wife) employed in the class to be reduced, shall be dismissed before any other persons employed in such a class are dismissed, if such husband or wife is also in the service of the United States or the District of Columbia." It also provided that in "the appointment of persons to the classified civil service, preference shall be given to persons other than married persons living with husband and wife, such husband or wife being in the service of the United States or the District of Columbia."[54] Although Franklin Roosevelt's administration revised the Economy Act in 1933, the married persons clause remained in effect.

While the clause did not specify whether the husband or wife should be targeted, agency bureaucrats interpreted the law to fit their own patriarchal perceptions of the proper place for women. Their views were not unusual and reflected a legal system that assumed men headed the family.[55] One congressional representative defended this assumption, claiming that he was getting quite a bit of mail from people complaining that women "were invading the domain of men and ought to retire to the home." But even without this patriarchal interpretation, the law affected more women than men because, as government officials were aware, of the two spouses, women usually held the lower-paying job. Similarly, even if the wife earned more than the husband, she was less likely to keep her job if it meant her husband would lose his. This law allowed government administrators to consider an employee's private life in personnel determinations.[56]

The law overwhelmingly affected women. Although women made up only 16 percent of the entire federal workforce between 1932 and 1935, they represented 78 percent of the separations effected under this legislation. During the same three-year period, Treasury Department officials, for instance, dismissed 220 women and only 47 men under section 213. And with few exceptions, resignations from women far outnumbered those from men. Of the 474 people who resigned under the law, 398 were women. To make matters worse, according to a study done by the U.S. Women's Bureau, the lowest-paid workers in government were "bearing the brunt of the provision," as 80 percent of those dismissed earned less than $2,600 a year, a salary significantly below the $3,500–$5,000 earned by middle-level managers.[57]

Women loudly asserted their displeasure with this measure. Federal agencies, especially during the expansion of state activity in the New Deal era, attracted many highly educated women who were articulate, literate, and confident. Their experiences in the federal bureaucracy, whether as home economists, pathologists, filing clerks, or typists, also gave them a sophisticated understanding of power and power relations. Individually, through unions, associations, and at times influential positions within the bureaucracy, women voiced their objection to section 213.[58]

Feminists had long been defending the rights of married women to work and strongly resented the use of statutory authority to negate that right.[59] Even though not all women who protested the law described themselves as "feminists," hundreds of individual women and scores of women's groups denounced the legislation as unjust.[60] They took to the airwaves, signed petitions, and organized delegations to visit elected officials.[61] Mae Wilson Camp, the only clerk in the Birmingham, Alabama, office of the Bureau of Mines, explained that because of her termination, the office would have to obtain a new clerk from Washington, D.C., or Pittsburgh. "Is that economy?" she asked presidential assistant Louis Howe.[62]

Organizations put forth a variety of arguments to challenge the legitimacy of section 213 on both private and public grounds. At hearings held in 1935 to consider repeal of the clause, one lawyer argued that the law encouraged "illicit" relationships between couples. "We know right here in Washington—without mentioning names—there are young people living together without the benefit of marriage because they can't live on one salary," he asserted. AFGE President Claude Babcock concurred, stating that he knew of nine such cases. The head of the National Women's Party was greeted with laughter when she claimed that the law was "unfair" because it required women to choose between their jobs and their husbands. In these instances opponents of the law constructed arguments that refuted the government's interpretation of family relations, not its right to examine them. Others, however, resorted to more public-oriented defenses. Rousing applause greeted a representative from the National Association of Women Lawyers when she emphasized that the law created a bad precedent for private industry and deprived women of their constitutional rights.[63]

Civil service unions, too, questioned the equity of the law. Although far from equal to their male peers, some female union members held influential positions and played key roles in civil service politics. Gertrude McNally, a founder of the female-dominated Bureau of Engraving and Printing Union, had joined NFFE during World War I and had become the union's long-time secretary-treasurer. Her union's journal criticized the law by calling attention to the "myth" that working wives were employed only to earn extra spending money. Helen McCarty, an employee of the navy, had a similarly high-ranking position within AFGE as the chair of the National Organizing Committee. Playing to legislators, she fought section 213 by arguing that the law equally applied to their wives. Unions, along with the League of Women Voters, forcefully pointed out that inquiries into a person's marital status weakened the concept of merit, supposedly the basis of the civil service system. One separated employee noted that whereas her efficiency rating was 100, workers with much lower ratings kept their jobs because they were not married to civil servants. AFGE Secretary Bernice Heffner simply stated that women should have "equal opportunity to compete for jobs for which they are physically and mentally qualified."[64]

Whether they relied upon morality, the Constitution, or the need to uphold a meritocracy, women ultimately earned repeal of the married persons clause through well-crafted arguments that revealed the hypocrisy behind the law. In a political setting that associated a merit system with democracy, government officials had difficulty constructing arguments to defend such gender-biased legislation. In a radio address, Heffner hammered away at this inconsistency, stating that to deprive women of the opportunity to have careers if they so chose was "pure reaction and pure Fascism, and has no place in America."[65]

Significantly, women such as Heffner believed the law corrupted the principles of American democracy. Unions, along with other organizations, supported the *right* of women to compete for jobs. Each individual woman, based upon her merit, deserved an *opportunity* to climb the career ladder. They did not attack the existence of those ladders; rather they believed that women, like men, should be judged upon their individual performance, however that was to be defined and evaluated by those in power. As historian Sharon Strom has noted in her work on private-sector office workers, "liberal feminists were often committed to the notion that class hierarchies were both natural and desirable; what they wanted was a chance to prove the competence of women so that they could take their proper place in those hierarchies alongside the professional men who were already in control." Politicians finally responded to this feminist vision and repealed the measure in 1937.[66]

Even after its repeal, some government officials still attempted to apply section 213 to married women. One senator requested that a woman in the Farm Security Administration be dismissed because her husband worked for the Soil Conservation Service. Agriculture administrators had to inform him that section 213 had been repealed three years before and they could not, therefore, dismiss her on that basis. Nevertheless, personnel managers continued to assume that married women who worked were not primary wage earners. Several admitted that financial status was a factor when determining who was to be laid off during a reduction-in-force. In almost all cases, married women were separated first.[67]

For feminists, repeal of section 213 served to discredit the idea that women worked only for "pin money" or to supplement the family wage. It also reinforced the notion that a merit system would not support hiring and firing on the basis of financial need. This meshed comfortably with merit reformers who viewed patronage as driven by a similar form of need. Even so, the struggle over section 213 left some government officials uncomfortable with the potential collective power of female civil servants. Women of all classes and political orientations had joined together to fight for a women's cause. Forceful, intelligent, and articulate women unnerved those who still felt that a sexual division of labor did not violate the tenets of a meritocracy.

Defining merit in the white-collar civil service was not a simple task. Because the work could be esoteric, supervisors could not simply measure productivity by counting output. Similarly, the dispute over section 213 had not challenged management's prerogative to assess an individual's performance. Increasingly, supervisors and personnel managers stressed the importance of personality in evaluating that performance.

Some government administrators portrayed women who questioned their subservient status as unfeminine, unstable, and unfit for public service. Women faced potentially severe consequences even for a verbal challenge to the status quo, as stencil cutter Nancy Luke discovered; her concern with promotional opportunities had initiated the Donovan case at the NRA. Luke's forthright tactics prompted her superiors to circulate a petition labeling her a "trouble-maker" and a "nuisance" and suggesting that she be reprimanded. Supervisors then dismissed her.[68]

Although gender was seldom directly discussed, it informed personnel decision making. Supervisors and personnel managers consistently penalized intelligent women who asserted their rights as workers. As Irene Walker discovered, personnel managers were prejudiced against self-assured women. After applying for a job in the Justice Department, Walker passed her stenographic and typing test with a score of 87 percent. Although personnel officers described her as "intelligent," "ambitious," and "resourceful," they also claimed she was "too self-possessed." Hence, the personnel manager commented, "it is doubtful whether she would be amenable to discipline."[69] Both Walker and Luke experienced discrimination because they crossed the boundaries of acceptable female behavior in the civil service.

In the late 1930s, government officials initiated new personnel programs to maintain the traditional system of female subordination.[70] As agency administrators sought to enhance their authority, they began to rely more heavily on social science theories to justify discriminatory practices and policies. By using psychological analysis to explain management decisions with respect to women, managers made women appear "naturally" less meritorious; this practice had the effect of preserving the male hierarchy. Under this new approach, personnel managers insisted that "personality" was a scientific category that had to be integrated into any sophisticated personnel program.[71]

Utilizing the language of psychology and sociology, managers began to label women with nontraditional values and nonconformist personalities as unstable, mentally deficient, or psychotic. In 1936 Emma Youngman, a fifty-five-year-old employee of the Agriculture Adjustment Agency (AAA), watched powerlessly as an argument over her dismissal turned into a referendum on her mental health. A long-time employee of the federal government, Youngman was targeted for separation after the Supreme Court declared the AAA unconstitutional. When she received her pink slip, she asked the local UFWA union to help her protest it. Meanwhile, administrators called in a psychiatrist who labeled her an unstable, psychopathic spinster who had "a tense, suspicious type of emotional make-up with rather strong paranoid trends." According to the psychiatrist, her "advancing age," her fear of "political discrimination," and the temporary nature of the AAA fostered in Youngman "an intense feeling of job insecurity and fear of being left economically stranded."[72]

The psychiatrist's diagnosis of Youngman as a "psychopathic spinster" suggests society's fear of economically independent unmarried women. In her position as an older working woman without a husband, Youngman threatened the traditional concept of the male as breadwinner and head of the household. When so many men were out of work and with a married persons clause in place, administrators were probably disturbed by Youngman's assertiveness in fighting her dismissal. At a time when the government was trying to bolster male self-esteem through job programs, Youngman's demands seemed even more impertinent.

Ultimately, the personnel manager (and union representative) accepted the psychiatrist's diagnosis. Youngman's protest was unsuccessful.[73] Terminated and without a position in the midst of a severe economic depression, Youngman had every reason to experience "an intense feeling of job insecurity." She also had every reason to believe she was being persecuted. As it happened, her "suspicions" and "paranoia" concerning management proved to be quite accurate.

In this case, Youngman had a very personal encounter with administrators. By 1940, these encounters become more frequent as personnel directors began to adopt a form of management theory and a body of techniques known as the human relations school of management. This school stressed the need for personal interaction between managers and employees. Some managers, as in Youngman's case, appropriated the language of psychology, sociology, and anthropology to demonstrate that women who challenged the status quo were unfeminine or unstable. In these instances, the rationalization for the subordination of women shifted from one of economic (and patriarchal) necessity to one of scientific inevitability.

Race and Fair Employment in the New Deal Civil Service

Social scientific rhetoric also factored into the government's treatment of African-American employees. For some employees, social science discourse and New Deal liberalism opened new doors in the civil service. During the 1930s, Roosevelt made some effort to draw black Americans into the federal government. He appointed blacks to prestigious positions in several departments, creating a small pool of administrators known as the "black cabinet."[74] Robert Weaver, for example, began a prestigious government career in 1933 as an assistant to Clark Foremen, an advisor on the economic status of black Americans under Interior Secretary Harold Ickes. Weaver later became a race relations specialist in the United States Housing Authority and then the Office of Production Management. Others in the black cabinet included

Robert Vann, an assistant to Attorney General Homer Cummings; William Hastie, a solicitor in the Interior Department and later a federal judge and race consultant to the War Department; Mary McCleod Bethune, a high-ranking administrator in the National Youth Administration; Edgar Brown, an advisor on Negro affairs in the Civilian Conservation Corps, head of the United Government Employees Union, and member of the National Negro Council; Harry Hunt of the Farm Credit Administration; Forrester B. Washington, a race advisor in the Federal Emergency Relief Administration; and Eugene Kindle Jones, executive secretary of the National Urban League and a Commerce Department employee. In 1936 this informal cabinet designated themselves the Federal Council on Negro Affairs, added new members, and began almost weekly meetings, usually at Bethune's home. Although they remained a rather informal group, their organization and attention to civil rights reflected a determination to move forward with this agenda during the depression.[75]

As historians John Kirby and Patricia Sullivan have demonstrated, white liberals in Roosevelt's administration also labored to bring the New Deal to black America. Economic and education reform, they continually argued, would elevate the status of black Americans and resolve the "Negro problem." A key member of their club, Ickes, broke ground with respect to fair employment by implementing racial quotas on public works projects. He likewise demanded equity in his own department and was one of the first cabinet secretaries to desegregate employee cafeterias.[76] Another important voice on race reform was Farm Security Administrator Will Alexander, who loudly insisted on a government commitment to elevating the standard of living for all Americans, white and black. He asked blacks to abandon their racial identity and to take advantage of opportunities made available by the New Deal. By demonstrating that they were capable of performing "white" work and contributing to "white" society, he argued, blacks could dispel the myth of racial inferiority.[77]

Eleanor Roosevelt echoed these views. Like many white liberals, she tried to steer a moderate course, warning black leaders not to push for special treatment but at the same time scolding employers who refused to hire or promote blacks. Government officials, she believed, had an obligation to plan programs that would ensure individual opportunity for all Americans, regardless of race. Like Ickes, she favored the use of quotas, suggesting that they be incorporated into civil service regulations in order to increase the number of blacks in federal employment.[78] Only by using government action to eliminate barriers to opportunity, these race liberals posited, could blacks shed their "inferior" culture, assimilate into what they perceived to be the mainstream, and eventually achieve equality in a white-dominated society.

These views were consistent with contemporary social science thought concerning American race relations. With increasing momentum, scientists of all stripes were disputing theories that maintained the biological inferiority of people of color. Arguing that environmental, not biological, factors kept African Americans from achieving equity within American society, social scientists embarked on studies that demonstrated a linkage between economic and political exclusion, ignorance and race discrimination.[79] Among the most prominent of sociologists studying race was Robert Park of the University of Chicago.

Park maintained that race prejudice was the product of economic conflict between whites and blacks. Until that conflict was eliminated, he maintained, blacks and whites could not live and work side by side. A one-time assistant to Booker T. Washington, Park believed that economic advancement, rather than militant action, would produce "progress" in race relations. Under his paradigm, assimilation would occur gradually without conflict when whites and blacks became economic equals. "Originally," he noted, "race relations in the South could be rather accurately represented by a horizontal line, with all the white folk above, and all the Negro folk below." But, he continued, with "the development of industrial and professional classes within the Negro race, the distinction between the races tends to assume the form of a vertical line." He thus encouraged the development of a strong, but separate, black professional and business class that would parallel white society. When vertical segregation replaced horizontal segregation, he said, racial barriers would begin to fall.[80] Like New Deal reformers in the federal government, Park believed that once blacks proved their capabilities, white racism would become illegitimate. Liberals consequently perceived equal employment opportunity as a means by which black Americans could prove their worth and eliminate prejudice.

Although social scientists began to critique eugenics and scientific racism in the interwar years, they also "naturalized" environmental forces. Park, among others, borrowed methodologies from the natural and physical sciences and adopted a "naturalist" perspective that cast race relations as part of an ecological cycle. Primitive societies, he claimed, began with an emphasis on kinship, customs, and traditions and eventually evolved into more sophisticated civic societies organized around the concept of citizenship and formal rules. Individuals as well as groups could move from a lower to a higher "cultural level." "Every country," he observed, "has a certain amount of culturally undeveloped material. We have it, for instance, in the Negroes and Indians, the Southern mountaineers, the Mexicans and Spanish-Americans, and the slums." Evoking Charles Darwin, he pointed out that "the struggle for existence terminates in a struggle for status, for recognition, for position and prestige." Eventually, he surmised, assimilation would be "progressive and irreversible." To him, assimilation—a concept he defined inconsistently—was the conclusion of an organic process. It would therefore be fruitless to thwart natural laws by forcing integration. [81] As Dorothy Ross explained, sociologists' desire to discover the social forces governing society meant that the "diverse sources and conflicting norms of social authority became blurred, obscuring just who was controlling whom." [82]

Sociologists also had difficulty defining assimilation within a pluralistic society. Park and William Thomas, another expert on race and ethnicity, espoused the virtues of assimilation but continued to perceive cultures and subcultures in hierarchical terms. In 1912, Park devised a study in order to measure "how a race rises from one level of culture to another, whether by internal stimulation and native ability, or by accepting and imitating the culture of the higher level of society; and more particularly, which races are fit to progress and which are not and why." Both Thomas and Park seemingly rejected the notion that mental ability was a function of race or gender, but they also maintained that the white race had clearly advanced over others. Rather than argue that America was a nation of diverse and equal subcultures, Park and Thomas promoted the ideal of cultural homogeneity in which they claimed that "inferior" subcultures, such as black America, would eventually become subsumed into "superior" white American culture. [83]

Many white liberals espoused these beliefs and thus tended to avoid the question of how various cultures might interact on equal terms. They continued to assume that the customs, speech patterns, educational system, and heritage they associated with black Americans represented an "other," inferior civilization. Hence, while they fought against certain aspects of economic segregation, they did not necessarily probe the problem of racial categories. They did not examine the frame of reference within which they judged African Americans. Nonetheless, in the New Deal civil service, social scientists along with white and black liberal activists began an important dialogue about economic opportunity and race.

They frequently had a difficult time convincing President Roosevelt to join that conversation. Fearful of alienating powerful southern politicians, the president trod gingerly around the race issue. His political concerns combined with his own prejudices and narrow definition of discrimination meant little would be done to elevate the low economic and social status of the vast majority of black government employees during the 1930s. An informal survey of the service in 1938 indicated that six agencies employed 29,046 people, of whom 1,078, or 3.7 percent, were black. Of these 1,078 African-American employees, only 3 had jobs in the professional service, and 870 labored in the custodial service. One scholar estimated that at the end of the decade, 90 percent of all black federal employees worked in the custodial service.[84] In response to a complaint that a white man had replaced a black man as elevator operator in the Treasury Department, the president asked Secretary Henry Morgenthau if he could "make an effort to correct a situation like this by taking on some colored people at the bottom?" It was perfectly acceptable to hire blacks as long as they remained in jobs coded as "colored."[85]

Within the federal civil service, the growing power of civil service reform after 1937 offered black leaders some hope. White and black reformers increasingly argued that race discrimination contradicted the fundamental principle of a meritocracy: to hire and promote individuals based only on their credentials and the quality of their work. Thus black intellectuals and interest groups like the NAACP strongly supported this reform movement during the New Deal era. To them the patronage system had failed to hold government officials accountable for racism. A merit system would not only break the hold powerful southern Democrats had over government jobs; it would also make agency officials responsible to a set of color-blind employment standards, thus offering worthy blacks job security and upward occupational mobility. In 1937, for instance, NAACP counsel Charles Houston scolded a Post Office Department official for his "complete disregard of the merit system" when he defended a Florida postmaster who had passed over an African-American applicant eight times, even though the applicant had the highest score on the mail carrier exam.[86] By 1941, the collective pressure of white liberals and black organizations—exemplified by A. Philip Randolph's planned march on Washington, D.C., to protest employment discrimination in both federal agencies and defense industries—paid some dividends as the Civil Service Commission finally abandoned the practice of requiring photographs for applications, begun under the race-conscious Woodrow Wilson Administration.[87]

Without a consensus on the meaning of merit and a strong commitment from government administrators and elected officials to ending discriminatory practices, however, merit reform and the standardization of personnel policies did little to alter traditional patterns of employment discrimination. Between 1932 and 1937, for instance, the percentage of African Americans working in the Government Printing Office hovered between 19 and 23 percent (approximately 1,100 of 5,300 total employees). Not one was employed as a clerical worker, and most worked as common laborers and janitors.[88] In some respects the rhetoric regarding the impartiality of the merit system obscured the variety of ways in which the system undermined the employment prospects of African Americans. Foremost among those mechanisms was the civil service's rule of three, giving appointment officials the authority to choose among the top three candidates on lists of eligibles supplied by the Civil Service Commission. Since the 1920s, Howard University dean and sociologist Kelly Miller had been publicly complaining about appointments that were based on "personal pulchritude," adding in 1937 that the "crux of the evil [of race discrimination in the civil service] lies in granting discretionary power to petty appointing officers." Waiting applicants did not have an endless opportunity to obtain a position, because civil service rules stipulated that if an eligible candidate were passed over three times for appointment, that candidate could be removed from employment registers. Frequently, the Civil Service Commission pointed to its rule of three in order to absolve itself of responsibility for discrimination.[89] In addition, the academic patronage of the 1930s disadvantaged those groups who had fewer educational opportunities, such as poor blacks and whites. With the growing emphasis on educational credentials, those entering the service at lower grades found it increasingly difficult to climb civil service ladders and cross occupational boundaries to higher-paying positions.

At times agency officials perceived jobs under the classified system in purely racial terms. For instance, according to Daniel W. Bell, acting director of the Bureau of the Budget in 1937, it was a matter of "common knowledge" that appointing officials hired "certain types" for "certain jobs." He cited the practice of hiring women exclusively as stenographers and nurses. Messengers, he said, "involve a selection of colored eligibles."[90] Standardization of personnel policies did little to break down a racial division of labor.

Economic and political forces conspired, however, to encourage some policy makers to broaden their commitment to a more liberal view of equal employment opportunity toward the end of the 1930s. Because of the continuing migration of blacks to urban northern communities, northern Democrats began to recognize the potential political power held by African Americans. African Americans mobilized their forces, engaging in demonstrations, boycotts, and letter-writing campaigns to protest the contradiction between the principles of democracy and equal opportunity and the prevalent practice of race discrimination. Political activism on behalf of African Americans was especially evident in Washington, D.C., where Howard University faculty and students vocally objected to local Jim Crow laws and vigorously pressed the Roosevelt Administration to take action. But perhaps most important, by 1940 a new war-induced labor shortage gave black Americans an important economic bargaining chip.

Depression era politics expanded the capacity of the federal government to address the needs of its ordinary citizens. In doing so, it forced federal officials to address a number of questions concerning ordinary citizens and their relationship to the federal bureaucracy: Who were ordinary citizens? Should the American civil service represent the ordinary or extraordinary? Was merit to be based on experience or academic credentials? And was a meritocracy gender and/or color blind? Mass unemployment spawned class conflict and encouraged Americans to consider the criteria by which one should be judged worthy of a job. Although some raised objections to the establishment of a "caste" bureaucracy peopled by those with "pockets full of college degrees," these concerns dissipated with the wartime labor shortage. Debates over caste shifted toward a discussion of the plight of women and African Americans.

At the same time that the Great Depression sensitized working people to their common economic plight, the New Deal highlighted—through its arts and writing projects, for instance—the cultural diversity present in the American mosaic. Friction between a desire to foster the common ties of citizenship and the reality of gender and racial separatism shaped the New Deal civil service. As an employer, the federal government grappled with this contradictory impulse on a daily basis. Politicians, agency heads, mid-level managers, and low-level servants labored to sort out conflicts over unionization and the employment of women and African Americans in an effort to form a strong, unified and committed American civil service capable of building a new national state. By the end of the 1930s, as debates over class and college degrees began to fade, questions concerning the proper role of unions and diversity became more pressing, and managers developed new strategies to control the federal workforce.

3 Managing Human Relations in the Wartime and Cold War Civil Service

In 1942 two occupational researchers surveyed federal employees about their jobs. Discontented employees, they reported, often cited poor supervision as the cause of their dissatisfaction. One young worker described her boss as "cranky" and "nervous." "She bawls you out as though you were in kindergarten and you can't defend yourself," she said. Another asserted that her supervisor "treats employees like children[; workers] can't stop to talk even for a minute, [and there is] no consideration for employees." And one editorial clerk simply observed that his supervisor was "old, senile, stupid and incompetent."[1] Personnel managers applauded these findings, not because they were pleased that supervisors were senile and cranky but because it reinforced their belief that poor supervision undermined morale. "Good supervision," wrote one personnel specialist, "is prized. The poor supervisor is a thorn in the flesh of the group."[2]

The use of employee attitude surveys and the emphasis placed upon the personal relationship between supervisor and employee signaled a shift in the managerial practices of federal officials. By World War II, many personnel administrators were touting these human relations techniques as the answer to poor employee morale and job performance. The federal employee, noted personnel administrator Raymond Zimmerman, was "not satisfied just to be a cog in a wheel." All employees, he said, craved a sense of "importance and recognition."[3] Essentially, personnel administrators sought to induce these feelings by improving supervisory leadership and promoting worker participation in the agency. From the late 1930s into the 1950s, federal personnel administrators absorbed and translated human relations techniques from business firms, where they had already gained in popularity, installing these in government agencies.

Employee counselor Margaret Barron outlined this trend in 1942, noting that the manpower crisis brought on by World War II increased interest among government administrators in "the problems of the individual and in a desire to assist him in solving these problems." Complex organizations and impersonal management, Barron believed, inhibited employees from functioning at "maximum capacity," for "people cannot be expected to develop the loyalty and faith . . . toward an institution or an individual employer who considers them mere machines. . . . In order to get each man to throw his full weight on the line, it is necessary first to recognize him as a personality, as a human being."[4]

The state premised its own managerial approach on personnel managers' concern with the "loyalty and faith" and hence productivity of civil servants. While a minority of administrators, often located in New Deal and later war service agencies, hoped that a more organic, personal, and democratic approach to management would achieve greater equity in the service, the majority used the human relations approach in a more conservative manner. The contours of this approach were shaped not only by industrial management practices (based on social science theories) but also by contemporary political, gender, and racial ideologies. On the one hand, new management schemes reflected a powerful political philosophy, validated by the New Deal and World War II, that emphasized executive management and rational planning within democratic institutions. On the other hand, these schemes also suggested a rejection of authoritarianism. As exemplified by Barron and Zimmerman, managers shied away from metaphors equating organizations with machines, because they tended to downplay the individuals who constituted the organization. As one member of Roosevelt's Committee on Administrative Management noted, "reorganization is not a mechanical task, but a human task, because government is not a machine, but a living organism."[5] The adoption of human relations management techniques not only promoted the federal bureaucracy as a "living" entity but also preserved the "loyalty" of civil servants to traditional bureaucratic power structures.

Some of the public administrators entering government in the late 1930s and 1940s were drawn to government work out of a sincere desire to make management more humane and egalitarian. Personnel official Frederick Davenport, an ordained minister and academic, had strong ties to Progressive and New Deal reform efforts, while Office of Price Administration (OPA) personnel directors Wallace Sayre and Kenneth Warner both advocated on behalf of minorities and women in their agency. Civil Service Commissioner Arthur Flemming, Bureau of the Budget management expert Elmer Staats,

Davenport, and Warner were all devout Methodists and proponents of various liberal causes. Warner later noted that he considered himself an "evangelist" on human relations. He continually emphasized the need for lateral rather than hierarchical relationships within agencies and stressed cooperation with unions and communication with employees. Although some of these human relations converts were Republicans, they were all strong supporters of New Deal welfare and regulatory programs. Progressive, social gospel, and New Deal liberal principles all found expression in the human relations philosophy and practices. For these officials, human relations promised to create a more equitable civil service and to advance the cause of social justice.[6]

As William Graebner has demonstrated, human relations was part of a larger "democratic social engineering" movement that joined social science knowledge and democratic principles with a faith in planning. Public managers worked to fuse a hierarchical bureaucracy with a decentralized democratic system. Insecure about the viability and legitimacy of democratic institutions, public managers championed the participatory aspects of human relations. Managers were to engage their employees in dialogue through suggestions systems, employee councils, or individual conferences. But "social engineering" implied control from above and managers rarely acknowledged that this school of management, like all others, was designed to enhance rather than destroy managerial authority. For some administrators, democratic rhetoric only served to mask the paternalistic orientation of human relations.[7]

American Industry, Social Science, and Human Relations

Elton Mayo, who directed a series of worker production experiments at Western Electric's Hawthorne plants in the late 1920s, pioneered and popularized the human relations school of management. Although other social scientists, most notably the psychometric pioneer Walter Dill Scott, had initiated the courtship between social science and management at the turn of the century, Mayo married the two in the field of industrial sociology.[8]

To interpret his observations of worker behavior, Mayo relied on sociological theories put forth by Emile Durkheim, Robert Park, and Park's colleagues at the University of Chicago concerning social anomie and criminal behavior. From these theories, Mayo argued that employee behavior and attitudes could be controlled by focusing on individual personality and small-group interaction at the workplace. According to Mayo, administrators were responsible for building a workplace conducive to "effective human collaboration"; they could do this by paying close attention to worker needs.[9]

In many respects, Mayo's outlook and hypotheses were a reaction against Frederick Taylor's earlier scientific management concepts, which had depersonalized the workplace. Yet Mayo was not rejecting Taylor's underlying objective of making business more profitable. Driven by a Progressive era faith that human behavior could be altered by external stimuli, Mayo set out to demonstrate how more attention to the day-to-day work environment of employees could make workers more motivated and, by extension, more productive. Unlike Walter Dill Scott, he avoided intelligence tests, instead advocating the establishment of an intensely personal relationship between supervisors and subordinates. Managers were to make "friends" with their employees and make the bureaucracy seem more like a "community."[10]

In essence, human relations specialists sought to socialize workers to the organization and the objectives of the firm. This process, Mayo believed, would alleviate the debilitating alienation fostered by employment in large-scale bureaucracies. His studies demonstrated the need to gather intimate details about the lives of each worker. Mayo, for example, described one operator as "a widow with two children both doing well at school." But he also observed that while she was "intelligent and conscientious" and informed about "child-welfare," she had few friends and was overly anxious about her children; "in a word, she 'overthinks' her situation in true obsessive fashion." These personal problems, he concluded, made her production output "erratic." The responsibility for assuaging these conditions fell to her supervisor, who was to ask questions of, listen to, and offer suggestions to the troubled employee.[11] Supervisors attentive to a worker's environment and "feelings" would foster in an employee a "sense of participation" and "a desire to cooperate."[12]

Ultimately industrial sociologists such as Mayo hoped to devise new systems of managerial control. Although supervisors were to govern in a gentle and personable rather than heavy-handed or brusque manner, they were clearly to be in charge. As one author noted, "nurturant supervision could adjust workers to bureaucratic life and get informal groups of workers to accept the formal goals of managers."[13] Control, Progressive era social scientists had argued, was a necessary element of social organization. According to Mayo's esteemed colleague at the Harvard Business School, Fritz J. Roethlisberger, managers had to be skilled at diagnosing "human situations," in order "to exercise effective control, to maintain authority [and] to obtain loyalty and confidence."[14]

Human relations provided managers with a way to apply social science to the sources identified in the Progressive era as inhibiting production output: poor morale, high turnover, and poor supervision. This school of management did not reject structural remedies but suggested that applied sociology and psychology would remedy another critical cause of organizational inefficiency, worker "pathology."[15]

While Mayo's work was targeted at factory workers, personnel managers also found it applicable to a growing federal work force. Human relations experts in the Agriculture Department urged supervisors to adopt the roles of scientific psychoanalysts and nurturing counselors. They linked morale not only to "good salaries, reasonable hours, . . . and job tenure" but also to the "imponderables of human relations—attitudes, omissions, commissions, suspicions, personalities, ambitions, and fears." To foster labor-management cooperation, the department's personnel office implored supervisors to recognize that employees had "feelings" and to understand that "what [an employee] thinks . . . may be determined by a complex of mental patterns only tenuously related to the real situation." Hence, personnel officers warned, "the real situation is not so important as what [the employee] thinks the real situation is." Because "the observed facts are filtered through mental stereotypes and a host of relevant, near relevant, and irrelevant experiences," supervisors would have to learn about each employee's personal life. Only then could supervisors successfully discern the difference between "fancied" and "real" grievances.[16]

Chair of the Council of Personnel Administration Frederick Davenport asked agency personnel directors not only to focus on the more mundane aspects of human relations—he urged directors to examine lighting conditions for federal employees "whom we represent mean a great deal to us"—but also to draw on their understanding of human relations and to investigate "human problems" before placing applicants in jobs. Personnel managers, he wrote in 1943, should "infuse the government service with enthusiasm," "motivate workers," and "develop morale."[17]

In 1942 the Employee Relations Committee of the council listed the simplification and humanization of administrative procedures as one of its key objectives. A year later, the council endorsed Ordway Tead's list of personnel management objectives. Tead urged managers to balance the aims of "production and personality"; to keep management "sensitive to human relations"; to recognize the "wholeness and integrity of the individual and his right to be dealt with as an end and not as a means only"; and to use scientific knowledge to improve human relations techniques and working conditions.[18]

To many federal administrators, human relations represented an advanced state of managerial civilization. According to one convert, those supervisors who refused to practice human relations were in a "prescientific stage." In this stage, he said, supervisors sought "ego satisfaction" by exercising arbitrary authority and denigrating their employees. That primitivism, in turn, resulted in resentment, low morale, apathy, and mediocre performances by employees; it was therefore imperative that supervisors learn the art of human "technology," defined simply as the skill of dealing with human beings.[19]

This managerial approach became especially popular in the Washington, D.C., federal workforce. As new employees poured into the city between 1939 and 1945, personnel managers believed that human relations techniques would help them adjust to urban life.[20] In April 1941, the Council of Personnel Administration invited Dr. McCartney of the First Presbyterian Church in Washington, D.C., to speak. He warned members that many of the new arrivals were ill prepared, both emotionally and physically, for life in the city. He called on departments to help new employees adapt "wholesomely" to life in Washington.[21] In response, personnel directors created orientation programs, including some called "induction councils," established a "travelers aid," organized recreation, and offered counseling to distraught and homesick employees.[22] By 1945 more than twenty-five agencies in the Washington, D.C., area employed 350 counselors.[23]

Agencies also organized employee relations divisions, built dormitories to house workers (particularly single women), provided transportation for employees to and from work, established child-care and recreation facilities, and sponsored such activities as dances and picnics.[24] Victory committees organized by the United Federal Workers of America (UFWA) and labor-management committees set up by the Civil Service Commission also reinforced the cooperative ideal and the united front that employees and administrative officials hoped to present to the world.[25] These morale-building exercises, administrators maintained, would elevate the government's production levels during the war against fascism.

Human Relations and Democracy

In the public service, administrators sought to promote loyalty and efficiency in a manner that would be consistent with democratic ideals. Human relations specialists emphasized the need for employee participation in decision-making processes. For example, they often referred to presidential statements regarding public employee relations as "magna cartas," thus evoking a sense of mutual agreement and understanding between leaders and servants.[26] But their emphasis on a more rigorous form of participatory democracy for employees obscured the degree to which some supervisors and elite administrators used human relations to enhance their authority over a growing pink-collar workforce.

Government administrators perceived themselves as preachers and teachers of the democratic way. Their mission was to spread the gospel of democratic management to their flocks. Aware of the rise of totalitarianism in Europe, public administrators perceived themselves as frontline warriors in the campaign against this system of governance.[27] Participatory management schemes would keep democratic principles viable. But these schemes would have to be balanced with the need for an efficient federal bureaucracy. If the civil service were not productive and effective, personnel administrators worried, democracy would be discredited. "The European dictators," asserted former Civil Service Commissioner Samuel Ordway, Jr., "taunt us with the inefficiency of our governmental administration." To ensure the survival of democracy, he called on administrators to build a civil service "founded on merit and training."[28] Thus, to save the system, and to maintain its legitimacy, administrators set out to erect a loyal and efficient workforce by using human relations techniques.

Roosevelt's Committee on Administrative Management had struggled with this dilemma in the mid-1930s. Public administrators had become enamored of the formal hierarchies and functional separation of work developed by highly successful business organizations in the late nineteenth century.[29] They found it difficult, however, to create strict hierarchies and to implement overall management schemes in a political system that dispersed power. Although local governments initiated city manager plans, federal officials found the national bureaucracy too decentralized to control from one source. But in the 1930s, reformers perceived an ineffective administrative structure as dangerous. Committee members believed that their assigned task—to reform the management and structure of the executive branch—was crucial to the survival of democracy. If they could make democracy work, totalitarianism would be discredited. This was a difficult task, as the head of the committee, Louis Brownlow, feared that democracy was a "form of organization that was futile and futilitarian and that inevitably selected governments that would not, could not, act."[30] Fundamentally, the committee believed that the office of the presidency, if strengthened, would be capable of providing the leadership necessary to make the federal government work and by extension to legitimize democracy.[31] Hence, the committee's recommendations reflected an executive orientation in management. It advocated, for example, the replacement of the Civil Service Commission with a single administrator responsible only to the president.[32]

With the reputation of democratic institutions damaged by the Great Depression, many American citizens, not just public administrators, were encouraged to debate the nature and structure of authority in their new, highly organized society.[33] Some expressed ambivalence about centralized power, especially in the context of European fascism.[34] Congress, run by many Southern Democrats who had a deep ideological affinity for a decentralized federal structure, expressed its ambivalence by voting down the president's 1937 reorganization legislation.[35]

To resolve this dilemma, public service managers turned during World War II to human relations, which sought to legitimate executive management through employee consent. According to Davenport, "the up-to-date philosophy of the personnel office is the philosophy of the democratic process."[36] That process included the acquisition of employee consent through participation in agency management. Public managers agreed that they were to teach office supervisors that autocratic methods of management were intolerable. "Supervision," as one personnel specialist claimed, "must be democratic if it is to serve a democratic society."[37] The first Hoover Commission on Organization of the Executive Branch of the Government concurred with this assessment, calling for employee participation in managerial decisions.[38] During and after the war, the Council on Personnel Administration heartily supported suggestion systems, employee councils, and grievance procedures as a means of securing employees a voice in the system.

But the type and nature of employee input was never clearly defined. The Hoover Commission, for instance, barely specified the parameters of employee participation. Its final report contained only two sentences on the subject. One called for the use of employee councils, which the second sentence noted would reduce "excessive red tape" in the personnel field. In practice, suggestion programs generated advice often on the level of what to do with the metal tips on the photocopy paper. (One employee proposed selling them for 5 cents apiece. Another thought they would make good ashtrays.)[39]

Employee councils often became a form of controlled pluralism or "democratic social engineering," especially in conservative old-line departments, such as the State and Agricultural departments. These plans assembled employees into advisory committees that met periodically with top agency administrators. Although the body was supposedly representative of the agency, a profile of the Agriculture Department's council in 1950 reveals a predominantly college-educated, professional, and career-oriented membership. Among the group's members were a division chief, an assistant division head, two lawyers, and a personnel officer.[40] Moreover, as Catherine Shea, a council representative from the office of the secretary, demurely revealed, councils were often ineffective. Qualifying her criticisms as merely her "two-cents worth," she noted that some members had demanding jobs that prevented them from attending meetings. And, she observed, discussions often reflected the sentiment of administrative or supervisory officials rather than lower-level employees.[41] Participatory programs were not premised on equality; they allowed public administrators to justify executive management as democratic. As Treasury personnel director Edwin C. Ballinger described it, the function of the personnel administrator was "predominantly one of *leadership* in human matters and human relations" (emphasis added).[42]

Just as the aim of welfare capitalism in the 1920s was "to attach individual workers to the corporate system by ties of self-interested 'loyalty' and frank dependence," public-sector human relations was designed to encourage civil servants to obey elite agency administrators and elected officials.[43] In one instance, Roy Hendrickson of the Agriculture Department lauded the "far-sighted" members of the business-oriented American Management Association, who "constantly seek to bring about harmony . . . between the management . . . and . . . the interests in many cases of rather clamorous groups of employees."[44] Similarly, even though Hendrickson's personnel newsletter in the Department of Agriculture described an organization in soothing words, the structure he outlined was clearly one of domination and subordination: "[organization is] the complicated series of channels—through which authority *flows* from the top to the bottom, and through which, *if management likes*, information and suggestions flow from the bottom to the top" (emphasis added). An in-service training program in the Farm Credit Administration required clerical and stenographic workers to attend classes in which *administrative* officials taught them the philosophy and purpose of the agency.[45] More conservative personnel administrators understood their world in hierarchical terms. Participatory programs designed to raise morale were undertaken within those terms.

Both the practice and the theory of human relations appealed to federal administrators because they believed this mode of activity validated American democracy. Its emphasis on personal problem solving negated the subordination of the individual to the state, a central tenet of totalitarianism. As one specialist in administration observed, "democratic internal administration," unlike the "*fuhrer prinzip*," represented the "modern way" for "civilized society."[46] Personnel administrators portrayed human relations as a fundamentally democratic and moral approach to employee relations. The system encouraged employee participation, making it appear as a microcosm of the larger American political universe.

But it was too often participation with conditions; it was "controlled" pluralism. For instance, independent and unlimited employee input into administrative personnel policy making was discouraged as "anti-democratic," for it suggested a civil service unaccountable to the public. Most personnel administrators used human relations to justify an administrative hierarchy that benefited the status quo, including, of course, their positions.

"As I understand it," council chair Davenport stated, "[democracy] represents two things, the common sense of the mass, which under certain methods shall finally control, but also it represents leadership of intelligent and honest people." Hence, he added, democratic societies needed to pick the "right" kind of people to do the "business" of government.[47] Along with other elites, Davenport was revitalizing a strand of Progressive thought (with roots in eighteenth-century American political ideals) maintaining that leadership in a democracy rested on the shoulders of an educated elite, albeit with the consent of the governed. Samuel Ordway and others like him reasoned that because the educational system was "democratic," by extension, the process of selecting administrative leaders from colleges and universities was also democratic.[48] Consequently, even though personnel managers promoted participation, they were advocating civil *service* to democracy, not civil *equality* within the bureaucracy.

Human Relations, "Company" Loyalty, and Subversion

Like their counterparts in business, government administrators linked productivity to employee morale and organizational loyalty. According to one federal personnel report, loyalty was an "emotional state" created through "indirect suggestion." Therefore administrators needed to create an environment "conducive to the development of attitudes." Once this was done, new employees would " 'feel' the attitude without it being directly discussed or even mentioned."[49]

During the late 1930s and early 1940s, personnel specialists attempted to construct this "emotional state" by building patriotic allegiance to the United States government. Public administrators therefore worked to promote institutional loyalty, not only to encourage productivity but also to fight radical elements within and outside the civil service. Frequently that fear of subversion was directed at unionized civil servants openly critical of the government. In one instance, officials of the CIO's UFWA argued that one of their members was targeted as a subversive, in part because he was a male employee who was "not in uniform." Apparently, in order to illustrate "company loyalty," eligible government employees were to serve their country as soldiers. In the context of war, issues of company loyalty in the federal government clearly became entangled with issues of patriotism, defined as employee support for democratic institutions and ideas.[50]

Sensitized to the possibility of communist and fascist subversion, many government administrators felt that they had a special mission to make employees accountable to Congress and the public.[51] As applied to government employee issues, then, human relations had a twofold, overlapping purpose: to create agency loyalty and to encourage patriotic allegiance to democracy among a "clamorous" group of civil servants.

A fear among public officials of political traitorism had been growing during the 1930s. According to Richard Fried, although there had been occasional governmental investigations of communist activities among public employees during the New Deal era, the reinvigoration of the House Special Committee to Investigate Un-American Activities under Texas Democrat Martin Dies in 1938 changed the tone of those probes. Dies and his committee often targeted federal employees who had been members of unions (especially the UFWA).[52] As fears of subversion intensified during World War II, the committee often singled out and harassed radical or left-leaning federal employees.[53]

In 1939 Congress responded to fears of communism by passing section 9A of the Hatch Act, which denied federal jobs to applicants who belonged to any organization or party that advocated the overthrow of the government. But the commission's interpretation of that clause was telling. Upon examination of the statute, the Civil Service Commission instructed agency heads to dismiss disloyal employees under a civil service rule authorizing removals in order "to promote the efficiency of the service."[54] Unconsciously or not, the commission had equated inefficiency with subversion and thus broadened the definition of traitorism. Two years later, Congress appropriated $100,000 for investigations of federal job applicants and employees suspected of violating this clause. And the secretaries of both the Navy and War departments were given the power to dismiss workers whom they deemed a threat to national security. To add more statutory force to the allegiance issue, Congress passed appropriation bills with riders forbidding agencies to use money to pay salaries of subversives and requiring employees to sign loyalty affidavits. By 1947, Truman formalized procedures in Executive Order 9835, which set up the federal employees' loyalty-security program.[55]

Agency personnel directors largely accepted the premises of section 9A. Hendrickson of the Agriculture Department sent a memorandum to each office in the department telling supervisors that if employees had information on colleagues who were engaging in action detrimental to the interests of the department or United States, they were to report this at once to the personnel office.[56] Employees complained that the investigations undermined rather than built morale and esprit de corps; one dismissed employee claimed that these policies resembled "the totalitarian doctrine that the State is all-important and the individual of little or no importance." Another noted that employees were "denied the fundamental right of a fair hearing." But personnel directors defended themselves by stating that they had a responsibility to the department, employees, and the government to examine all charges and would do so "honestly and fairly."[57]

Protestations of honesty, however, often obscured the real issues of power involved in loyalty cases. Definitions of loyalty and patriotism were often entwined with political debates concerning the proper relationship between the private and public sector as well as with views toward race and labor.

At times, investigators and members of the Dies committee seemed unable to distinguish between American liberalism and subversion. Personnel managers and administrative elites often investigated and hassled civil servants who did not conform to a particular image or political view, or who did not respect existing authority structures. Opponents of loyalty investigations claimed that some administrators were attempting to "smear" the New Deal. Significantly, a number of those targeted by the Dies committee worked for New Deal and war agencies involved in either regulatory or welfare activities. Among those targeted for investigation was Mary McCleod Bethune, the well-respected head of the National Youth Administration, as well as three employees of the Federal Communications Commission, four from OPA, and several from the War Production Board and Social Security Board. Individuals with more liberal views probably gravitated toward these agencies and, not surprisingly, many belonged to unions. One FBI investigator, for instance, described a senior economist in the Office of Price Administration as an active "left-winger." He derisively noted that the economist had brought in a "group of agitators" to take part in demonstrations protesting a labor leader's dismissal from the National Recovery Administration in 1934 and that he had carried on union membership drives among clerks, messengers, and other lower-level employees. It took a year for the OPA personnel office to determine that he was "loyal."[58]

UFWA officials continually complained about the loyalty program and Dies committee, insisting that their members were disproportionately investigated and dismissed. They adamantly defended one Federal Security Agency (FSA) employee, Morris Tepping, who had been a member of their Local 10. On the basis of his reading habits, investigators accused Tepping of having connections with "people, causes and organizations of a radical or communistic nature." Tepping countered that his interest in organizations advocating for civil liberties, as well as labor and minority rights, was evidence of his commitment to democracy. In another case, the union asserted that investigators had unfairly attacked OPA employee David Ginsburg, a "New Deal Democrat," because they resented his and his agency's commitment to price and rent controls. UFWA members suspected that it was their union membership and liberal politics, rather than their alleged allegiance to another country, that prompted their dismissals.[59]

In a sense, the advent of these investigations presented the Civil Service Commission with a predicament concerning politics and government employment. As staunch advocates of the merit system, they continually opposed the introduction of politics into the selection process. Hence, these inquiries were reminiscent of the "evils" of patronage, in which employees gained or lost jobs on the basis of their political beliefs rather than their talents. Yet Civil Service Commissioner Flemming reasoned that support of a nonpartisan federal service gave the commission the right, and duty, to purge its ranks of rabidly political employees, such as Nazis and communists. It apparently did not matter if they expressed these opinions at work. Unlike "ordinary" Democrats and Republicans, Nazis and communists could not "be" nonpartisan. Federal officials did not consider nazism, fascism, and communism to be political orientations but rather saw them as "un-American" creeds because advocates of these systems were loyal to another country. As un-Americans, adherents thus could not be protected by free speech doctrines. Still, civil service commissioners recognized that Americans were allied with a country opposed to "American" values—the Soviet Union. They therefore reassured the public that although they sought to ban communists from the government, they deeply appreciated the "tremendous contribution the Soviet government and people have made to the winning of the war." Their loyalty policy, they stated, was simply a recognition that an individual could not serve "two masters." Certainly, commission officials added, the Soviets would likewise object to a Soviet citizen who pledged allegiance to another country.[60]

Commission ambivalence toward this issue was reflected in its 1943 order banning investigators from asking applicants "general questions about their political philosophy," including whether they believed in "capitalism" or whether they belonged to a union. Investigators could inquire about membership in the Communist Party, but only if this was followed by questions regarding membership in fascist and Nazi organizations. Because the commission remained sensitive to public and congressional opinion, it felt the need to justify its decision. When Illinois Republican Fred Busbey complained about the new policy, asserting that the commission had bowed to pressure from UFWA members to implement the plan, the commission responded that it was not relinquishing its right to ask applicants and employees about their political affiliations. It dropped these questions, said the commission, because they were ineffectual and only served to give "ammunition" to critics who claimed the commission was targeting political progressives.[61]

Commissioners engaged in a balancing act between their support of civil liberties and their desire to maintain a credible government. On the one hand, they worried that unions such as UFWA would undermine their investigatory authority by convincing others that these activities constituted a witch hunt. On the other hand, commission officials were also certain that investigations were necessary to maintain the legitimacy of the government. One stressed that determining the fitness of a job candidate was far from an "exact" science and that the commission had to respond to congressional inquiries, especially those from Representative Dies. Commissioner Arthur Flemming recognized the sensitivity of these investigations. In one instance, he resisted turning over some personnel records to Dies, feeling that it would be unethical to respond to Dies's subpoena. Fortunately for Flemming, Dies indicated that he had received the pertinent documents from another source. Concerned about his role in the assessment process, Flemming prepared for loyalty hearings on the hill "more thoroughly" than for almost any other hearings in which he participated. Even so, stressed Flemming, overall, the commission had to offer this service because "the country was in a frame of mind that . . . if you didn't face that [loyalty] issue then the country would lose confidence in you."[62]

Maintaining the legitimacy of the service with the public remained a top priority for the Civil Service Commission. Loyalty investigations frequently overlapped with the government's right to oust employees whose personal lives did not fit the "image" of the public service. The commission had long claimed the authority to investigate the "character" of its employees and to deny appointments to those who did not uphold the standards of the service. In 1941, 560 civil service candidates were denied jobs because their loyalty was questionable, but 2,400 were disqualified on the basis of character investigations. While these standards included attention to criminal activity, they also shifted over time as social mores and cultural values changed. During World War II, one investigator, for instance, inquired whether a white employee entertained blacks in her home. Those employees who displayed a more liberal, tolerant orientation toward social and political issues were deemed socially flawed or perhaps mentally incompetent. Representative Dies frequently used the term *crackpot* to describe radicals. They were unstable extremists whose mental health was greatly impaired.[63]

"Crackpot" labels and questions concerning social customs revealed the extent to which the line between private and public affairs had been blurred. The human relations emphasis on personality adjustment along with character and loyalty investigations politicized the personal in the federal civil service. In 1946, Civil Service Commissioner and former Labor Secretary Frances Perkins opposed the commission's statutory right to conduct periodic health examinations and give medical advice to civil servants, the use of "impertinent and uncalled for questions on [commission] application blanks, particularly about physical defects," and the implementation of government-sponsored after-hours recreation programs. These practices, she asserted, were an intrusion on the employee's right of privacy. Perkins argued that the government engaged in "too much snooping," probing into areas that were "none of [the government's] business." While acknowledging that civil servants should behave "in a manner befitting ladies and gentlemen," she wondered "what difference" it would make "if a man entertains a lady in his room? How is this going to reflect on his ability to do his job?"[64]

Henry Madurga had already received an answer to that question. In 1942, he found himself barred from taking a civil service exam for one year because he did not meet the "standards of general qualifications, suitability and fitness maintained by Government employees." The commission considered Madurga "immoral" for living with a woman to whom he was not married.[65]

One of the most controversial character investigations involved a professor and his wife, both economists for the federal government. After their maid as well as their neighbor accused them both of excessive drinking and the wife of infidelity—the neighbor alleged that the wife had sex on her kitchen table with a man while her husband stood by and laughed—the Civil Service Commission began an investigation. From this, commission investigators concluded that the wife was unfit for public service and dismissed her. The commission was then bombarded with letters from colleagues and friends who insisted that the couple were simply social drinkers and would never engage in "lewd" sexual behavior. Eventually the agency for which they worked conducted its own investigation into the charges and decided that the accusations were unfounded. Several top officials, including Harold Ickes, lambasted the commission for failing to conduct a proper investigation. While the Civil Service Commission eventually exonerated the couple of all charges, the objections raised during this controversy centered on the commission's failure to accord the defendants due process. No one questioned the commission's authority to define proper "moral" behavior for employees outside the office setting.[66] Private lives hence became a public concern when citizens went to work for the federal government.

Longtime civil service employee Maurice Parmelee found himself in a protracted battle with the commission and Dies committee over his employment qualifications. Although Parmelee had received the highest efficiency ratings possible and had just been promoted at the Railroad Retirement

Board, commission officials claimed that Parmelee should be dismissed, not because of "disloyalty" but because he lacked "qualification[s] for the work." In addition to his involvement in a number of civil rights causes, Parmelee was apparently "unqualified" because he extolled the benefits of nudism in a 1931 article.[67]

By 1946, civil servants, the Civil Service Commission, elected officials, and other federal administrators were hotly debating the relationship between public employment and privacy. UFWA officials complained that legislators were using information from personnel files to smear and embarrass individuals, and the officials argued that congressional requests for personnel files constituted a breach of confidentiality.[68] Commissioner Flemming argued with Perkins over the matter of privacy, contending that the government could not eliminate "certain restrictions that we [the government] impose on Federal employees and still have a career service." Classification expert and commission employee Ismar Baruch concurred. In commenting on the Hatch Act, he noted that employees gave up certain "free rights" when they entered government employment. Flemming avoided making a clear distinction between privacy and the public interest, except to state that national security interests superseded concerns with personal freedoms. Because civil service employment was a privilege, not a right, Flemming maintained, an employee's freedom could be curtailed "by those principles which are an integral part of the developing code of ethics in the federal civil service." Officials waffled on whether that "code of ethics" included advocacy for a specific political agenda and/or conformity to certain mainstream social beliefs and cultural customs. Flemming, for instance, admitted that the government needed to avoid "excessive restrictions," but the definition of *excessive* remained disputed.[69]

Postwar politics clouded rather than clarified the meaning of *subversive*. After UFWA's successor union, the United Public Workers of America (UPWA), pushed through a convention plank supportive of the Soviet Union's foreign policy, Civil Service Commission officials considered investigating the body. Although union leaders were not federal employees, the commission declared it had jurisdiction. Both Perkins and Flemming expressed their opposition to federal workers' right to strike, another provision adopted by UPWA.[70]

Character investigations and the adoption of human relations techniques brought the personal lives of employees into the workplace. When elected officials authorized the use of loyalty investigations, the lines between political views, personal habits, public actions, and work activities became extremely hazy. Certainly the construction of an elaborate loyalty apparatus gave elite government administrators and elected officials the opportunity to expand their character examinations. But because human relations experts suggested that personal problems affected worker efficiency, supervisors felt that they had additional justification to examine an employee's personal life, especially during the war, when officials were constantly worried about productivity. Human relations specialists also suggested that "company loyalty" would increase worker productivity. In the federal government, loyalty to the work-place meant loyalty to a specific set of political, social, and economic values defined by administrative elites. These included a belief in capitalism and an acceptance of mainstream white, middle-class values, which in the late 1930s and 1940s included segregation.

Civil servants were well aware of the contradictions and blurred lines be-tween private and public space involved in human relations and loyalty issues. In a protest directed at limitations on the political activities of civil servants, one government forester passionately declared: "The events leading up to this world conflict seem to me to prove that every citizen of a democracy, including civil servants, must be politically alert and active if we are to protect our liberties and retain our rights. . . . Can we set the civil servant apart from the rest of our people? I believe the lessons of the past few years are sufficient warning that the mere creation of an efficient burocracy [sic] is not the goal of democratic government."[71] As this forester revealed, the public and private beliefs of employees became magnified in the civil service. Similarly low-level employees, middle-level managers, and elite administrators often defined the relationship between "company" loyalty and patriotism in radically different terms.

After World War II, public personnel directors broadened their commit-ment to a public version of human relations. They increased their dedication to research and scientific methodology as a means of solving employee pro-ductivity problems.[72] They sponsored many new studies of morale and mo-tivation between 1944 and 1948. They looked to books by human relations specialists Ordway Tead, Elton Mayo, F. J. Roethlisberger, and Alexander Leighton (who spoke at a council meeting in 1947) for guidance on em-ployee relations in the civil service.[73] As the Cold War against communism intensified, personnel administrators became more sensitive to the symbolic importance of the decision-making *process* but also to issues of loyalty. Loyalty policies, employee suggestion programs, and participation plans multiplied in the years following 1945.

Gender, Race, and Human Relations

Like political ideologies, contemporary gender and racial ideologies had a powerful influence on managerial strategies. While some human relations experts shaped their theories to fortify prevailing gender and racial categories, others used them to unsettle these categories and dispute discrimination. On the one hand, human relations introduced a managerial approach that many personnel experts associated with feminine welfare activities. They valued feminine behaviors and sought to use them to ease the plight of low-level workers. Similarly, other practitioners emphasized inclusion and argued that employees—regardless of their sex or their skin color—should be treated equally. On the other hand, this management school tended to reproduce essentialist categories that kept women and African Americans divided and unequal. As demonstrated, in the hands of federal administrators, human relations proved to be an elastic managerial philosophy, promoting both progressive and conservative behavior among managers. Women and African Americans took advantage of various aspects of the human relations program, but in the end, it did not help them erase the boundaries between male and female, black and white.

Although women tended to be the primary recipients of human relations welfare programs, both men and women became its purveyors. Nevertheless, the sex of those constructing human relations programs and discourse was not irrelevant to its development or to the evolution of the personnel occupation. At the beginning of the century, women played an active role in establishing personnel or employment management, while men generally promoted Frederick Taylor's scientific management. Scientific management served to reinforce late Victorian social definitions of "manly" behavior, including individualism, aggression, ambition, and competitiveness within new corporate structures. It also promoted rationality, standardization, and efficiency as masculine traits. Personnel work that focused on the welfare of workers was deemed a more appropriate concern for female white-collar workers, because it coincided with contemporary perceptions of women as natural caregivers.[74]

Even so, the relationship between masculine and feminine approaches to management remained ambiguous and contested. In an effort to assert a more professional image, male personnel practitioners began to stress the more "masculine," technical aspects of their occupation. They emphasized the need to systematize personnel functions by devising organizational charts, standardizing job classifications, quantifying work output, and devising tests to determine the fitness of job applicants. By the 1920s, the "feminine," more welfare-oriented approach to personnel management had become increasingly peripheral to the field. Despite the growing numbers of women entering the employ of America's corporations, few controlled the development of management programs. These gender distinctions, of course, pervaded the bureaucracy. As white-collar work became divided between elite, intellectual labor and routine office work, women provided organizations with a large pool of low-cost labor.[75]

Likewise, a segmentation of personnel duties during the professionalization process left most women in the field performing routine clerical tasks while male personnel officers conducted research and engaged in program development. Task segmentation widened the distance between professional men and amateur women within the new field of personnel administration. Because of the privilege accorded to corporate experience and education over civil service tenure in the appointment of personnel directors, many women were denied these prestigious personnel positions. The one notable exception prior to the Second World War was Julia Atwood Maulding, personnel director for the Interior Department. Although Maulding was active into the 1940s in government personnel issues, she was relatively silent at the male-dominated meetings of the Council of Personnel Administration. In effect, the professionalization process minimized the input women had into personnel policy making.[76]

In one important respect, human relations gave women new access to this work. By revising the "feminine" approach to personnel management popular before World War I, human relations offered women occupational opportunities as counselors, orientation advisors, or training specialists. For example, Dr. Helen Pallister, a psychologist who had served as an instructor at Barnard College and research specialist at St. Andrew's University in Scotland, became the Civil Service Commission's employee counselor in 1943. Dorothy Bailey, a Phi Beta Kappa graduate of the University of Minnesota, also had distinguished academic credentials before entering government service as a clerk in 1933. By 1947, she was earning nearly $8,000 a year as a training specialist with the United States Employment Service. At the time, only a few dozen women in the entire service earned over $8,000 a year.[77]

Those who made it to the top of the profession often justified their contributions along gender lines. Interior Department personnel director Julia Atwood Maulding, the only female member of the Council of Personnel Administration in 1939, said she could not deny that there was "some prejudice against women" in executive jobs, but she said this was "diminishing each year." Even though she felt that an individual's qualifications rather than sex determined success, she also conceded that women were "more emotional and sensitive than men." Men might display these traits too, she said, but "the very sensitiveness, or fine-fiberedness, . . . of women, often enables them to handle [some] situations more successfully [than men]." The qualities that each sex brought to the workplace, she concluded, created a balanced social environment.[78]

In its World War II form, human relations often promoted values associated with female behavior. Some managers hoped to create a more nurturing environment based upon cooperation rather than conflict. In fact, the sympathetic environment officials hoped to create was associated with an ideology of maternalism. As Molly Ladd Taylor has explained, this ideology stipulated that women had a special value system based upon nurturing and caring. Yet both male and female personnel administrators recognized that this would undermine their status as professionals.[79] Government practitioners denied that the human relations approach to management was an attempt to coddle employees. One human relations supporter, for example, denied that counseling constituted maternalism, which she described as the desire to "direct" or "manage" the affairs of another.[80]

As Sharon Strom has revealed in her study of early-twentieth-century office work, personnel managers who advocated a more "sentimental (and effeminate)" approach to employee relations had to temper these aspects of their profession in order to be accepted in a masculine business environment. She also reminds us that both men and women expressed feminine and masculine elements of personnel management. "Men and women contributed to the feminine aspect of personnel management, and both women and men sought to toughen the profession."[81]

Hence the feminine approach to management proved problematic for the field of public personnel administration. At times, personnel officials likened morale-building exercises to those of the military. But this association with a masculine institution could not obscure the feminine, welfare roots of these exercises. Human relations therefore acted as a bridge between an extremely "masculine" organizational style based upon the military and an extremely "feminine" style based upon maternalism. It allowed managers to appear professional but not domineering or authoritarian.

Human relations experts had a tangled relationship to race-related issues as well. Their emphasis on participation opened possibilities for the inclusion of African-American viewpoints in labor relations. In some agencies, for example, human relations supporters encouraged consultation with unions, including the interracial UFWA. At OPA, some personnel officials strongly supported the involvement of UFWA Local 203, particularly in settling racial discrimination charges. One personnel administrator argued that managers simply would not respond to race discrimination charges without union pressure. As he observed, "some poor girl comes in here with a complaint of discrimination and you feel sympathetic, but as soon as you begin to think about doing something you realize you can't prove her boss has given her a raw deal." Eventually "the human and moral realities are obscured by a definition of the problem in terms of formal responsibility and lines of authority. And nothing gets done." Until, he claimed, the union gets involved, which "forces management back into an awareness of the real meaning of the problem." At this point, the personnel official becomes the " 'disinterested' referee or advisor" and effects a reasonable agreement.[82] At the Department of Labor, UFWA Local 1 responded positively in 1943 to the department's human relations initiatives but insisted that "all dances or other social functions be open to all employees— Negro as well as white." Similarly, the focus on the individual employee and personal problems offered African-American employees an opportunity to lay bare the devastating impact of race discrimination. A black employee at OPA recalled his gradual integration into the organization's social life, while another reflected on OPA's "real regard for people as individuals," a critical element of the human relations philosophy.[83] Nonetheless, because most human relations practitioners concentrated on productivity, they shied away from encouraging open debate about racial tensions in the workplace. Instead, many sought to avoid racial conflict by maintaining segregation.

Some personnel managers and supervisors used human relations as a justification for accommodating the perceived racist notions of employees below them. They argued that harmony and productivity—two key aims of the human relations school of management—would best be achieved by mimicking rather than challenging conventional patterns of social relations, including racial separatism.[84] A form of sociologically justified racism legitimated physical and occupational segregation and thus the subordination of African Americans on the labor hierarchy.

Frequently production managers refused to hire blacks into positions because they claimed that it might cause resentment among white employees. This argument was not new and was used frequently to justify an aversion to hiring African Americans in the federal government, particularly after 1913 when segregation became commonplace. Entrenched beliefs about the denigration of labor done by blacks convinced government managers that they should, for the sake of productivity, segment blacks into low-paying menial jobs so as to elevate the status of "white" occupations.[85] One supervisor declined to employ black men as machinists' helpers because operators, who worked closely with these workers, would not accept it. At the TVA, officials denied blacks positions as lab assistants because they might then be promoted to lab technicians, a "white" job. This disruption of employment patterns, they asserted, would cause inefficiency. They likewise refused to hire black machinists or journeymen because they did not want to alienate white workers.[86] Supervisors in the Civil Service Commission refused to promote black messengers to clerical positions because many of its southern employees "simply couldn't put up with" occupational integration. Ordway objected to the practice but apparently felt powerless to change it.[87] Meanwhile, supervisors of the stenographic pool in the Social Security Board would not send black stenographers to offices in which "officials had definitely said that they would not receive colored stenographers." Pool supervisors defended their decision, claiming they were saving black stenographers from "harassment." Some supervisors couched their decisions in economic terms, claiming that they could not risk the resignation of white women if they hired African Americans.[88]

This kind of discrimination reverberated throughout agency ranks, harming even those African Americans who had managed to climb the labor hierarchy. During an extensive review of discriminatory promotion policies in the Veterans' Administration, the only two black adjudicators in the agency testified that they were often denied stenographic help because the supervisor of the stenographic pool would not assign them white stenographers and there were not enough black stenographers. This proved damaging to their careers because they were unable to get clerical help when important decisions had to be made. Thus, they said, they often "missed the boat." Their supervisor defended this segregationist practice by noting that he had to factor racial attitudes into his management decisions. Some white stenographers, he claimed, threatened to resign if assigned to black executives. "Since there is a shortage of stenographers it seems advisable to keep them [the white stenographers] on." While racism had been eliminated from management and from policy, he asserted, it remained among individual employees.[89]

In most departments, programs aimed at alleviating employee stress, such as recreation associations, either segregated or excluded black employees. In one agency a threatened messenger strike in the immediate postwar era led the personnel director to establish a parallel recreation association for black employees, but the director continued to assert that integrated recreation was an impossibility. Even office parties were frequently for white employees only.[90] Many personnel managers did not perceive a link between social separatism and occupational segmentation. In 1948, for example, reporters revealed that a member of the Fair Employment Board (the civil service successor to the Fair Employment Practices Committee) participated in an effort to exclude a black woman from the Washington, D.C., chapter of the American Association of University Women. Annabel Matthews defended her action by distinguishing between social activities and employment rights. While recognizing that "discrimination exists against Negroes and other minorities in an economic way," she said, "there is no discrimination involved in choosing your own friends and associates in social activities." Yet she also noted that in addition to "merit and ability," employers needed to consider how job applicants would get along with other employees.[91]

Black civil servants therefore had few opportunities to negotiate for benefits such as housing offered under the human relations approach. Although the government provided one dorm for "colored girls," it segregated them and placed the dorm a significant distance from downtown offices. Resistance to further assistance was strong. As Democratic chairman of the Senate District of Columbia Committee, Theodore Bilbo (MS), a vocal racist, opposed all measures designed to aid blacks in the nation's capital. Typically, housing for black residents was scarcely habitable. A wartime OPA report on District housing for African Americans concluded that no effort had been made to provide blacks "even the minimum essentials of bearable living." Conditions were getting worse, the report stated—whole families lived in single rooms, and only those getting eviction notices were eligible for new housing. Neighborhoods were deteriorating. One OPA employee lived with her husband and three children in an uninsulated house with peeling plaster, a leaky roof, and rats. Some workers who earned salaries of $1,220 lived in rooms without water and cooking facilities. Street crime was a daily occurrence in many areas, and space was at a premium; the construction of the Pentagon displaced two hundred black families, and a predominantly black neighborhood in Foggy Bottom was destroyed to make room for luxury apartments, government buildings, and George Washington University. Thus the only places to move, for those who could afford it, were so far from the city center that employees were habitually late for work. By 1947, President Harry S. Truman's Committee on Civil Rights reported that 40 percent of all black-occupied housing was substandard, while only 12 percent of white-occupied housing earned that status.[92]

Legal and de facto segregation in Washington, D.C., further distanced African Americans from human relations programs. Although the city temporarily desegregated recreation facilities during the war, Washington remained a Jim Crow town with restaurants surrounding government agencies usually off-limits to black employees. When OPA asked to use a school building to hold a training class, district officials denied their request because the class consisted of white and black clerks.[93] African Americans in Washington, D.C., resented the treatment they received and were active in promoting integration. Howard University students launched sit-down strikes in segregated restaurants, theaters, and stores, and the UFWA insisted that agencies refrain from sponsoring any employee activity that excluded black workers. Not surprisingly, officials and city leaders labeled these men and women "agitators" and "fellow travelers." More than a few were investigated by the FBI.[94]

In more liberal agencies, administrators used human relations techniques to examine the myriad difficulties confronting African-American workers. In this manner, OPA administrators both broadened the understanding of the causes of race discrimination and reversed the rationale underpinning sociological racism. They argued that segregation, rather than integration, caused conflict and lowered employee morale, although personnel director Warner admitted that in divisions where significant numbers of black employees worked with whites, racial friction occurred. Still, OPA's personnel office rejected the argument that segregation promoted harmony and productivity.

To further assist employees, OPA's managerial staff suggested hiring a black counselor and at times probed the personal problems of African-American workers. African-American women were particularly vulnerable as they struggled to cope with both gender and racial inequities. One executive recalled the case of a young woman whose performance was "just intolerably" bad. Through his detective work, he found that she was a single parent with a three-year-old child. For a time the woman had placed the child in a nursery school, but when she became dissatisfied with the school, she began to leave her child at home. "It was a couple of months," the administrator recalled, "before we discovered that she used to dash out of the office two or three times a day and run a few blocks to feed the child and see that it was all right. She didn't even eat any lunch. And of course the place she lived in was impossibly small and dirty." Upon discovering this, the administrator decided not to fire her for incompetence. Instead he discussed the problem with her, at which time she concluded that she should return to her family in New York, because "her situation was hopeless."[95] In this instance, counselors unveiled the severe hardships endured by some employees.

Significantly, OPA's personnel officials traced the tardiness and poor performance of African-American women to economic deprivation: many of these employees lived in squalid conditions and worked two jobs in order to send money home to their families. These problems, one personnel manager noted, were ones many black women faced because "the family ties are likely to be quite strong, the families in greater need, the girl's knowledge of decent nutrition standards smaller, and of course Negroes have less chance to find a place to live or a decent-paying job." Although managers tried to reach a compromise for the employee whose work suffered under these trying circumstances, these compromises rarely involved financial compensation. If an employee continued to draw unsatisfactory ratings, managers put the worker on a thirty-day trial period, at the end of which the personnel manager and supervisor decided whether or not to initiate dismissal proceedings. If they did, they placed a document stating the "facts" of the case in the employee's file. "We then try to help the employee with her problem, but there's often nothing we can do."[96]

OPA's professionally oriented personnel managers were among the few who used human relations techniques in an effort to improve race relations. They believed a personal approach to fair employment was far more effective than an impersonal statistical one. They thus shunned an emphasis on such "technical" tasks as testing and classification. According to one personnel official, technically oriented personnel people "either try to sidestep the problem [of race] entirely, or, if they are concerned to implement fair employment practices, they ask: 'What is the ratio of Negro to white employees?'—and they make free use of such sanctions as they have at their command. They may do a good deal in pushing the hiring of Negroes, but they don't touch the real problem at all." But those who did understand the race problem from the perspective of human relations "always placed a low value on the use of formal techniques and directives, policy statements, statistical ratios, and the like. . . . We never regarded discriminatory attitudes as evidence that the people involved were evil people, but rather inferred that they didn't understand the problem. Consequently, we used long-term, gradual pressure by subtle methods." Some African Americans working at OPA also found these methods subtle. Arline Neal, who fought successfully for a promotion, eventually left government work, embittered by her experience in the civil service. The head of OPA's employee relations branch later confessed that he and his colleagues had difficulty convincing other personnel officers to remain committed to the more liberal human relations agenda. Many of these officers, he lamented, "retreated to the old authoritarian attitude" and "hid behind their personnel manuals" when confronted with racial inequities.[97]

Human relations techniques often produced contradictory impulses. While the emphasis on personal relations rather than statistics broadened administrators' understanding of the relationship between race prejudice in society and at the workplace, it also tended to focus attention on the individual worker and supervisor rather than on the large-scale effects of, and solutions for, discrimination. In the 1940s, social scientists reinforced this trend by attributing racial prejudice to psychological disturbances. According to this model, race prejudice resulted from individual psychosis rather than collective cultural biases.[98] In this sense, the "personal" human relations approach to management proved to be interpreted in highly idiosyncratic ways.

Human relations as a management style promised to establish a productive workforce through democratic mechanisms and therefore emerged from the war years strengthened. As the World War ended and the Cold War began, elected officials and top government administrators became even more worried about maintaining a motivated workforce. Without the unity and urgency provided by a common enemy and a "hot" war, managers had to find new incentives to keep civil servants "efficient." An overpadded, underutilized, and ineffective bureaucracy, government officials believed, was exactly what the Soviets had under communism. Americans would not accept it under democracy. But having defeated fascist regimes, Americans also found centralized and unilateral power structures dangerous. Although they wanted the "trains to run on time," they also wanted to preserve symbols of egalitarianism and democracy. As Davenport mused in 1950, "democracy . . . is essentially and morally a spiritual philosophy of life which gives primary place to the human being as a unique organism. This is the great issue which now divides the world."[99] From 1946 into the early 1950s, public personnel officials emphasized the need for a pluralistic system of labor relations that would also commit bureaucrats to efficient public service.

That system was to promote harmony through teamwork. Organizational conflict, caused by union-management friction, racial prejudice, or gender issues, was therefore "bad," and cooperation was "good."[100] By demanding consensus, however, administrative specialists stifled debate about the means used in public-sector human relations. Unfortunately, these cooperative concepts were superimposed on a system in which some were more equal than others. In structure, if not always in spirit or practice, top administrators considered the federal bureaucracy a business organization, the ultimate goal of which was to produce services and commodities. Whether these were social security checks, business regulations, or aid to farmers, federal personnel managers used a supervisory system to oversee production of federal goods and services. At times, personnel administrators realized that Mayo and the original human relations school "implicitly" denied the existence of authoritarianism in the factory system.[101] But these critiques meant little in practice, for ultimately, managers were unwilling to abdicate their responsibility to decide whether employee "suggestions" were compatible with the public good.[102]

After all, productivity was still their primary concern. As OPA personnel director Wallace Sayre explained, the war made personnel people less concerned with control, rules, and policy making and more interested in "how to motivate [civil servants], how to manage them in such a way as to get maximum production results over the long period."[103] After the war, they had to keep American civil servants committed to production and public service in order to fight the red menace.

The war against a fascist regime and pervasive anticommunist feelings powerfully legitimated the democratic ideology espoused by the personnel managers. A relatively rigid system of hierarchy existed in the federal government; personnel managers believed clear lines of authority to be most efficient. But they were able to use human relations to balance the necessity of consolidated power and thus calm their audience's fear of totalitarianism. Centralized authority would be developed with the "consultation of employees themselves."[104] Employee participation would reinforce the public servant's patriotic commitment to democracy at a time when its foundations were being challenged by "subversives."

By the postwar period, personnel directors had developed a language to address their conflicting interests in strengthening executive leadership and promoting employee participation. The creed they developed, adopted from the human relations school of business management, had a particularly "public" hue to it. Supervisory concern with an employee's lifestyle, personality, and psychology intersected with fears of political subversion. Civil servants who failed to observe the proper code of conduct as written by department heads, personnel managers, bureau chiefs, and office supervisors were labeled "deviant," or worse, "communist," and thus unfit for public service. Vocal union members were "agitators"; employees with confrontational personalities, "malcontents," "cranks," or psychologically deformed; and free spirits, "immoral." Congress, absorbed by wartime concerns, often stood on the periphery of these issues, allowing departments to micromanage their workforce. This enabled personnel managers and line managers to have a significant impact on the tone of employee relations within each agency. They institutionalized the concept of controlled pluralism within the federal bureaucracy, thus fostering the development of internal interest groups. As we shall see in the next chapter, these groups included civil service unions, the very existence of which challenged the professional and managerial power of personnel administrators.

Managers used the human relations philosophy to strengthen and legitimate their authority and to demonstrate that they could use "democratic" management techniques to create an efficient bureaucracy. These human relations concepts had a fragile claim to democracy, for they relied on an artificial and unobtainable consensus between a growing (and vocal) pink-collar and organized workforce and the managers who controlled the terms of employment. For quite some time, however, human relations would continue to mask the fundamentally inequitable distribution of power between employees and managers in government agencies.

Women war workers at the Quartermaster Corps enjoy a break in the lounge built with money given by an anonymous donor, who worried that employees did not have convenient access to recreational facilities (November 1942). Photo courtesy of the Washingtoniana Division, D.C. Public Library.

Women found work in old-line as well as war agencies during World War II. In the Federal Bureau of Investigation, women dominated the Identification Division, where among other duties they processed fingerprint files. The arrangement of desks and expanse of the room reveal the routinized nature of this work. Photo courtesy of the Still Picture Branch, National Archives and Records Administration.

Women perform clerical duties in an integrated workspace at the War Production Board (October 1942). Photo courtesy of the Washingtoniana Division, D.C. Public Library.

The attire, posture, and demeanor of these African-American women working in an Agricultural Adjustment Agency file room in 1944 suggest their desire to present themselves as professional, middle-class white-collar workers. Photo courtesy of the Still Picture Branch, National Archives and Records Administration.

Office of Price Administration employees James T. Taylor and Anne Mason discuss cost of living issues with Professors R. E. Martin and C. E. Crawford from North Carolina A&T. Perhaps reflecting the individualist ideology embedded within the merit system, these speakers argued that individual citizens bore most of the responsibility for keeping the cost of living in check. Photo courtesy of Still Picture Branch, National Archives and Records Administration.

A landlady shows off a furnished room to two Washington, D.C., war workers, who then show off their living arrangement to a photographer. Photos courtesy of the Washingtoniana Division, D.C. Public Library.

4 Unions and Federal Labor Policy

Agriculture administrator Paul Appleby was one of the first departmental managers to recognize the consequences of the New Deal's commitment to organized labor. While reviewing an administrative order on work conditions in the Resettlement Administration during February of 1937, he complained that the order too closely resembled industrial labor relations policies and was therefore inappropriate for the public sector. He went on to urge that agency administrators be given the power to prevent employees from using their organizational memberships in "an offensive way." This he defined as carrying out an organizational campaign, pestering members of Congress, or being, in general, a "nuisance." Not surprisingly, United Federal Workers of America (UFWA) grievance chair Louis Matasoff informed Appleby the following month that officials in the Department of Agriculture had not been as "cooperative and straight-forward" regarding an employee complaint as he had expected.[1]

Without a formal, congressionally sanctioned labor policy for civil servants, agency executives and unions struggled to define their roles in the federal government. Appleby understood that New Deal labor policies had blurred the boundaries between public and private employee relations. Civil service union members had become increasingly vocal in their desire to negotiate with administrators regarding grievances and agency personnel policies. A few months after Appleby had received Matasoff's scolding, he wrote to Wisconsin Progressive Senator Robert LaFollette, asking for advice on government policies concerning civil service unions. "It is altogether likely," he penned to the senator, "that without determinations in the executive agencies they [the executive branch agencies] will inch along in the direction of accepting completely the thinking and relationships that enlightened people have come to accept in the field of industrial labor." While he noted that the government needed a "progressive" and "enlightened" labor policy of its own, he also claimed that there were fundamental differences between public and private employment. Hence, he wanted LaFollette's views on the limitations that should be placed on government unions with respect to such issues as collective bargaining, administrative negotiations, and union political activity.[2]

Others were deeply concerned about these same issues. By 1937, agency administrators, elected officials, union leaders, and rank-and-file members faced critical problems involving the government's policy toward its own workforce. At a time when industrial labor was capturing headlines with dramatic strikes and when the Committee (later Congress) of Industrial Organizations (CIO) was emerging in full force, federal civil servants were demanding a more explicit labor policy statement from agency administrators and elected officials. Government officials had at least to address, if not fully answer, questions about the right of federal employees to organize and bargain collectively. Did unions have the power to negotiate with agency administrators? If so, under what circumstances and on what issues? Did the interests of unionized employees conflict with their duty to serve the people?[3]

Managers often answered these questions by employing a double standard. First they emphasized the similarities between government agencies and private firms, insisting that business management techniques, such as human relations, could be used successfully in the executive branch. But having made that comparison, they proceeded to explain to civil service employees that unlike the private sector, the public sector could not tolerate strikes and collective bargaining. Because civil servants were accountable to taxpayers and their representatives, managers asserted, organized labor had to operate under special restrictions in the public sector.

Chair of the Council of Personnel Administration Frederick Davenport, for example, argued that public "industry" was "tied down by rules and traditions and by standards" that differed significantly from the private sector. Government consultant and labor relations specialist Otto Beyer, while supporting civil service unionization for employees paid by wage boards, believed that private-sector labor practices had to be modified to suit the particular needs of the classified civil service. Hence, he advocated consultation with the National Civil Service Reform League and Civil Service Assembly of the United States and Canada rather than the National Labor Relations Board on issues involving government labor relations.[4]

As in business management, some personnel directors hoped that grievance procedures and other bureaucratic controls would atomize employees and hence provide a check on autonomous union power.[5] Other directors pursued grievance procedures as an appropriate and necessary substitute for bargaining rights in a public service they saw as unable to offer those rights to employees. But still others supported limited forms of collective bargaining, arguing that the state had to remain consistent in its approach to labor. All agency administrators, however, remained opposed to a closed shop that would have given unions the power to regulate entrance and perhaps promotion standards as well. This, they deemed, would negate the government's merit-based personnel system.

Government labor relations tended to shift during the 1930s and 1940s from a politically based paternalism rooted in patronage to an administratively based paternalism linked to contemporary business management ideals. In a mid-twentieth-century bureaucratic context, paternalism referred to managerial strategies that sought to personalize authority structures. After the emergence of impersonal bureaucracies, business executives, for instance, created company towns, company stores, and welfare capitalism to ensure employee loyalty and make the company appear more benevolent.[6] In the government, an administratively based paternalism emerged from a struggle between agency officials and union members for control over employee relations as the patronage system diminished in scope. In theory, the Civil Service Commission was to step into the vacuum left by the congressional retreat from patronage and establish a uniform personnel system guided by impersonal bureaucratic controls. In reality, the commission was too weak to overcome the powerful centrifugal force of agency administrators who were used to operating under personal, and political, control.[7] With strict congressional oversight waning, agency elites worked to broaden their discretion over personnel issues, as did the president in his role as chief executive. Indeed, President Franklin D. Roosevelt asserted considerable authority over civil service issues and as such set the tone, if not the firm policy, for governmental employee relations.

Government Labor Policy in the New Deal Civil Service

After the passage of Robert Wagner's National Labor Relations Act in 1935, a small group within the administration favored passage of a "Little Wagner" bill for government employees. Some members of Roosevelt's Committee on Administrative Management drafted a special section on employee relations for inclusion in the president's reorganization bill. This section established the right of federal employees to organize and bargain collectively with administrative officials "on matters within the administrative discretion of such officials that relate to working conditions, hours of service, or compensation schedules." It also provided for the creation of a Federal Service Personnel Relations Board, modeled on the National Labor Relations Board. Significantly, these employee relations provisions were absent from the bill as it was presented to Congress in 1937. Their removal left the relationship between private- and public-sector labor relations unresolved. Hence, the issue continued to fester.[8]

In response to repeated strikes in New Deal agencies, especially the Works Progress Administration (WPA), to the organization of the CIO's UFWA, and to general discontent among civil servants, the president moved to clarify the government's position on unionization.[9] First, on July 9, 1937, Roosevelt held a news conference at the White House in which he addressed the issue. Recalling his days as assistant secretary in the Navy Department, Roosevelt explained how he sought, in 1913, to work with employees to set wages and improve work conditions. According to Roosevelt, administrators had no authority to enter into *contracts* with labor unions. Only Congress, he said, had the power to set wage standards. Although Roosevelt's argument failed to elucidate the difference between having pay determined by a wage board versus having wage scales set by congressional statute, he clearly believed employee unions had no legal right to bind agency administrators to an agreement. But employees, he also noted, were not without power. They could freely organize and choose representatives to petition Congress or wage boards for a raise in pay or a change in work conditions. Citing civil service rules, he maintained that government workers did not possess the right to strike.[10]

A week after his press conference, Roosevelt had occasion to put his governmental labor philosophy into writing. In response to an invitation from Luther Steward, president of the National Federation of Federal Employees (NFFE), for Roosevelt to attend the union's annual convention, the president and his advisors chose to issue a clear statement on the relationship between the government and public employee unions. Roosevelt asked Civil Service Commissioner Harry Mitchell to draft a reply that would explain why government employees did not have the right to strike or bargain collectively. The president then called union leaders into his office for a discussion of the letter. NFFE President Steward praised it, later claiming that "there must be a definite recognition of the fact that in the public service, unlike private employment, there can be no such thing as collective bargaining," though he claimed to support negotiations and conferences between management and labor. UFWA President Jacob Baker made several conservative suggestions to Roosevelt, who rejected all of them. Baker lauded the letter for its "proper" condemnation of employee strikes, but asked Roosevelt to make the statement more supportive of union organization. The presence of unions and frequent conferences between administrators and union representatives, he wanted the president to emphasize, could be used to improve employee morale and personnel policies. Finally, he asked that the letter explain that the "values of common action and representation gained by [government employee] organization are not to be confused with the more militant efforts common to unions in industry."[11]

Instead, Roosevelt used the letter to make a forceful statement about the restrictions under which government unions operated. Noting that employee organizations had "a logical place in Government affairs," Roosevelt added that the desire of civil servants for reasonable pay and working hours, safe working conditions, opportunities for advancement, grievance reviews, and hence a "proper" employee relations policy was little different than the desire of employees in the private sector. However, he continued, government employees were to be aware that:

> the process of collective bargaining, as usually understood, cannot be transplanted into the public service. It has its distinct and insurmountable limitations when applied to public personnel management. The very nature and purposes of Government make it impossible for administrative officials to represent fully or bind the employer in mutual discussions with Government employee organizations. The employer is the whole people, who speak by means of laws enacted by their representatives in Congress. . . . Particularly, I want to emphasize my conviction that militant tactics have no place in the function of any organization of Government employees. Upon employees in the Federal service rests the obligation to serve the whole people, whose interests and welfare require orderliness and continuity in the conduct of Government activities.[12]

While the statement resulted from a collaborative effort, its content reflected Roosevelt's longtime experience as a political figure. Harkening back to his tenure as assistant secretary of the navy (1913–20) during an era of internal civil service strife, Roosevelt elected to support the government's long-standing traditions with respect to employee unionism. The timing of this statement was important because the president in 1937 was trying desperately to strengthen his hand as chief executive. He was attempting to streamline civil service administration (as exemplified by the recommendations of the Committee on Administrative Management) and to transfer emergency appointments he had made early in his presidency to the career civil service. His employee relations policy statement was consistent with his overarching desire to tighten presidential control over the government's civil servants.[13]

One can hardly overestimate the impact of this statement on the future of union-government relations. For more than twenty-five years, Roosevelt's letter was cited repeatedly as the "magna carta" of government employee relations by personnel administrators, agency heads, elected officials, and some union leaders. In 1941, AFL President William Green told public sector employees that they could not approach department heads with demands for shorter hours, higher pay, or better work conditions, because "department officials have no power to grant your demands." Roosevelt's letter was used to rein in unions during World War II and to get "no-strike" legislation passed in Congress. Similarly, administrators used it to fight off legislative proposals to "recognize" government unions as bargaining agents and to justify the government's "open shop" and "right to work" policies.[14]

Public personnel managers translated Roosevelt's philosophy of accountability into administrative authority. When administrators spoke of accountability, they meant accountability to agency elites and agency objectives. Hence, they believed that as paternal stewards of the government, they, more than lower-level employees, represented and protected the public interest. They, in turn, used their authority to explore and exploit sophisticated techniques to regulate communication, and thus union power, within their organizations. Grievance procedures, participatory programs, and regulations about union activity allowed personnel managers to undermine the potential autonomy and hence the authority of the unions.[15] Personnel specialists, in cooperation with political officials, limited the power of unions to bargain collectively. Managers established a pluralistic labor system in which unions constituted only one of the many legitimate voices being heard.

Agency Labor Relations, 1938–1945

From the perspective of those working on the office floor, the employee relations issue took on different contours than it did when viewed from the White House or Capitol Hill. At the point of production, personnel managers and administrative elites worked together and grappled with one another on a daily basis in an effort to establish control over work conditions. Until the UFWA and the militant new lodges within the American Federation of Government Employees (AFGE) took the initiative, civil service unions hesitated to contest or use administrative discretion to obtain their objectives. Once militant unions emerged, the situation changed decisively. When Roosevelt created personnel divisions in 1938 under Executive Order 7916, he called upon personnel directors to draft policies for their respective agencies. Threatened by activist union lodges, several managers devised policies that they hoped would minimize confrontation between agency officials and union members. Adopting techniques from business management, personnel administrators worked to develop a sense of paternal authority—a mutual respect between employees and agency elites that would preserve the power of the elites and legitimate the subordination of employees. They attempted to coopt unions by giving them a voice but no substantive decision-making power. Personnel directors and agency management maximized their power by defining elected officials (Congress and the president) *and* themselves as the "employer." Thus, agency administrators could wield against unions the powerful argument for civic responsibility.

Throughout the 1930s, 1940s, and 1950s, government officials continued to address the nature of union participation in the public sector, but the link between union participation and racial equality was rarely articulated as an explicit issue. Instead, government administrators and union leaders negotiated over the terms of collective bargaining with little attention to how those policies would combat race discrimination. On occasion, some unions made a noise about the subject. During the 1940s, the UFWA-CIO vocally protested discrimination in various agencies, and a good deal of the hostility it encountered from administrators, and sometimes other union leaders, stemmed from its progressive stand on race. Because the union was integrated, its efforts to earn union representation at the bargaining table, a grievance hearing, or an efficiency rating appeal had the potential to pull African-American employees into the negotiating process. Consequently, while the fight over a labor relations policy did not directly address race, the existence of an integrated UFWA helped draw attention to the repercussions of racial exclusion by other unions. In this area, as in the area of collective bargaining, pressure for change largely came from below, although administrators worked to control the pace and direction of policy.

Personnel managers relied heavily on administrative authority to curb union activity within agencies. In the Department of Labor, personnel director Robert Smith reacted negatively to a UFWA-circulated memo calling for increased publicity of department vacancies; promotions, he stated, were to be determined by bureau and division heads and reviewed by the personnel department. The circular, he remarked with distaste, was designed "to make it possible for the [UFWA] Adjustment committee to have a list of available jobs, a list of applicants, a list of aggrieved employees who were not promoted, and an opportunity to harass bureau heads by forcing them to justify the selections made for promotions and requiring reasons for passing over other qualified candidates."[16] Despite his professed open mind toward employee organizations, Smith expressed resentment toward union efforts to participate in decisions involving weather-related leave, department appropriations, and administrative promotions. "I am perfectly willing to admit," he proclaimed, "that they [unions] should not be concerned with some of these points."[17]

During a discussion of standardized holiday, sick, and annual leave rules, Navy Department personnel director Charles Piozet worried that if administrators did not take the initiative in developing new regulations, they would be coopted by organized employees. "It seems as though everything gotten through in recent years," he complained, "has been solely by the efforts of the employees and not by the administrative officials. . . . [The five-day, forty-hour week] was put over in '34 by the employee groups over the protests of a good many departments." Davenport agreed with Piozet, noting that "there isn't any wonder the employees feel the need of organization if everything they get that is rational comes from pressure of employee groups and not from pressure of administrators."[18]

Uniformity remained a problem. A broad survey of governmental labor policies, undertaken by the Council of Personnel Administration in the spring of 1939, uncovered widespread discrepancies between and within departments. Treasury Department officials, for instance, candidly admitted that none of their divisions accorded employee groups absolute or limited veto power over personnel policies. Bureau of the Mint regulations frankly stated that "employee groups [were] not permitted to participate in the formulation of basic personnel policies" and that the Division of Disbursement's local AFGE lodge had no official relationship to the division. They "never interfered in any way in connection with personnel administration. . . . The operations of the Division are as if the union did not exist." Even the Post Office

Department, which had a highly unionized workforce, had no procedures for unions to negotiate formal labor agreements.[19] Likewise the Interstate Commerce Commission (ICC) refused employees the right to present grievances through union representatives.[20] In the Agriculture Department, on the other hand, the official employee relations policy, Memorandum 753, set forth the right of employees "to join or refrain from joining" a union and allowed employees to use union representatives when consulting supervisors.[21]

To remedy these inconsistencies, the Council of Personnel Administration established an employee relations committee, chaired by State Department personnel director Edward Yardley and staffed by Dick Carlson (Civil Aeronautics Authority), Russell Cook (U.S. Housing Authority), and Roy Hendrickson (Agriculture). According to Smith (Labor), the development of an overall statement establishing the degree and nature of employee participation in personnel management had become absolutely necessary because, despite Roosevelt's statement, unions were still "trying to participate in management."[22] Nevertheless, at the insistence of several members, the council and employee relations committee agreed to start on a narrower project called for by Roosevelt's Executive Order 7916: the construction of grievance procedures. Hendrickson, for instance, favored a more specific statement, similar to Memorandum 753, that prioritized grievance procedures.[23]

When the council discussed the grievance issue, Smith recognized its fundamental importance. At issue, he noted in one meeting, was the nature of the relationship between subordinates and supervisors: how much, he wanted to know, should employees be involved in the decision-making process?[24] He did not want to know, apparently, whether a reordering of hierarchical relationships might improve operations; instead he and his colleagues hoped to fortify management authority.

Several council members had extensive experience with the grievance issue. The Treasury Department had a grievance committee, while the Civil Service Commission and Labor Department used conciliation committees to address complaints. The Secretary of Labor charged the department's conciliation committee, which consisted of four supervisory and four nonsupervisory employees, with the task of investigating cases submitted in writing. It had the authority to summon witnesses, gather written statements, hold hearings (which were to be transcribed), and issue opinions. The Department of Agriculture's Memorandum 753 included grievance procedures that personnel director Hendrickson claimed made the government a "model employer" and fostered esprit de corps among employees.[25]

In practice, these procedures did not significantly empower federal workers. In 1936 the Labor Department's conciliation committee expanded to include five supervisory employees and six union representatives (two from each civil service union). Perkins directly appointed all five managerial members and, on the basis of nominations made by union members, selected those representatives as well. After 1937 the personnel director, who was frequently antagonistic to union demands, became a permanent member.[26] Moreover, the committee had no power to enforce its rulings, and between 1936 and 1940 it acted favorably on only three of the fourteen employee petitions on which it agreed to rule. Usually the committee gave bureau chiefs discretion in remedying grievances. In one instance, committee representatives recommended a raise in an employee's efficiency rating but denied the reclassification request, mandating only that the bureau chief give the employee preference in any future vacancies. When the complaint involved a financial reward, as in a job reclassification or transfer to a more lucrative position, the committee almost always endorsed the original decision of the bureau chief or office supervisor.[27] Secretary of Labor Frances Perkins viewed the committee only as a court of last resort. She emphasized that employees were always free simply to approach supervisors with problems; she encouraged them to visit the committee only if they were unhappy with the result of those meetings.

A number of agencies lacked formal, written procedures and instead relied on vague "open door" policies to resolve personnel problems. These policies left most of the power in the hands of administrative officials, as they retained the discretion to close the door when they pleased. Post Office personnel director Frank Ellis captured the essence of the open door: "Certainly," he said, "the administrative officer should have something to say about whom he will see and how long he will see them."[28]

Committed to the human relations school of management, council members encouraged dialogue between individual employees and supervisors. As classification expert and Civil Service Commission employee Ismar Baruch proclaimed, the purpose of the grievance procedure was to prevent the escalation of a complaint by encouraging the participation of employees in its resolution at the lowest possible level.[29] This, the personnel directors believed, would minimize the number of complaints moving through the cumbersome appeal procedure and would, in turn, undermine unions. As Hendrickson worried, unless administrators accepted responsibility for employee relations, "someone else will—employee organizations, outside 'interference,' and eventually Congress."[30]

Accordingly, council members stressed supervisory performance in maintaining labor harmony. Davenport urged personnel managers to undertake a special mission: to train supervisors in the art of conflict management.[31] The Federal Security Agency grievance procedure (devised under personnel director Robert Barnett) stated forcefully that an employee has the "right, and is expected, to consult freely at all times with his supervisor. . . . Supervisors will make themselves available and will grant to employees under their supervision courteous and sympathetic interviews."[32] In this manner, the council hoped union participation would be unnecessary.

As the accent on supervisory participation in grievance procedures revealed, directors were caught between two contradictory goals: one was a standardized, routinized, bureaucratized system of labor relations; the other preserved discretion, personal interaction, and paternalism. Even former Civil Service Commissioner Samuel Ordway Jr., who eventually championed standard procedures as a safeguard against employee revolt, recognized the potential power of employees in a standardized system: "Once you define [a procedure] in writing you create a right on the part of the employee to go to the head of the organization." He initially hesitated in supporting formal grievance and appeal procedures for "just as there are arrogant, stupid and selfish department and division heads, sometimes, there are also a great many disgruntled and crackpot employees. . . . I believe that the danger of increasing the opportunity of the latter group to make the administrative task difficult, outweighs the advantage of seeking to solve the problem by placing the appointing official 'on trial.' "[33] Some administrators initially resisted formalized procedures because they worried about upsetting established agency hierarchies. Personnel director John Switzer (ICC) saw little reason to create a third party apparatus to handle complaints; supervisors, he said, were not "bums," and most charges were "unfounded" and "unjustified."[34]

But while many council members agreed that supervisors were not bums and would give employees sympathetic interviews, they recognized that in some cases more stringent and uniform bureaucratic control would be necessary to maintain harmony. Not all favored union participation in the general appeal procedure. Switzer worried that if the agency required union participation in grievance procedures, unions would use these procedures as a "club" over management's head. He also expressed fear that employees might pick a low-level clerk to represent them and the clerk would not be able "handle" the case, or worse yet, they might choose an "outsider." Farm Credit Administration (FCA) personnel director Theodore Wilson expressed hostility toward any union participation. He did not think personnel administrators "should encourage employees to go to union representatives and have them [the representatives] take the cases up with their supervisors." Rather he wanted to shield supervisors, especially those in lower grades, from contact with unions. In the FCA, he explained, administrators employed a special liaison officer to deal with unions.[35] Overall, the council's recommendations reflected a belief widespread among personnel administrators that in an individualized, merit-based system, civil service unions were not the legitimate voice of employees.

Unions, nevertheless, struggled to retain a voice. In the private sector, grievance procedures may have helped undermine the shop steward system, an important force of labor radicalism, but public-sector unions did not have an extensive steward system. Hence, employees generally welcomed grievance procedures as a means of limiting the arbitrary rule of office supervisors, division heads, and bureau chiefs. NFFE had been calling for arbitration boards at least since the early 1930s. They most often advocated a system similar to Great Britain's Whitley Councils, whereby an equivalent number of civil service management and staff representatives met to discuss and make binding decisions on personnel issues. Charles Stengle of the AFGE admired the Labor Department's conciliation committee, hoping that Congress would use it as a model when (and if) it set up an appeal board for the entire service. When the council held hearings on the grievance policy, they sought input from administrators and union leaders, although the council was free to accept or reject their suggestions.[36] According to Civil Service Commission guidelines, if an informal resolution to a grievance failed, agency administrators were to establish an "impartial" board that incorporated "adequate employee representation." (The commission deliberately left the concept vague so that the Council of Personnel Administration would define it.)[37] This provision engendered much debate among council members. According to Clive Palmer of the Federal Home Loan Bank Board, simply allowing employees to serve on a board was "as far as we should go on the question of employee representation on such committees, and . . . it is as far as we have any right to go. . . . I feel that employee representation is adequately provided if the employee himself can choose his representative from among his co-workers."[38]

Council members also realized that a formal grievance procedure would not necessarily force agencies to resolve racial inequities. In 1940, Piozet told council members that the AFL craft unions often found in various navy yards would only admit whites and that, in general, the AFL did not charter black unions. A year later, Caso March, personnel committee chair of AFGE Lodge 421 in the Federal Power Commission (FPC), asked black messenger Clarence Strong to withdraw his application to the union. Instead March offered to create an all-black organization, "unit B of Lodge 421," with separate officers and funds. When Strong refused, noting that segregation was "not in accordance with the purpose of the Union," March campaigned against Strong's membership, rejecting his application a week later because a majority of the lodge members voted against it. March's attempt to segregate black union members highlighted the connection between administrative procedures, union power, and race. Prior to Strong's petition for membership, Lodge 421 representatives had earned the right to meet with the FPC chairman every other week to discuss vacancies, grievances, and personnel problems. Representatives for the meeting were chosen by lodge members, but the proposed unit B was to have no "voice in the election of the officers of the main union." Hence, black employees would have no voice in choosing a representative and thus no voice on personnel issues. As a Fair Employment Practices Committee (FEPC) investigator later noted, "when it is realized that the present chairman of the personnel committee, Mr. Caso March, is also the promoter of the idea of a separate unit for colored persons . . . it does not seem probable that the colored employees of the [Federal Power] Commission would receive impartial treatment as far as his committee is concerned." The investigation revealed that while the constitution and by-laws of Lodge 421 did not specifically exclude black employees, the lodge was not interested in recruiting African Americans. Not surprisingly, the AFGE lodge—unlike the UFWA—also lacked a committee devoted to race discrimination.[39] The lack of such committees in NFFE and AFGE lodges further isolated the issue of race discrimination from the union movement, divorcing the cause of class equity from the cause of racial justice.

A fear of class conflict no doubt made council members reluctant to give unions any specific role in the grievance process. After promulgation of the commission statement on appeal boards, some agencies, such as the Labor Department, provided for union representation on general grievance appeal boards, but they were not obligated to do so.[40] But the Federal Security Agency, as was the case with many other agencies, merely stipulated that its three-member appeal board consist of an employee chosen by the agency head, one named by the aggrieved employee, and the last chosen by the other two.[41]

In their draft on grievance procedures, the Civil Service Commission and the council took the opportunity to insert caveats on employee unionization. They noted that employees were free to join employee groups but that these organizations could not assert the right to strike against the government of the United States. Some council members criticized the antistrike clause as unnecessary. Others, however, defended its inclusion because of the statement's prior reference to union representation.[42] Although personnel managers accepted the existence of civil service unions, neither the commission nor the council wanted to yield to the unions a primary position in labor-management relations.

Labor relations expert Otto Beyer urged the commission to highlight the role of unions by tempering the tone of its statement. According to Beyer, the commission's policy should reflect the notion that employee organizations facilitated rather than inhibited conflict resolution. Hence, its explicit open shop statement—employees were free to "join or refrain from joining employee organizations"—he said, was too negative and potentially destructive to cooperative union-management relations. While the commission rejected his advice on this issue, it did accept Beyer's suggestion to make specific the right of employees to use representatives and appeal boards to resolve grievances.[43]

The eight principles designed to guide agencies in formulating procedures minimized union representation and employee input. In the opening paragraphs of the final statement on grievance procedures, the commission reiterated the government's restrictions on employee organization. The paragraph began with the open shop stipulation to which Beyer objected. It then reminded employees that they were not to join organizations that supported the right to strike against the government and restated section 9A of the Hatch Act, prohibiting employees from joining organizations that advocated the overthrow of the government.[44]

In the end, the commission's principles contained no provisions for enforcement and were written as guidelines rather than as mandates. Agencies submitted their procedures to the Civil Service Commission for approval, and while most council members agreed that "progressive" and "professional" personnel management demanded the establishment of formal grievance procedures, they left personnel directors some administrative discretion. They had less discretion with regard to efficiency rating review boards, but here too, the debate over employee representation reflected considerable ambivalence and some hostility toward union power.

Efficiency ratings represented the most powerful means with which supervisors controlled employees. The Classification Act of 1923 mandated the establishment of a uniform rating system for retention, dismissal, demotion, and promotion purposes in the departmental classified service (field employees came under the rating system in 1941). Between 1924 and 1935, the government employed a "graphic scale" that used standard adjectives (ranging from "very superior" to "dull") to describe an employee's ability to learn and perform job-related skills specified by the Bureau of Efficiency. Employee dissatisfaction led to a revision in 1935 that introduced an adjectival and numerical scheme. Advocates of the rating system proclaimed it as objective and impartial and therefore consistent with the merit ideal. But because these ratings were often used as a basis for promotion and reduction-in-force ladders, low-level employees resented the power that ratings placed in the hands of office supervisors. Their decisions were final. According to UFWA members, ratings were based "solely on the personal opinions and prejudices of supervisors" and were often used to intimidate or dismiss union members. Stating that New Deal principles gave working men and women a "right to a direct voice in matters concerning their economic well being," UFWA members challenged the authority of supervisors to rate them.[45]

To address widespread disgruntlement over rating procedures, Congress passed the Ramspeck Act in November 1940, directing the Civil Service Commission to establish three-member efficiency rating review boards and to determine the manner in which employees were to be represented on review boards. Under the law, the commission had to designate the chairman of the three-member board. This was a narrowly focused grievance program—the law stipulated that review boards hear only cases involving disputed ratings. Unlike grievance procedures in the Civil Service Commission guidelines, Congress gave these review boards the power to adjust ratings as they "may find proper."[46]

When the council members took up the issue of efficiency rating review boards, they again agreed that union representation should be permitted but not *privileged*. Soon after the passage of the Ramspeck Act, UFWA leaders insisted that in all cases involving their members, a UFWA member should be present on the review board.[47] This annoyed personnel managers. Davenport retorted that unions were to function as lawyers, not as judges.[48] Unions, several personnel directors pointed out, did not represent a majority of employees. In the State Department, for example, the combined membership of NFFE, UFWA, AFGE, and an independent employee association did not constitute a majority of the personnel. Hence, Yardley stated, he made a conscious effort to confer with unorganized employees.[49] Council staff member Henry Hubbard likened unions to political parties and worried that the presence on the board of a union member representing a minority group of employees would deprive the majority of recognition and be "detrimental to the policies with respect to collective bargaining in industry."[50] William Bowen of the Railroad Retirement Board (RRB) stated that it was "undemocratic" for agencies to mandate that union members who represented "small minorities" be placed on the board.[51] None of the personnel directors suggested a closed shop as a means of ensuring majority representation.

While a special committee researched the issue for the council, members debated the merits of various plans to select an employee representative to the board. Among the provisions suggested were appointment by a union; a general election by employees; employee designation of a representative on a case-by-case, rotating basis; or selection from a panel designated by employees. Personnel staff of the RRB called for a "panel" approach whereby the agency head, commission, and employees would designate panels of "qualified" people from whom to choose a representative. They believed this would "professionalize" the work of the review board.[52] Hendrickson favored a petition and nomination system. The nominating petition, he asserted, would both eliminate the problem of union representation and enervate the union movement. "The unions can get busy and nominate all they want to," he told his council colleagues. "We've got unions that will be carrying petitions around for a long time; they enjoy it; it will be good experience for them. This democratic process, as it always does, will knock them down and bring them in line."[53]

Many directors pointed out that eligibility for board service was complicated by the unclear line that existed between management and labor. As Oliver Short noted, two of the unions in the Commerce Department were headed by assistant division chiefs. Piozet, too, wondered about the ethics of allowing supervisors to be employee representatives. Interior personnel director Julia Maulding concluded with exasperation that the most democratic procedure would be to have a general and open election in which nominated employees ran against one another. This, she said, would eliminate charges of discrimination and favoritism with regard to unions. Piozet agreed it was democratic but also recognized that in agencies that were highly organized, union members had in the past refused to participate in or to recognize an election if provisions were not made for their representation.[54]

Despite these reservations, the council ultimately decided to compromise: it reinforced a belief in employee participation while it fortified the administrative hierarchy. "Employees themselves," the committee researching the issue declared, "[must] have confidence in the appeals system established under this Act. Employee participation, as provided in this law, is essential to the attainment of this confidence." Rather than recommend one method by which employees could appoint their representative to the board, the committee offered several, including direct primaries, general elections, and preferential balloting. While the committee recommended the use of a referendum to determine which plan employees preferred, it also made it clear that the department head had the final authority to select the method used. Further, the report reminded council members that "the heads of departments and agencies [should] be regarded as the appropriate authority for determining the number and jurisdiction of boards to be established within each department or agency." One council member worried that the existence of appeal boards might be illegal because their decisions would essentially usurp the authority of the department head. This would be the case even though the department head still retained the power to choose one board member, while the Civil Service Commission was to choose the chair (who was not to be an employee of that agency). As with grievance procedures, union representation was not guaranteed in the appeal process.[55]

At the recommendation of the commission, Roosevelt issued Executive Order 9252 in October 1942 prescribing the regulations for efficiency rating review boards. The order stipulated that employees who received ratings were to use a general election to determine who would be their representative on the board. Even when union members were elected to review boards, they were often AFGE and NFFE members who were more representative of management than of staff. The Department of Agriculture's employee representative in 1941 was NFFE member Dr. Howard Edson, head of the Mycology and Disease Survey Division. In 1942, AFGE Local 228 member and former professor Molly Ray Carroll was elected to the Labor Department's efficiency rating appeal board.[56]

Personnel directors worked hard to preserve administrative authority. They could, for instance, restrict the flow of communication with regard to the review board's deliberations. Hence the council committee suggested that hearings be conducted "on an informal basis, generally without stenographic notes." The committee stipulated that the board's decision be submitted in writing to the department head, but since there was no way to appeal the board's decision, "it would appear unnecessary," committee members wrote, "to maintain a complete stenographic record or to include in its written decision formal or detailed reasons for the decision. It is legally unnecessary and administratively undesirable that the procedures or records of appeal boards be kept in detailed and formalistic manner."[57] Control over the flow of information provided an important source of power for elite administrators.

Particularly in political bureaucracies, access to information frequently determined who had power and authority and who did not. Control over employee files became a powerful tool in the hands of elite administrators. Recognizing this, former AFGE president Babcock (who had since become head of a privately funded study group called the Federal Personnel Association) requested that the president issue an executive order mandating that employee files be opened. A survey conducted by the Civil Service Commission, however, revealed that departments felt the proposal would "cause misunderstandings, disturb harmonious relations, and result in the disruption of efficient administration." Departmental administrators argued that it was essential to protect the anonymity of sources in order to get accurate information on employees. Roosevelt honored their wishes by rejecting Babcock's request. Hence, employees were often denied promotions, raises, and sometimes their jobs without benefit of an explanation, substantiation of the derogatory information in their files, or an opportunity to refute charges made against them.[58]

Because managers held a monopoly on personnel information, employees were at an inherent disadvantage in any grievance they pursued. Smith, for instance, recognized the need for increased communication but favored the dissemination of an agency bulletin informing employees of rules, regulations, and statutes so that there would be no misunderstanding as to the position of management.[59]

Pressure from unions gradually broke the code of silence. By 1941 AFGE's Lodge 421 in the Federal Power Commission had obtained the right of employees to examine their own files. And in a dramatic reversal of the closed file tradition, the UFWA coaxed Office of Price Administration (OPA) officials in 1943 into opening all of the agency's files during an investigation of racial discrimination.[60] To this point, however, the progress was agency by agency, and that promised a long, slow campaign.

African-American organizations also worked on a case-by-case basis to remedy discrimination. The National Association for the Advancement of Colored People (NAACP) remained an active force in the campaign for racial justice in the civil service through the 1920s, 1930s, and 1940s. Often, they worked closely with the National Alliance of Postal Employees, a black union formed in reaction to the all-white practices of its AFL counterparts. Both organizations doggedly investigated cases brought to their attention, collecting affidavits, writing letters, and imploring administrators, on the basis of democratic principles and the merit system, to act on cases of discrimination.[61] A number of other, smaller, and sometimes more informal groups worked at the agency level to root out discrimination. In the New York City office of the Customs Bureau, the Phalanx Club, an organization consisting of African-American guards, undertook a campaign in 1938 to win promotions for meritorious black employees.[62] During World War II another group, calling itself the Committee for Economic Advancement of Messengers, similarly publicized the lack of promotional opportunities for African-American public servants, particularly in Washington, D.C. On occasion, the collective pressure of an organization produced results, but more often than not, agency administrators and the Civil Service Commission responded to these cases with a reference to the rule of three, or as NAACP official Roy Wilkins indicated in 1933, they avoided charges of discrimination through the use of "tricky rules and regulations."[63]

Perhaps because of the existence of the UFWA and other specialized unions such as the National Alliance of Postal Employees, few general unions existed for African Americans. Two organizations appear to have formed in the early 1940s—the United Government Employees and the National Employees and Tenants Union (NETU)—but both seem to have disappeared before the end of the war. These unions voiced strong support for the Roosevelt Administration and, like the NAACP and National Alliance, preferred to work within the system rather than overturn it. The head of the NETU, Andrew Wicketts, had been educated at Northwestern University and LaSalle Extension University in Chicago and worked for the Census Bureau, but he was also well-versed in union causes, having worked with A. Philip Randolph in the sleeping car porters union and having organized for the United Government Employees. While Wicketts advocated for collective bargaining rights, fought for an explicit nondiscrimination policy, and complained about the "disastrous consequences" of segregation, he also offered support for all-black units within specific departments if these units offered opportunities for blacks to become supervisors and/or professionals. Like the AFGE and NFFE, his organization also denounced the use of strikes and pickets and condemned black Republicans who criticized the Roosevelt Administration for "setting up 'Jim Crow' in government," instead casting the blame on William Howard Taft and the subsequent Republican administrations of Warren Harding, Calvin Coolidge, and Herbert Hoover.[64] The existence of these unions and informal organizations signaled the growing strength of the civil rights movement during the war and the movement's willingness to use government procedures to implement a color-blind merit system. Nevertheless, the low survival rate of these unions suggests the enormous obstacles they faced in financing their organizations, winning new members, and mounting a successful challenge to race discrimination in the federal government.

Personnel officers showed little support for black unions, but they did not always appear overtly anti-union. Most allowed unions to use specified bulletin boards, occupy conference rooms outside office hours, and distribute union literature in government offices as long as it was not on government time. Unions tried to take advantage of every such provision. UFWA organizers, for instance, began signing up low-paid workers on lunch hours and leave time; they solicited membership from cleaning women at the elevator when the women ended their shifts at midnight; and they called meetings on shift breaks and in the evenings.[65]

Some management officials were perturbed about these incursions and revealed their proprietary feelings by expressing significant concern over issues such as the use of "outside" speakers at union meetings. As Post Office personnel officer Frank Ellis put it, "Is the administrative officer going to allow any speaker in there that he thinks is a detriment to *his* employees [?]" (emphasis added). Council members also agreed that outside organizations should be prohibited from conducting membership drives or general meetings in government offices.[66] One set of instructions for unions organizing in the Bureau of Internal Revenue limited speeches to "certified" union representatives and forbade individual canvassing or membership solicitation in bureau offices.[67]

Union literature also made administrators nervous. The Treasury Department allowed unions to post announcements and circulars on bulletin boards as long as they were not offensive to "non-union" employees.[68] When a union in the Agriculture Department printed a leaflet that discussed the Spanish Civil War, personnel director Hendrickson protested that the department could "hardly provide for the expenditure of Government money for such purposes."[69] OPA administrators, on the other hand, decided to let a union questionnaire be distributed even though they had not approved it. They tried reverse psychology: "Actually, we are able to exert considerable influence without exercising authority. This would most certainly disappear if we tried to adopt a control attitude."[70] Ironically, personnel administrators who wanted to disassociate themselves from union activities refused to review documents because they were afraid it would seem as though the department sponsored the material.[71]

Restrictions on meeting space and time and the distribution of literature had a significant impact on the strength of government unions. Worker ties maintained *outside* the workplace, especially in ethnic communities, often bolstered private-sector unionization. Union hall meetings and neighborhood activity reinforced solidarity. Government workers, however, did not have the same neighborhood structure to bond members together. They were to a considerable extent members of an atomistic middle class that scattered to the suburbs after work. For them, the *workplace* was the only common thread tying them together. If they did not hold union meetings or distribute union literature at government offices, they had virtually no opportunity to do so outside the office, given their scattered residential patterns.[72]

In the end, administrative regulations governing grievance procedures, efficiency ratings reviews, and union activities combined with the powerful arguments of public accountability and individual merit to limit union influence over employee relations. Hence, despite a new focus on administrative negotiation over legislative lobbying, unions failed to become the sole voice of employees.

The Struggle for Union Recognition, 1937–1953

Members of the Council of Personnel Administration realized that Roosevelt's letter did not resolve the controversy surrounding employee negotiating rights. International Association of Machinists members who worked in the Newport Torpedo Station, for instance, did not interpret Roosevelt's letter as an abrogation of their rights as laborers. They wrote to the president claiming that the administration's collective bargaining commitment with regard to private-sector unions should apply equally to government employees. They charged the navy with "vigorously carrying out a Company union policy" and suggested "a return to the workers [of] the right of collective bargaining to be administered by a Personel [sic] director as of your executive order of June 24, 1938."[73] UFWA locals, likewise, banded together on several occasions to confront and negotiate with administrators on a variety of issues. This included frequent trips to the Bureau of the Budget, where they pressured officials to raise appropriation requests.[74] In 1941, seven locals researched and presented reports to Agriculture personnel director Roy Hendrickson in an effort to keep the administration from slashing $142 million from the department's budget. That summer, UFWA members also called for formal collective bargaining rights after one of their members was abruptly dismissed from the Labor Department. A few months later, both Representative Robert Ramspeck (D-Ga.), chair of the House Civil Service Committee, and Civil Service Commissioner Mitchell reiterated the government's (and Roosevelt's) "official" opposition to bargaining and striking rights for federal civil service unions.[75] Unions thus often verbalized their concerns to administrators even though their voices were not officially recognized.

In response, some New Deal bureaucrats argued for a new flexible policy with regard to unions in the federal service. A report from the National Civil Service Reform League in 1941 emphatically denying public employees the right to bargain collectively sharpened the debate among personnel administrators. TVA personnel director Gordon Clapp told league president Samuel Ordway (who had stepped down as Civil Service Commissioner in 1939) that the report was a "disappointment." He called the statement "superficial" and inconclusive and argued that the denial of exclusive recognition missed the practical point of majority representation. "Majority representation and exclusive recognition," he said, "is a device for fixing responsibility and encouraging leadership and the acceptance of obligations." Clapp spoke from personal experience. Since 1935, TVA administrators had engaged in collective bargaining with the authority's employees through a trade and labor council. But Clapp, like Beyer, also believed there was a difference between agencies that established wages through special boards and those under the classified civil service. The use of wage boards, Beyer and Clapp argued, allowed administrators the authority to bargain with employees and enter into contracts.[76]

William Leiserson of the NLRB, and one of the authors of TVA's labor relations policy, explained to the council members that they should stress administrative negotiation with employees. He explained to them the values of, and limitations on, collective bargaining for civil servants. Leiserson vociferously supported the right of public-sector employees to make contracts with their employers, but he noted that "insofar as the legislative body has acted finally on a question, there is no room for bargaining on that." In the classified civil service, he stated, the legislature took the issue of minimum wages out of the bargaining arena. On the other hand, he wanted to insulate administrators from restrictive legislation. He worried that a dissatisfied workforce would turn to Congress, which in turn would pass laws on issues that should not require legislation. By promoting negotiation between agencies and unions, Leiserson believed that agency administrators would prevent employees from bothering Congress with their problems. "Within the limits of our authority," he concluded, "we have got to bargain with employees and thru their unions. We must not hide behind the Government and say the Government can't bargain."[77] Eric Nicol of the War Production Board urged personnel directors to work out "a way in which collective bargaining can be made effective in the Federal Government." But like Leiserson, he also suggested that the real obstacle to administrative power was congressional authority, not union power. He felt there was "still too much emphasis on maintaining privileges and getting legislation through for sick leave and vacations and retirement."[78]

War encouraged government administrators to try to extend their authority over some personnel matters. Council members were unsure of how best to keep legislative interference in administrative planning to a minimum. Representative Robert Ramspeck (D-Ga.), for example, had requested advice from the Council of Personnel Administration before he drew up legislation for the efficiency rating review board, but council members declined to advise, claiming that it would be improper for them to comment because of the overlapping and contradictory interests of the agencies they represented. A month after the legislation was enacted, however, Hendrickson complained that it was defective because it provided no time limit for an appeal. Errors such as this, Hendrickson told Davenport, could be remedied by the designation of a legislative expert who would analyze and follow bills of this sort. Some council members believed that it would be imprudent to express their views on this legislation because it might compromise their image as representatives of employees and of management.[79]

Increasingly, informal personnel committees operated outside congressional channels. A few months prior to the bombing of Pearl Harbor, the Civil Service Commission agreed, at the urging of the UFWA, to set up a labor-management advisory committee, modeled on the British government's Whitley Councils. Among the management representatives on the committee were Commissioner Arthur Flemming, Librarian of Congress Archibald MacLeish, Post Office administrator Jesse Donaldson, and Leiserson. National Association of Letter Carriers (NALC) President William Doherty, AFGE President James Burns, NFFE President Steward and his assistant, Gertrude McNally, along with UFWA administrators Eleanor Nelson and Allan Haywood, represented labor. Charged with investigating such concerns as night pay differentials, employee transfers, and wartime wages, the committee tried to create a more uniform, equitable system of personnel administration throughout the government.[80]

The committee's agenda, expanded by the UFWA in 1942 with its "Victory Plan for Wartime Conversion," advocated bureaucratic control as the means of harmonizing the interests of management and labor. The plan was designed to make war production more efficient while raising wages and protecting employees from the arbitrary authority of agency administrators. This program called for a centralized personnel system headed by a single administrator, who would be advised by a Victory Committee consisting of representatives selected by the Bureau of the Budget, the Civil Service Commission, the Council of Personnel Administration, and organized labor. Each agency was to establish its own smaller version of this victory committee.[81] Despite the wartime emphasis on cooperation, some agencies politely refused to organize committees; Agriculture administrators said that Memorandum 753 provided an adequate "channel for employees' suggestions and recommendations."[82] By December of 1942, the Council of Personnel Administration reported that of the eleven committees established under the plan, only four "seriously" confronted the production problem.[83]

Unions took advantage of sympathetic administrators to effect change. In war agencies, where the morale of government workers was critical, and both workers and managers tended to be more progressive, unions effected numerous administrative deals. At OPA, personnel director Kenneth Warner informed one acting administrator that the agency endorsed unions, although it did not recognize one as the sole representative of employees. In 1943 the UFWA reported that the OPA branch of Local 203 had signed an agreement with OPA officials covering the pay and promotion of twelve stenographer-typists. The agreement tied pay increases to specific speed rates and mandated that management promote stenographers and typists when they reached designated speeds.[84]

Even in these agencies, nonetheless, friction often developed between administrators and union leaders. UFWA's active locals, like 203, were emboldened by their successes and initiated several lengthy investigations into alleged management abuses. In the case of Adassa Balaban, a typist in the OPA's stenographic pool, the union faced stiff resistance from the supervisor who dismissed Balaban for inefficiency and poor attitude. Balaban's supervisor, E. Buckner Blackerby, voiced outrage that a union representative called her without first "clearing it through the proper channels" (those being the bureau chief and the personnel office). She later complained that the union had no "business" conducting activities during office hours. When UFWA representative Henry Beitscher explained that union activities improved the morale of the workers and that they were aiding the war effort directly by giving blood, Blackerby informed Beitscher that blood donations were "not winning the war." Even though personnel director Warner supported union activity, he felt constrained by his desire to decentralize authority and give operating supervisors greater discretionary powers. In the end, he sided with Blackerby against the union on this case and allowed her to refuse a meeting with union representatives.[85] Relations between the UFWA and OPA managers deteriorated after the war, especially when Congress began cutting appropriations to the agency.[86] Nevertheless, the UFWA leadership and rank and file did not give up the fight for recognition when the war ended and their blood was no longer needed.

As the war drew to a close, negotiation rights became, once again, a matter of political concern. In 1944 Roosevelt's personnel specialist, William McReynolds, asked the council to examine the issue of collective bargaining more closely. UFWA locals pushed this study.[87] In preparing their "Statement of Policy Governing Relations of Federal Agencies with Organized Employees," council members fiercely debated whether agencies could enter into contractual agreements and accord preferred recognition to unions. Most public personnel administrators still defended the position that contracts for classified civil servants undermined the sovereignty of Congress and that they were therefore undemocratic and illegal. A few—including Beyer, Nicol, and Leiserson—tried to find a middle ground, but in an early 1946 draft of the statement, the employee relations committee of the council remained adamant in its denunciation of exclusive recognition:

> Administrative officials cannot accord any one employee organization exclusive or preferred status. . . . In the public service, the prohibition of preference to any individual extends to the prohibition of preferment to any one group. The agency, as an instrument of the government and of the people, can only

recognize and accord to the employee organization the right to act as the representative of its members employed in that agency, safeguarding to the other employees of the agency the full right to deal with the agency on their own behalf either singly or collectively.[88]

Pressure from Beyer and representatives of TVA, the AFGE, and UFWA moved the council to reconsider its stance. Thus, under certain circumstances, the council now concluded, administrators could "accord a particular employee organization preferred status in representing all employees . . . when such organizations have been designated by a majority of employees."[89] In turn, the designated group would be the only organization consulted in the drafting of personnel policy. Bargaining would apply to every issue with the exception of wages, which Congress determined.

The statement immediately generated controversy. Gerard Reilly of the NLRB vigorously rejected the extension of exclusive bargaining rights to public employees. He argued that government officials who had the power to appoint employees could not make an agreement with an organization that would bind their successors in office. Noting the differences in function of private and public agencies, Reilly rejected the applicability of the Wagner Act's principles to employees classified under the professional, clerical, administrative, or fiscal services. Although the council's statement forbade agreements that contradicted existing statutes, the policy, Reilly said, did not make any provision for the primacy of Civil Service Commission regulations.[90]

Beyer tried, unsuccessfully, to arrange a compromise. Ever the voice of reason, he countered Reilly by suggesting that the Wagner Act would actually facilitate the negotiation of working conditions between unions and administrators. But he conceded that exclusive recognition should only occur in places where it was "feasible."[91] National Civil Service Reform League Executive Secretary Henry Kaplan took a conservative stance. Employee organizations, he explained, could negotiate but not bargain with their government employers. So-called collective bargaining in government agencies could not result in enforceable written contracts.[92]

These civil service issues became especially volatile in the postwar era, as unionism and radicalism became entangled with issues of loyalty and accountability in the executive branch. As noted, government officials expressed concern after the newly formed United Public Workers of America (a merger of the UFWA with the CIO's state and local government employee union) adopted convention planks that implicitly supported the right of government employees to strike and explicitly endorsed the policies of the Soviet Union.[93] Reilly questioned the prudence of allowing employees who knew military secrets to join potentially "subversive" unions: "I do feel it is dangerous . . . to make any mandatory rule that the Government can have no concern at all with the type of labor organization to which employees may belong."[94]

A week after the UPWA convention, the council issued its new liberally phrased report on union recognition. The *Washington Evening Star* ran a front page article on the report under the headline: "Collective Bargaining for Federal Unions Suggested by Council." Civil Service Commissioners claimed to be "horrified" by the report and denounced it as "ill considered." Their concern, they said, lay with those non-unionized civil servants who would be disempowered by the recognition of a single union.[95] Not surprisingly, personnel administrators backed off the issue. Former council member Raymond Zimmerman, who had become an aide to President Harry Truman in the fall of 1945, told the president to refrain from making a statement on exclusive recognition for unions.[96]

Once again, the council revised its statement. In its November 1946 draft, submitted to the Civil Service Commission as an official rule, the council called for administrators to "recognize and confer . . . with duly constituted representatives of employees at their request on matters of policy."[97] This nebulous statement, the council and league rationalized, was a democratic compromise that would allow majority group representation without stifling the voice of the minority.

Public administrators and civil service reformers continued to express fear that the closed shop, a corollary of collective bargaining, would destroy the principle of merit. If agency appointment officers could only hire union members, merit reformers argued, the open competitive system of examinations would be annulled. Most opposed to the closed shop were the Civil Service Assembly and league.[98] Unions tried to compromise by asking for union shops, but the league countered that this would also restrict employees and undermine the sanctity of merit. In the end, the league asserted "only capacity to do that job, or some other broad criterion, is appropriate to democracy."[99] Without a closed shop, civil service unions reasoned that they would have little chance to control work conditions in federal offices. But the closed-shop concept proved impossible for many of the reformers and managers to accept.

The debate did not end, despite the council's retreat on the collective bargaining issue. Beyer completed an extensive report on collective bargaining in Interior Department subsidiaries such as the Bonneville Power Administration. With the Cold War expansion of defense activities and resulting influx of industrial workers into federal employment, Beyer argued, came an opportunity to extend bargaining power to agencies outside the classified civil service.[100] In 1948 the Department of Labor concurred. Roosevelt's 1937 employee relations statement, the department explained, failed to distinguish between rights for federal employees performing sovereign functions and those engaging in proprietary functions of government. Roosevelt's letter was therefore directed only at classified civil servants.[101]

The council, by contrast, began to retreat after members realized what a storm had brewed. They had originally hoped that President Truman would issue an extensive executive order promulgating new personnel policies. As the union issue became heated, however, the council backed down and wrote a weak, broadly worded "Federal Personnel Policy." Essentially a restatement of the Civil Service Commission's 1941 grievance procedure circular, this document was intended to serve as an amendment to the civil service rules. Truman's Executive Order 9830 of February 24, 1947, replaced Roosevelt's Executive Order 7916 and numerous others. It consolidated civil service rules and reaffirmed the Civil Service Commission's and council's right to issue personnel regulations.[102]

The failure of government administrators to agree on a formal bargaining program reinforced the commitment of personnel managers to the participatory programs advocated by the human relations school of management. Spurred on by the Hoover Commission's recommendation in 1949 that employees have a greater voice in the formulation of personnel policies, the council and commission began working on a comprehensive participation plan.[103] Although personnel managers made it clear that the program was not to interfere with the rights of organized employees, they did not consult unions or employees during the policy-making process. The chair of the employee relations committee, Virgil Couch, suggested that the committee invite an NFFE representative to sit on the subcommittee studying the issue, but the whole committee voted down the proposal. At an appropriate time, council members said, a union representative could be invited as their guest. A few months later, in January 1950, the council agreed that they had "some obligation" to find out how employee groups would react to policies the council initiated.[104]

Council members debated two versions of the employee participation plan, both of which resembled the employee council system that had already been implemented in many departments. In the first version, the "direct participation" plan, all employees were automatically considered to be members of an advisory committee. (Each committee was limited to twenty-five; additional committees were established to absorb the overflow.) Officers were selected by secret ballot. And although the plan discouraged supervisors from holding office, it did not prohibit them from doing so. The second, the "elected representative" plan, directed managers to divide employees into groups from which employees chose someone to present their views to their respective administrators. Both initiatives called for administrators to set meeting agendas. Administrators permitted employees to present their own grievances, but employee representatives could not call meetings with the employees they represented—they had to secure employee recommendations and concerns informally.[105]

Even though these plans obviously did not threaten the administrative hierarchy, many field personnel managers reacted negatively to them. While some wanted to encourage employee esprit de corps, many considered the plans an encroachment on management prerogatives. One was shocked at the "revolutionary" proposal and complained that "lower level personnel" would not be able to offer useful advice because they were unable to grasp the significance and consequences of broad policies; another simply stated that administrative decisions were "clearly the responsibility of management and as such should not be exposed, in effect, to general plebiscites." Others worried that meetings would degenerate into individual grievance sessions or that employee turnover would make it impossible to obtain consistent employee recommendations. One field council member said that the time had come to dispense with theory. In practice, he asserted, existing suggestion and award programs and Civil Service Commission provisions for counseling, grievance, and appeal procedures created a "fair and impartial" workplace. If a plan had to be effected, he conceded, it should be a representative plan that would not become individualized and cumbersome; besides, he offhandedly added, management *might actually use* some of the recommendations made at meetings.[106]

Unions also objected to the participation plan. They felt that it was at best management driven and at worst a new form of management control. Advisory councils reminded them, they said, of company unions and shop committees. One union leader questioned the value of the plan if management dictated the agendas of the meetings. NALC leaders reminded the council that in the past management had refused to discuss problems about which employees had strong opinions. As the CIO leadership saw it, this was a shop plan designed to "divide and conquer" employees.[107]

The council meanwhile wrote a "Suggested Guide for Effective Relations with Organized Employee Groups." Once again, the statement relied on standards developed a decade earlier. Despite a slightly different organization and the inclusion of new sections defining terms and the rights of employee organizations with respect to bulletin board usage, literature distribution, membership canvassing, and business meetings, the council's principles repeated the familiar mantras against the right to strike, the right to join or refrain from joining an organization, and the right of union representatives to consult agency administrators. One addition made the guide actually somewhat more conservative than its predecessors. At the beginning was an explicit statement that any arrangements negotiated between employees, their unions, and administrators were to be "in conformity with and subject to, the laws of the United States." This clause drew a strong reaction from AFGE President James Campbell and representatives from the CIO, who found it unnecessary. Only a subversive organization, Campbell claimed, would question the authority of legislative statutes over federal agencies and employees. CIO legislative representative Richard Shoemaker picked apart the guide section by section. He was particularly galled that it did not establish any "rights" for employees, except the right to join a union. "This right becomes meaningless," he wrote to Davenport, "when it is considered that *any* activity in which the union might engage is not a right, but a privilege granted by management. Boiled down to its essence, the 'Guide' is nothing but a statement for 'Company Unionism.'" He also bristled at the fact that the council distributed the guide to the press before unions could comment on it.[108]

For their part, most personnel directors considered grievance procedures adequate substitutes for public-sector collective bargaining rights. But in the postwar period, both unions and agency administrators found much to criticize in these bargaining substitutes. Because of the emphasis on personal negotiation, agency procedures remained nebulous. Managers perceived them as too complex, "over-democratic" and biased in favor of employees. Employees, on the other hand, claimed to have little confidence in these managerially oriented procedures. UFWA Local 203, for example, complained about the interference of the personnel division in one of its OPA cases.[109] By 1952 even the AFGE was calling for a new approach to grievance resolution, since "in practically every Federal agency, the grievance appeal board is composed entirely of the members appointed by the head of the agency, and . . . consist[s] of top supervision."[110]

The council's decade-long attempt to establish a comprehensive employee relations policy unraveled as the 1940s drew to a close. By 1949, unions, even the relatively conservative AFGE, had become more contentious in denouncing the federal government's internal labor policies. While the UFWA had originally extended the boundaries of negotiation at the agency level, by the postwar period, union leaders (with the exception of the NFFE) were looking to Congress to validate their right to be recognized as bargaining agents. Fearful that divisions between public- and private-sector labor relations might be obliterated, one National Civil Service Reform League member complained that "the main barrier [to effective public personnel policy] has been hamstringing legislation that attempts to control administration. . . . [W]e all need to work together to convince the lawyers and farmers in Congress—who for the most part have had little or no experience in running large enterprises—of what it takes to run a modern personnel program."[111]

After years of rhetoric about cooperation, the divisions between personnel directors and agency administrators on the one hand and union members on the other sharpened rather than softened. Caught up in the postwar red scare and antilabor atmosphere, the council was unable to develop effective federal personnel policies that would accommodate collective bargaining rights. When the council's most progressive members lost their bid for a more liberally worded statement on government unions in 1946, they retreated and steered a safe middle course. Human relations provided them with an agenda that at least allowed them to portray their grievance procedures, participation plans, and suggestion systems as progressive approaches to labor-management relations. But without a validated union voice, these human relations policies became nothing more than Band-Aids for individual wounds.

Throughout this period, personnel managers continued to struggle to define the proper sphere for governmental unions. Many had a commitment to New Deal labor policies that prevented them from opting simply to banish employee organizations from the government. At the same time, professional concerns drove them to preserve the status of management within the agency hierarchy. Deeply conflicted, they sought to include unions in managerial functions without giving them the unilateral power to change those functions.

Civil service unions, as we have seen, did not always dispute this role. The NFFE, for example, remained comfortable in its advisory and lobbyist functions. But the UFWA was committed to industrial unionism. It hoped to unify civil servants across agency boundaries and bargain with a central personnel agency. Agency administrators and personnel managers fended off that effort, maintaining departmental autonomy and forcing union lodges to negotiate as best they could on an agency by agency basis. Although private-sector labor relations influenced those of the government, the government refused to accord public employees the right to bargain collectively. Political accountability, administrators continued to argue, made this impossible.

Personnel policies thus reflected not some inevitable trend toward rationalism but instead a long power struggle among various factions within the federal bureaucracy. Employee relations, hence, were far from the Weberian ideal type. In devising policies for their agencies, personnel administrators often emphasized the informal, not the formal, relationship of supervisors to subordinates. In this manner, they individualized and personalized employee relations and undercut the potential power of employee collectives. Likewise, managers seldom gave any impression that the government as a whole was one employer. Fragmentation served their purposes too well.

The policies and practices of public administrators reveal their concern with the preservation of administrative discretion in an era of declining patronage. Rather than erase paternal authority and replace it with impersonal, bureaucratic authority, managers created a form of administrative paternalism similar to that which existed in America's large business corporations. Their efforts to engage supervisors in personal interaction with employees, to enhance administrative discretion at the expense of statutory authority, and to relegate unions to a subordinate role reflected this paternal orientation. Ironically, the distinctions managers made between public- and private-sector unions eventually drew legislators back into the debate. Armed with legislative support, unions would ultimately achieve limited recognition from agency administrators.

5 Gender and the Civil Service

Gender played a critical role in the construction of federal labor policies and practices. Patriarchal values did not disappear after the repeal of the married persons clause and end of the Depression, but the growing supremacy of a conservative version of human relations managerial techniques and a new stress on patriotic service to the state submerged the patriarchal ideology and brought a new paternalistic orientation to federal labor practices.[1] As a result, women found it more difficult to locate and challenge the source of their oppression within the bureaucracy. Historian Susan Ware has observed that the feminism associated with New Deal politics began to wane after 1936 due to the aging of a generation of feminist reformers, a retrenchment in New Deal programs, and passage of the Hatch Act, which curtailed the political activities of women in the New Deal civil service. This environment laid the foundation for the development of such management practices as psychological paternalism, which in turn further weakened feminism.[2]

Rather than argue, as managers had during the 1930s, that women held lower-paying jobs because their wages only supplemented family income, personnel managers began to adopt a psychological rationale in the 1940s to explain why women were not suited to hold or wield authority. According to managers (both male and female), a woman's psyche, rather than her place in the family, became responsible for her inability to move up the labor hierarchy. By appropriating social science language to evaluate women's performance, managers appeared "objective." Claims of objectivity made the sexual division of labor seem more "natural" and thus more impenetrable.[3]

The conservative form of human relations philosophy adopted by some managers embedded in federal labor relations an image of women who were emotionally and financially dependent upon men. In addition, the onset of war evoked patriotism and an increasing intolerance for radicalism. The war enabled government officials to legitimate the oppression of union women fighting for work equity and to mute a more progressive interpretation of human relations. Attacks against union members, socialists, and communists stifled the open debate about gender equity that women had engaged in during the Depression.

A wartime labor shortage brought many women to Washington, D.C., in search of work. One of those, described by a personnel specialist as Miss "A," found work at the Federal Security Agency, where superiors described her as bright, attractive, and capable. Initially she performed exemplary service, but after a year, her work began to suffer. Her co-workers began to observe her wandering around the office, jerking her shoulders and swinging her arms in a "peculiar way." During interviews, a staff counselor discovered Miss A to be a "lone wolf" who rarely socialized with others in or out of the office. After a further investigation, the counselor concluded that Miss A, who had been a talented pianist in her home town, was suffering from lack of attention. Indeed, her jerky movements were not, as first thought, a nervous tic, but an attempt by Miss A to "imitate one of the motion picture actresses!" To compensate for her feelings of inadequacy in her new urban environment, Miss A was engaging in "affected mannerisms." As soon as the counselor introduced Miss A to the agency's choral group and a local drama troupe, her peculiar mannerisms apparently disappeared.[4]

Psychological counseling was a relatively new phenomenon in government agencies. Along with other management-sponsored activities, it constituted part of the larger movement to use human relations management techniques in federal agencies. From questions about marital status (divorced people were considered maladjusted) during the hiring process to the evaluation of "nervous tics" during the work day, public personnel officers sought to evaluate individual employee problems in an effort to create a more stable and productive workforce.[5]

Although federal employees did not have the right to bargain or strike, they had access to counseling, welfare and recreation associations, grievance machinery, and employee councils. Through these programs, managers portrayed the state as a benevolent and impartial employer.

That portrayal was especially evident, and important, during the Second World War, when the government actively recruited thousands of women to work in the federal war machine. From 1939 to 1945, the percentage of women working for the federal government in Washington, D.C., increased by half, from 40 to 60 percent. In some agencies, such as the Office of Price

Administration (OPA) and Selective Service, between 70 and 85 percent of the workers were female.[6] With women pouring into the city, government officials began to worry about the ability of young women from rural America to adapt to an urban environment. Human relations management policies, claimed officials, visibly demonstrated the state's commitment to protecting female workers. Counseling and orientation programs, for example, were designed to provide women with a protective shield against the harsh realities of city life. In this sense, personnel managers used these techniques to address and remedy real employee problems. At times, human relations techniques assisted female civil servants in their quest for independence and stability and promoted egalitarian principles in the civil service. Yet, the simple act of offering these programs suggested that women were emotionally unstable and incapable of handling stress. "Benevolence" was in this sense a code word for paternalism.

As other scholars have detailed, gender as a concept operates on two levels. On one level, gender is equated with the biological sex of individuals. Public personnel administrators, for instance, responded to the women moving into the service by constructing new managerial strategies to address the changing sex composition of the workforce. On another level, however, gender, according to one author, "refers to the social construction of sex: the cultural and psychological traits different societies attribute to being male and female." As we have seen, for example, the management strategies developed by administrators were articulated in gendered terms. Gendered notions of employment, including masculine and feminine definitions of authority, influenced the sexual division of labor. Because the sex of a worker and the "cultural construction of sex" are distinct, albeit related, categories, men can promote "feminine" values and engage in behavior coded as "feminine." Women likewise can adopt "masculine" social and cultural traits. When this happens, however, there are often sanctions, as these actions contradict social norms regarding the proper behavior for men and women. This chapter examines gender on both levels to uncover the story of gendered management discourse and its impact upon white-collar female workers.[7]

The conservative paternalism associated with the human relations school of management was closely tied to masculine authority systems, including the social sciences. As they had done with Miss A, government managers (and counselors) frequently appropriated psychological rhetoric to analyze the experiences of female civil servants. The counselor's description of Miss A as a "lone wolf" in need of social activities, especially artistic ones, reflected the gendered terms upon which these management strategies were constructed. During the Second World War "psychological paternalism" characterized the relationship between conservative managers and their female subordinates. Psychological paternalism was not simply a passive description of the labor-management relationship but an active force that enabled more conservative managers to cast women as emotional cripples and therefore unfit for high-powered, decision-making positions. Consequently, although the wartime labor shortage allowed some female civil servants to engage in jobs tradition-ally assigned to men, most remained concentrated in positions within the clerical, administrative, and fiscal service (CAF) and clustered at the lower end of employee grades.[8]

But new management programs also evolved from liberal and feminine traditions associated with New Deal politics and welfare work. Progressive managers emphasized the democratic principles in the human relations doc-trine, insisting on a more open communication system and a gender-neutral merit system. In asserting a strong commitment to equal opportunity, these managers labored to eliminate gender inequities through promotions and child care provisions for working mothers. Many of these liberal personnel managers encouraged women's participation in their field and felt confident that the war would promote workplace equity.

Because the public sector was not driven by the profit motive, these lib-eral, "feminine" management strategies actually had some chance of success. Politically charged battles over management of the bureaucracy, however, modified feminized management approaches and ultimately strengthened the civil service hierarchy. In the civil service, hence, management strategies were both gendered and politicized as personnel administrators sought to advance liberalism, preserve democracy, and retain a sexual division of labor.

With large numbers of female workers flooding into the Potomac region after 1941, personnel managers focused even more intently upon women's perceived needs. Through the establishment of counseling programs, recre-ation facilities, dormitories, and social clubs, personnel directors hoped to build a nurturing environment for the civil servants they referred to as "our girls."[9] As Daniel Nelson observed, in the private sector, businessmen with large numbers of female employees constructed welfare programs to fit the perceived needs of women. Hence, these firms built lunch and "rest" rooms, offered classes in child care and home economics, and established social clubs. In contrast, programs for male-dominated firms emphasized financial security (through the establishment of pension, saving and stock-sharing plans) and physical recreation.[10] During World War II, government personnel directors urged federal officials to build dormitory and recreation facilities and hire counselors as a means of easing disoriented girls into a stressful urban environment.[11]

Human relations experts stressed the need for personal interaction. Counseling, they argued, was a necessary element in any successful personnel program. Counselors, personnel managers maintained, could improve morale and productivity by aiding female employees with personal problems.[12]

By trumpeting the success of counseling programs, personnel managers reinforced an image of emotionally frail female workers. Unless they were provided with emotional support, personnel managers suggested, women's work would suffer. One personnel director, for instance, detailed how the resolution of a landlord-tenant dispute restored the productivity levels of three "girls." According to him, an irate landlord had threatened to have the three fired if they did not pay their phone bill. Once their counselor informed them that this was not possible, the personnel officer noted that their efficiency increased again.[13]

At times the focus on personal problems as the root of worker discontent obscured more relevant and substantive causes of discontent, such as lack of autonomy. In one case, a single mother of two who earned $1,260 a year complained to her counselor that her supervisor often made her shoulder the blame for problems for which she was not responsible. She told the counselor that she was thinking of resigning. When the counselor learned that the woman needed $50 for an emergency, she deduced that it was this, rather than the supervisor, that was causing stress. The counselor, therefore, arranged a loan for the woman. Then, according to the counselor, the woman was able to "adjust" to her job.[14] From the perspective of the counselor and personnel officer, her adjustment had little to do with her conflict with her boss. Under psychological paternalism, there was no need to change the system, only the person.

In addition to counseling, the human relations school of management included recreation and housing programs, making this school a close cousin to the welfare capitalism of the 1920s. Although public personnel managers denied that human relations policies had paternalistic overtones, their policies aimed, like welfare capitalism, to control employee behavior and strengthen employee commitment to the organization. Under public-sector human relations practices, employers hoped to bind employees to the established hierarchy.

Personnel officials argued that the human relations school of management was not paternalistic because participation in agency associations was voluntary. Managers, one practitioner noted, were simply helping employees help themselves.[15] Yet, at least one source contended that agency welfare associations were often run by supervisory employees. Since supervisors controlled efficiency ratings and thus promotions, demotions, and dismissals, employees probably felt obligated to support such programs.[16]

Managers legitimated paternal authority by linking it to scientific objectivity. Because the labor movement had discredited company paternalism in the 1930s and 1940s, government personnel managers rejected the comparison between public-sector human relations and private-sector paternalism. Human relations personnel programs, they argued, were not based upon arbitrary, personal authority but upon scientific sociological and psychological studies of employee behavior.

By objectifying this management school, administrators succeeded in *depersonalizing* management strategies without making managers seem *impersonal*. The close relationship between a manager and subordinate was to be based on scientific analysis of personality. Employees were therefore described as "organisms." Terms such as this one were to convey a sense of concern with an employee's complete physical and mental health—mind and body were to be attended to in scientific ways under this new management approach. Nevertheless, these "organically" oriented programs, like their counterparts under welfare capitalism, sought to build organizational loyalty by providing workers with educational, residential, and financial aid.[17]

Personnel officers consistently portrayed women as naive and homesick and thus believed that these recreation and housing facilities were "essential safety valves for fatigued bodies and frayed nerves."[18] By providing dormitories, like the Arlington Farms complex in Virginia, the state was able to nurture its image as a conscientious employer. Severe housing shortages in Washington, D.C., created problems, as many women were forced to double, triple, and quadruple up in rooms. For instance, four single women who were on two different shifts might share a room with two beds. Thus, the construction of public housing was, in many respects, a responsible reaction to the crisis, for it offered some women affordable housing located conveniently for their jobs. Yet government officials also took the opportunity to impose curfews, mandatory meal plans, and guest restrictions on residents in order to make certain that these government girls lived in a wholesome environment and presented a moral image to the public.[19]

Morality became a contentious issue in employee relations. In 1942, hiring officials asserted that "girl workers" were kept happy by "pleasant and continuous association with young men." One guest home owner whose boarders included men and women boasted that there were five or six marriages a month, and ten to fifteen every June. But others were more pessimistic about the availability of men and expressed concern that this shortage would cause domestic distress for the government girl. As evidenced by the diagnosis of Miss A's curious behavior, personnel officials worried that women lacking a social life would become dysfunctional and unproductive or leave their jobs. One Civil Service Commission employee suggested that a series of parties in the same place would do more than an isolated dance in establishing "steady social contact" and a feeling of "belonging" for the "girl worker."[20]

Although many stressed the importance of a social life, others differed.[21] Representative Earl Wilson (R-Ind.) recommended that government girls have a 10:00 P.M. curfew in order to combat inefficiency. Too many female workers, he complained, came to work sleepy, then spent an hour in the rest room putting on makeup before going to lunch. When they did work, he explained, their work was full of mistakes because they were probably a little "woozy." His suggestion brought forth a storm of protest as women wondered why the curfew would not apply to men and how government officials proposed to force female workers into bed at a reasonable hour. Finally, several women pointed out that they often worked ten hours a day or longer, leaving little time for shopping, cooking, and cleaning, let alone parties. In an "Ode to Mr. Wilson," one government worker penned:

> Since Washington women
> Outnumber the men
> Just who is to keep us
> All out after 10?

Wilson denied that he was questioning the wholesomeness of working women, claiming that they were "the cream of the Nation's crops, mentally and morally." Nevertheless, concerns with morality surfaced frequently.[22]

The "problem" of morality was brought into sharp relief by the rape and slaying in October 1944 of seventeen-year-old Pentagon employee Dorothy Berrum. Berrum, who had come to Washington, D.C., from Wisconsin, was a resident at the Arlington Farms dormitory complex. She had gone into town one evening to meet a friend but instead joined a stranger, a young marine. After taking her on a walk near the Jefferson Memorial, the marine raped and strangled her.[23] The crime resulted in an outpouring of anger and concern that the United States government had been careless in recruiting teenage girls and in failing to protect them from the seedy side of the city.

Letters and editorials on young female war workers dominated the papers for weeks. Members of the Washington, D.C., community engaged in lengthy debates about the responsibility of the government to safeguard morality. Several suggested that the government send home all women under twenty; Eleanor Roosevelt urged parents to keep their daughters at home unless the daughters were mature enough to handle living in the city; and others implored the Civil Service Commission to screen recruits more carefully. Many referred to the government's recruiting practices as "reckless" and "irresponsible."[24]

The debate demonstrated a wartime preoccupation with the emotional health of female civil servants. Public assessment of these young women, implicitly and at times explicitly, revealed the widespread belief that "promiscuous" (and thus "immoral") women were emotionally unbalanced. Perhaps, one person stated, "girls from church homes" would be better "risks" because they would be able to avoid the temptations the city offered. Writing to the editor of the *Evening Star*, District resident Evelyn Drayton argued that if parents had "properly trained" their daughters, these young women would be more discriminating about their social activities. As anyone trained in psychology would know, she said, governmental educational campaigns would do little to alter the behavior of wanton women.[25] A woman who conducted orientation seminars at OPA agreed. Neither churches nor government agencies, nor the Civil Service Commission, should assume the "duties of parenthood," she wrote. A child's emotional makeup was the direct result of parental guidance: "If the parents so sheltered a daughter that she still needs sheltering [when she is recruited by the government], then let them keep her home until they have trained her in the art of living without such shelter." While she did not believe the government should be responsible for the "moral training" of women workers, she also explained that in her orientation program, she offered to help women with personal problems and asked them to maintain, at all times, "the standard of morals which they had had back home and which they had brought here with them."[26]

One editorial writer made more explicit the link between moral behavior and psychological stability: "It has been argued, of course, that it is mostly girls of naturally unstable personality who become sexually amoral or who get into serious trouble in Washington. However, since personality defects of this sort are said to be detectable by psychiatric examination, it is hard to see why girls, and especially minors, in this category were ever accepted in the first place by the civil service."[27]

Underlying these arguments was the concept of gender difference, for as this quote reveals, the problem was perceived to be *hers* rather than his. Women who were victimized needed better moral training; they were psychologically unbalanced to begin with and therefore put themselves in danger. It was a woman's responsibility to retain a chaste image and to resist "temptations." Nowhere did the commentators describe the rapist-murderer's behavior as abnormal.

Despite assertions that the government could not change the behavior of young women, officials did concentrate effort on securing the psychological stability of their female workforce. The same woman who denied that the government should be involved in "parenting" lauded OPA's employee relations staff for assisting employees with "practically every type of personal problem." And during orientation meetings she gave women information on cultural events, church services, and agency-sponsored recreational activities. Through these efforts, she concluded, the agency had become "organized as one large family." All employees were "sincerely interested in helping each other to be happy in a strange new territory." Arlington Farms officials targeted similarly "immature" women and lectured them against getting into cars with people they did not know, picking up people, and spending money frivolously.[28]

According to many personnel administrators, men were perfectly able to cope with the uncertainties and strains of city life. As a group, for instance, personnel directors rejected suggestions that recreation facilities and accommodations be constructed for men. Several managers maintained that unlike women, most men in the civil service headed stable family units. Issues of job insecurity and social disorientation, said one, were specific to women. When one administrator pointed out that most government "girls" were over thirty, another noted that although these "older" women might be more "stable," they were not necessarily "happy, because [they were] not so adaptable as the younger group."[29]

A paternalistic management orientation afforded women some opportunity to negotiate for needed programs. While the participation encouraged by the human relations school of management did not make employees equal to their supervisors or alter the agency hierarchy, it allowed employees to lobby for some reforms, including child care.[30] Due to the severe labor shortage, personnel managers expressed repeated concern about absences among working mothers. The council collected story after story of women who had to quit their government jobs because they could not find or were entirely dissatisfied with day care facilities. The United Federal Workers of America (UFWA) confronted the issue by setting up a conference to address the needs of women with children. Along with the government, they sponsored "Working Mothers' Clubs" that helped reconcile conflicts between work shifts, shopping schedules, and household duties.[31] These agency programs helped women achieve short-term relief from the rigid work schedules imposed by the war.

By attempting to address the child care needs of working mothers, government officials opened up some opportunities for women in the civil service. For instance, the council supported training seminars for women to become junior engineers, typewriter repair workers, administrative assistants, personnel officers, and map makers. They agreed that women would have to be paid more than the base clerical salary of $1,440, and as one Agriculture Department official noted, administrators would have to emphasize the "employment and training of women for a wider range of types of work in the Department." Despite "conventional prejudices," he concluded, "adequately trained women are well qualified to handle the duties in many lines of work."[32]

Those opportunities, however, did not mean that the occupational map had lost its gendered compass. Although the war disrupted traditional patterns of men's and women's work, Ruth Milkman has noted that "*new* patterns of occupational segregation developed." Thus the boundaries between men's and women's work simply "changed location."[33] Managers never eliminated the fundamental concept of gender differences. One labor specialist told the council that in his field of industrial placement, "we approach the placement of women in some . . . jobs about the same as you would physically handicapped." Likewise, one Department of Agriculture official "recognized" that in a normal labor market "physical limitations of strength and endurance" prevented women from engaging in many types of work. He, along with most others, believed that using women in high-paying skilled-craft work was a temporary expedient. As it turned out, the passage of the Veterans Preference Act of 1944—which ensured former civil servants who served in the military that they would have their jobs when they returned and which added points to the civil service exam score of any veteran—codified the temporary nature of women's wartime employment into law.

Most assumed that a sexual division of labor was still necessary in some fields. Consequently, the Civil Service Commission never disputed the right of any agency to determine whether it wanted a man or woman for any particular position. Roy Hendrickson, personnel director at the Agriculture Department, told one female union official that "many positions in the Department involve duties too arduous or otherwise unsuitable for performance by women." He explained that women could not be fruit inspectors because these inspectors had to work in refrigerated railroad cars, at cold storage plants, or on exposed piers and had to move crates and sacks. Of course, he added, the department's policy "is, and has been, dead set against discrimination of women's employment in capacities for which they are qualified." Similarly, the Commissioner of the Bureau of Internal Revenue refused to sanction the use of women as zone deputy collectors, citing safety concerns as well as fears that taxpayers would disregard instructions from a woman. An official from the bureau's employee organization concurred, noting that men and women should be assigned jobs for which they were "temperamentally best fitted."[34] As late as 1951, India Edwards, chair of the Women's Division of the Democratic National Committee (DNC), complained that defense agencies and the State Department specified "males only" when requesting civil service registers for analysts, political scientists, and historians. White House aide Donald Dawson assured Edwards that 31 percent of requests from these departments were without restriction on women. "As a matter of fact," he wrote, "5% specify that they shall be women."[35] Throughout the 1940s, then, government managers had both the latitude and the *right* to determine the physical or mental qualifications for any position—and thus its gender dimensions as well.

More critically, human relations legitimated the authority of managers to evaluate and define appropriate personality traits for government workers. This proved to be especially damaging to women, whose job descriptions and training often mandated that they focus on developing such personal traits as appearance, poise, deference, and gentility rather than cultivating their intellectual or technical skills. Personnel officers couched these personal traits in the scientific language of psychology and sociology, lending authority to the claim that these characteristics were innately female. Job evaluations, thus, had little to do with technical or professional performance and everything to do with personality and appearance. In a training guide for secretaries written by the Farm Credit Administration's (FCA) personnel office and released by the Civil Service Commission, personnel managers argued that the difference between an effective and ineffective personal secretary was one of personality and political skill. Contrasting "Jane," the "good" secretary, to "Ruth," the "bad" one, the guide asserted: "Jane has a way of doing things and dealing with people that makes business with her office a pleasure, while people who work with Ruth often become irritated or indifferent." Like a "coiffure," personality took "determined effort" to develop.[36]

The FCA training manual insisted that female secretaries be efficient, tough, and hardworking but appear soft, accommodating, and subservient. They had to play dual roles—the private role as the boss's ruthless protector and partner and the public role as his subservient, genteel helpmate. Furthermore, the manual considered secretaries responsible for the emotional and psychological health of their co-workers and bosses. To maintain this emotional equilibrium, a secretary was to treat her boss as both son and husband, catering to his every need yet also steering him away from trouble and subtly helping him create a successful image. All of these mandates assumed a woman's innate ability to "read" other personalities and her feminine responsibility to arbitrate disputes and ease friction.[37]

The characteristics assigned to the "good" secretary were those that ultimately limited her upward mobility in the federal bureaucracy. On the one hand, personnel officers urged secretaries to be ambitious. An individual's pursuit of a promotion, however, was to be achieved through efficiency, enthusiasm, a knowledge of the organization, and a serious commitment to her job. She was not, the FCA training manual warned, "to show discontent with her present job, curry favor with higher-ups, or play office politics." Nor was she to appear so efficient "as to seem managerial to her supervisor, for most men put bossy women in the same class with rattlesnakes." Thus, the very maneuvers that men had to perform to gain promotions within the business and political world were deemed inappropriate for women.[38] Accordingly, the guide implied that women who used these political maneuvers were not meritorious and would not be promoted.

As the rattlesnake metaphor reveals, management programs conveyed a tension between a desire to encourage individualism through personality, on the one hand, and a concern, on the other, that too much individuality would threaten the organization. Democracy encouraged individuality and individual achievement, but too much nonconformity threatened the stability of the community. Women who became too ambitions were "rattlesnakes"; they acted alone and could poison the group. Frequent use of the term *lone wolf* also suggested that those who deviated from the behavior accepted as normal by management were dangerous and needed to be reintegrated into the pack. One woman on the staff of the Democratic National Committee criticized a female candidate for vice chair because she appeared "unable to adapt herself to either work in a group or with a group, or to delegate authority to another." She categorized the candidate as a "lone wolf," just as had happened to Miss A, indicating that women who tried to establish a strong, separate (and perhaps aloof) attitude were considered maladjusted.[39]

Many public servants considered bossy women—or rattlesnakes—unsuited to supervise other employees. When Gertrude Magill Ruskin requested a transfer, the Civil Service Commission initiated an investigation because Ruskin had alleged ties to the Communist Party. Although Commissioner Arthur Flemming absolved her of these charges, he concluded that she was "totally unfit" to be a supervisor. He quoted extensively from interviews with a dozen former co-workers who described her not only as "brilliant," "bright," and "conscientious" but also as "too aggressive," "too self-directed," "overbearing," and "bossy." Their accounts portray a woman who was both demanding of herself and others:

> Witness No. 3: She was bold and had a tough attitude. She cussed and swore around here like a tramp. She was very uncouth. . . . She was very bossy.
> Witness No. 7: She was pretty rough and crude in handling people. . . .
> I personally liked her very well.
> Witness No. 10: She's very aggressive and does not like to subordinate herself to anyone. As far as ability, she's a very good clerk. . . . Tactics resemble a steam roller. I have had no complaints from any subordinates made to me. She assumes responsibility very readily. Conscientious, but very tactless. She flies off easily— no control of her emotions. . . . I think she is capable and conscientious and has a lot of ability along routine lines or paper work, but may be handicapped in handling people in regards to being too rough and crude. She uses bull methods.
> Witness No. 11: She wasn't polished enough in the way she talked, in language and mannerisms. . . . Within the first two weeks . . . all the supervisors didn't like her. Her manner was too forward, too aggressive. She would probably have been O.K. to handle laundry girls, somebody to kick around. . . . She's not a good person for administrative personnel because of her crude way of handling people.[40]

Along with Flemming, these witnesses assumed that Ruskin's mannerisms were inappropriate for a woman or for someone who managed women. By using the word *handicapped* with reference to Ruskin's interpersonal skills and noting the lack of control she had over her emotions, the language used by

Witness No. 10, for instance, indicated that female supervisors were judged by their temperaments, including their ability to get along with people. As with Witness No. 11's reference to laundry workers who could be "kicked around," their assessments implied that white-collar women should act and be treated gently.

Meanwhile, many of Ruskin's co-workers and subordinates felt ambivalent about her. While they respected and admired her work, they had difficulty with her brusque manner. Words like *trooper* and *tramp*, furthermore, suggested that they considered Ruskin's behavior unbecoming for a woman in her line of work. While Flemming was a staunch advocate of the hiring and promotion of women, his evaluation revealed the strength of gender categories in the personnel decision-making process. This gendered language revealed the contemporary belief that female executives, especially those supervising other white-collar women, should be "refined."[41] Aggressive male managers evoked a different response. One OPA supervisor was characterized by his subordinates as having a "brusque" and "contemptuous manner." When he returned from military service and proceeded to dismiss one third of his staff, employees revolted. But outside observers described him as a "brilliant, tough man utterly devoted to an effective program of national rent control." Indeed, "to most taxpayers he would have seemed an unusually public-spirited, even a heroic bureaucrat!"[42]

Management experts insisted that the successful (and well-balanced) female worker remain modest and, in some ways, invisible. According to one contemporary article about women and office promotions, "Mrs. Rhoades," a supervisor of a large number of women, was resented by her subordinates because "they unconsciously realize that her efforts [to be a perfect supervisor] spring not from a spontaneous interest in them and their welfare but from a self-interested desire to advance herself." Her individual ambition threatened to disrupt the equally low status shared by women at the bottom of office hierarchies.[43]

Female executives were never to demonstrate feelings of superiority. Those who did were depicted as authoritarian. Another executive continually failed to reach the top ranks because of one "fatal flaw": her blatant ambition. Subordinates, said the author, labeled her a "dictator" because she wanted to "dominate and control." They also described her as "haughtily aloof from all but the big shots in the office," with whom she engaged in "shameless efforts to curry favor." Thus, the author concluded, she was afflicted with "an all too common disease" among women known as "executivitis." This disease attacked "women with particular frequency and virulence" because female executives suffered from deep insecurities about their position in the organizational hierarchy. Once women forgot about their own ambitions and concentrated on their job and their associates in a detached, objective way, the author claimed, they would earn the recognition they deserved. Hence those who demonstrated initiative and individual ambition were criticized and categorized as dysfunctional. Managerial experts not only overly scrutinized the personalities of female workers; they also insisted that women with strong personalities were unfit for leadership roles.[44]

During the 1940s, the psychological language of management reinforced the concept that men and women had inherently different dispositions. That concept became integral to personnel policies and enabled managers to control more forcefully the sexual division of labor. Women, for instance, were perceived as natural conciliators by human relations experts; as office subordinates committed to group effort, they would be capable of protecting democracy at its roots. Women were to facilitate cooperation among members in a group by establishing a common purpose and a sense of equity among office workers. Without such an effort, said one author, "personal ambitions and jealousies [would] grow like weeds" and destroy democratic principles.[45] Women were to nurture and serve democracy at its lowest levels. Men, in contrast, were to lead (and save) democratic institutions.

Those women who might have protested gender inequities would surely have found the civil service during World War II antagonistic to most forms of feminism. Frequently, feminism was equated, or at least associated, with socialism and communism. Although elected officials had long demonstrated hostility toward socialists and communists, the late 1930s witnessed a revival in intensity of antiradical rhetoric and investigations. As noted, from the late 1930s through the 1940s, various government bodies increased their character and loyalty probes among civil servants.

The war further heightened the commission's desire to hire public servants who were not tainted by "sex perversion" and who thus upheld the commission's ideal of American decency. Government officials were particularly worried about the "problem of homosexuals and sex perverts," especially those in sensitive positions. In 1950 Dr. Robert Felix, head of the National Institute of Mental Health, spoke to personnel officers about the psychological makeup of homosexuals as well as "promiscuous persons, gossips, thieves, alcoholics and horseplayers." Although he claimed that employees who fit in any one of these categories should not be dismissed unless they had done something to bring discredit on the government, he added that none should be employed in positions dealing with national security. Personnel directors reiterated this view to bureau chiefs in their "school for scandal," a seminar "so popular, it had to be conducted in three jam-packed sections." Taught by trained experts in abnormal psychology, it was designed to "acquaint [bureau chiefs] with the whys and wherefores of sexual aberration."[46] White House officials, on the other hand, expressed a fear that any public discussion regarding the "problem" of homosexuality would give the impression that "government rolls are replete with sex perverts." According to the White House assessment, discussion would cause some people, including Senator Joseph McCarthy, to insist that "only red-blooded Americans should be employed by the government."[47]

By distinguishing homosexuals from "red-blooded" Americans, officials (and doctors) suggested that homosexual men were effeminate. Often, they used the same psychological language applied to women to discuss homosexual men, whom they referred to as "neurotic," "weak," and "fickle." Officials also observed that gay men were "characterized by emotional instability." And as one official explained, "some experts hold that where the mores of a people have condoned homosexuality . . . the vigor and virility of that people have been emasculated."[48]

Many equated sexual identity with sexual behavior and argued that homosexuals should not be hired for any position in the civil service. A senior official in the State Department pointed out that civil service rules stipulated that anyone who was guilty of "criminal, infamous, dishonest, *immoral* or notoriously disgraceful conduct" could be separated. Homosexuals fell into this category because they engaged in "acts of perversion which are legion and which are abhorent [sic] and repugnant to the folkways and mores of our American society."[49] By analyzing sexuality and sexual identity through the lens of psychology, federal officials further legitimated their authority to define not only morality but also normal "male" and "female" behavior. Anyone who fell outside their narrowly construed categories was labeled not only abnormal but also disloyal.

The hot war against German and Japanese fascism and the Cold War against Soviet totalitarianism validated the equation of dissent with nonconformity and led to the oppression of feminist rhetoric. Personnel officials and agency administrators who had the power to define "dissent" used it to label outspoken critics of federal labor policies as "communists." This proved especially damaging for union members, like those from the CIO's UFWA, who championed gender equity as one of their causes.[50] Helen Miller, an employee with high efficiency ratings in the Labor Department, was targeted for investigation after she raised questions about the department's promotion policies. As chair of the UFWA's adjustment committee, Miller was a vocal and visible supporter of worker rights. When the Dies committee labeled her a "subversive," department administrators questioned Miller for nine hours without benefit of counsel or union representation. They then dismissed her from the department (with one hour's notice) and denied her the right to an open hearing.[51]

The government's loyalty concerns deepened after the war, as evidenced by the president's 1947 executive order establishing a loyalty-security program in each agency. In contrast to Roosevelt's wartime program, Truman's order called for an investigation of all employees, not just new applicants. One of the first employees dismissed under that program was a ten-year veteran of the civil service, Dorothy Bailey. A highly paid training supervisor at the United States Employment Service (USES), she was also a member of the Society for Personnel Administration and the Society for the Advancement of Management as well as an activist union leader. As president of UFWA Local 10, a general vice president of UFWA, and a member of the International Executive Board of UFWA's successor union, the United Public Workers of America (UPWA), Bailey aggressively pursued racial and gender equity. In 1945 she had assisted the union in devising reconversion policies that would minimize the impact of layoffs on women and minority workers. She had also engaged in a fight to halt her employer, the USES, from separating black and white job candidates on lists they released to potential employers.[52]

Unlike many, Bailey decided to fight her dismissal in the courts. But while she drew attention to civil rights violations within the loyalty program, others focused on her forceful personality. One newspaper reporter commented on her "active" social life and claimed that although she was not married, she was not the "spinster type." A judge, ruling on whether she could have her job back while her case was under consideration, wrote that she asked for "too much" and was "too impatient." In the end, in a four to four decision, the Supreme Court let stand Bailey's dismissal and the constitutionality of the president's loyalty order.[53]

Bailey's case underscored the attack made in the postwar era on the more liberal form of human relations. Bailey was a social reformer who became interested in personnel administration while at the University of Minnesota. She majored in psychology, the basis of human relations, and clearly benefited from this more feminine approach to personnel management as she worked her way up from clerk to supervisor of the USES training section. Her active work in the Society of Personnel Administration and Society for the Advancement of Management similarly illustrated her commitment to this field. Yet ultimately she, like Helen Miller before her, became threatening because she chose to link her feminism to organizational power. In the postwar era, Bailey's collectivist, liberal, and activist orientation to her work proved incompatible with prevailing political ideologies and cultural norms.

This case also revealed how the loyalty issue marginalized the radical feminism linked to the CIO and to groups supporting forms of socialism and communism. Along with psychological paternalism, loyalty cases like Bailey's narrowed the debate over sex discrimination. Administrators pointed to the success of individual women who occupied professional or high-ranking managerial positions but failed to acknowledge that institutional biases against women existed in the civil service. This, in turn, made it more difficult for feminists to unearth the deep-running roots of gender bias in the workplace.[54]

The new style of employee relations in the civil service had both debilitating and liberating consequences for women. By arguing that supervisors should not dominate employees with an iron fist, personnel managers softened the tone of labor relations. An emphasis in human relations on personal interaction further reinforced a notion that employees were to be treated with respect. Human relations experts rejected as counterproductive an impersonal relationship between managers and workers. This resulted in a tempering of the harsh environment often associated with the workplace. Recreation, housing, and social programs also provided important services to the many employees who sought camaraderie with co-workers, needed shelter, or enjoyed organized activity. Finally, human relations programs gave women personnel positions as counselors and orientation advisors.

But paternalism as it was practiced by many in the federal government entrenched an image of female frailty into political institutions. Attempting to "sell" state activism—including a larger civil service—to the American public, managers and supervisors tried to demonstrate that the federal government took care of those who could not care for themselves, especially female civil servants. The rationale used to develop these programs required managers to assign traits to women that made them appear naturally less supervisory. Highlighting women's alleged physical and emotional infirmities, the concept of gendered difference harmed the long-term employment prospects for female civil servants.

In addition, federal managers appropriated psychological language and paradigms to evaluate the "nervous tics" of women in the government. Those deviating from the behavior delineated as socially acceptable by doctors, academics, and managers were categorized as abnormal or immoral and either "treated" or dismissed. By adopting the language and theories of the social sciences, conservative agency administrators reinforced the concept that women were naturally volatile and subordinate to men. Because of the authority accorded professional social scientists, those arguments were difficult to dispute.

Politics also stifled the more gender-friendly tenets of human relations. Generally, the more progressive personnel managers worked for war agencies, such as OPA, with more liberal mandates. Elected officials abolished most of these agencies when the war ended. More important, the war validated the use of patriotism as a powerful means of maintaining cultural uniformity and allowed agency administrators to label nonconformist feminists as "disloyal." Human relations, in many respects, became merely another means of keeping women "in their place."

Depression era proclamations that women's work was secondary to that of husbands did not disappear from management rhetoric. For the most part, this patriarchal argument against the employment of married women was temporarily suppressed because of the wartime labor shortage. During demobilization and the onset of the Cold War, however, traditional patriarchal arguments returned in full force. In a 1953 study of employee attitudes at the Department of Agriculture, researchers reported that morale among women was especially low because they did not have the same promotion opportunities as men and were often assigned rather routine tasks. But apparently "women adjust[ed] reasonably well to this division of labor, accepting business and industry as a man's world and recognizing the male's position as the principal breadwinner in the family." The report further stated that women regarded their work as a "strictly temporary venture to be terminated when they marry, become pregnant, or save enough money to supplement the family income." It blended this analysis with psychological paternalism by claiming that women "don't want to work under pressure."[55]

It would be a mistake, however, to assert that only male managers held a gendered view of the workplace. Although this was often the case, women also absorbed these stereotypes and then recapitulated and reinforced them in the work world. Edwards of the DNC, who continually fought for women's employment opportunities, rejected a suggestion in 1951 that she become chair of the entire committee. "I know there are some jobs that can be handled better by the masculine sex . . . I make a better Vice-Chairman than I would a Chairman, believe me," she wrote to one of her supporters. In the tough political years ahead, Edwards thought it best to have a man at the "helm."[56] Psychological paternalism successfully incorporated the notion of gendered difference—different female and male temperaments—into the language of management. Consequently, it recast the sexual division of labor along new, socially scientific lines.

At times women contested their role in the new management structure, but they also participated in the construction of the new gendered management philosophy, human relations. The erection of gendered management structures resulted from neither unassailable forces nor a conscious conspiracy to deny women employment equity. A complex interaction of cultural traditions, political ideologies, labor market shifts, state expansion, and the popularization of psychological theories and methods in the 1930s and 1940s produced new federal management programs and practices. Significantly, these same forces would help redefine the meaning of merit and race discrimination in the civil service.

6 Race and Merit

In 1920 John Alexander joined the civil service as a messenger. Eight years later, on the basis of seniority and performance, his superiors promoted him to general utility clerk at the Federal Farm Loan Bureau. Alexander's responsibilities expanded until he became head of the publications storeroom, supervising messengers, supply clerks, and mimeograph operators at the Farm Credit Administration (FCA). In 1942 the FCA moved its headquarters from Washington, D.C., prompting Alexander to seek another civil service position. Eager to benefit from an expanding war bureaucracy, he began searching for a position at least two grades higher than the CAF-2 grade he held at FCA. After several months, he found a post at the Office of Price Administration as a CAF-3 assistant file clerk, although his duties were those of a storekeeper. Although Alexander complained about his erroneous job title at OPA, officials insisted that his file clerk classification made the payroll less complicated. It also made it appear that he did not have supervisory duties, which he did. After twenty-two years in the service, his salary of $1,680 per annum equaled what he had earned as a CAF-2 at FCA.[1]

While at OPA Alexander repeatedly earned praise and high efficiency ratings from his immediate supervisor, who promised to promote Alexander to a CAF-5 post. But Alexander was an African American, and each time a CAF-5 vacancy occurred, branch managers gave it to a white employee. In one case, an agency official told him that a white employee with less seniority would be promoted because the job entailed supervising white "girls" who would not work for a black supervisor. When agency officials questioned the women about their views, however, one named Madge from Tennessee thought that having Alexander as her supervisor would be "just wonderful." Administrators then told Alexander that because the "girls" were young, an "older" man should have the job. At the time Alexander was forty-three; the previous white supervisor (who had not been dismissed but had joined the military) was twenty-two. At least the replacement was older than Alexander. He was sixty-one. Alexander continued to press agency officials for a promotion, but each time a position opened, officials continued to refuse him. Once they told Alexander that the job involved supervising white southerners who would refuse to work for a black man. Another time, branch chief Walter Jacobsen questioned Alexander's supervisory experience. In the end Jacobsen split a CAF-5 vacancy into two CAF-4 positions. Alexander obtained one of these positions and a white employee the other.[2]

When Arline Neal came to Washington, D.C., in 1941, she too found work at OPA. After scoring 92 percent on her clerical exam, Neal was hired in the bindery section, collating papers at a salary of $1,260 a year.[3] Because she excelled in her job, Neal gradually acquired more responsibility. She began typing, operating and fixing mimeograph machines, and supervising the work of other employees. Her salary never rose, however, because administrators informed her that she had "reached her peak." When she left to take a short-term typing class, the chief temporarily assigned her duties to a woman earning $1,620 a year.[4]

United Federal Workers of America Local 203 urged Neal and Alexander, both members, to lodge a formal complaint. With some hesitancy, Alexander and Neal agreed, and they were joined by a third plaintiff, James Hargrove. After compiling their case, the union's grievance committee presented department administrators with a document detailing a consistent pattern of race discrimination and maladministration in OPA's Printing and Distribution Branch. Soon afterward, Edward Hay, a deputy division administrator, and Durant Rose, a division chief, took the unprecedented action of appointing a special fact-finding committee consisting of agency and union representatives to investigate these charges. Agency officials opened files to the committee and allowed them to interview nineteen witnesses for some twenty-eight hours over eight days.[5] Faced with overwhelming evidence of discrimination and mismanagement in the Printing and Distribution Branch, OPA officials agreed to reclassify ten employees—including Alexander and Neal—and remove Jacobsen from his post.[6]

As this case illustrates, some government officials displayed a willingness in the 1940s to root out race discrimination in federal agencies.[7] President Franklin D. Roosevelt's fair employment policy, created through an executive order in 1941, included a formal procedure through which African Americans could dispute discriminatory practices. This policy applied to industries holding government contracts and to government agencies. Available evidence suggests that this policy had a rather limited impact on government contractors.[8] An examination of the federal government's own efforts to define and enforce fair employment policies within the executive branch reveals how advocates and critics of fair employment policies developed competing definitions of the word *merit*. To Alexander and Neal, who successfully fought discrimination at OPA, "fair employment" meant the opportunity to compete for jobs and promotions on the basis of performance and ability rather than skin color. In this case, at least, the system upheld their interpretation of merit.

Their interpretation of merit was not the dominant one. As discussed, from the establishment of a merit system for the government service under the Pendleton Act of 1883 until the early 1900s, African Americans, along with some government officials, believed that the exam system provided a color-blind means of evaluation.[9] But once a racial caste system became firmly established in American society, the evaluation of merit diverged along racial lines. Even into the 1930s, most white liberals, along with conservatives, maintained that African Americans were not socially, culturally, or intellectually equal to whites. During the New Deal, however, a growing chorus of black activists, accompanied by a small group of white liberals, began to call for universal standards by which to assess merit. These standards included attention to previous work experience and training; academic credentials; civil service test scores; and efficiency ratings. From the late 1930s through the war years, calls for a single, color-blind standard of merit competed with a caste system that had created a racially tiered perception of merit. While liberals increasingly criticized this perception, race conservatives, such as Alexander's and Neal's supervisors, viewed it as fully consistent with their support for the merit system.

Because white liberals and black activists were still in a process of redefining the concept of equal opportunity, there remained a wide discrepancy between fair employment policy and managerial practices at the agency level. Despite the president's 1941 fair employment order, Jacobsen, for instance, had continually refused to promote blacks in his division. Even when employees used grievance procedures to lodge a complaint, agency officials hesitated to rule against line supervisors. In their first assessment of the Alexander case, for example, managerial members of the fact-finding committee acknowledged that the investigation uncovered evidence of maladministration. But they pointedly added that the case did not really "prove" race discrimination. Even after the conclusion of the case, OPA officials were slow to remove

Jacobsen as branch chief. Over the UFWA's objections, officials did not fire Jacobsen but transferred him to another division.[10] Even if some employees "proved" discrimination, occupational segmentation remained. At the end of 1943, most of OPA's black employees were still classified as messengers and low-level clerks. As of July 1944, OPA employed 476 African Americans in its departmental service, 88 percent of whom were in the CAF service. Of those, 70 percent were employed in grades 1 through 3. They also continued to receive the most undesirable shifts. Officials assigned black employees to the night shift and white women to the day shift.[11] According to William Bradbury, in mid-1945, African Americans constituted approximately 13 percent of the 3,800 employees in the Washington, D.C., office. Occupationally, they represented 2.8 percent of professional, administrative, and supervisory positions (P 1–8 and CAF 5–15); 30 percent of skilled clerical positions (CAF 3–4 and SP 4–8); 59.3 percent of routine clerical positions (CAF 1–2 and SP 1–3); and 90 percent of all custodial and labor positions (CPC 1–8). Most African Americans (64.3 percent) who worked in the agency were in skilled clerical positions.[12]

According to liberals, a meritocracy gave each individual the right to compete for jobs and promotions, regardless of skin color. A violation of this principle was therefore a violation of an individual's rights.[13] In their minds, race discrimination was a problem to be addressed in each individual case; it was not a problem of "institutional racism" in which a host of structural impediments, such as lack of access to education and training programs, prevented groups from competing on an equal basis with other groups. Neither scholars nor the general public perceived the problem of race discrimination in those terms. As a result, the vast majority of race liberals within the federal government failed to support programs like job training, aimed at leveling the playing field.[14]

Unlike race liberals who argued that race discrimination polluted a color-blind merit system, conservatives maintained that race had to be factored into some personnel decisions. The government's personnel system worked, they contended, because everyone knew their place—black employees, if hired at all, belonged at the bottom of the labor hierarchy. Some still believed that separate but equal was a real possibility; it allowed administrators to voice support for equal opportunity without claiming that blacks and whites were the same.

Even though southern conservatism did not dominate the Council of Personnel Administration, members sympathetic to this perspective were able to temper liberal policy suggestions. For the most part southern-born personnel directors worked in small, independent agencies that were not under civil service regulations. For example, from 1936 to 1940 Kentuckian Justice Chambers was personnel director of the Maritime Commission, an agency with only about 1,000 employees, as compared to the more than 45,000 employed at the Interior Department.[15] Although conservative personnel directors did not have the collective power to persuade the council to take a stand against the appointment of blacks, they did exercise negative power over decision making with regard to race relations.

Several southern personnel directors were in a position to keep liberal reformers from seeking strong oversight of fair employment regulations. South Carolinian T. Roy Reid was appointed head of Agriculture's powerful personnel office in December 1941, a move that was protested by the National Association for the Advancement of Colored People. In a letter to White House aide Wayne Coy, NAACP Secretary Walter White commented that "the general impression among Negroes who are in a position to know is that they will stand little chance to get appointments, promotions, or other recognition in any department which Reid controls." Any executive order barring discrimination, White said, "will be virtually a dead letter so far as Negroes are concerned in any matter which Mr. Reid will handle."[16] Although he headed the personnel office of a small agency, Kentucky-born Robert Barnett of the Social Security Board was appointed a member of the council's race relations committee, organized in 1940 after President Roosevelt expressed an interest in the subject. Chairing that committee was A. J. Sarré, personnel director of the Federal Works Agency, who had been an undergraduate at Tulane and was probably from Louisiana.

As members of the race relations committee, Sarré and Barnett, for instance, blocked race relations proposals that seemed to suggest too radical a shift in the color line. They helped stymie the use of quotas and centralized enforcement of fair employment policies. Federal employees recognized a distinctly southern orientation with regard to race issues. One administrator noted that if one person in the labor hierarchy had traditional southern ideas, then he or she could fairly easily block efforts to enforce fair employment. Without constant pressure, this individual noted, it was difficult to implement these policies.[17] Sarré reassured his fellow directors that neither the council nor the president's nondiscrimination statement would attempt to "police" department practices. Instead, he suggested that the Civil Service Commission appoint a specialist to advise personnel offices on minority employment, analyze reactions, and initiate a program for cooperation with agencies to end discrimination. "We are not," he said, "making a statistical study in the number of cases of discrimination in any agency. If that were the purpose of the committee, I [would] ask to be relieved."[18]

According to conservatives, who also included personnel directors Charles Piozet from the Navy Department and George Henderson Sweet of the Veterans Administration, a segregated and segmented labor force reflected established race relations and therefore kept harmony within the labor force. And harmony, according to human relations experts, equaled productivity. These personnel administrators believed that morale was elevated when supervisors worked with, not against, the informal social patterns established by their employees.

As noted in chapter four, some managers, then, used human relations to construct a crude sociological justification for race discrimination. Sociological racism preserved a racial division of labor and hierarchy. Despite incremental upward mobility during the war, most African Americans continued to serve as custodians and messengers, particularly in highly professional departments such as Agriculture. Department administrator Paul Appleby remarked in 1937 that "so many whites would refuse to work under the supervision of a negro that this fact—important to the underlying job of administration—simply must be recognized." Hence, he concluded, acceptance of black employees on a level equal to whites was an "ideal impossible of early attainment."[19] Others expanded on Appleby's sentiments, arguing that white workers had the right to participate in managerial decisions or to "state their preferences" regarding the hiring and placement of black workers. At OPA, Jacobsen never placed blacks in new positions without first canvassing the opinions of white workers who were to work under or with them.[20] These views limited opportunities for African Americans, even when economic necessity demanded their labor.

This type of sociologically based racism nevertheless replaced a more virulent form of scientific racism popular in the early twentieth century. By the late 1930s social scientists, such as psychologist Otto Klineberg, sociologists Alfred McClung Lee and Norman D. Humphrey, and anthropologists Melville Herskovitz and Robert Lowie, among others, were more likely to claim that racial differences were not linked to biology.[21] As these scholars adopted new environmental paradigms to explain racial differences, most personnel managers shied away, at least in public, from arguing that people of color were innately unable to handle complex tasks. However, in their search for timeless laws governing society, social scientists often implied that social forces were fixed. References to social conditions and culture therefore frequently cast employment inequities in "natural" terms.

The issue of race, like that of gender, exposed the fragility of the concept of a "science" of administration based upon universal principles. Administrative techniques and the ideologies supporting them reinscribed existing inequalities in a new historical and intellectual context rather than transforming these. Discrimination based upon skin color alone threatened the legitimacy of the liberal understanding of an "objective" merit system. Race liberals were therefore able to criticize (if not always punish) managers who manipulated classification schedules, exam scores, efficiency ratings, and other "objective" criteria to preserve the racial division of labor and racial hierarchy. But the views of fair employment advocates were also limited because many divorced the concept of equal employment opportunity from the concept of social equality. Moreover, they focused on discovering individual culpability for racist acts rather than attempting to uncover and address how and why social structures and institutional culture contributed to a racial division of labor. Yet, despite these limitations, white liberals joined black activists in an uneasy alliance to challenge a traditional color-based definition of merit. Their efforts within the civil service opened up the conversation concerning office race relations and laid the terms for a discussion of the economic as well as social consequences of race discrimination.

Race and Fair Employment in the Wartime Service

In 1940 progressive Georgia Democrat Robert Ramspeck, who also chaired the House Civil Service Committee, moved to include a provision in his comprehensive civil service legislation that would outlaw discrimination on the basis of race. Not to be upstaged, the president issued an executive order effecting such a policy in the weeks before the legislation passed through Congress.[22] In response to Roosevelt's interest in the subject, the Council of Personnel Administration established a committee to study race relations in the civil service. While the council clearly hoped to make policy recommendations to the president, they soon discovered that they could not forge a consensus on this issue.

Personnel directors such as Piozet, Sweet, Chambers, and Henry Hubbard, a council staff member, had begun their government careers as messengers and low-level clerks during the first two decades of the twentieth century.

They tended to favor a version of sociologist Robert Park's ecological cycle. These administrators advocated for a slow introduction of blacks into the civil service. This often reflected their experience working in a predominantly segregated civil service.

They suggested that the creation of separate black enclaves—havens "safe" from discrimination—would nurture black professional development. The director of the Census Bureau, for instance, provided a defense against charges of discrimination in 1941 by noting how he had organized "by mutual agreement with Negro employees and many prominent Negro leaders . . . Negro employees into solid Negro sections consisting of 20 clerks, a section chief, and an assistant section chief" in population division offices. These units, he said, allowed African-American employees to become supervisors. He said they also assured that "Negroes would be recommended and judged by their own people. This," he concluded, "is far from being racial discrimination."[23] Veterans Administration personnel director Sweet approved of this kind of approach, cautioning other agency personnel directors against any swift movement toward integration. He maintained that segregated units of black clerical workers enabled these employees to demonstrate their capabilities and to "advance on an individual basis." In one instance, he noted, a black clerk at the CAF-2 level was actually promoted to attorney (grade P-2) and assigned a black stenographer, "thus widening job opportunities for negroes."[24] Managers could easily adapt this "separate sphere" view to contemporary sociological thought, maintaining that over time, separatism would prepare blacks to enter the white mainstream as equals.

According to these conservatives, practices such as these eliminated discriminatory employment patterns while maintaining harmony in the workplace. A separatist approach, maintained Sweet, would avoid "the sudden shock of attempting to force a large number of negroes into all parts of an organization working side by side and mixing indiscriminately with white workers." Like many, he favored a gradual approach that would eventually allow a select few black workers to "filter" through the entire organization with a minimum of friction.[25] Personnel managers thought the idea best for departments in which few or no blacks were employed. As they saw it, it would encourage agencies that would not otherwise hire blacks to do so, it would provide opportunities for blacks to become supervisors, and it would help introduce individual black employees into "non-traditional" occupations.[26] These administrators believed that a single standard of merit applied separately would preserve democratic principles; a separate but equal merit system was a desirable intermediary stage on the evolutionary trail toward assimilation, which would occur in the distant future.

Reaction from black leaders to this suggestion ranged from diplomatically lukewarm to explicitly cold. Departmental race advisors, for instance, flatly rejected a proposal by one department that a separate unit of ten thousand blacks be established.[27] Yet Andrew Wicketts, head of the pro-Roosevelt National Employees and Tenants Union, concluded that separate black units could be established "without the administration being accused of setting a precedent of jim-crow or segregation in the civilian branch of the government service." He complimented personnel director Charles Piozet for initiating such a plan in the Navy Department. This, he said, was essentially the only way to "create an outlet for the intelligent energies of these qualified, yet unemployed Negro eligibles."[28] Race relations advisor William Trent of the Federal Works Agency remained fundamentally opposed to segregation and agreed instead to introduce fully competent black employees into the agency at a slow pace.[29] The accomplished and passionate William Hastie, a race relations advisor in the War Department during the 1940s, found the suggestion that blacks enter separate units an "insult" to civil service laws and the merit system. He saw separate units not as enclaves of opportunity but as "blind alley[s]" created to accommodate minorities. Supremely frustrated at the lack of integration, Hastie resigned from his War Department post in January 1943.[30]

Other administrators sympathized with Hastie's frustration. Some New Deal and wartime bureaucrats had ties to liberal Protestantism (including the social gospel) and liberal academic circles in which support for fair employment was growing. Among these reformers were Council of Personnel Administration Chair Frederick Davenport, a Columbia Ph.D. and a native of Salem, Massachusetts, and Harvard-educated Samuel Ordway, Jr., a New Yorker by birth. Former business executive Heath Onthank, one of the most outspoken and influential members of the council as personnel director for the War Department, hailed from Massachusetts. Although their numbers were small, these men perceived merit reform and race discrimination as mutually exclusive. To them, one system of merit should be applied to all potential and current employees. Davenport urged the council to face the race issue "squarely," while Ordway scolded supervisors in the Civil Service Commission for failing to promote black messengers with ten years of service. White employees who could not deal with the promotion of black messengers to clerks, he said, should leave the service.[31]

Race liberal Isaac McBride of the National Archives described race discrimination as "a disease which ought to be quarantined." McBride perceived race prejudice as pathological and linked it to white ignorance. Fair employment laws were necessary, McBride argued, in order to bring management practices in line with democratic principles. "If minorities cannot hope for recognition and decent treatment in a democracy," he stated, "there certainly is no place for them to turn." Kenneth Warner, a westerner who headed OPA's personnel office between 1942 and 1943, expressed significant distress at the race discrimination he witnessed in federal offices in Washington, D.C.[32] While they were not always able to agree on what practices constituted race discrimination or how to enforce fair employment, these outspoken liberals kept racial issues prominent.

These race progressives adhered to a strong individualistic perspective of merit, in which civil service exams, efficiency ratings, and outside credentials served as impersonal measures of individual worth. Most felt little need to examine social and economic handicaps endured by marginalized groups. Nor did anyone conceive of merit as a "socially constructed categor[y]" that reflected the biases and culture of the white majority.[33] Their strong commitment to individualism, along with their suspicion of centralized authority (heightened by the fight against totalitarianism), set the parameters for the liberal debate over discrimination.

While liberals favored regulation, they remained skeptical that a deeply entrenched sociological and psychological phenomenon like racism could be eliminated simply by issuing a fair employment edict. Julia Maulding, personnel director of the Interior Department, for example, explained that the forced integration of clerks in her department resulted in cooperation between black and white employees, but then added that authoritarian proclamations alone could not change behavior.[34] Personnel administrators, she asserted, had a responsibility to provide equal employment opportunity but nothing more. It was up to the black civil servant, she said, "to sell himself . . . because they themselves are the people that are going to overcome prejudice, not us."[35] Another council member cautioned his colleagues against pushing race policies "faster than Congress and administrators are prepared to accept." Personnel directors remained quite cognizant of the power of southern legislators who controlled a number of oversight and appropriation committees.[36]

Liberal administrators had to balance their desire to jettison "authoritarian" management structures and techniques with their desire to enforce fair employment. Many believed that supervisors should be persuaded rather than forced to follow fair employment policies. Maulding encouraged her colleagues to "sell" non-discriminatory policies to agency employees.[37] Proper leadership, personnel directors maintained, would remedy discriminatory problems; according to Warner of OPA, the personnel officer should be responsible for stimulating "progressive thinking" among supervisors. By arguing that they had only a "positive responsibility for providing guidance and advice" to administrative officials, personnel administrators inadvertently lodged the ultimate responsibility for fair employment with the people who often engaged in discrimination: office supervisors.[38] While personnel administrators who perceived racism as a blight on the civil service were more open-minded, they, like the more conservative accommodationists, were unwilling to promise strict enforcement of fair employment.

President Roosevelt's fair employment executive order attempted to address this blight. Roosevelt ultimately bypassed the Council of Personnel Administration's race relations statement, which urged federal agencies "to translate into practical procedure the democratic principle of non-discrimination against minority groups in government employment in existing legislation, executive orders, and regulations" in favor of an executive order.[39] On June 25, 1941, after pressure from civil rights activist A. Philip Randolph, who had threatened a massive march on Washington, D.C., to protest employment discrimination, the president issued Executive Order 8802 establishing a committee to ensure fair employment in government agencies and war industries. The president relied upon a specially appointed subcommittee, whose members included New York politician Fiorello LaGuardia, National Youth Administrator Aubrey Williams, and labor leader Sidney Hillman, to draw up the order.[40] Two months later, the council and White House personnel specialist William McReynolds drafted separate letters for the president to consider sending to federal department heads. The council's draft (which the Civil Service Commission sent to the president) requested that department heads examine personnel policies as a means of eliminating race discrimination. McReynolds's draft did not mention race but asked agency heads to examine personnel policies and practices in order to ensure equity. The president's letter, sent to agency heads in September, recommended that they take "immediate steps . . . to put into effect this policy [E.O. 8802] of nondiscrimination in Federal employment."[41]

Although the executive order creating the Fair Employment Practices Committee (FEPC) was a powerful moral and political statement about the injustice of race discrimination, the order failed to ensure equal employment opportunity. Because Roosevelt created the committee as an advisory agency, it had no enforcement authority. Its only tools were those of investigation, persuasion, and on occasion publicity. One supervisor referred to the fair employment order as simply a "piece of paper."[42] Like the grievance procedures written by personnel administrators, the fair employment procedure attacked discrimination on a case-by-case basis; it never provided for a widespread assault on the racial division of labor. Moreover, the committee often upheld the original decision of agency managers accused of racist employment practices and failed to take an aggressive stance against pervasive race discrimination in field offices. Overwhelmed by their mandate, the FEPC staff held hearings on only a fraction of the cases submitted, and cases involving government employees had low priority. Of all cases filed, only 25 percent involved government employees. All government agency hearings, furthermore, were to be conducted in private, thus depriving the FEPC of publicity. Because the FEPC lacked a field staff, it had to rely upon the Civil Service Commission to investigate federal cases outside Washington, D.C. Generally, the commission, while cooperative, refused to limit the discretion of agency administrators with regard to work assignments and employment conditions. Between October 1941 and March 1946, the Civil Service Commission found race discrimination to be proven in only 58 of the 1,871 cases it investigated. Institutionally, the FEPC also suffered. In the status-conscious world of bureaucratic politics, the FEPC was viewed as a temporary, low-priority war agency. Initially placed in the Office of Production Management, the committee soon became a bureaucratic nomad, shifted from department to department before acquiring its independence in 1943.[43]

The committee lacked the political support necessary to expand its activities. Congressional opponents employed a variety of political strategies to undermine the agency's legitimacy. Southern legislators likened the committee to bureaucracies within totalitarian regimes—as the offspring of an executive order, the committee, they charged, was not publicly accountable. Legislative enemies of the program created a special committee—the Smith Committee—to investigate agencies acting beyond statutory limits. In addition to targeting regulatory agencies such as OPA, the committee spent extensive time investigating the FEPC and listening to complaints about the agency from government officials and industrial clients.[44] Faced with uphill appropriation battles every year, the committee probably logged more time testifying before Congress than it did reviewing charges of discrimination.

Most agency managers never envisioned fair employment regulation as a mandate for dramatic social and economic change. Personnel administrators perceived race as an issue that threatened to upset the delicate social balance of the workforce. As human relations converts, they placed a premium on cooperation, shunning conflict as "inefficient." Thus, personnel managers repeatedly stated their desire to support an "evolutionary" rather than "revolutionary" approach to race relations. While the refrain was used by many in the white establishment to preempt a radical shift in employment practices, its usage was deliberate and revealing. The scientific paradigm evoked by the word *evolution* suggested that race relations would follow a natural progression, mapped out by unbending social principles, from separatist conflict to harmonic assimilation. Indeed, the term *progress*, which administrators often deployed, implied that the status of African Americans was following a linear trajectory. Even though personnel managers perceived race discrimination in social rather than biological terms, it was still a "scientific" issue. Given the existence of scientific principles, "radical" integrationist policies would have little effect on established patterns of race relations. Finally, by associating immediate integration with the specter of "revolution," especially during a period in which totalitarian regimes threatened western democracies, personnel administrators implied that integration would lead to disastrous political, social, and economic upheaval.

Some government agencies rejected even evolutionary policies. Because enforcement of fair employment rules within the civil service depended upon the goodwill of agency administrators, fair employment practices varied considerably from agency to agency. Merit issues were complicated by the implementation of war service regulations that allowed agencies to circumvent civil service exams and hire employees on a temporary basis, particularly in war agencies. As one commissioner noted, this expedited staffing by enabling the government to hire "well-qualified" people, not necessarily the "best qualified" people. Perhaps agency appointing officials felt that they had more power to hire according to their desires.[45]

Several studies on race relations in the federal government have linked agency culture, rather than abstract fair employment policies, to office race relations. Scholars have concluded that during the 1930s and 1940s, old-line agencies were the least willing to hire black employees. During the New Deal, the Agriculture Department under Henry Wallace had the smallest percentage of black employees and was the last of the departments to appoint a black advisor. In September 1941, the department had a total of 275 (2.1 percent) African Americans in its departmental service. A year later, the number had risen to 500 (4.7 percent). Little had changed by the end of the war. In September 1945, the Department of Agriculture counted only 89 (0.5 percent) blacks in professional grades. The dearth of African-American employees in old-line agencies and elite occupations was not necessarily reversed during the war-induced labor shortage partially because appointment officers more frequently began to hire credentialed professionals from outside the civil service. By doing so, they blocked the upward mobility of experienced and qualified black employees who had been forced, because of occupational discrimination, to begin their government employment as messengers and elevator operators. In contrast, civil rights activists often lauded OPA for its exemplary record. In 1942, more than a hundred of the agency's approximately 170 black employees working at its headquarters served in the clerical service, although most of the remaining employees worked in the custodial service. Only seven were classified as professionals.[46] The agency's comparatively good record improved over time and at the end of the Second World War, OPA administrator Chester Bowles complained to Civil Service Commissioner Arthur Flemming that few agencies seemed willing to offer employment to OPA's African-American workers, who were losing jobs as the agency reduced its workforce. It would be an "injustice" and "tragedy" not to maintain employment opportunities for blacks, Bowles concluded. Flemming responded to repeated charges with a personal investigation of five cases, and found that one constituted discrimination.[47]

An agency's record on race discrimination was also related to its constituency; those that served financial and business clients (e.g., the Federal Trade Commission) were more likely to discriminate than those that attended to the needs of lower-income groups (e.g., the Federal Security Agency). And departments with routinized tasks (e.g., Treasury and Tennessee Valley Authority) were more likely to employ large numbers of blacks in segregated divisions.[48] The wartime employment of African Americans varied considerably from agency to agency and was higher in the departmental than in the field service. As of March 1943, only 1.1 percent of OPA's 46,422 field service employees were black. Nearly all of the forty-nine black employees hired in its southern office were in custodial positions.[49]

Office, Human, and Race Relations

Depending on the agency, managerial practices either weakened or maintained the liberal principle of fair employment. Conservative personnel managers actively resisted enforcement of the policy. This was not hard to do. They continually emphasized the right of supervisors to make decisions regarding the hiring, placement, and work assignments of lower-level employees. Many personnel managers stressed their professorial role, asserting that as teachers, rather than police, they were to *persuade*, instead of coerce, supervisors to follow fair employment edicts. Even OPA's more liberal personnel staff admitted that they limited their authority over employment decisions to an occasional veto. Some remarked that they preferred to rely on "peaceful persuasion." Occasionally, if that did not work, they would impose some penalty but never dismissal. In one instance, the personnel office penalized the Accounting Department for refusing to hire African Americans by halting the certification of any department recruits until the department began to accept employees on merit, regardless of race.[50] This gave supervisors and conservative personnel managers an opportunity to perpetuate the existence of a merit system founded upon a belief in "natural" social and cultural inequalities. Ideological and structural deficiencies, expressed through management programs and policies, combined to reinforce occupational segmentation based upon skin color, despite the wartime labor shortage. An examination of one agency with a highly professionalized staff, the Smithsonian, highlights the dearth of African Americans in elite positions. In 1943, the Smithsonian had 106 black employees, three of whom were classified as professional; the remaining 103 were in the custodial, protective, and craft service. In 1951 the institution had five black "professionals": a preparer of exhibits (GS-7), two library assistants (GS-5), a mimeograph operator (GS-2), and a museum helper (GS-2).[51]

Many supervisors believed that skin color "naturally" factored into merit. If the combination of seniority and efficiency ratings that determined reduction-in-force ladders privileged African Americans, conservative supervisors simply constructed an alternate system of evaluation. At the end of the war, for instance, one supervisor decided to rate all of his attorneys as "excellent," in order to increase their chances for retention. When he found out that under reduction-in-force rules, a black attorney in the office was slated to get a desirable position, he ordered the attorney's rating lowered to "very good." Another supervisor coded race into the very concept of efficiency: "In our reduction in force, *of course* [Negroes] suffered more than the whites did, because they're just not as efficient as a group. And if you could juggle efficiency ratings to keep the people you wanted, you did it. Everybody did it—an administrator naturally tried to keep his most competent people when he cut down." Nor was this sentiment new. One Richmond postmaster declared in 1935 that "all Negro employees" were "inefficient."[52] Tapping into pervasive myths concerning African-American laziness, these supervisors ignored the hard work done by thousands of black civil servants—many of whom were grossly overqualified for their jobs—striving to move up civil service ladders. Instead, these managers equated competence with pale skin. One administrator, for example, expressed surprise that a black professional he knew "worked . . . not as a Negro at all, but as an able guy"; indeed, he was "one in a million."[53]

In order to be "one in a million" African Americans had to deny their racial identity. A white race relations specialist praised Robert Weaver because he was a man who "wasn't interested much in the race problem." Another described him as a "thoroughly emancipated Negro."[54] In a similar vein, administrators attributed the success of one black professional to the fact that he "recognizes no color barrier at all." Significantly, according to later accounts, he impressed his white peers as a "brown-skinned white man."[55] Implicit in these remarks was the belief that only cultural assimilation into native-born white society could lay the foundation for equality. During the war, when government officials stressed unity, they meant cultural homogeneity. In this sense, the unity they often encouraged, perhaps inadvertently, reinforced the notion that minority cultures were not sufficiently "American." Ideally, then, integration would result in assimilation rather than a pluralistic society in which difference was tolerated and each group recognized as equal. Under this assimilation model, officials emphasized the need to hire blacks who would not challenge the domination of white culture.[56]

Race liberals often retreated to similar merit-based arguments to explain the dearth of African Americans in professional and management posts. As James Anderson has illustrated with respect to northern white academics in the 1940s, liberal personnel managers also argued that merit prevented many African Americans from entering government service as professionals. Although Davenport supported the hiring of black skilled workers when labor shortages threatened war production, he defended the lack of black interns recruited by the National Institute of Public Affairs (NIPA). None, a spokesmen contended, survived the "stiff competition." Even Will Alexander, a champion of racial equity, cautioned agencies against hiring unqualified black employees.[57] Many surmised that because blacks had little experience in positions of authority, they were generally unqualified for these positions. One division director explained the problem: "The fact that [Negroes] have been excluded from a whole slice of our civilization seriously handicaps them for many kinds of work."[58] Because of the malleability of the term *merit*, it was extremely difficult for employers to distinguish between intentional racism and the application of impartial standards. In his study of academics, Anderson observed that the term *merit* became a "fragile bridge" joining racist practices with a rhetorical commitment to equality. The construction of that bridge made the endeavor to create a single, color-blind standard of merit for the civil service virtually impossible to achieve.[59] As long as the term *merit* was used to justify discrimination *and* promote equality, its use became more of a hindrance than a help to advocates of fair employment.

Most liberal personnel managers did not believe that race discrimination required a wide-scale reeducation program for white supervisors and employees. They often personalized discrimination, claiming that it was the result of aberrant individual prejudice, not institutional culture. OPA personnel director Warner maintained that racial tension was traceable to isolated individual episodes rather than to "group tensions." After discussing a charge of discrimination with his department head, one bureau chief accepted blame, claiming it was caused by his "personal feelings" and had nothing to do with department policy.[60] And in a statement from the head of the Fair Employment Board (established under the Civil Service Commission in 1948 to replace the then defunct FEPC), director James T. Houghteling wrote:

> In our experience, discrimination is usually something personal. It may be a conscious process of thought on part of some person who controls the appointment or promotion or some personnel action, or it may be a traditional and quite unconscious act or process of thought, but it usually is the act of one or more persons and we have tried in our investigation of complaints to find who is discriminating. The whole government is not discriminating, or we would not be here. I do not think there is any government agency where everyone is discriminating.[61]

Regulations were designed to find individuals, not whole agencies or the executive branch, responsible for discriminatory acts. This regulatory approach prevented a large-scale, centralized assault on the problems of underemployment and unemployment in the African-American community. It failed to examine the standards supervisors used to evaluate the performance of African Americans or to attack the sociologically oriented arguments they made to demonstrate the value of separatism. Personnel managers often accepted the argument supervisors made that lower-level employees would not "accept" African Americans. According to personnel managers, these were not "group tensions" but the feelings of individual employees. Finally, the emphasis placed upon individual acts of discrimination veiled the existence of a broader work culture that demeaned people of color.

Workplace culture contributed significantly to black economic stagnation. As one African-American stenographer in the Treasury Department explained, her work environment was so poisoned by racism that she did not think she could endure her job much longer. On occasion, she said, her immediate supervisor told her that she had "no brains." But the same supervisor also chastised her for attending a training class designed to improve job skills and then threatened to withhold her efficiency rating, a rating necessary to obtain promotions and pay increases. In addition, the stenographer complained that the other women in her section ignored her. "It's just a clear case of discrimination, because I am the first colored girl who has ever been employed in this capacity in this building. . . . I am in that room with five other whites and they are trying to freeze me out, mostly by not talking to me, ignoring me, and in those very subtle ways they can use."[62] While personnel administrators might try to enlighten supervisors about race discrimination, they rarely tried to elevate the morale of African-American workers.

As we have seen, participation was emphasized as a vital element in the human relations program. Consequently, the Council of Personnel Administration consulted various black leaders and the UFWA, a champion of fair employment, about race relations policies. During its discussions in 1941 on the fair employment issue, the council's race relations committee held hearings in which race relations advisors Robert Weaver (Office of Production Management), William Hastie (War), and William Trent (Federal Works Agency) testified. Likewise, race relations expert Will Alexander spent a day with the council discussing the approach they should take. And OPA managers routinely sought union input regarding the development of race-related policies.[63]

Even with their consultative roles, agency race advisors often lacked the power to desegregate agencies and enforce equal employment. In 1942 OPA chief Leon Henderson wrote a letter informing division and branch chiefs that violations of the president's fair employment order would result in dismissal. His successor vested enforcement of this policy in the personnel office, and in particular with T. Arnold Hill, the agency's race relations advisor. Personnel managers, however, later succeeded in deleting the penalty clause from the agency's written policy, despite protests from OPA's local UFWA lodge.[64] Hill's duties as race advisor, therefore, were greatly circumscribed. According to his job description he was to: canvass "black opinions and reactions" to OPA policies and operations; act as a spokesman for black groups; communicate OPA policies and aims to black groups; and implement OPA's nondiscriminatory policy by educating and advising operating officials. In theory Hill was to be the agency's spokesperson and liaison to African-American employees. He was to help personnel managers market their program to employees. Officials urged the staff to respect his authority, even though he actually had very little. Apparently, African Americans respected him a great deal; they brought their problems to him so frequently that his office became a "center of pressure for the placement of Negroes."[65]

Personnel officers viewed Hill's race relations efforts as an infringement upon their own prerogatives. In fact, they protested so loudly that Henderson's successor, Chester Bowles, abolished Hill's position the following year. Bowles eventually hired another advisor on race relations whose "chief weapons were those of the luncheon-table and the informal conference, not of authority or overt pressure." He praised her efforts in "interpreting our organization to minority groups." Rather than have employees visit her with their complaints about discrimination, she insisted that they use the regular grievance machinery set up by the personnel office. Personnel officers praised her for the advisory role that she played. She did not tread on their turf.[66]

Turf battles and a lack of authority frustrated those race relations advisors who were committed to ending race discrimination in government agencies. They were often excluded from personnel policy debates by white administrators. Davenport felt it better to contain within the council room deliberation on the race issue because, he said, "we do not discuss it acrimoniously here."[67] Another policy maker expressed a sentiment similar to Davenport's: "In policy discussions there are many times when we have to let down our hair and talk pretty bluntly about racial problems. . . . You may say it's wrong, but the fact is that we simply feel unable to talk bluntly and to the point about these problems if there is a Negro . . . present." Exasperated by their exclusion from power and by the lack of support for fair employment, many race advisors left government service when the war ended, leaving white administrators firmly in charge of the government's fair employment program.[68]

Others remained within the government, however, to fight these battles. An integrated UFWA-CIO played a central role in the struggle against race discrimination in the federal service. UFWA leaders, for instance, pressured agencies to refrain from holding parties in segregated hotels and from segregating recreation programs. In a case resembling Marian Anderson's unsuccessful bid to sing in Constitution Hall, the union vigorously objected to the

1945 decision by the Daughters of the American Revolution to stop black pianist Hazel Scott from performing in that same building.[69] Union officials were also acutely concerned that agencies follow fair employment practices. In addition to pursuing the Alexander case at OPA, the union petitioned to stop the United States Employment Service from maintaining separate rosters for black and white employees and referring employees on the basis of race if the employer requested it. Government agencies that used this service, the union pointed out, were violating civil service rules concerning discrimination. After an investigation, the Civil Service Commission agreed that the service had to be reformed, although it preferred that the service reform itself.[70]

To some degree the union's lack of formal power inhibited their efforts. "When we complain to Personnel about the total segregation of employee recreation," one union official stated, "they reply that 'the Negroes organized their own ball team, we didn't organize it for them.'" Union members often felt overwhelmed by the race relations problem and the resistance toward integration: "If the segregated set-up were abolished outright, the simple truth is that the Negroes would have nothing. The real answer is that Personnel should take a positive attitude of encouraging the development of integrated activities, but it's very hard to get them to do anything like that. I think those people just don't understand the problem enough to be willing to do that."[71] Another claimed that while personnel officials were "nice, helpful [and] amiable," they "want to keep everybody happy, and they don't understand the full significance—or meaning to the Negroes themselves—of racial discrimination. Consequently, they don't fight on it." Many UFWA branches felt that they lacked the resources necessary to engage in lengthy battles with agency officials.[72] Despite these handicaps, the UFWA remained one of few organizations willing to discuss and combat race discrimination publicly. Along with race advisors, the union at least provided some barrier against a sea of prejudice in the federal government. The union's ability to provide this shield, however, was severely restricted in the postwar era by weak federal oversight of fair employment and by the red scare.

Fair Employment, Unions, and Loyalty in the Postwar Era

Reconversion to a peacetime economy adversely affected the employment prospects of the government's African-American employees. The many who had been hired as temporary war workers were dismissed and the few lucky enough to have regular civil service status in war agencies found it difficult to transfer to other permanent agencies. Most government officials demonstrated little concern with equal opportunity employment, and in December 1945 President Truman turned the FEPC into a fact-finding agency. Several months later, conservative legislators succeeded in dismantling it altogether. Truman pledged support for a "true" merit system and urged agency heads to adhere to the government's rules against discrimination, but neither he nor sympathetic government officials had any means to enforce these policies. While many agencies were engaging in massive layoffs, the federal government provided no oversight for fair employment practices.[73]

UFWA's successor, the United Public Workers of America (UPWA), reacted strongly to this lack of oversight, urging the Civil Service Commission to centralize hiring and investigations of race discrimination for the federal service. Commissioners pledged to support the nondiscrimination provisions of civil service regulations but resisted any suggestion that they take the lead in the fight against race discrimination.[74] When asked by the White House to draft a new fair employment executive order, the commission devised a simple statement that declared race discrimination to be against the policy of the United States government, gave the commission the authority to investigate complaints and submit recommendations to agencies, and mandated nondiscrimination clauses in government contracts. The Bureau of the Budget and Civil Service Commission were to set forth rules in order to administer the program. White House aides rejected the order, calling it "weak" and politically damaging, "for it would incur as much wrath as a stronger order and yet would not gain any favor."[75] In July 1948 Truman issued an executive order providing for a special board to monitor fair employment. In a promising move, the president named two African Americans—a member of the Urban League and a former government official—to the first board, which was headed by public administrative specialist Guy Moffett. Although under jurisdiction of the commission, the board was to be composed of "representative" private citizens. Nevertheless, weak federal enforcement along with a zealous concern with loyalty undermined civil rights efforts.[76]

Truman's Fair Employment Board (FEB) established by the executive order defined fair employment in specifically economic terms, although it still left standards of evaluation vague. Reflecting a stronger emphasis in liberalism on individual rights, Moffett believed that the board was designed "to protect the economic rights of the individual." Agency officials, asserted Moffett, were to evaluate individual employees "objectively" on their "capacity, industry, and personal conduct," without regard to race, color, creed, or ethnicity. Any personnel action that affected an employee's "opportunity for advancement or financial reward," said Moffett, was to be made solely on the basis of "merit and fitness." Personnel actions, as defined by the board, included decisions involving appointment, separation, work assignment, and participation in training programs. Discrimination could not be charged in cases where "preference in appointment and differences in conditions of employment, such as pay, leave, hours of work, etc., [were] based upon law."[77] Board members hoped that their regulations would provide equal opportunity for each individual to rise or fall according to his or her ability, although terms such as *fitness* and *personal conduct* gave appointment officials and supervisors some latitude in judging performance.

While the liberal notion of a single evaluation process for both whites and blacks gained greater acceptance under the FEB, structural and statutory deficiencies made it difficult for the board to alter existing patterns of discrimination. Faced with an anti–New Deal Republican backlash, President Truman hesitated to expand bureaucratic authority. Like the FEPC, the FEB had few enforcement powers, although it could appeal to the president if an agency failed to carry out FEB recommendations "promptly and fully." Even so, agency authority generally prevailed. Each department was left the responsibility of designating a fair employment officer and designing fair employment procedures. This officer remained responsible to the agency head, who had to make a written ruling before an employee could appeal to the FEB.[78] Voluntarism rather than coercion remained a central tenet of the fair employment program.

Fair employment officers as well as employees often found it difficult to administer and negotiate fair employment grievance procedures. Once an individual employee submitted a detailed written complaint to the fair employment officer outlining the details of the adverse personnel action(s) and the individual(s) involved, the fair employment officer was obligated to conduct a three-month survey of personnel actions in order to determine whether the problem was one of "personality" or racism. Aside from the difficulties involved in determining the consciousness of the individual accused of discriminating, fair employment officers found the procedures time-consuming and cumbersome. One officer in the Agriculture Department explained its impracticality: "Forest fires need to be put out, meat needs to be inspected and passed, [and] quarantine inspections need to be given to incoming airplanes. . . . These activities cannot wait while somebody in Washington is making reviews and pre-audits."[79] Agency heads, moreover, often designated personnel directors to be fair employment officers, thus asking them not only to do two jobs but also in some instances to police themselves. Fair Employment Board members estimated that these officers spent only 5 percent of their time on employment equity issues. Many of them felt that the small number of formal complaints reflected the lack of discriminatory practices in their agencies.[80]

Decentralized authority made it relatively easy for agency administrators to resist the board's rulings. Officials in the Post Office, for example, refused to place a statement explaining fair employment practices with each employee's paycheck. It was unnecessary as well as expensive, they argued, because employees were already aware of their rights. Similarly, even after board officers notified the Department of Agriculture's fair employment officer that the department's policies failed to comply with board regulations, the officer expressed reluctance to alter them. They were, he said, clear, simple, and liberal. FEB's standards, he explained, merely spelled out what was implicit in the department's statement. Rather than comply immediately, the department's officer drafted another statement and submitted it to "interested" groups within his agency for approval.[81]

Nevertheless, the board existed and African-American employees availed themselves of this administrative channel in order to address grievances. Because the procedures were elaborate, employees who had organizational support were in a much better position to prove their complaints. Many relied upon the expert, moral, and financial support provided by UPWA to help them negotiate this process.[82] Even with the union's expertise, black employees achieved only minimal redress for years of discrimination. On occasion the FEB ruled in favor of employees, allowing individuals to step up the labor hierarchy, but the majority of African Americans remained in low-level positions.

Civil rights activists found themselves without organizational strength as the UPWA fended off attacks from anticommunist foes in the postwar era. In response to the new UPWA constitution, which tacitly supported strikes by government employees, legislators attached antistrike riders to the 1946 appropriation bills. These clauses forbade the employment of any person who belonged to a union or organization that asserted the right to strike against the United States.[83] The following year, Congress formally banned strikes by federal employees through a provision in the Taft-Hartley Act. And Truman's loyalty-security program, implemented in 1947, authorized departmental investigation of employees suspected of disloyalty. Under the program, each agency created a Loyalty Review Board for such purposes.[84]

UPWA members became frequent targets of loyalty investigations. Loyalty investigators often focused on civil rights activists. They considered the UPWA a "radical" organization and described one member, a lawyer at OPA, as a "spark plug in union activities" as well as an "ardent and aggressive union leader." Authorities charged twenty-two members of the Cleveland Post Office with subversion; all were members of the National Alliance for Postal Employees and participants in civil rights campaigns. Similarly a leader of the NAACP and postal employee in Santa Monica, California, was dismissed for disloyalty after he led an antidiscrimination picket line in front of Sears, Roebuck and Company.[85]

During loyalty hearings, all-white loyalty review boards frequently inquired about the racial attitudes of employees. Board members often asked whether an employee attended integrated social functions. One board member even questioned Labor Department employee and UPWA activist Dorothy Bailey about letters she had written to the Red Cross protesting their policy of segregating black and white blood. UPWA President Abram Flaxer complained bitterly that government officials were using the loyalty program to weaken the fair employment program. In the four months since the president had issued his fair employment order, observed Flaxer, nearly seventy loyalty cases had involved "Negro employees who have been active in the fight for civil rights." Questions posed by loyalty investigators regarding civil rights activists, charged Flaxer, were not the result of ignorance or personal prejudice but of "official policy."[86] In answer to complaints about questions regarding race during hearings, the chairman of the loyalty program responded that "any element relating to race which creeps into any loyalty hearing is purely accidental and entirely out of harmony with our procedures."[87]

By 1950 "official policy" enabled unsympathetic bureaucrats to eviscerate the UPWA. Treasury personnel director and fair employment officer James Hard recommended that agency officials only recognize complaints from unions whose officers had signed anticommunist affidavits. At the time he made this suggestion, Hard was in the midst of fighting the UPWA over the postponement of an apprentice plate printers exam in the Bureau of Engraving and Printing that had blocked the promotion of dozens of black employees.[88] Congress also took up the crusade and began consideration of a bill to give statutory authority to Hard's recommendation. In response, the UPWA decided to reduce the number of its national vice presidents from six to one, leaving the organization with a president, vice president, secretary-treasurer, and director of organization. Several days later, the union issued a statement noting that they were victims of "the most oppressive witch-hunt hysteria the nation ever witnessed." Truman's 1947 loyalty order, said UPWA President Abram Flaxer, had "poisoned the air." Once Senator Pat McCarran's Internal Security subcommittee labeled UPWA President Flaxer a "fanatic" communist and linked several other top union officials to the Communist Party in 1952, the union quickly lost political legitimacy.[89]

Attacks on the union, however, did not come from government officials alone. The CIO expelled the union in February 1950 for alleged subversive activities. The union's plummeting reputation hindered the campaign for racial justice. Of course the loss of UPWA organizational strength made it more difficult for African Americans to negotiate the grievance process. At the same time, however, civil rights activism became "tainted" by the union's "red" reputation. The red scare solidified the association many had already made between the civil rights struggle and political subversiveness. The idea that African-American employees were not to be trusted with state secrets was a strong one, and it was applied especially to those who tried to assert their rights. One government executive explained that his office got "a lot of hot communications . . . and you never could know when a Negro was going to start reading them as a Negro rather than a civil servant." Another explained that he could not hire some black women displaced from their government jobs at the end of the war, because the job that was available was "pretty 'hot'. . . . [They would] have access to a lot of secret documents."[90] In the tension-filled postwar era, government officials became increasingly intolerant of any threat to white authority.

During its existence, the CIO's government union had acted as a check on pervasive discrimination. From its founding the union spurred a healthy dialogue about the meaning of racial equality, and its work on behalf of minority rights tested the racial status quo. It suggested that a single color-blind system of merit should create an integrated workplace, replacing the ideals of both vertical and horizontal segregation. When the union was purged out of existence in 1952, African-American employees lost an important advocate in the battle against race discrimination and for integration.[91]

By committing to fair employment through an executive order, Roosevelt seemed to have made the executive branch a liberal force in the struggle by African Americans for equal rights. His order and the creation of the FEPC gave black employees access to an administrative channel that promised to protect their rights. In 1941, the federal government seemed poised to make the merit-based civil service the supreme model of equal opportunity employment.

But officials at the top as well as those in the middle remained deeply divided over the definition of merit and consequently over the enforcement of the order. Conservative personnel managers responded with a prescription that followed the separate but equal doctrine; liberal personnel managers trumpeted fair employment and integration but hesitated to dictate fair employment practices. As many personnel managers interpreted it, the human relations school taught them to adopt personnel policies that fit the informal social structure and relations of office workers. From the perspective of conservative administrators, racial interaction was therefore to be kept to a minimum because it would only lead to conflict. They claimed that they needed to respect the wishes of their white employees, who allegedly opposed occupational and spatial integration. These personnel managers followed contemporary and regional patterns of segregation, thus reinforcing the concept that the races were socially and culturally—if not biologically—different and incompatible. Their actions solidified a racial division of labor that kept many African Americans working far below their "merit."

Of course managers did not have complete control over the system. Avenues of resistance existed. African Americans in general and the UFWA specifically consistently contested race discrimination in the 1940s. The willingness of employees to exercise their rights under grievance procedures and the fair employment order kept the issue of race in sharp focus for government officials. Importantly, the cases that African-American employees and the union successfully prosecuted reversed blatant acts of discrimination. The situation also stimulated a critical dialogue regarding the meaning and nature of race discrimination in employment.

But the policies enacted did not eliminate long-standing patterns of underemployment and unemployment among African Americans. Fair employment policies were difficult—at times impossible—to administer, and enforcement remained sporadic. Administrative channels, for one thing, were designed to handle complaints on a case-by-case basis and therefore did little to assault the white power structure. The decentralized nature of the grievance process, furthermore, left supervisors and personnel managers with significant discretionary power. Fair employment policies did not overturn the right of managers to determine the "merit and fitness" of their employees. As we have seen, the definition of merit was informed by cultural attitudes that devalued the work performed by African Americans and that allowed some to perceive race separatism as part of the "natural" social order. By omitting African Americans from certain occupations, social spaces, and management programs, government officials perpetuated the notion that blacks and whites were different and unequal. Despite the federal government's fair employment policies, the civil service color bar remained firmly in place.

During the Second World War and the Cold War, African Americans found few whites willing to overhaul the racial division of labor. Within the federal government, efforts to achieve racial equality became even more difficult as officials used the fear of communism to stifle any criticism of the government. President Dwight Eisenhower, moreover, abolished the FEB and replaced it with an organization that had even less power—the President's Committee on Government Employment Policy.[92] But the contradictions between racial discrimination in the workplace and democratic principles remained. While the state mandated collective bargaining in the private sector, it continued to deny union rights to its own employees. While the state claimed to have a civil service based on merit, it endorsed a sexual and racial division of labor. Even though officials periodically purged liberals, including communists, from the civil service during the late 1940s and early 1950s, resistance did not disappear. Instead civil servants began to marshal their forces for a challenge to managerial authority—a challenge that would begin to reshape this aspect of American society and government during the "placid" 1950s.

Conclusion

Between 1901 and 1940, over 790,000 employees were added to the federal payroll, reflecting the influence of Progressivism and New Deal liberalism.[1] World War II broadened this expansion significantly, making the federal government one of the most influential employers in the country. In 1953, President Dwight D. Eisenhower together with Congress presided over a federal bureaucracy employing over 2.5 million people in more than fifty-five agencies.[2] This bureaucracy not only provided welfare services, regulated industry, maintained national defense, and delivered mail to millions of Americans but also acted as an employer. In this capacity, it became an arena in which employees and politicians hotly contested the meaning of American pluralism.

As a national institution, the federal bureaucracy served as a powerful symbol of civic life. Its employment patterns therefore reinforced and at times fostered private-sector employment trends. For instance, as Desmond King and other scholars have argued, by segregating African-American employees at the beginning of the century, the government legitimated an American caste system.[3] And by employing large numbers of women during World War II, it encouraged diversity in the workplace. Hence the state's employment policies demonstrated the permeable boundaries between state and society that a number of scholars have also observed in the state's economic and welfare activities.

Paul Van Riper has observed that heated debates over American identity have often coincided with crises in the development of the civil service. In the 1830s and 1840s when the Jacksonian spoils system took hold, ordinary Americans were attacking the patrician class. The advent of the merit system in the 1880s was tied to efforts to malign immigrants and political machines. And finally, the anticommunist purges of federal employees in the late 1940s and 1950s reflected an assault on civil rights activists, homosexuals, and independent women in society at large. In each instance, battles over the construction of the civil service system involved contention over the role of diversity in American society.[4] Depression and wartime developments established the parameters for the midcentury debate over pluralism and liberalism. The onset of the Depression directed the attention of the American public and politicians toward issues of class mobility, including its operation in the federal civil service. Once engaged in a national conversation over class and economic rights, segments of the population—women, African Americans, CIO union members, and political liberals in general—broached questions of race and sex discrimination. The labor shortage induced by World War II encouraged liberals to seek answers to these questions, as they did with the creation of the Fair Employment Practices Committee. Ironically, while class issues provided the initial forum for a discussion of diversity, class concerns became less visible in the 1940s.

Domestically, the Depression and New Deal reforms intensified liberal concerns with class mobility, but internationally, the rise of fascism accentuated a fear of caste systems and authoritarianism. Committed to preserving democracy, government bureaucrats therefore sought ways to address not only class inequities but also race and gender discrimination within the federal civil service. By the late 1930s, liberal administrators undertook a three-pronged approach to accomplish these objectives: they promoted an interpretation of the merit system that suggested that sex and race were irrelevant to assessing worth; they considered recognition of unions; and they adopted the human relations school of management.

Merit reform was central to the construction of the modern administrative state. Advocates of a meritocracy believed that their democratic society allowed for the establishment of a "natural" aristocracy that would rule by virtue of talent. The creation of a meritocracy in the federal bureaucracy fortified values associated with a capitalist system. With its emphasis on performance and output (or a measured potential to perform well), the merit system fostered an individualist and utilitarian perspective toward work. Although lacking a profit motive, administrative reformers focused on the efficient production of government services as their prime objective. Perhaps unintentionally, the late-nineteenth- and early-twentieth-century introduction of entrance and promotion exams, based upon the emerging field of psychometrics, offered a potential challenge to beliefs regarding the innate inferiority of various groups, although cultural biases continued to guide administration of exams, interpretation of scores, and hiring practices. Early in the century, scientific racism and sexism held that African Americans and women were "naturally" excluded from this aristocracy. Significant challenges to these beliefs did not occur until the 1930s and 1940s, when increasing numbers of liberals rejected scientific racism and elements of scientific sexism, instead arguing that the merit principle rested upon a gender- and color-blind assessment of worth.

Even so, multiple interpretations of merit continued to exist, and criteria other than test scores or efficiency ratings often determined who was hired, promoted, or fired. Government officials believed that an individual's character, personality, academic credentials, and work experience all factored into a decision concerning worth and fitness for federal work. Personal networks extending into the academy, business, and local and state governments also influenced hiring and promotional decisions. Often credentials and networks reflected larger societal patterns of race and sex segregation, leaving African Americans and women without access to the schools or contacts needed to secure well-paying civil service positions. Despite calls for implementation of a merit system based upon universal principles, the playing field remained far from level. Class segmentation, along with racial and gender caste divisions, resulted in uneven ground that left some groups behind.

Administrators used the rhetoric of class mobility to justify their vision of hierarchical authority within a democratic political system. While some civil servants equated occupational compartmentalization and New Deal intellectual patronage with a "caste" system, elite administrators portrayed this segmentation as the outgrowth of a democratic society and the development of a natural aristocracy. In this manner, civil service employment was to reflect the end result of mobility; it was not to serve as a mechanism to effect that mobility. Administrative efforts to recruit well-educated professionals highlighted that process.

On the surface, public administrators shunned the use of ideology, favoring instead a technical, nonpartisan approach to administrative state issues.[5] By portraying an arbitrary patronage system as the polar opposite of an impartial merit system, administrative reformers obscured the subjectivity and cultural biases informing the merit principle. Their behavior, however, unveiled a particular vision of democracy that guided their efforts to manage the public workforce. This was especially evident in their approach to civil service unionization.

Between 1939 and 1953 personnel officials had succeeded in weaving an elaborate tapestry of regulations and forming protective structures for workers, including rating, fair employment, and loyalty review boards. These developments had multiplied the levels of management and expanded the number and nature of regulatory controls managers had over workers. But a basic inconsistency between the government's labor policy in the private sector and its policy toward executive branch employees plagued administrators through the late 1930s and 1940s and continued to characterize these policies as late as 1953. In the 1950s, labor-management conflict energized the federal civil service unions and encouraged them to seek statutory recognition for bargaining rights.

During the late 1940s and 1950s, federal civil service unions developed a set of opposing institutions and a competing ideology regarding labor-management relations. As congressional edicts, technological innovations, and economy drives threatened government jobs, union militancy increased. In an attempt to prevent workers hired during the Korean War from becoming permanent employees, Congress passed the Whitten Amendment in 1950, mandating that all government hiring, promotions, and transfers be on a temporary basis.[6] Four years later, the Eisenhower Administration briefly considered implementing a plan whereby the Republican National Committee would have to approve all new civil service appointments. The Willis Plan, named after its chief architect, White House aide Charles Willis, brought forth a hail of protest. Unions and the National Civil Service League decried it as a return to the spoils system.[7] The American Federation of Government Employees vigorously protested not only these attacks on the permanent career service but also the growing tendency for defense agencies to contract out for work and to adopt technology that displaced workers.[8]

Hostile government officials succeeded in restricting union behavior and purging "radicals" out of government service, but they also succeeded in fortifying union opposition. Unable to achieve their aims through the Federal Personnel Council (formerly the Council of Personnel Administration) or White House, unions took their cause to Congress, lobbying for formal recognition and bargaining rights. Beginning in 1949 and continuing through the 1950s, sympathetic senators and representatives introduced a series of "Little Wagner" bills for government employees.[9]

Stiff opposition from government executives, personnel agencies, and the White House, however, frustrated union attempts to gain statutory recognition. Both the Federal Personnel Council and the Civil Service Commission felt legislation to be unnecessary, and the Bureau of the Budget, General Accounting Office, and White House voiced their opposition as well. Personnel managers claimed that while they agreed in principle with union recognition, they feared that a legislative mandate would limit administrative discretion. They favored issuance of an administrative rather than a legislative edict on the matter, and in 1958 Rocco Siciliano, a special White House aide on personnel management, sent a letter to all agency heads emphasizing the need for smooth employee relations and encouraging them to deal with unions.[10] During 1956 hearings on the recognition and arbitration bills, Civil Service Commissioner and White House personnel specialist Philip Young warned legislators that formal recognition of unions would lead to "chaos." Drawing out the concept of civic responsibility, he asserted that arbitration boards would infringe upon the authority of Congress and agency heads. If, as one bill stipulated, these boards had the power to dismiss officials who refused to follow decisions or provisions of the act, said Young, it would encroach upon the rights of agency heads to discipline workers. If arbitration boards had the power to rule on pay, leave, and reductions-in-force, they would impinge on congressional authority in these matters. Moreover, he noted, board decisions might conflict with existing veteran preference statutes.[11] As late as 1959, the National Civil Service League continued to argue that unions were lobbying bodies only and that bargaining rights would subvert the merit system as well as violate the principle of public accountability.[12]

Continued union agitation and congressional concern throughout the 1950s encouraged newly elected President John F. Kennedy to organize a fact-finding task force on employee-management relations in the federal government. Led by Labor Secretary Arthur Goldberg, the group began an extensive investigation of the union recognition issue as well as a host of other related employee concerns. National Civil Service Reform League officials felt encouraged by the willingness of the task force to solicit their views. They were also buoyed by the presence of Daniel Patrick Moynihan, then an assistant to Goldberg, on the committee. Moynihan, noted league officials, favored an approach that emphasized improved supervision as the key to harmonic employee relations. According to these officials, he did not support "some unreal concept of 'collective bargaining.'" In fact, said league officials, he followed the "*public* administration line' rather than the union stress on 'collective bargaining' as an end in itself."[13]

Weighing evidence from government officials, business concerns, public-sector unions, and foreign countries as well as from interest groups like the league, the task force attempted to tailor a program to fit the unique needs of the federal service. "Unique," of course, indicated that the task force believed that private-sector models of labor arbitration could not be applied in their entirety in the federal government. The task force report, "A Policy for Employee-Management Cooperation in the Federal Service," largely cloaked old concepts regarding voluntary negotiation in the public sector in new rhetoric. The authors even admitted this, noting in their cover letter that most of the proposals in the task force report already existed as "established policy" in one agency or another.[14]

Although the report paid heed to the league's work and rejected the union and closed shop and the right to strike, it did introduce some changes, including an expansion of the league's concept of recognition, which was defined in the report on three levels: informal, formal, and exclusive. Informal recognition, already followed in many agencies, stipulated that any organization had the right to articulate its views to agency management, but managers had no obligation to seek these views. Under formal recognition, if 10 percent of the employees "in a unit or activity of a government agency" were organized, then that organization had "the right to be consulted on matters of interest to its members." Exclusive recognition, finally, provided that if a majority of employees in an "appropriate unit" belonged to a single employee organization, then that organization had the right "to enter collective negotiations with management officials." Agreements resulting from these negotiations could not conflict with existing federal laws, agency regulations, federal personnel policies, or congressional authority.[15] Coordination and voluntary cooperation, rather than compulsion, remained the themes of federal labor relations.

Two months later Kennedy incorporated the task force recommendations into two executive orders—one that provided for recognition of federal employee organizations and the other mandating implementation of an "adverse action" appeal system. His orders represented a departure in their imposition of a government-wide policy recognizing unions and their right to negotiate at the agency level. These orders did not, however, diminish management authority. Section 7 of the recognition order, E.O. 10988, confirmed the right of managers to hire, promote, retain, dismiss, transfer, and discipline employees. Much of the authority for administering the order and determining its contours remained with agency officials. In this sense, administrative authority at the agency level emerged strengthened rather than weakened by the orders.[16] Government officials designed these orders to impose standardization on union-agency relations, not to offer a radically new program for federal labor relations.

When personnel managers introduced human relations techniques and programs into the civil service in the late 1930s, they had hoped that this management school would preempt the need to accord workers these formal bargaining rights. At the time, human relations appeared to be a revolutionary new approach to labor-management conflict. It promised to create a new order in which employees "participated" in management. Through employee councils, suggestion systems, efficiency rating review boards, and grievance procedures, managers would canvass the views of union members without the need for a formal system of collective bargaining. In this manner, managers highlighted the participatory aspects of human relations as a democratic management program consistent with American political principles.[17]

According to public personnel administrators, human relations followed a middle road between mob rule, anarchy, and inefficiency on the one side and totalitarianism on the other. Uncomfortable with both rigid, hierarchical structures and loose, egalitarian ones, public personnel administrators suggested that human relations would promote leadership, individualism, and efficiency within the organization. The American bureaucracy, they maintained, could be effective without mimicking authoritarian forms. Davenport even suggested that human relations resolved productivity problems while simultaneously instilling working Americans with a sense of patriotism and citizenship. These feelings, he stressed in a speech in 1942, were necessary if Americans were to ward off external threats as the British and Chinese had been doing in fighting the Germans and Japanese. If workers felt tired, frustrated, and unjustly treated in the workplace, Davenport observed, they would not strive to be better citizens. To Davenport, human relations was a crucial cross beam linking work to citizenship.[18]

Accordingly, postwar research into human relations accelerated. An interdepartmental committee on employee motivation—including as members Kenneth Warner, then with the Office of Education; two employees of the Bureau of the Budget; one from the council's permanent staff; and Alexander Leighton, a human relations expert representing the Guggenheim Foundation—sought to "inject greater awareness of human relations into the work of the council and its committees." It was to do this primarily through research into the "fundamentals of human relations."[19] In response to the Civil Service Commission's proposed revisions to the efficiency rating appeal process in 1948, Davenport also urged on research, complaining that the "whole field" of employee performance appraisals rested on a "series of untested hypotheses and exchanges of opinions." "Comprehensive controlled experiments" or other scientific techniques, he suggested, should be used to determine the relationship between employee evaluations and motivation. This, he claimed, would "make a significant contribution to the whole approach to work improvement and human relations in the Federal Service."[20]

Davenport's retirement in 1953 and the demise of the council that same year did not dampen the federal managers' enthusiasm for human relations, even though Elton Mayo's writings came under increasing scholarly fire during the 1950s.[21] Francis Brassor, one of the first personnel managers appointed in the 1930s, remained active in government administration during the postwar era. In his capacity as a high-level administrator in the Civil Service Commission, he became a tireless advocate of human relations. Although many of its basic tenets remained the same, the liberal, welfare roots of this management school diminished at midcentury as managers chose to articulate its aims in more conservative terms.

Articles collected by Brassor and memoranda he distributed in the 1950s continued to reflect the notion that emotional instability contributed to low productivity. On the one hand, many assumed that cooperation and harmony represented a natural state of human existence and that "just as a cold is a mild form of upper respiratory disorder, so a temporary fit of anger or a day-long feeling of the 'blues' is a mild form of emotional disorder." Brassor described troubled employees as those who "cannot seem to cooperate & be pleasant." On the other hand, human relations experts suggested that supervisors, counselors, and personnel directors had to understand that employee emotions were often generated by radically different perceptions of work conditions or situations.[22]

This assertion did not lead human relations experts to adopt a form of cultural relativism. Rather, they maintained that with training, supervisors could discern the "reality" of the situation and use it to promote morale. In 1953, clinical psychologist Dr. Arthur Rautman, for example, detailed how a company changed tires on its wheelbarrows but soon received complaints that the wheelbarrows had become too difficult to push. Rather than switch back to the original tires, managers took the valve stems from them and attached them to the new tires. "Here," observed Rautman, "you changed the material things, fooled the workers, and got the results you wanted." Ultimately, management's perception of reality overrode labor's perception.[23]

Both the influx of women into the service and gendered notions of power contributed to the development of these new management theories and

programs in the postwar era. Human relations programs easily accommodated the presence of women in the workplace. An emphasis in human relations on worker behavior encouraged managers to examine the perceived
sources of behavior, including in this era one's sex. For example, according
to Rautman, men and women reacted differently to changes in room lighting. In one instance, he noted, male workers found that a new blue-green
light installed above their work stations reduced eye fatigue and increased
productivity. Female workers, however, complained and were absent more
frequently after the company installed the lights. Rautman reasoned that
although the lights reduced eye strain for all workers, it also "ruined" the
"appearance of the women's make-up" as the "blue-green light made them
look positively ghastly." Women, he concluded, were more "emotionally . . .
concerned about their physical appearance than about their eye strain!" Rautman and others like him easily incorporated gender stereotypes into human
relations management theory.[24]

Many advocates of the human relations school of management perceived
it as a more nurturing, "feminine" approach to labor relations. Both male and
female personnel workers championed this school as one that cared about
the welfare of workers and sought to understand their perspective. Many
stressed the need for personnel workers to resist siding with "the man who
pays their salary." These egalitarian ideals were often couched in feminine
terms. Rautman, for instance, likened morale to "the virtue of one's wife,"
because both "should be taken for granted." He went on to note that morale
"will not respond to your direct caress, nor come at your strident call. But
wherever you have democratic and sympathetic administration, wherever
you have men working cooperatively for a common ideal, there will you have
morale also—not like a guardian angel to protect either workers or management, but like a goddess of beauty to give point to the works of man."[25] In
this case, the personal, cooperative dimensions of human relations, especially
with respect to morale building, were categorized in feminine terms. Yet the
act of producing was reserved for "men." Just as female symbols such as
Columbia, or "republican mothers," protected the virtue of the nation, so
too would the "goddess of beauty" guide the "works of man." In this case,
though, the emphasis on physical beauty and appearance overshadowed the
powerful political messages associated with depictions of Columbia. Postwar
Americans accepted women's presence in the voting booth, the workforce
generally, and the civil service specifically, but few were ready to view human

relations techniques as a challenge to traditional gender categories or a sexual division of labor.

Although human relations was potentially progressive, it ultimately failed to produce a new gender or racial order in the federal bureaucracy. Brassor and others continually emphasized inclusion over exclusion. Supervisors, stated Brassor, should promote a "feeling of belonging to the organization and of being of value to it."[26] If applied to race relations, this attitude may have encouraged integration. Instead, human relations experts frequently stressed the contradictory and more conservative goal of supervisory adjustment to informal employee relations. Observing that "worker groups" often developed a "definite caste system, based upon the individual's standing among his fellows," Rautman recommended that the "wise personnel worker" recognize and respect these systems. Rautman did not define caste in racial terms, but others applied this principle in that manner.[27] Ironically, by doing so, personnel workers absolved themselves of responsibility for creating workplace culture. Their often passive role with respect to race relations did little to hasten equal employment opportunity, even in a "merit"-based civil service.

Ultimately, a renegotiation of the concept of merit rather than human relations ideals or the recognition of unions had the most potential to alter the course of equal employment opportunity in the civil service. With the rise of rights-based liberalism, progressive administrators and civil rights activists equated a single definition of merit with democracy. They rejected scientific racism and encouraged the employment of African Americans, as well as women, in the civil service. This rejection destabilized existing patterns of discrimination and encouraged a significant challenge to labor segmentation based upon gender and race. During the war, the government made some effort to recognize the sociocultural context of the labor market and to dictate that agencies remedy the workplace inequities that often resulted from social and cultural forces. But this ideological sea change failed to produce a significant redistribution of power in the workplace.

In part, this was because the debate over the meaning of merit was far from resolved. The new interpretation of a color-blind merit system evolved without a critical evaluation of what determined merit. While liberals objected to the use of skin color as a criterion for evaluation, they often supported an assessment of personality and character. But many people associated personality and character with race. This was reinforced in social science disciplines such as anthropology, which began to stress the study of American subcultures in the postwar era. Consequently, it became difficult for public administrators to untangle the relationship between merit and race discrimination. Moreover, attention to group categories, and efforts to interpret their construction, often implied that these categories were fixed and unyielding. Accordingly, when explaining "difference," social scientists replaced biological forces with equally powerful social and cultural forces; these abstract forces often obscured the mechanisms and location through which institutions and administrators exercised power.

Within the civil service, departmental administrators shifted between two paradigms of evaluation. At times they employed a set of assessment criteria associated with a utilitarian and capitalist vision of merit. Performance and output, therefore, informed their hiring, firing, and promotion decisions. Ideally then, this merit system ignored a servant's gender and race, although as we have seen, these categories could easily be incorporated into evaluation standards. At other times, however, government managers perceived a broader mission for the federal bureaucracy. As an institution, the government's administrative arm both received and generated political objectives, such as a desire to promote social justice. Hence, a group of reform-minded public administrators, sensitive to gender and racial inequalities, constructed new management programs and policies to eliminate discriminatory practices. What is critical, however, is that as a whole, the federal bureaucracy embraced both of these assessment paradigms, often simultaneously. Government administrators adhered to one or the other depending upon their personal viewpoint or departmental traditions and culture. Others, however, frequently shifted between these two paradigms, uncertain as to how to bridge them.

World War II provided them with a temporary bridge. In the midst of the wartime labor shortage, capitalist motives concerning output and performance expressed themselves in an egalitarian manner. Marketplace demands encouraged administrators to hire and promote people who had previously not had equal access to decent jobs—people such as women and African Americans. But with the exception of a small group of committed liberals devoted to social justice, administrators did not perceive the hiring and promotion of women and African Americans as a statement of their opposition to discrimination.

Other problems contributed to the perseverance of discrimination. A declining faith in civic engagement as the basis for liberalism accompanied the rise of rights-based liberalism. The new emphasis on individual rights, in particular, discouraged collectivism, especially collectivism rooted in class.[28] Postwar liberals, hence, developed fair employment procedures that relied on a case-by-case assault on discrimination. According to public administrators, only individuals committed discrimination, and only individuals suffered from it. Few addressed structural deficiencies, such as class inequities born of economic and cultural forces, and few discussed the need for a rejuvenation of civic culture. By the 1950s, Davenport's identification of work with citizenship, which harkened back to a producer-oriented culture, faded from view. Strained employee relations within the service along with the consumer aspirations of postwar workers turned government work into a job rather than a public service. Increasingly, the "bureaucrat," much like the "overpaid" assembly worker, became an object of derision in America; postwar bureaucrats were not worthy of praise but of scorn.

In crucial respects, however, Davenport's 1942 speech anticipated postwar cultural developments. His emphasis on the personal fulfillment of workers was later echoed in New Left and counterculture ideologies. Women's rights groups and the Students for a Democratic Society, for instance, championed career fulfillment as a key to self-actualization. Human relations advocates' utilization of psychology and attention to an individual's emotional health found expression as well in the postwar boom in psychotherapy. Hence, human relations reintegrated the personal into the workplace.

Twentieth-century labor relations within the government reflected the tensions between capitalist and democratic values. While some federal officials emphasized efficiency, others stressed equality of opportunity and employment security. Proponents of these viewpoints often openly clashed over values, but at times, they also tended to slide between these two systems of thought. More critically, those who stressed efficiency often failed to perceive the ways in which the measurements for performance reflected deeply entrenched racial and gender biases.

At certain points, as in the early twentieth century, the state mimicked private-sector labor relations, and at other moments, as in the World War II era, the state asserted its own political agenda. It acted as an innovative and model employer, emphasizing its power as it regulated personnel policies in private firms.[29] Liberalism and the influx of women and African Americans into the service created new opportunities for democratic management styles and the extension of citizenship rights. But while the intellectual context for labor relations shifted as a result of these trends, a hierarchical management structure remained in place. The advent of the Cold War and the growing influence of more conservative political ideals weakened democratic management styles. Ultimately, state authority helped reproduce gender and racial inequalities within the civil service and, by extension, in society.

As in the private sector, authority remained deeply fragmented in the public sector, and hence there was little centralized or long-term planning for the civil service. Nonetheless, throughout Davenport's thirteen-year tenure as head of the Council of Personnel Administration (later the Federal Personnel Council), he had led personnel directors in an intense effort to gain full control over the government's sprawling civil service. Their views and actions profoundly informed the shape of the service at midcentury.

In the eighty years since the government had begun the shift from a patronage to a merit-based civil service system, the personnel system had not accorded more power to low-level government workers. Administrative reformers had promised that the merit system would protect government workers from the arbitrary authority of politicians. They promised workers that the merit system would award promotions and pay raises to those of proven ability, thus eliminating personal favoritism—which characterized nineteenth-century patronage—from personnel decision making. A merit system, they asserted, was inherently based upon objective, impersonal systems of evaluation. But when reformers traded patronage for merit, they did not eliminate the authority of managers to make employment decisions. Instead, they simply changed the location of the employee-management struggle from the legislative to the executive branch, where agency officials, rather than elected officials, determined the definition of merit. As we have seen, merit became a concept constructed and contested along class, gender, and racial lines.

Federal managers helped promote pluralism as a positive value in American society. Many advocated for the rights of women and African Americans, supporting their hiring and promotion within the civil service. New management theories and practices often reinforced the connection between pluralism and liberalism, allowing lower-level employees, many of whom were women and minorities, to challenge their subordination. Indeed, the struggle over union recognition was itself a dramatic symbol of the shift that was taking place in power relationships during the late 1950s and 1960s.

Despite this acceptance of pluralism, administrators reinscribed rather than transformed hierarchical power structures within the federal government. Into the 1950s and 1960s, Americans therefore continued to wrestle over the tension between bureaucratic structures and democratic values. Rather than fully engage in a structural and institutional overhaul of the federal civil service, however, federal officials chose to use management strategies, such as human relations, to promote pluralism. These efforts to personalize management were themselves a reflection of the escalating debate over the meaning of individualism and equality in a pluralistic society dominated by large organizations. Subsequent social and political movements would alter the terms but not the substance of that debate.

NOTES

Abbreviations

ACC.	Accession
AFGE	American Federation of Government Employees
AFL	American Federation of Labor
AHC	American Heritage Center
BIA	Brookings Institution Archives
CIO	Congress of Industrial Organizations
CPA	Council of Personnel Administration
CSC	Civil Service Commission
ERC	Employee Relations Committee
FDRL	Franklin D. Roosevelt Library
FEB	Fair Employment Board
FEPC	Fair Employment Practices Committee
FM & CS	Federal Mediation and Conciliation Service
FPC	Federal Personnel Council
GMLA	George Meany Labor Archives
HSTL	Harry S. Truman Library
LC Mss.	Library of Congress Manuscript Division
NAACP	National Association for the Advancement of Colored People
NARA	National Archives and Records Administration
NCSL	National Civil Service League
NCSRL	National Civil Service Reform League
NFFE	National Federation of Federal Employees
NIPA	National Institute of Public Affairs
NLRB	National Labor Relations Board
NRA	National Recovery Administration
OF	Official files
OPA	Office of Price Administration
OPML	Office of Personnel Management Library
RG	Record Group
SUA	Syracuse University Archives
UFWA	United Federal Workers of America
UPWA	United Public Workers of America
WHCF	White House Central File

Introduction

1 Johnson, "The Administrative Career of Dr. W. W. Stockberger," 50–64, quotes from 62, 61 respectively. See also MacMahon and Millett, *Federal Administrators*, 47–49.

2 Scott et al. to FDR, 5/4/33, OF 93 Colored Matters (Negroes) 1933, FDRL; FDR to J. Roosevelt, 3/13/37, OF 4 Government Printing Office, 1937–42, FDRL.

3 S. Herrell, Memo to Chiefs of Bureaus and Offices, 7/9/42, RG 16, Office of Secretary, Box 689, Personnel, Mar. 7 to Aug. 31, NARA; Minutes of staff conference, 5/20/43, Work Improvement Program, Papers of William McReynolds, Box 6, CSC-CPA Training Committee, 1941–44, FDRL; Minutes of staff conference, 3/12/43, U.S. Civil Service Committee, McReynolds Papers, Box 3, Committee on Admin. Personnel—II, FDRL.

4 Perkins to Smith, 4/28/41, RG 174, Sec. of Labor, Box 1, Administrative—Robt. Smith, Dir. of Personnel, 4/28/41, NARA; *Washington Post*, 3/16/39; Report on the manpower situation in the Department of State, Dec. 31, 1942, McReynolds Papers, State Dept., 1941–45, FDRL.

5 Census Bureau, *Historical Statistics of the United States*, 1102–3.

6 *New York Times*, 11/15/91.

7 Ibid.

8 *Los Angeles Times*, 8/11/89; *Washington Post*, 2/12/92.

9 Brinkley, *End of Reform*, 165–66.

10 E. Coit, Philadelphia Federal Council of Personnel Admin., "Causes of Unrest among Federal Employees," 5/31/45, RG 146, Council Files, 1938–54, Prior to 1944, Box 9, Employee Relations (Gen'l), 1945, NARA. Rights-based liberalism is discussed in Brinkley, *End of Reform*, 10–11, 164–70; Lichtenstein, "Epilogue: Toward a New Century," in Lichtenstein and Harris, eds., *Industrial Democracy in America*, 275–83.

11 Young, *Rise of Meritocracy*; Lemann, *The Big Test*, 117.

12 Smith, *The Culture of Merit*, 21–39, 65–81.

13 Ibid., 34, 123–79, 216–29, quotes from 34, 171.

14 Silberman, *Cages of Reason*, 91–92, 114–16; Vaughan, "The Grandes Écoles," 74–75, 78.

15 National Civil Service Reform League, *The Civil Service in Modern Government*, 37; I. Jennings, "The Achievement of British Bureaucracy," in Dalby and Werthman, eds., *Bureaucracy in Historical Perspective*, 22–27; O'Malley, *The Indian Civil Service*, 238–56; Chester, *English Administrative System*, 157–61; Silberman, *Cages of Reason*, 289, 293, 313–14, 326–31.

16 While the European and American adoption of exams to determine fitness for public service was essentially a nineteenth-century phenomenon, the Chinese had established training schools and merit ratings for government officials un-

der the Han dynasty (206 B.C. to 220 A.D.). See, for instance, E. A. Kracke Jr., "Bureaucratic Recruitment and Advancement in Imperial China," in Dalby and Werthman, eds., *Bureaucracy in Historical Perspective*, 34–39; Miyazaki, *China's Examination Hell*, 16.

17 Silberman, *Cages of Reason*, 91, 136–40, quote from 91; Sutherland, *Ability, Merit and Measurement*, 98–99.

18 Chester, *English Administrative System*, 159–60. At various times, Chinese officials required that candidates have sponsors or individuals vouch for the reputation of the family. They also rated a variety of personal characteristics of potential mandarins and inquired about their physical appearance. Kracke, "Bureaucratic Recruitment and Advancement in Imperial China," 35–37; Miyazaki, *China's Examination Hell*, 19, 74.

19 Fish, *The Civil Service and Patronage*, 1–13.

20 Emerson, "Aristocracy," 958–59; Lemann, *The Big Test*, 43, 45.

21 Emerson, "Aristocracy," 959–65.

22 Ibid., 961.

23 Lemann, *The Big Test*, 50–52.

24 Haney and Hurtado, "The Jurisprudence of Race and Meritocracy."

25 Van Riper, *History of the United States Civil Service*, 307.

26 Aron, *Ladies and Gentlemen of the Civil Service*, 139–50, 160–61.

27 *Washington Post*, 3/16/39.

28 Van Riper, *History of the United States Civil Service*, 100–101, 144, 207; on affirmative action and various forms of preference, see Horne, "Reversing Discrimination," 7–14.

29 Brown, *Definition of a Profession*, 42.

30 Mumby, *Communication and Power in Organizations*, 91–94.

31 Weber, *The Theory of Social and Economic Organization*, 328–63. For a critique of Talcott Parsons's interpretation of Weber see Mumby, *Communication and Power in Organizations*, 1–4.

32 Ferguson, *The Feminist Case against Bureaucracy*, 5, 7, 27. For an additional gendered perspective on large organizations see Witz and Savage, "The Gender of Organizations," in Witz and Savage, eds., *Gender and Bureaucracy*; Kanter, *Men and Women of the Corporation*.

33 Aron, *Ladies and Gentlemen of the Civil Service*, 25–39; Zunz, *Making America Corporate*, 39.

34 Baker, "The Domestication of Politics," 628n; Stivers, *Gender Images in Public Administration*, 109–13.

35 Green, *Secret City*, 158–59; Hayes, *The Negro Federal Government Worker*, 23.

36 Douglass, *Frederick Douglass*, 683–84.

37 Lynch, *The Facts of Reconstruction*, v–lvi, 240–42, 275.

38 Green, *Secret City*, 165–66.

39 King, *Separate and Unequal*, 16, 40, 48.

40 Yinger, *Ethnicity*, 41.

41 Ibid.

42 *Washington Evening Star*, 4/10/35.

43 Ibid.

44 For a theoretical explanation of the emergence of formal personnel systems, particularly in the private sector, see Sanford Jacoby, "Masters to Managers: An Introduction," and Walter Licht, "Studying Work: Personnel Policies in Philadelphia Firms, 1850–1950" both in Jacoby, ed., *Masters to Managers*. For works emphasizing the importance of labor unrest and unionization in explaining the emergence of formal personnel rules, see Lescohier and Brandeis, *History of Labour in the United States, 1896–1932*, 323–35; Montgomery, *The Fall of the House of Labor*, 236–44.

45 Waring, *Taylorism Transformed*, 6. Additional scholarship that provides excellent analysis of twentieth-century managers, their ideology, and their policies includes Gillespie, *Manufacturing Knowledge*; Zunz, *Making America Corporate*; and Jacoby, *Employing Bureaucracy*.

46 This is a form of what William Graebner has identified as "democratic social engineering." Graebner, *Engineering of Consent*, 3–6.

47 Mosher, *Democracy and the Public Service*.

48 Weber, *Economy and Society*, 212–26, 956–75, 978–80, 987–1005, quote from 975.

49 Silberman, *Cages of Reason*, 313–14.

1 Scientific Administration of the Civil Service Prior to the New Deal

1 Trachtenberg, *The Incorporation of America*, 163.

2 Van Riper, *History of the United States Civil Service*, 98–110.

3 Bederman, *Manliness and Civilization*, 17–25.

4 Stivers, *Gender Images in Public Administration*, 103–4; 109–12; Bederman, *Manliness and Civilization*, 15, 25.

5 Bederman, *Manliness and Civilization*, 198; Dyer, *Theodore Roosevelt*, 97.

6 Murphy, Reconstructing the Nation, 170–71, 256.

7 Murphy, Reconstructing the Nation, 130–32; see also Bederman, *Manliness and Civilization*, 123–24.

8 On debates over citizenship and national identity during the late nineteenth and early twentieth centuries, see Smith, *Civic Ideals*, chapters 11 and 12; Murphy, Reconstructing the Nation, 7–9, 76–91.

9 Higham, *Strangers in the Land*, 117–23, 131–57, 183, 205–18, 237–43; Bederman, *Manliness and Civilization*, 199–200.

10 Wilson, "The Study of Administration," 481, 493–94; Goodnow, *Politics and*

Administration, 17–27, 25–39, 44–46, 72–132; Henry, "The Emergence of Public Administration as a Field of Study," 39–42.

11 Trachtenberg, *The Incorporation of America*, 163–64.

12 Ross, *The Origins of American Social Science*, 276; Ingraham, *Foundation of Merit*, 7–8; Furner, *Advocacy and Objectivity*, 278–81, 287–89.

13 Van Riper, *History of the United States Civil Service*, 141, 178–79, quote from 141.

14 Aron, *Ladies and Gentlemen of the Civil Service*, 106; Skowronek, *Building a New American State*, 177–211; Dodd and Schott, *Congress and the Administrative State*, 23–29, 38–42.

15 Goodnow, *Politics and Administration*, 85.

16 The Rockefeller Foundation also supported the Institute for Government Research and, in the 1930s, the National Institute of Public Affairs. Dahlberg, *The New York Bureau of Municipal Research*; Kahn, *Budgeting Democracy*, 4, 29–58.

17 "An Institute for Government Research," 5/1/15, Governmental Studies–Institute for Government Research, Official Papers, 1915–35, BIA. See also Critchlow, *The Brookings Institution*, 24–40; Kahn, *Budgeting Democracy*.

18 Avery to Goodnow, 11/5/15, Governmental Studies–Institute for Government Research, Correspondence of Chair of Board, F. J. Goodnow, Nov. 1915–June 1916, BIA.

19 Critchlow, *The Brookings Institution*, 21–24.

20 Susman, *Culture as History*, 273–74, 280. For a contemporary example, see Theodore Roosevelt, "Character and Civilization," *Outlook* 105 (Nov. 8, 1913): 526–28.

21 Susman, *Culture as History*, 271–85.

22 As quoted by Critchlow, *The Brookings Institution*, 36.

23 Ingraham, *Foundation of Merit*, 27; Titlow, *Americans Import Merit*, 204, 207–8, 305–10; Leupp, *How to Prepare for a Civil Service Examination*, 1, 10–17, 11–14, 45–54, 333.

24 Leupp, *How to Prepare for a Civil Service Examination*, 55–296; "Personality as a Test for Public Service," *Survey* 35 (Oct. 2, 1915): 3.

25 Smith, *Civic Ideals*, 414–15.

26 Schinagl, *History of Efficiency Ratings in the Federal Government*, 18–40. Some agencies were more analogous to business organizations than others. The functions of the Post Office (mail service) and Treasury (currency production) departments, for example, could more easily be compared to manufacturing concerns than could the activities of the Interior or Agriculture departments.

27 Jacoby, *Employing Bureaucracy*, 140–42; Noble, *America by Design*, 298–99.

28 Noble, *America by Design*, 207–8; Alchon, *The Invisible Hand of Planning*, 43; Brown, *Definition of a Profession*, 106–12.

29 Lynch, "Walter Dill Scott,"160–63; Brown, *Definition of a Profession*, 109–12; Jacoby, *Employing Bureaucracy*, 144–47; Noble, *America by Design*, 221, 298–99.

30 Brown, *Definition of a Profession*, 38–40, 127–30.

31 White, *Trends in Public Administration*, 247. To tighten commission administration of these functions, Lewis Meriam of the Brookings Institution (formerly the Institute for Government Research) suggested a substantial reorganization of the U.S. Civil Service Commission in 1933. (The Bureau of Efficiency had been dissolved and its duties transferred to the commission in 1932.) McMillen and Mitchell to Roosevelt, 7/10/33; Meriam to Civil Service Commissioners, 7/7/33, and attachments, both in OF 2, Civil Service Commission, Jul.–Dec. 1933, FDRL.

32 Van Riper, *History of the United States Civil Service*, 222–23; Skowronek, *Building a New American State*, 182–85; MacMahon and Millett, *Federal Administrators*, 79.

33 Skowronek, *Building a New American State*, 186–94; Mansfield, "Reorganizing the Federal Executive Branch," 475–78; Arnold, *Making the Managerial Presidency*, 42–48.

34 White, *Trends in Public Administration*, 246–47.

35 Van Riper, *History of the United States Civil Service*, 144–49, 151–53, 248; Skowronek, *Building a New American State*, 188–89, 197–98; MacMahon and Millett, *Federal Administrators*, 16–27. On management practices in the Gilded Age civil service, see Aron, *Ladies and Gentlemen of the Civil Service*, 96–135.

36 Stockberger, *Personnel Administration Development*, 135; MacMahon and Millett, *Federal Administrators*, 32–35.

37 *Federal Employee* 24 (Mar. 1940); Spero, *Government as Employer*, 168–80; Johnson, "General Unions," 24–28. (Trade newsletters such as the *Federal Employee* are here cited the same way as newspapers, with names and identifying dates.)

38 Mayers, *The Federal Service*, 548; Spero, *The Labor Movement in a Government Industry*, 96–97, 113.

39 Spero, *The Labor Movement in a Government Industry*, 138–39.

40 Ibid., 143–46. The 1909 French postal strike caused great consternation and engendered much debate among National Civil Service League Reform members. Secretary to Gutterson, 2/3/16, Papers of the National Civil Service Reform League (NCSRL), Acc. 7947, Box 20, Organization of Employees Leagues Law Committee, AHC.

41 Proceedings of the Convention of the National League of Government Employees, January 8–14, 1912, Civil Service Commission Historical Collection, OPML; Aiken, *Taylorism at Watertown Arsenal*, 227–36; Spero, *Government as Employer*, 96–97; Mayers, *The Federal Service*, 551.

42 Spero, *Government as Employer*, 141–43; Skowronek, *Building a New American State*, 191–94.

43 Secretary to Gutterson, 2/3/16, NCSRL, Acc. 7947, Box 20, Organization of
   Employees Leagues Law Committee, 1916, AHC.

44 Meeting of Special Committee to Consider Organization of Employees, 2/7/16;
   see also Secretary to Gutterson, 2/3/16, both in NCSRL, Acc. 7947, Box 20,
   Organization of Employees Leagues Law Committee, 1916, AHC.

45 Stewart, *The National Civil Service Reform League*, 106–7; Stivers, *Gender Images in Public Administration*, 109–13; Baker, "The Domestication of Politics,"
   628n.

46 Stivers, *Gender Images in Public Administration*, 117.

47 Furner, *Advocacy and Objectivity*, 287–89. On the faith in evolution see Smith,
   Civic Ideals, 349–50, and Murphy, Reconstructing the Nation, 21, 27.

48 Stockberger, *Personnel Administration Development*, 41; Aron, *Ladies and Gentlemen of the Civil Service*, 50–55.

49 Van Riper, *History of the United States Civil Service*, 159; Aron, *Ladies and Gentlemen of the Civil Service*, 82–86, 93, 125.

50 In 1880, women in the departmental service (Washington, D.C.) made up approximately 22% of all workers; in 1893, 32%, and in 1903, 27%. Aron, *Ladies and Gentlemen of the Civil Service*, 5. In 1904, women made up 7.5% of all government workers (workers in the field and departmental services). Van Riper,
   History of the United States Civil Service, 160.

51 Aron, *Ladies and Gentlemen of the Civil Service*, 124.

52 Van Riper, *History of the United States Civil Service*, 160.

53 *Federal Employee* 19 (Apr. 1934); MacMahon and Millett, *Federal Administrators*, 342–43. McNally quickly became a force in NFFE, and in 1925 became its
   secretary-treasurer, a post she held until 1953.

54 Van Riper, *History of the United States Civil Service*, 260.

55 Alchon, "Mary van Kleeck and Social-Economic Planning," *Journal of Policy History*, 1–9; Greenwald, *Women, War and Work*, 73–75. Van Kleeck's participation
   was particularly noteworthy as she, along with Mary Anderson of the Department of Labor, demonstrated the political contributions women were making
   to social reform issues, including the plight of female industrial workers. Van
   Kleeck pioneered in personnel management, arguing that better management
   would ameliorate the harsh conditions under which women worked.

56 *Federal Employee* 16 (Apr. 1931).

57 Mayers, *The Federal Service*, 357. Avice Marion Saint, "Women in the Public
   Service, 4—The Federal Service of the United States," *Public Personnel Studies*
   9 (Jan.–Feb. 1931): 14–19.

58 Strom, *Beyond the Typewriter*, 138–39.

59 Avice Marion Saint, "Women in the Public Service, 1—A General Survey,"
   Public Personnel Studies 8 (Apr. 1930): 53.

60 Krislov, *The Negro in the Federal Employment*, 19; Green, *Secret City*, 129; Gate-

wood, *Aristocrats of Color*, 64; Aron *Ladies and Gentlemen of the Civil Service*, 30; King, *Separate and Unequal*, 45–46.

61 The 1891 estimate is taken from Green, *Secret City*, 129–30, 159, and the 1892 estimate from Gatewood, *Aristocrats of Color*, 64. The latter number appears to have been obtained from Hayes, *The Negro Federal Government Worker*.

62 Van Riper, *History of the United States Civil Service*, 161–62; Krislov, *The Negro in Federal Employment*, 19–20. The NCSRL's newsletter *Good Government* estimated the number of African-American civil servants in Washington, D.C., at one in nine. *Good Government* 25 (Sept. 1908).

63 Green, *Secret City*, 156–59; *Washington Bee*, 1/21/05, 2/11/05.

64 Green, *Secret City*, 157–58. On discrimination under the Taft Administration, see also *Washington Bee*, 4/27/12, 5/7/12.

65 King, *Separate and Unequal*, 51–57; Green, *Secret City*, 159, 166–67.

66 Dyer, *Theodore Roosevelt*, 97–99.

67 Brown, *Definition of a Profession*, 45.

68 Krislov, *The Negro in Federal Employment*, 18.

69 Apparently fearful of a backlash, black civil servants refrained from vigorous protest. Green, *Secret City*, 171–75.

70 Krislov, *The Negro in Federal Employment*, 20–21; Green, *Secret City*, 175.

71 Krislov, *The Negro in Federal Employment*, 21.

72 Critchlow, *The Brookings Institution*, 36–37; Skowronek, *Building a New American State*, 206, 208; Van Riper, *History of the United States Civil Service*, 298–300; Ismar Baruch, *History of Position Classification and Salary Standardization in the Federal Service, 1789–1941*, P.C.D. Manual No. A–2, U.S. Civil Service Commission, Personnel Classification Division, OPML 1941.

73 Baruch, *History of Position Classification*, 50.

74 U.S. Senate, Committee on Appropriations, *Hearings before the Subcommittee of the Committee on Appropriations on H.R. 8928, Reclassification of Salaries*, 1922, 67th Cong., 2d and 4th sess., 91–95, 116–17.

75 Stewart, *The National Civil Service Reform League*, 224–25; Van Riper, *History of the United States Civil Service*, 273–77; Skowronek, *Building a New American State*, 204–9.

76 Employees had not always supported uniform procedures. See Aron, *Ladies and Gentlemen of the Civil Service*, 106–15, 120–35.

77 "Women in Political Affairs," n.d. (circa 1920s), Papers of Frederick M. Davenport, Box 41, Writings, Speeches, T–Z, SUA.

78 Mayers, *The Federal Service*, 356–57. On women, see also Saint, "Women in the Public Service, 1—A General Survey," 52, and Helen H. Gardener, "Status of Women in the Civil Service," *Proceedings at the Fortieth Annual Meeting of the National Civil Service Reform League*, 4/14/21 (New York: National Civil Service Reform League, 1921), 52–60.

79 Feldman, *A Personnel Program for the Federal Civil Service*, a report transmitted to the House Committee on the Civil Service, 71st Cong., 3d sess., 1931, House Document no. 773, 238–39.

80 In some post offices, the percentage of blacks rose to between 15% and 20%. Krislov, *The Negro in Federal Employment*, 22.

81 Bradbury, Racial Discrimination in the Federal Service, 32–34, 120–21, quote from 124.

82 "Some Trends in Public Personnel Administration," *Public Personnel Studies* 7 (Nov. 1929): 151–52, 157.

83 Murphy, Reconstructing the Nation, 43.

84 Brown, *Definition of a Profession*, 101–2; Tichi, *Shifting Gears*, 55–63.

2 Building the New Deal Civil Service

1 "On Teaching a Method of Government," 8/30/35, Papers of the National Civil Service Reform League (NCSRL), Acc. 7947, Box 70, (6700) Committee to Educate the Public as to the Practical Value of the Merit System 1935, AHC.

2 Leffingwell to Burlingham, 5/25/36, NCSRL, Acc. 7947, Box 86, 1936 Misc. Correspondence, A to M, AHC.

3 Morgenthau to Gulick, 1/16/34, RG 56, Office of Secretary, Box 90, Personnel (General), 1933–56, NARA; Commissioner to FDR, 10/17/34, Papers of Frederick Davenport, NIPA Correspondence, Box 18, Oct. 1935, SUA. That concern with recruiting the best "men" was reiterated in the commission's final report. *Federal Employee* 20 (Feb. 1935).

4 "Union Activities," *Personnel Administration* 1 (Mar. 1939): 9; Van Riper, *History of the United States Civil Service*, 326–32; Collier to Davenport, 7/12/38, Davenport Papers, NIPA Correspondence, Box 8, Jul.–Dec. 1938, SUA; *Washington Post*, 5/29/38.

5 *Washington Post*, 2/15/39.

6 Steward to Rhudy, 4/8/37, Acc. 7947, Box 91, (5000.2) National Federation of Federal Employees, 1937, AHC.

7 See, for example, Kirby, *Black Americans in the Roosevelt Era*, 106–51; Leuchtenburg, *Franklin D. Roosevelt and the New Deal*, 186–87; S. Ware, "Women and the New Deal," in Sitkoff, ed., *Fifty Years Later*, 115–22; interview with Isabelle Gichner by Suzanne Helfand, 7/30/80, Jewish Historical Society of Greater Washington Oral History Project, copy in Martin Luther King Library, Washington, D.C., 9–11, 25–26.

8 A. Lawson, "The Cultural Legacy of the New Deal" in Sitkoff, ed., *Fifty Years Later*, 156.

9 See, for example, Harris to Elliot et al., 4/28/36, President's Committee on Administrative Management, Box 22, A-II-22, FDRL.

10 *Washington Post*, 3/12/39.

11 On the establishment and findings of the Reed committee, see Cummings to FDR, 1/4/37; Emmerich, "Integrating Federal Personnel Services with Operations," n.d., EXII-3; Brookings Institution, Investigation of Executive Agencies of the Government, Report to the Select Committee to Investigate Executive Agencies of the Government, Report on Government Activities in the Field of Public Personnel, n.d., EIV, all in President's Committee on Administrative Management, Box 11, FDRL.

12 Mitchell telephone call, 1/2/39, OF 2, Civil Service Commission, Jan.–May 1939, FDRL; Baker to Davenport, 7/29/40, Davenport Papers, NIPA Correspondence, Box 23, July–Sept. 1940, SUA.

13 Miller to Smith, 2/19/40, Davenport Papers, NIPA Correspondence, Box 23, Jan.–March 1940, SUA; *Washington Evening Star*, 11/9/35.

14 *Washington Post*, 3/5/39.

15 82nd Council Meeting, 12/12/40, RG 146, FPC Meetings, Box 9, NARA. Piozet was responding to a suggestion that unskilled laborers be segregated in a separate service.

16 Silberman, *Cages of Reason*, 291–93. Members of the President's Committee on Administrative Management, headed by Louis Brownlow, spent a significant amount of time examining the British public service and also traveled to France and Germany. Davis, *FDR: Into the Storm*, 25; Davenport to Brownlow, 10/21/37, Davenport Papers, NIPA Correspondence, Box 8, Aug.–Dec. 1937, and Brownlow, "Public Administration," 9/26/36, NIPA Subject File, Box 36, Lectures, both in SUA.

17 See, for instance, Scott, "One Woman's Experience of World War II."

18 Nienburg to Hyde, 9/11/41, RG 86, Women's Bureau Bulletins, 1918–63, Box 524, #181–182, NARA.

19 Workers may not have perceived the need for unions, because as Aron pointed out, the development of rules did not prevent employees from negotiating with their supervisors over issues such as hours and leave. That style of negotiation eroded between the 1910s and 1930s. Aron, *Ladies and Gentlemen of the Civil Service*, 115–35.

20 Spero, *Government as Employer*, 17, 141–43; Spero, *The Labor Movement in a Government Industry*, 171–73; Aron, *Ladies and Gentlemen of the Civil Service*, 13–61, 158–60.

21 "The National Federation of Federal Employees, Twentieth Anniversary: Our Organization," 1937, NCSRL, Acc. 7947, Box 91, National Federation of Federal Employees, 1937, AHC.

22 NFFE's commitment to the extension of the merit-based classification system over the objection of unclassified laborers and the AFL executive council precipitated NFFE's break with the AFL. By a vote of 16,335 to 11,406, the rank

and file agreed to become an independent union. Attentive to the close vote, the AFL took the unusual step of setting up a parallel union, the AFGE in 1932. Spero, *Government as Employer*, 188–92; Nesbitt, *Labor Relations*, 65–69; Johnson, "General Unions," 28–31; Nevin and Nevin, *AFGE Federal Union*; and *Federal Employee* 16 (Nov. 1931) and 17 (Oct. 1932).

23 Nesbitt, *Labor Relations*, 68.

24 Johnson "General Unions," 31; Nesbitt, *Labor Relations*, 69.

25 *Federal Employee* 18 (Apr. 1933; Aug. 1933); NFFE, "Summary of Proceedings of the 12th Convention," September 4–7, 1933, Micro 37, Reel 125, Proceedings, GMLA.

26 *Government Standard*, 1 (Mar. 9, 1934); *Postal Record* (National Association of Letter Carriers) 48 (Apr. 1935). Steward made the same remarks concerning consumption in 1933. NFFE, "Summary of Proceedings of the 12th Convention," September 4–7, 1933, Micro 37, Reel 125, Proceedings, GMLA.

27 McReynolds to Babcock, 1/2/34; McReynolds to Babcock, 1/9/34, both in RG 56, Office of Secretary, Box 90, Personnel (General), 1933–56, NARA.

28 Donovan's career and case were reconstructed from the following documents: "Memorandum for the Board Re: Donovan Case," n.d.; NLRB, "Arbitration, Case No. 39," 8/21/34; NLRB Hearing, 8/10/34, all in RG 25, NLRB Case No. 39, New Series, Donovan, John, L., Washington, D.C., NARA (hereafter cited together as Case 39).

29 Ibid.

30 Ibid.

31 Ibid. Dr. Leo Wolman, chairman of the Labor Advisory Board, along with Peck, had been very critical of Donovan's work on the labor provisions of the paper and paper pulp code. *Washington Evening Star*, 8/10/34.

32 NLRB, "Arbitration, Case No. 39," 8/21/34, Case 39; *Washington Evening Star*, 8/10/34.

33 Rhine and Stabler to FDR, 6/19/34, OF 1094, Donovan, John L., FDRL; Johnson to NLRB, 8/11/34, Case 39.

34 Babcock to Wagner, 6/27/34, Case 39. The National Labor Board (NLB) had initially declined to hear the case, claiming it had no jurisdiction over federal employees. Although the NLRB heard the Donovan case, it later agreed with its predecessor, the NLB, that it had no jurisdiction over federal employees.

35 In the 1930s, Agriculture Department administrative assistant Paul Appleby advocated a similar "open-door" policy whereby employees brought complaints at any time to the agency head. But he also recognized the difficulty of this approach: "with the numbers of unions growing," he explained, "[each] demanding and needing administrative time, the physical problem becomes a most considerable one." A more formal procedure, however, was out of the question. He said the suggestion that arbitration committees hear employee

complaints was an "absurd" abrogation of the secretary's authority, noting that it was "asking too much of human nature, to ask executives invariably not to discriminate against employees for making complaints. There are instances in which employees should be fired for making complaints." Appleby to Rhine, 7/31/37, Box 2450, Agriculture Department Employees; Appleby to Baldwin, 2/16/37, Box 2606, Personnel [Jan.–July], [3 of 3], both in RG 16, Office of Secretary, NARA.

36 E. A. Symmes, Henry Rhine, John Donovan, Margaret Stabler, et al., "Affidavit of NRA Lodge No. 91, AFGE," 8/10/34, Case 39.

37 One union sent a resolution to Secretary of Labor Frances Perkins stating that the dismissal of Donovan "raises serious doubts in the minds of organized labor in the Recovery Administrator's attitude toward AGGRESSIVE labor unions" and called on Johnson to refrain from further participation in strike settlements until he agreed to have Donovan's case settled by the NLRB. Mills to Perkins, 8/13/34, Case 39.

38 "Memorandum for the Board Re: Donovan Case," n.d.; Donovan to NLRB, 8/11/34, both in Case 39; *Washington Evening Star*, 8/10/34; FDR to Nye, 6/28/34, OF 1094, Donovan, John L., 1934, FDRL. It appears that Roosevelt asked Johnson to draft this letter to Congressman Nye; nevertheless, it went out over the president's signature, indicating his approval.

39 *Government Standard* 3 (June 22, 1934).

40 *Government Standard* 3 (June 29, 1934).

41 Babcock had this proclamation printed on the masthead of the *Government Standard*. "Constitution of the American Federation of Government Employees," *Government Standard*, 11/5/37, copy in NCSRL, Acc. 7947, Box 265, Constitutions of Public Employee Organizations, AHC; Spero, *Government as Employer*, 193. The relationship between Lodge No. 91 and AFGE's national officers deteriorated in 1935. The national organization was especially critical of the lodge's methods of agitation concerning excessive and uncompensated overtime at the NRA. *Washington Evening Star*, 4/18/35, 4/19/35, 9/19/35.

42 Several federal employee unions tested the limits of public service restrictions on their rights. In September 1936, clerks in the Inland Waterways Corporation joined longshoremen unions and stopped work at the St. Louis terminal over wages and use of non-union workers. Local AFGE president Nicholas Fillo told the president that the experience at the barge lines was "exactly opposite to the New Deal views you expressed on Labor Day." This strike was arbitrated by the Federal Conciliation Service. Fillo to Perkins, 6/7/36; White to Kerwin, 6/24/36; Fillo to FDR, 9/10/36; White to Kerwin, 9/26/36 and White to Kerwin, 11/9/36, all in RG 280, FM & CS, 182–1077, Federal Barge Lines, NARA.

43 UFWA, *The History and Structure of the United Federal Workers of America CIO*; *Organizer* (Jan.–Feb. 1937), copy in Box 2450, Agriculture Department

Employees; *Organizer* (June 1937), copy in Box 2606, Personnel [Jan.–July] [1 of 3], both in RG 16, Office of Secretary, NARA.

44 *Organizer* (Jan.–Feb., 1937), copy in Box 2450, Agriculture Department Employees; *Organizer* (June 1937), copy in Box 2606, Personnel [Jan.–July] [1 of 3], both in RG 16, Office of Secretary, NARA; Bell to McIntyre, 5/7/37, OF 252 Government Employees, 1937, FDRL.

45 *Government Standard* 4 (Sept. 21, 1934).

46 *Government Standard* 9 [misnumbered] (Mar. 19, 1937).

47 *Government Standard* 3 (Aug. 31, 1934).

48 *Washington Evening Star*, 5/3/36; "Discrimination by Labor Unions," n.d., n.a., Papers of the National Association for the Advancement of Colored People (NAACP), Group II, Box A-348, General Office File: Labor Unions General, 1940–41, LC Mss.

49 *Government Standard* 4 (Sept. 7, 1934).

50 *Federal Employee* 22 (Mar. 1937).

51 Iler to Green, 12/16/37, Papers of William Green, 1891–1952, Box 2, Folders 13–16, Reel 9, Ohio Historical Society, copy in Micro 13, GMLA.

52 Lemons, *The Woman Citizen*, 179–208; Chafe, *The Paradox of Change*, 45–78.

53 Strom, *Beyond the Typewriter*, 137–40. On the efforts of professional women to ensure upward mobility, see Ware, *Beyond Suffrage*.

54 *U.S. Statutes at Large*, vol. 47, 406. On the clause see Scharf, *To Work and to Wed*, 46–53; Kessler-Harris, "Gender Ideology in Historical Reconstruction"; Hobbs, "Rethinking Antifeminism of the 1930s"; Kessler-Harris, "Reply to Hobbs."

55 See, for instance, a 1907 interpretation of a statute prohibiting more than two members of a family from holding government jobs, in which the attorney general defined family as those living under the same roof as "pater familias," or those who formed *"his"* fireside" (emphasis added). The clause referred to by the attorney general is section 9 of the 1883 Civil Service Act in *U.S. Statutes at Large*, vol. 22, 403. The attorney general's interpretation is in *Official Opinions of the Attorneys-General of the United States*, vol. 26 (Washington, D.C.: Government Printing Office, 1908), 301–3.

56 *Washington Evening Star*, 4/18/35.

57 Women's Bureau, Department of Labor, "A Preliminary Study of the Application of Section 213 of the Economy Act of June 30, 1932," April 1935, OF 252 Government Employees, Jan.–June 1935, FDRL; *Washington Evening Star*, 3/7/35; Women's Bureau, *Women in the Federal Service, 1923–1947, Part I*, 19; see also Ware, *Beyond Suffrage*, 79. For a detailed study of the law's impact see RG 86, Women's Bureau, Division of Research, Unpublished Studies and Materials, 1919–1972, Box 17, Effects of Dismissing Married Persons from the Civil Service, 1932–36, NARA. One woman labeled the clause "class legislation" because husbands and wives in upper-level government positions were allowed to keep

their jobs. Patterson to Roosevelt, n.d. (circa Feb. 1935), OF 252, Government Employees Jan.–June 1935, FDRL. On class issues, see also Hobbs, "Rethinking Antifeminism of the 1930s."

58 Well-connected women within the Roosevelt Administration, like Molly Dewson, also fought against what they termed the "dumb clause." Ware, *Beyond Suffrage*, 79–82.

59 On the feminism associated with the right of wives and mothers to work, see Scharf, *To Work and to Wed*.

60 The National League of Women Voters publicly denounced the feminine interpretation of the law, and women in the Census Bureau opposed the law by presenting a petition to the president. Hundreds of women also wrote to the president asking him to repeal the law. See documents in OF 252, Government Employees, Apr.–July 1933, FDRL.

61 See, for example, *Government Standard* 4 (Nov. 23, 1934); McIntyre to FDR, 6/12/33, OF 252, Government Employees, Apr.–July 1933, FDRL.

62 Camp to Howe, 7/14/33, OF 252, Government Employees, Jan.–June 1933, FDRL.

63 *Washington Evening Star*, 4/18/35, 4/19/35, 4/25/35.

64 Heffner quoted in *Washington Evening Star*, 9/28/35. See also *Federal Employee* 18 (Sept. 1933); Nevin and Nevin, *AFGE Federal Union*, 14–15; *Government Standard* 6 (May 3, 1935); *Washington Evening Star*, 4/18/35. Coleman to FDR, 4/25/33, OF 252, Government Employees, Apr.–July 1933, FDRL.

65 *Washington Evening Star*, 9/28/35.

66 Strom, *Beyond the Typewriter*, 116.

67 Wickard to Bulow, 8/14/40; Appleby to Bulow, 9/28/40, both in RG 16, Office of Secretary, Box 129, Personnel, Aug. 23–Nov. 15, NARA; 35th Council Meeting, 12/7/39, RG 146, FPC Meetings, Box 4, NARA.

68 Hearing, 8/10/34, RG 25, NLRB Case No. 39, New Series, Donovan, John L., Washington, D.C., NARA.

69 Bernstein, *Loyalties*, 62.

70 As Lisa Fine has observed, private-sector firms often established separate hierarchies for men and women, thus preventing women from entering elite positions within the firm. Fine, *Souls of the Skyscraper*, 92–96.

71 Conservative social scientists and feminists used psychology to argue their cases against and for the employment of married women in the period after 1920. Weiner, *From Working Girl to Working Mother*, 98–107. On the intersection between gender and psychiatry see Lunbeck, *The Psychiatric Persuasion*.

72 Matasoff to Appleby, 1/27/37; Matasoff to Stockberger, 2/8/37; Klein to Bernhardt, 2/4/37; Gladmon to Tolley, 2/17/37; Harvey to Gladmon, 2/23/37; and Gladmon to Matasoff, 2/26/37, all in RG 16, Office of Secretary, Box 2606, Personnel [Jan.–July] [3 of 3], NARA.

73 Matasoff to Stockberger, 2/8/37; Gladmon to Matasoff, 2/26/37, both in RG Office of Secretary, Box 2606, Personnel [Jan.–July] [3 of 3].

74 Kirby, *Black Americans in the Roosevelt Era*, 16–21. In 1933 Alphonzo Harris, an employee in the Registers Office at the Treasury Department, wrote to the president requesting that he appoint black cabinet assistants to attend to the needs of black employees. Harris to Roosevelt, 8/31/33, OF 93, Colored Matters (Negroes) 1933, FDRL.

75 See, for instance Kirby, *Black Americans in the Roosevelt Era*, 109, 111–112, 133–147; Sitkoff, *A New Deal for Blacks*, 77–79.

76 Kirby, *Black Americans in the Roosevelt Era*, 22–23; Sullivan, *Days of Hope*, 41–67; Krislov, *The Negro in Federal Employment*, 23.

77 Kirby, *Black Americans in the Roosevelt Era*, 49–62.

78 Ibid., 76–96.

79 Sitkoff, *A New Deal for Blacks*, 190–96; Wacker, Race and Ethnicity in American Social Science, 58. On the issue of race in the natural sciences, see Barkan, *The Retreat of Scientific Racism*.

80 Park, "The Bases of Race Prejudice," (1928) in *Collected Papers of Robert Ezra Park*, vol. 1, *Race and Culture*, ed. Hughes, 233–34, 243; Ross, *The Origins of American Social Science*, 360, 438–40; Persons, *Ethnic Studies at Chicago*, 82–84, 114–15; Wacker, Race and Ethnicity in American Social Science, 88.

81 Park, "The Nature of Race Relations," in *Race Relations and the Race Problem*, ed. Thompson, 3–17; Miller and Park, *Old World Traits Transplanted*, 262–65; Park, "Our Racial Frontier on the Pacific" (1926), in *Collected Papers of Robert Ezra Park*, vol. 1, *Race and Culture*, ed. Hughes, 150.

82 Ross, *The Origins of American Social Science*, 247–49, 358–71, 437–40, quote from 248.

83 Park, "Race Psychology," 725–26; Miller and Park, *Old World Traits Transplanted*, 262–65 (Dorothy Ross notes that this book was drafted by William Thomas); William I. Thomas, "The Mind of Woman and Lower Races," 438–39; 440–41. Ross also states that at times Park equated assimilation with acculturation, while at other times, he maintained that they were distinct concepts. Ross, *The Origins of American Social Science*, 118n, 348–71, 437–40.

84 The six agencies were State, Commerce, War, Agriculture, Veterans' Administration, and Maritime Commission. Hayes, *The Negro Federal Government Worker*, 105, 131–51, 153–54. See also FEPC, "Tables and Summary of Employment of Negroes in the Federal Government," December 1943, and FEPC, "The Wartime Employment of Negroes in the Federal Government," January 1945, both in RG 228, Office of Committee, George M. Johnson, Box 74, Entry 11, Employment of Negroes in the Federal Government, NARA.

85 Harris to McDuffy, n.d.; FDR to Morgenthau, 6/5/36, both in OF 21, Department of Treasury, 1936, FDRL. Roosevelt rarely publicized statistics and fre-

quently accepted the explanation that the dearth of black employees was the result of uncontrollable market forces. See, for example, FDR to James Roosevelt, 3/13/37; Giegengach to FDR, 3/16/37, both in OF 4 Government Printing Office, 1937–42, FDRL; FDR to Civil Service Commission, 12/28/36; Mitchell, McMillen, and White to FDR, 1/8/37, both in OF 2 Civil Service Commission, 1936, FDRL; Grant, *TVA and Black Americans*, xxi–xxii.

86 See for example, Miller to Kaplan, 12/6/37, NCSRL, Acc. 7947, Box 94, 1937, Misc. Corresp. A to Z, AHC. On the Post Office, see Borras to Houston, 12/30/36; Howes to Houston, 1/14/37; and Houston to Howes, 1/19/37, all in NAACP Papers, Group I, Box C-229, Civil Service Cases, B–C, LC Mss.

87 Kammerer, *Impact of War*, 50n. Because this was the era of black and white photographs, the Civil Service Commission required job candidates to list eye and hair color on their applications. Hayes, *The Negro Federal Government Worker*, 52–56; King, *Separate and Unequal*, 57–59. As late as 1942, the commission was still issuing some personnel forms that referred to race, and not all agencies abandoned the use of photographs. TVA required photos until 1955. When the FEPC questioned the practice, officials claimed it was used merely for record-keeping purposes, an explanation the FEPC accepted. Washington *Evening Star*, 4/23/42; Grant, *TVA and Black Americans*, 143; Van Riper, *History of the United States Civil Service*, 241. On objections to the use of photos, see, for example, Love et al. to FDR, n.d. (circa June 1937), OF 2, Civil Service Commission, June–Dec. 1937, FDRL.

88 Giegenach to FDR, 3/16/37, OF 4, Government Printing Office, 1937–42, FDRL.

89 Miller to Foulke, 9/18/23, NAACP Papers, Group I, Box C-273, Discrimination: Employment—Federal Service, 1929, LC Mss.; Miller to Kaplan, 12/6/37, NCSRL, Acc. 7947, Box 94, 1937 Misc. Corresp. A to Z, AHC. On the rule of three see, for example, Mitchell and McMillen to FDR, 8/23/37; Bell to FDR, 9/4/37, both in OF 2, Civil Service Commission, June–Dec. 1937, FDRL; King, *Separate and Unequal*, 51–57; Burk, *The Eisenhower Administration and Black Civil Rights*, 75.

90 Bell to FDR, 9/4/37, OF 2, Civil Service Commission, June–Dec. 1937, FDRL.

3 Managing Human Relations in the Wartime and Cold War Civil Service

1 Charles Cofer and Eleanor Cohen, "Job Attitudes of a Hundred and One Federal Employees," *Public Personnel Review* 4 (April 1943): 96–102, quotes from 99–100. The interviews were limited to D.C. workers and were conducted in August and September 1942.

2 Raymond R. Zimmerman, "More Teamwork in Management," *Personnel Administration* 8 (June 1946): 28.

3 Ibid.
4 Margaret Barron, "Employee Counseling in a Federal Agency," *Personnel Administration* 4 (Mar. 1942): 1–10, quote from 8–9.
5 Luther Gulick as quoted in Davis, *FDR: Into the Storm*, 23n.
6 Greene, "Frederick Morgan Davenport," 12–21; phone interview with Kenneth Warner, May 22, 1995; interview with Arthur Flemming, Washington, D.C., June 19, 1995; interview with Elmer Staats, Washington, D.C., June 13, 1995.
7 Graebner, *Engineering of Consent*, 3–5, 73–78.
8 On the influence of the social sciences on industry, see Baritz, *The Servants of Power*; Lynch, "Walter Dill Scott"; Gillespie, *Manufacturing Knowledge*, 29–36.
9 Mayo, *The Human Problems*, 122–43, 183. Mayo also drew on other disciplines including psychology, psychiatry, physiology, and anthropology. Gillespie, *Manufacturing Knowledge*, 96–126.
10 Waring, *Taylorism Transformed*, 15. On the emergence of industrial psychology and human relations, see Gillespie, *Manufacturing Knowledge*, 28–32; Lynch, "Walter Dill Scott"; Harris, *Right to Manage*, 162–63. Andrew Abbott has explained that psychiatrists used a barrage of tests, including IQ and personality tests as a means of "helping" individuals adjust to life in the new organizational society emerging at the turn of the nineteenth century. Industrial psychology and psychiatry, he notes, were also employed to defuse potential strikes. Abbott, *The System of Professions*, 148–49.
11 Mayo, *The Human Problems*, 55–56, 70, 103.
12 As quoted in Waring, *Taylorism Transformed*, 15.
13 Ibid.
14 Roethlisberger, *Management and Morale*, 178–80, 193. On Mayo and social control theories, see Mayo, *The Human Problems*, 122–27, quote from 126–27.
15 Public personnel managers drew upon the ideas of both Frederick Taylor and Elton Mayo. On "post-Taylorist" and "post-Mayoist" traditions within scientific management, see Waring, *Taylorism Transformed*, 6–7, 14–19. On the use of human relations in industry during the 1940s and 1950s, see Fones-Wolf, *Selling Free Enterprise*, 72–78.
16 Hendrickson, "Employee Relations," 5/6/40, RG 16, Office of Secretary, Box 875, Personnel (2 of 5), Feb. 1–May 31, 1943, NARA.
17 "We Pay Tribute to Frederick M. Davenport," *Personnel Administration* 7 (Jan. 1945): 19–20; Davenport, "The Pulpit and Its Relations to [Some Questions of] Social Science," n.d., Papers of Frederick Davenport, Writings, Sermons, Box 39, SUA; *Washington Post*, 2/26/39; 85th Council Meeting, 1/15/41, RG 146, FPC Meetings, Box 9, NARA; Frederick Davenport, "The Personnel Office and the Full Use of Manpower," *Personnel Administration* 5 (Jan. 1943): 3–5, quotes from 4–5.

18 Tead, "The New Trends in Characterizing Personnel Management," RG 146, FPC Project Files, Box 1, C43–16, Personnel Director, Place of, NARA.

19 Rogers to Division and Bureau Chiefs, Administrative Officers, n.d. (circa Mar. 1946), RG 188, OPA Management Offices, Box 5, Entry 4, Meetings, Policy Staff, Personnel Division, 1946–47, NARA. For an explanation on how the social sciences became wedded to natural science models of inquiry, see Ross, "The Development of Social Sciences" and her *The Origins of American Social Science*.

20 Despite incremental increases in gross federal employment throughout the 1930s, government payrolls swelled starting in 1939 when Congress began appropriating more money for defense. Between 1936 and 1938, civilian federal employment in Washington, D.C., actually declined by a net of 2,200 employees (from 122,937 to 120,744). Between 1939 and 1941, the federal government added 60,000 workers to civilian payrolls and by 1942 another 85,000. Census Bureau, *Historical Statistics of the United States*, 1102.

21 98th Council Meeting, 4/24/41; 100th Council Meeting, 5/8/41, both in RG 146, FPC Meetings, Box 10, NARA.

22 See, for example, "Excerpt from CPA Meeting," 2/5/42, McReynolds Papers, Box 5, Council of Personnel Administration, FDRL; Hubbard to Davenport, 5/6/42, RG 146, FPC Meetings, Box 14, 141st Council Meetings, 5/7/42, NARA; LaDame to Perkins, 4/14/42, RG 174, Office of Secretary, Box 140, Government Employees, NARA.

23 Margaret Barron, "The Emerging Role of Public Employee Counseling," *Public Personnel Review* 6 (Jan. 1945): 11; "Preliminary Check List No. 10," received 10/9/45, RG 146, FPC Project Files, Box 16, Education for Personnel Work—Training 1945, NARA.

24 Kammerer, *Impact of War*, 288–302.

25 See, for instance, UFWA, "Victory Plan for Wartime Conversion in the Federal Service," attached to Nelson to Perkins, 2/24/42, RG 174, Office of Secretary, 1940–45, Box 113, Administrative—Personnel UFWA (1942), NARA; *Federal Record* 4 (Feb. 27, 1942).

26 See, for example, 26th Council Meeting, 9/13/39, RG 146, FPC Meetings, Box 3, NARA. This language was also used by business personnel. Bernstein, *The Lean Years*, 166.

27 For an overview of the twentieth-century crisis of democracy, see Purcell, *Crisis of Democratic Theory*, especially chapters 6 and 7. In the 1930s, the president's administrative advisors, like Louis Brownlow, linked management and structural reform in the executive branch with the survival of democracy. Davis, *FDR: Into the Storm*, 4, 20–23. See also Brinkley, *End of Reform*, 154–64. On the relationship between intellectuals and fascism in the 1920s, see Diggens, "Flirtation with Fascism."

28 Ordway to Reining, 3/25/41, Davenport Papers, NIPA Correspondence, Jan.–Apr. 1941, Box 23, SUA.

29 For an example of the business bias of those studying the public service, see Friedrich, "Introduction: The Problem and Its Setting," 4.

30 Louis Brownlow as quoted in Davis, *FDR: Into the Storm*, 23.

31 Ibid., 21–23, 34.

32 See, for example, Davenport to Brownlow, 10/21/37, Davenport Papers, NIPA Correspondence, Aug.–Dec. 1937, Box 8, SUA; President's Committee on Administrative Management, *Report of the Committee*, especially 74–84, 95–101.

33 Graebner, *Engineering of Consent*, 91–109.

34 Many feared that Roosevelt's court packing plan, reorganization program, and attempted party purge revealed his dictatorial tendencies. Others disagreed. Purcell, *Crisis of Democratic Theory*, 117–38; Diggens, "Flirtation with Fascism," 487–506; Davis, *FDR: Into the Storm*, 36; Leuchtenburg, *Franklin D. Roosevelt and the New Deal*, 148–66, 340–45; Best, *Pride, Prejudice, and Politics*, 143–55, 194–95.

35 Davis, *FDR: Into the Storm*, 33.

36 Davenport, "The Personnel Office and the Full Use of Manpower," 3.

37 Bradford White, "Article Abstracts: 'Social Theory Involved in Supervision,'" *Public Personnel Review* 5 (Oct. 1944): 256.

38 *The Hoover Commission Report on Organization of the Executive Branch of the Government*, 127–28.

39 Ibid., 128. On suggestions systems see, for example, documents in RG 16, Office of Secretary, Box 875, Personnel Jan.–May 20, 1943 (4 of 5), NARA.

40 "Biographical Sketches of Members of the Employee Council," 7/29/50, RG 16, Office of Secretary, Box 2110, Employee Council Material, NARA.

41 Shea to Reid, 6/29/52, RG 16, Office of Secretary, Box 2110, Personnel (Gov), NARA. Other agencies had slightly different participatory programs. The Library of Congress had a mandatory staff discussion group during which employees spent half the session discussing a topic handed down by the librarian and the other half discussing issues, as long as they were not individual grievances. Zapollo to Couch, 5/24/50, RG 146, Council Files, Box 14, 3 (14) Employee Relations, 1950, NARA.

42 Ballinger to Davenport, 5/25/44, RG 146, FPC Council Files, Box 5, (35) Personnel Management, NARA.

43 Harris, *Right to Manage*, 169.

44 45th Council Meeting, 2/21/40, RG 146, FPC Meetings, Box 5, NARA.

45 *Personnel Bulletin* (July 1940), copy in RG 16, Office of Secretary, Box 129, Personnel 3 Bulletin of Personnel Administration (Correspondence re:), NARA. William Grelle, "Article Abstracts: 'Telling a Clerk About His Agency: Class Method,'" in *Public Personnel Review* 2 (Oct. 1941): 358.

46 Reining to Clapp, 11/8/37, Davenport Papers, NIPA Correspondence, Box 21, Oct.–Dec. 1937, SUA.

47 104th Council Meeting, 6/5/41, RG 146, FPC Meeting, Box 10, NARA.

48 Ordway to Spivak, 1/13/40, and Ordway to Wilkie, 3/5/40, both in Acc. 5003, Papers of Samuel Ordway Jr., Box 16, Civil Service #1, AHC; Richard Cooper, "A Limitation on 'Career' Promotions," *Personnel Administration* 1 (April 1939): 9–10.

49 U.S. Department of Agriculture, "The Development of Administrators: An Interim Report on Training in Administrative Management," June 1941, McReynolds Papers, Box 18, Agriculture, Executive and Judiciary Departments (Agencies), FDRL.

50 *Federal Record* 4 (Mar. 15, 1943).

51 Les K. Adler and Thomas G. Paterson claim that the word *totalitarianism* did not come into general academic use until the late 1930s. Adler and Paterson, "Red Fascism," 1046.

52 Fried, *Nightmare in Red*, 45–49. Despite the U.S. wartime alliance with the Soviet Union, the federal government continued to demonstrate little tolerance for the employment of "communists." For a general overview see Latham, *The Communist Controversy in Washington*.

53 See, for example, *Federal Record* 4 (Aug. 15, 1941; Mar. 15, 1943; Sept. 23, 1943).

54 Bontecou, *The Federal Loyalty-Security Program*, 14. The Civil Service Commission interpreted this law to include fascist and communist organizations.

55 On anticommunism, the Dies Committee, and the loyalty issue in the 1940s see Fried, *Nightmare in Red*, 45–49, 52–56, 59–86; Bontecou, *The Federal Loyalty-Security Program*, 1–34; Leuchtenburg, *Franklin D. Roosevelt and the New Deal*, 280. The loyalty affidavit was written by the Bureau of the Budget, Civil Service Commission, and Council of Personnel Administration. *Washington Evening Star*, 6/22/41.

56 Hendrickson to Thatcher, 9/24/40, RG 16, Office of Secretary, Box 129, Personnel, Aug. 23–Nov. 15, NARA. Roosevelt did not admire the Dies committee tactics but apparently ordered investigators to rid the National Labor Relations Board of communist sympathizers in 1940. See Levenstein, *Communism, Anticommunism, and the CIO*, 131. Procedures for investigating applicants and employees varied, and involved, at times, the Dies Committee, agency administrators, and the FBI. After the fall of 1941, the FBI no longer needed agency approval to investigate war service appointments, but the final decision regarding retention rested with agency officials. Applicants for federal jobs, on the other hand, were investigated by the Civil Service Commission, which then determined eligibility. In 1943, the president established an Interdepartmental Committee on Investigations to review cases and act as a liaison to agencies. See, for instance, *Washington Evening Star*, 2/16/42, 2/7/43, 2/24/44.

57 Richter, Evans, and Jordan to Perkins, 10/16/42; "Resolution on Dismissals of Anti-Fascist Trade Unionists," attached to Berkowitz to Roosevelt, 6/11/42; and Smith to Richter, 12/8/42, all in RG 174, Office of Secretary, Box 113, Administrative—Personnel, UFWA 1942, NARA; Parmelee to Kelley, 9/6/43, Papers of National Civil Service Reform League (NCSRL), Acc. 7947, Box 147, (3200) Subversive Activities, 1943, AHC. On loyalty investigations see Drury, Separations of Federal Employees, 1937–1947, 112; Fried, *Nightmare in Red*, 55. On the ambivalence Americans felt regarding the exercise of power during an era of dictatorships, see Graebner, *Engineering of Consent*, 98–109.

58 Other targeted employees worked in agencies such as the Rural Electrification Administration, the Interior Department, Office of Strategic Services, and Federal Security Agency. *Washington Evening Star*, 2/7/43; Sherwood to Henderson, 7/16/41, RG 188, OPA Management Offices, Box 12, Entry 11, Leander Bell Lovell, NARA.

59 *Federal Record* (Aug. 15, 1941); *Federal Record* 4 (Mar. 15, 1943). On Representative Dies's association of union activity with radicalism and call upon the president to oust Nazis and communists from union leadership, see *Washington Evening Star*, 3/10/41. Carl Bernstein offers a more personal account of UFWA/UPWA-CIO activities and loyalty purges in *Loyalties*. Significantly, the AFL's AFGE pledged their allegiance to the government and urged Congress to purge the government of subversives. It suggested, for instance, placing employees with "dual sympathies" at the top of reduction-in-force rosters. *Washington Evening Star*, 3/30/41, 5/9/46.

60 *Washington Evening Star*, 1/4/44. In a 1942 case involving Labor Department employees investigated by the FBI, department officials stipulated that employees could not be dismissed for "political reasons." But, they added, "the protection offered political views by the Civil Service Rules relates to the orderly political processes of the nation and not to activities designed to overthrow or undermine those processes." Richter, Evans, and Jordan to Perkins, 10/16/42, Smith to Richter, 12/8/42, and attachments, RG 174, Office of Secretary, Box 113, Administrative—Personnel, UFWA 1942, NARA.

61 *Washington Evening Star*, 11/30/43, 12/3/43, 1/4/44.

62 Flemming recalled how he and Commissioner Frances Perkins agonized over these cases. Interview with Arthur Flemming, Washington, D.C., June 19, 1995.

63 *Washington Evening Star*, 12/3/41; *Federal Record* 4 (Sept. 23, 1943); *Washington Evening Star*, 2/7/43, 2/9/43, 7/14/46.

64 *Washington Evening Star*, 11/17/46.

65 Kaplan to Hull, 6/19/42; Hull to Kaplan, 6/30/42, both in NCSRL, Acc. 7947, Box 140, (3300) Federal Complaints, 1942, AHC.

66 This case was from 1944. See, for example, Ickes to McReynolds, 3/3/44; Daniels to Roosevelt, 2/3/44, and other documents in McReynolds Papers, Box 24, Confidential File, FDRL.

67 Doyle to Kaplan, 6/20/40; Kaplan to Doyle, 6/24/40, both in NCSRL, Acc. 7947, Box 127, Federal Service Complaints, AHC; Parmelee to Kelley, two letters of 9/6/43, 10/13/43, NCSRL, Acc. 7947, Box 147, 3200 Subversive Activities, 1943, AHC; Brinkley, *End of Reform*, 150.

68 Sayre to Potter, 3/31/46, Congressional Correspondence; Stafford to Sayre and Axtelle, 4/17/46, Files, Personnel; and Axtelle to Reimer et al., 5/24/46, Civil Service Commission, all in RG 188, OPA Management Offices, Box 1, Entry 1, NARA.

69 Perkins expressed reservations about the investigation process. *Washington Evening Star*, 11/17/46; 71st Council Meeting, 9/12/40, RG 146, FPC Meetings, Box 8, NARA.

70 *Washington Evening Star*, 5/9/46, 11/17/46.

71 Mollenhauer to Department of Agriculture Office of Personnel, 4/23/42, NCSRL, Acc. 7947, Box 140, (3300) Federal Complaints, 1942, AHC.

72 Henry Hubbard, "The Elements of a Comprehensive Personnel Program," *Public Personnel Review* 1 (July 1940): 8–13.

73 See, for instance, 96th Council Meeting, 4/11/41, Box 10; 357th Council Meeting, 4/3/47, Box 33, both in RG 146, FPC Meetings, NARA; and documents in RG 146, FPC Project Files, Box 13, C118, NARA.

74 Kwolek-Folland, *Engendering Business*, 72–76.

75 Strom, *Beyond the Typewriter*, 5–6, 109–171. Those in the public administration field followed a similar path to professional status. See Stivers, *Gender Images in Public Administration*, 109–18.

76 Strom, *Beyond the Typewriter*, 112–13; Jacoby, *Employing Bureaucracy*, 39–97, 126–47. In a sample survey of government personnel workers, Harold Clark found that women constituted 29% of all personnel workers in 1941, but they were not represented in these occupations in proportion to their employment within various agencies. In the Department of Agriculture, women made up 48% of the workforce and 14% of the personnel staff. Clark, An Occupational Study of Personnel Workers, 91–92.

77 *Washington Evening Star*, 2/11/43, 3/27/49. On women and personnel work in the private sector, see Strom, *Beyond the Typewriter*, 146–54; on human relations and gender, see Fones-Wolf, *Selling Free Enterprise*, 77–78. On women's salaries, see Women's Bureau, *Women in the Federal Service, Part II*, 17.

78 *Washington Post*, 6/11/39.

79 Ladd-Taylor, *Mother-Work*, 3.

80 Barron, "Employee Counseling in a Federal Agency," 10.

81 Strom, *Beyond the Typewriter*, 111–13.

82 Bradbury, Racial Discrimination in the Federal Service, 366–71.

83 Goody to Perkins, 5/15/43, RG 174, Office of Secretary, Box 113, United Federal Workers of America, 1943, NARA; Bradbury, Racial Discrimination in the Federal Service, 392–93.

84 In 1951, business personnel managers asserted that fair employment procedures threatened to disrupt congenial work groups and hence undermine the efficiency of the workforce. William Thomas, "Problems under FEPC," *Personnel Journal* 30 (May 1951): 14–19.

85 Grant, *TVA and Black Americans*, 140.

86 Deviny to Houghteling, 1/9/52, RG 146, Fair Employment Board (FEB), Box 10, Winston H. Luck, NARA.

87 98th Council Meeting, 4/24/41, RG 146, FPC Meetings, Box 10, NARA.

88 Davidson to Cramer, 12/17/41, RG 228, Office of Committee, Lawrence W. Cramer, Box 81, Entry 12, Dec. 1941, NARA; Bradbury, Racial Discrimination in the Federal Service, 140, 182–83.

89 "Summary of Testimony at Hearing on Appeal of Theodore A. Brown," n.d., RG 146, FEB, Box 7, Theodore Brown, NARA.

90 Bradbury, Racial Discrimination in the Federal Service, 154–55, 158–59.

91 *Washington Evening Star*, 10/31/48.

92 Brinkley, *Washington Goes to War*, 77–79, 235–36; "Report on Negro Housing as It Effects [*sic*] Employees at OPA," 4/18/44, RG 188, OPA Management Offices, Box 55c, Entry 32, Racial Relations, NARA. For a description of housing for African Americans, see Green, *Secret City*, 233–37; Borchert *Alley Life in Washington*; President's Committee on Civil Rights, *To Secure These Rights*, 87, 91.

93 On the steady deterioration of black standards of living, see Green, *Secret City*, 270–73, 287–88; interview with Martin McNamara, Washington, D.C., June 14, 1995; interview with Tom Page, in Hoopes, ed., *Washington at War*, 56–57; President's Committee on Civil Rights, *To Secure These Rights*, 87, 90.

94 Roche to Files, 9/14/44, RG 228, Administrative Division, Box 110, Entry 25, Complaints against Government Agencies, NARA; Brinkley, *Washington Goes to War*, 247–51; "Position of UFWA Local 203 on Employee Discrimination, OPA," 7/13/42, RG 188, OPA Management Offices, Box 55c, Entry 32, Racial Relations, NARA; Gody to Perkins, 5/15/43, RG 174, Office of Secretary, Box 113, Administration—Personnel, United Federal Workers of America 1943, NARA; Sitkoff, A New Deal for Blacks, 156–58; interview with Arline Neal, Washington, D.C., July 18, 1991.

95 Sayre to Stafford, 8/20/45, Box 55c, Racial Relations; Warner to Cramer, 5/10/43, Box 55a, Fair Employment Practice Commission, both in RG 188, OPA Management Files, Entry 32, NARA; Bradbury, Racial Discrimination in the Federal Service, 329, 339.

96 Bradbury, Racial Discrimination in the Federal Service, 339–40.

97 Ibid,, 326, 323; interview with Arline Neal, Washington, D.C., July 18, 1991.

98 See, for instance, M. F. Ashley Montagu, "Some Psychodynamic Factors in Race Prejudice," *The Journal of Social Psychology* 30 (1949): 175–87. The use of statistics in demonstrating race discrimination has proven to be a double-edged sword.

On the one hand, statistical evidence often uncovers the effects of racism (associated with institutional racism). On the other hand, social scientists often champion the statistical methods associated with standardized tests as "objective," although they may contain hidden cultural biases.

99 Davenport to Dawson, 7/18/50, President's Personal Files 2820, HSTL.

100 For an example of the emphasis on consensus in organizations, see the book written by one-time Justice Department personnel director Brownrigg, *The Human Enterprise Process*, and Zimmerman, "More Teamwork in Management," 24–29.

101 Reinhard Bendix and Lloyd H. Fisher, "The Perspectives of Elton Mayo," *Personnel Administration* 14 (Jan. 1951): 15–25.

102 For an example of participation as a means of motivating workers, see "Notes of Employee Motivation Subcommittee," 10/18/46, Box 13, C118 Human Motivation, Employee Morale, 1944; Maulding to Davenport, 1/12/50, Box 15, C156, Collective Bargaining, Labor Unions 1944, both in RG 146, FPC Project Files, NARA.

103 Sayre, "Relationship of Personnel Management to Overall Management," 7/9/46, RG 146, FPC Project Files, C-104, Personnel Management, Functions and Responsibilities of Organization and Management, 1944, NARA.

104 CPA, Employee Relations Committee Minutes, 5/16/45, RG 146, FPC Project Files, Box 48, P485–1 (cont.) Effective Relationships with Organized Employee Groups, 8/1/49, NARA.

4 Unions and Federal Labor Policy

1 Appleby to Baldwin, 2/16/37; Matasoff to Appleby 3/5/37, both in RG 16, Office of Secretary, Box 2606, Personnel [Jan.–July] [3 of 3], NARA.

2 Appleby to LaFollette, 6/22/37, RG 16, Office of Secretary, Box 2606, Personnel [Jan.–July], [1 of 3], NARA. Appleby sent an identical letter to Gordon Clapp, personnel director of the Tennessee Valley Authority (TVA).

3 Many of these issues are discussed in Mosher, *Democracy and the Public Service*, 176–82, 186–201.

4 106th Council Meeting, 6/19/41, RG 146, FPC Meetings, Box 11, NARA; Otto Beyer, "Employee Relations in the Public Service—Present and Future," *Public Personnel Review* 7 (June 1946): 19–24; Beyer to Zimmerman, 12/28/45, Papers of Otto Beyer, Box 15, Employer Opinions, LC Mss.

5 Many labor historians have perceived personnel administration and bureaucratic control as an effort to undermine unionism and radicalism. See, for instance, Edwards, *Contested Terrain*, 105–10; Montgomery, *The Fall of the House of Labor*, 236–44. Howell Harris, on the other hand, asserted that scientific management reflected the rationalization of the bureaucracy, although he recognized that

merit systems and grievance procedures were designed to limit union influence. Harris, *Right to Manage*, 160–66.

6 In his study of clerical workers in England, David Lockwood has drawn a more divisive line between paternalistic and bureaucratic organization. Lockwood, *The Blackcoated Worker*, 143–55.

7 In their study of the civil service system, the President's Committee on Administrative Management made a distinction between "personnel operations primarily concerned with the enforcement of the law," which belonged to a strong central agency, and personnel activities concerning "individual and group adjustment for the purpose of greater efficiency and higher morale." The latter tasks were to be the responsibility of the agencies. See "Memorandum," n.d., President's Committee on Administrative Management, Box 11, EXII-4, Memorandum by Leonard White, FDRL.

8 The bill has neither date nor author but was probably drafted in 1936. "Right to Organize and Negotiate: Conciliation and Adjustment of Disputes," President's Committee on Administrative Management, Box 11, EXIII-1, Draft of a Bill on Rights of Federal Employees to Organize, etc., FDRL. See also the committee's published report: President's Committee on Administrative Management, *Report of the Committee*, 111–14.

9 Ziskund, *One Thousand Strikes of Government Employees*, 133–84.

10 Press Conference #380, 7/9/37, in *Complete Presidential Press Conferences of Franklin D. Roosevelt*, sections 21–33.

11 Steward to FDR, 7/14/37; Hassett to Mitchell, 7/16/37; Mitchell to FDR, 7/27/37; and Baker to FDR, 8/10/37, all in OF 252, Government Employees, 1937, FDRL; *Federal Employee* 22 (Nov. 1937). Gerard Reilly, in 1937 a solicitor in the Department of Labor and later a member of the NLRB, claimed responsibility for some of the letter's content. 319th Council Meeting Summary, 4/25/46, RG 146, Meeting Summaries, Box 2, Extra Copies, NARA.

12 FDR to Steward, 8/16/37, copy in Micro 05, Reel 18, Government Employees, American Federation of, GMLA. Copy of letter also in OF 252, Government Employees 1937, FDRL. Roosevelt not only consulted with union leaders; he also sent each a copy of the final draft. Despite the letter, the UFWA continued to press the administration for a comprehensive statement with regard to unions.

13 See, for instance, Milkis, "The New Deal, Administrative Reform, and the Transcendence of Partisan Politics," 434, and more generally his *The President and the Parties*, especially chapters 5 and 6. Roosevelt supported TVA's labor relations policy, which provided for collective bargaining through a trade and labor council. Spero, *Government as Employer*, 346.

14 *Government Standard* 26 (Jan. 31, 1941).

15 In the language of government administration, "rules" were made by the pres-

ident whereas "regulations" were devised by the Civil Service Commission in consultation with the departments to be affected by them.

16 Smith to Perkins, 4/26/40, RG 174, Secretary of Labor, Box 1, Administrative—Robert C. Smith, Director of Personnel, NARA.

17 29th Council Meeting, 9/28/39, RG 146, FPC Meetings, Box 3, NARA. In the spring of 1939, Smith had met with union heads of the NFFE, AFGE, and UFWA to discuss classification and pay issues. *Washington Post*, 5/9/39, copy in RG 280, FM & CS, 195-155, NARA.

18 45th Council Meeting, 2/21/40, RG 146, FPC Meetings, Box 5, NARA.

19 Summary Report of Surveys: Personnel Survey, 3/1/39, Box 1; Personnel Survey, 4/23/39, Box 5; Personnel Survey, 8/24/39, Box 7, all in RG 146, Personnel Survey, NARA.

20 11th Council Meeting, 4/27/39, RG 146, FPC Meetings, Box 2, NARA.

21 A copy of the original Memorandum is reprinted in the *Federal Employee* 23 (June 1938); a revised version can be found in RG 16, Office of Secretary, Box 375, Personnel [2 of 3], NARA.

22 11th Council Meeting, 4/27/39.

23 Ibid.

24 Ibid..

25 32nd Council Meeting, 11/16/39, Box 3; 40th Council Meeting, 1/18/40, Box 4, both in RG 146, FPC Meetings, NARA (hereafter cited as 32nd Council Meeting, 11/16/39); Perkins to all Officers and Employees of the Department of Labor, 12/22/33 and 10/12/37, both in RG 174, Office of Secretary, Box 114, Administrative—Conciliation Committee, Department of Labor, NARA.

26 Samuel Gompers chaired this conciliation committee for a time. Perkins to all Officers and Employees of the Department of Labor, 12/22/33 and 10/12/37; Smith to Perkins, 3/8/41, Box 1, Administrative—Robert C. Smith, Director of Personnel, all in RG 174, Office of Secretary, NARA.

27 Parker to Perkins, n.d. (circa 1940), RG 174, Office of Secretary, Box 32, Conciliation—General, 1941, NARA.

28 32nd Council Meeting, 11/16/39.

29 11th Council Meeting, 4/27/39.

30 Hendrickson, "Employee Relations," 5/6/40, RG 16, Office of Secretary, Box 875, Personnel (2 of 5), Feb. 1–Mar. 31, 1943, NARA.

31 26th Council Meeting, 9/13/39; 32nd Council Meeting, 11/16/39, both in RG 146, FPC Meetings, Box 3, NARA.

32 Federal Security Agency, "Employee Relations Policy," n.d. (circa 1941), McReynolds Papers, Box 18, Federal Security Agency, Executive and Judiciary Departments (Agencies), FDRL. On the role of supervisors, see also 26th Council Meeting, 9/13/39.

33 Ordway's remarks come from 32nd Council Meeting, 11/16/39, and Ordway to

Berman, 11/22/40, NCSRL Papers, Acc. 7947, Box 124, League 1940, A to F, AHC.

34 4th Council Meeting, 8/31/39; 32nd Council Meeting, 11/16/39, both in RG 146, FPC Meetings, Box 3, NARA.

35 32nd Council Meeting, 11/16/39.

36 Edsforth, *Class Conflict and Cultural Consensus*, 193–94; *Federal Employee* 18 (Oct. 1933, Dec. 1933), 19 (Mar. 1934), 22 (Oct. 1937); Stengle to Perkins, 11/19/37, RG 174, Office of Secretary, Box 114, Administrative—Conciliation Committee, Dept. of Labor, NARA. On Britain's Whitley Councils see, for example, Humphreys, *Clerical Unions in the Civil Service*, chapters 7 and 8.

37 See, for example, 59th Meeting, 5/29/40, RG 146, FPC Meetings, Box 6, NARA.

38 Palmer to Davenport, 11/30/39, RG 146, Council Files, Box 7, Council—General, NARA.

39 98th Council Meeting, 4/24/41, RG 146, FPC Meetings, Box 10, NARA. On the Strong case, see Excerpt of AFGE #421 Meeting Minutes, 9/4/41; Austin to Strong, 9/9/41; Constitution and By-Laws of Federal Power Commission Lodge No. 421 (AFGE); Deposition by Clarence Strong, n.d.; and Memo to G. Johnson, 11/19/41, all in RG 228, Entry 25, Complaints against Unions, Box 114, Fair Employment Practices 1–4, American Federation of Labor, American Federation of Government Employees, NARA.

40 Smith to Perkins, 3/8/41, RG 174, Secretary of Labor, Box 1, Administrative—Robert C. Smith, Director of Personnel, NARA.

41 Federal Security Agency, "Employee Relations Policy," n.d. (circa 1941), McReynolds Papers, Box 18, Federal Security Agency, Executive and Judiciary Departments (Agencies) File, FDRL.

42 59th Council Meeting, 5/29/40, RG 146, FPC Meetings, Box 6, NARA.

43 Beyer to Mitchell, 9/20/40, Papers of Otto Beyer, Box 5, M—Miscellaneous [1934–43], LC Mss.

44 Departmental Circular No. 251, 2/24/41, McReynolds Papers, Box 3, C.S.C. Departmental Circulars, FDRL. William McReynolds asked the commission to change its original statement regarding strikes. He said that it implied that employees were not allowed, by law, to affiliate with organizations that supported the right to strike against the United States. The Lloyd-LaFollette Act, upon which the statement was based, applied only to postal workers, he told the commission. The words "by law" were deleted, although the gist of the paragraph remained the same. McReynolds to Mitchell, 2/1/41, McReynolds Papers, Box 2, Civil Service Commission—1941–42, FDRL.

45 The adoption of a new 1 to 5 rather than 1 to 10 rating system in 1941 did little to quell discontent. Schinagl, *History of Efficiency Ratings*, 44–58; Thomas Love, "Resolution," n.d. (circa 1937), RG 280, FM & CS, 195–233, United Federal Workers, NARA. Other UFWA locals passed the same resolution.

46 *U.S. Statutes at Large*, vol. 54, pt. 1, 1215–16.

47 *Federal Record* 3 (Nov. 22, 1940).

48 83rd Council Meeting, 12/19/40, RG 146, FPC Meetings, Box 9, NARA.

49 Employee Relations Committee Meeting Minutes, rec'vd, 11/4/40, RG 146, Council Files, Box 4, Council—Committees (14) Employee Relations Prior to 1944, NARA.

50 82nd Council Meeting, 12/12/40, Box 9; 103rd Council Meeting, 5/29/41, Box 10, both in RG 146, FPC Meetings, NARA.

51 83rd Council Meeting, 12/19/40, RG 146, FPC Meetings, Box 9, NARA.

52 Memo prepared by Personnel Staff, Railroad Retirement Board, 12/4/40, McReynolds Papers, Box 1, Ramspeck Act and Related Executive Orders, FDRL.

53 82nd Council Meeting, 12/12/40, FPC Meetings, Box 9, NARA.

54 82nd Council Meeting, 12/12/40; 83rd Council Meeting, 12/19/40, both in RG 146, FPC Meetings, Box 9, NARA.

55 "Report of Special Committee on Efficiency Rating Appeal Review Boards," 1/14/41, RG 146, Council Files, Box 1, Efficiency Rating Committee No. 11, NARA; 81st Council Meeting, 12/5/40, FPC Meetings, Box 9, NARA.

56 Spero, *Government as Employer*, 197; *Government Standard* 33 (July 31, 1942).

57 "Report of Special Committee on Efficiency Rating Appeal Review Boards," 1/14/41, RG 146, Council Files, Box 1, Efficiency Rating Committee No. 11, NARA.

58 Babcock to FDR, 7/11/38; Mitchell to Bell, 10/27/38; McIntyre to Babcock, 11/19/38, all in OF 252, Government Employees, 1938–39, FDRL; *Washington Post*, 6/27/38, 3/14/39.

59 Smith to Perkins, 4/24/40, RG 146, Secretary of Labor, Box 1, Administrative—Robert C. Smith, Director of Personnel, NARA.

60 *Government Standard* 28 (June 21, 1941); interview with Arline Neal, Washington, D.C., July 18, 1991.

61 See, for instance, Anderson to Houston, 4/8/38, Group I, Box C-273, Discrimination: Employment—Federal Service, 1937; Hunton Delegation to Civil Service Commission, 8/6/40, Group II, Box A-194, General Office File: Civil Service—President's Committee on Civil Service Improvement, 1940, both in NAACP Papers, LC Mss. For examples of the NAACP's assistance to individual civil servants complaining of discrimination, see, for instance, NAACP Papers, Group I, Box C-228, Civil Service Cases, M–N, and Box C-229, Civil Service Cases, B–C, LC Mss.

62 Robinson to Houston, 6/21/38, and Memorandum Re: case histories, n.d. (circa June 1938); Gibbons to White, 5/5/39; and Phalanx Club "Reply to Mr. Gibbons," 5/31/39, all in NAACP Papers, Group I, Box C-229, Cases: Civil Service Customs Guards, May 1939–1940, LC Mss. On groups, such as the Committee for the Economic Advancement of Messengers and their fight for civil rights in

the Washington, D.C., civil service, see NAACP Papers, Group II, Boxes A-235 and A-236, LC Mss.

63 Wilkins to Baugh, 2/3/33, NAACP Papers, Group I, Box C-273, Discrimination: Employment—Federal Service, 1933, LC Mss.

64 Brown to Early, 6/9/42, McReynolds Papers, Box 10, Alphabetical File (Individual) BM–BZ, FDRL. On the National Employees and Tenants Union, see Wicketts to McReynolds, 9/6/41; Wicketts Answer to Dr. Scott's Letter against Roosevelt Administration, 5/12/41; Constitution of the National Employees and Tenants Union, adopted 7/14/41, all in McReynolds Papers, Box 17, Minority Groups—Robert Weaver, FDRL; Wicketts to Felker, 1/4/42, RG 188, OPA Management Offices, Box 55c, Entry 32, Racial Relations, NARA.

65 98th Council Meeting, 4/24/41, RG 146, FPC Meetings, Box 10, NARA; Bernstein, *Loyalties*, 53.

66 24th Council Meeting, 8/31/39, RG 146, FPC Meetings, Box 3, NARA.

67 Treasury Dept. P-Mimeograph, Coll. no. 4674, 10/12/37, RG 56, Office of Secretary, Box 102, Personnel—Union Membership 4/17/39, NARA.

68 Ibid.

69 Employee Relations Committee Meeting Minutes, rec'vd 11/4/40, RG 146, Council Files, Box 4, Council—Committees (14) Employee Relations Prior to 1944, NARA.

70 Reimer to McCullough, 9/14/46, RG 188, OPA Management Offices, Box 2, Entry 3, Reports, Personnel Division, 1946–47, NARA.

71 18th Council Meeting, 6/22/39, RG 146, FPC Meetings, Box 2, NARA.

72 See, for example, Cohen, *Making a New Deal*.

73 Decker to FDR, 11/15/38; FDR to Green, 12/3/38, both in OF 18b, Navy Yards—Stations 1938, FDRL.

74 *Washington Times Herald*, 4/1/40; "Union Activities," *Personnel Administration* 1 (Jan. 1939).

75 *Federal Record* 4 (Jan. 25, 1941); *Washington Evening Star*, 7/9/41, 9/10/41, 10/11/41.

76 NCSRL, "Government Employee Relationships," n.d. (circa May 1941); NCSRL, "Report of Special Committee of National Civil Service Reform League on Government Employee Relationships," n.d. (circa 1941); Ordway, "Government Labor Relations," August 1941; Clapp to Ordway, 7/1/41; and Ordway to Clapp, 7/5/41, all in NCSRL, Acc. 7947, Box 135, (6500) Committee on Labor, 1941, AHC. On the debate over the definition of "collective bargaining," see also Ordway to Clapp, 12/3/41; Clapp to Ordway, 12/15/41, both in Papers of Samuel Ordway, Acc. 5003, Box 22, OO/Ordway S. H., 1941, File 84667, AHC; Beyer, "Personnel Management," n.d. (circa 1941–46), Beyer Papers, Box 15, LC Mss.

77 96th Council Meeting, 4/11/41, RG 146, FPC Meetings, Box 10, NARA.

78 140th Council Meeting, 4/30/42, FPC Meetings, Box 14, NARA.

79 6th Council Meeting, 3/23/39, RG 146, FPC Meetings, Box 1, NARA; Hendrickson to Davenport, 12/26/40, RG 146, Council Files, Box 7, Council—General, NARA. See also, for example, Civil Service Commission, Departmental Circular no. 442, 10/19/43 and no. 454, 11/27/43, both in McReynolds Papers, Box 3, C.S.C. Departmental Circulars, FDRL.

80 *Federal Record* 4 (June 17, 1941); Kammerer, *Impact of War*, 318.

81 *Federal Record* 4 (Feb. 27, 1942); UFWA, "Victory Plan for Wartime Conversion in the Federal Service," attached to Nelson to Perkins, 2/24/42, RG 174, Secretary of Labor, 1940–45, Box 113, Administrative—Personnel, UFWA (1942), NARA; and Nelson to Roosevelt, 5/1/42, OF 252, Government Employees, Jan.–May 1942, FDRL.

82 Assistant Secretary to Thorkelson, n.d. (circa Mar. 1942), RG 16, Office of Secretary, Box 689, Personnel Activities, 1942, NARA.

83 Employee Relations Committee, "Interim Report," 12/15/42, RG 146, Council Files Box 4, Council—Committees (14) Employee Relations Prior to 1944, NARA.

84 Warner to Hay, 6/30/43, RG 188, OPA Management Offices, Box 55c, Entry 32, UFWA-CIO, NARA; *Federal Record* 4 (Sept. 23, 1943); phone interview with Kenneth Warner, May 22, 1995.

85 Blackerby to Carolan, 9/8/42; Warner to Benson, 9/28/42; and "In the Matter of Adassa Balaban," 9/16/42, all in RG 188, OPA Management Offices, Box 11, Entry 11, Adassa Balaban, NARA; phone interview with Kenneth Warner, May 22, 1995.

86 For an assessment of OPA labor relations in the postwar period see Axtelle to Sayre, 2/27/46, RG 188, OPA Management Offices, Box 5, Meetings, Policy Staff Personnel Div., 1946–47, NARA.

87 Gould, "Chronology of FPC Work on Relations of Federal Agencies with Organized Employees," 4/16/52, RG 146, FPC Project Files, Box 15, C156 Collective Bargaining Labor Unions, 1944, NARA. Navy Department officials had been pressuring the White House for a formal union policy due to labor friction in Navy Yards, involving a dispute over whether supervisors could join unions. Draemel, "Order No. 13/45," 1/22/45, Micro 05, Reel 18, Government Employees, American Federation of, GMLA; *Washington Evening Star*, 10/14/45, 5/6/46.

88 Lawton to Davenport, 4/18/46, Beyer Papers, Box 40, U.S. Govt. Labor Policy, 1946–47, LC Mss.

89 For extensive discussion of the bargaining issue, see 262nd Council Meeting Summary, 1/25/45; 271st Council Meeting Summary, 4/12/45; and 285th Council Meeting Summary, 7/26/45, all in RG 146, FPC Meeting Summaries, Box 2, Council Meetings Extra Copies, NARA. See also 319th Council Meeting, 4/25/46, RG 146, FPC Project Files, Box 48, P485–1 (cont.), Effective Relation-

ships with Organized Employee Groups, 8/1/49, NARA (hereafter cited as 319th Council Meeting, 4/25/46). A summary of the views of some labor leaders is in Subcommittee on Collective Bargaining Meeting Minutes Summary, 12/4/45, also in Box 48, P485–1, and in "What They Are Saying at the Society Meetings," *Personnel Administration* 7 (Feb. 1945): 20; "What They Are Saying at the Society Meetings," *Personnel Administration* 8 (May 1946): 21–22; CPA, "Proposed Statement of Policy Governing Relations of Federal Agencies with Organized Employees," 4/18/46, Beyer Papers, Box 40, U.S. Govt. Labor Policy, 1946–47, LC Mss.

90 319th Meeting Summary, 4/25/46, RG 146, Meeting Summaries, Box 2, Council Meetings Extra Copies, NARA. Reilly believed TVA's labor relations policy to be atypical and therefore not applicable to other federal agencies.

91 Ibid.

92 Ibid.

93 *Washington Post*, 5/2/46, 5/3/46. See also unnamed articles in RG 146, FPC Project Files, Box 15, C156 Collective Bargaining, Labor Unions, 1944, NARA.

94 319th Council Meeting Summary, 4/25/46.

95 *Washington Evening Star*, 4/30/46, 5/3/46. For the council reaction see Hubbard to Davenport, 5/9/46, RG 146, FPC Project Files, Box 48, P485–1 (cont.).

96 Zimmerman to Truman (draft letter), 5/7/46; Zimmerman to Truman, 5/8/46, RG 146, FPC Project Files, Box 15, C156.

97 "Proposed Statement of Policy Governing Relations of Federal Agencies with Organized Employees," 11/13/46, Beyer Papers, Box 40, U.S. Govt. Labor Policy, 1946–47, LC Mss. A new guide issued in 1953 also directly avoided the issue of collective bargaining. "Suggested Guide for Effective Relationships with Organized Employee Groups in the Federal Service," 1953, RG 146, Committee Files, Box 3, P584-B, Pamphlets on Participation and Communications, ERC, NARA. In fact, a proposed executive order (circa 1955) actually had a clause prohibiting agencies from requiring or forbidding membership in an organization as a prerequisite for hiring, promotion, demotion, transfer, or dismissal. "Revised Draft on Executive Order on Recognition of Federal Employe Organizations," n.d. (circa 1954–55), Micro 07, Reel 14, U.S. Govt. Depts., GMLA.

98 NCSRL, Meeting Minutes of the Council, 10/29/40, NCSRL, Acc. 7947, Box 129, (6100.10) Council Meeting, Oct. 29, 1940, AHC; Stanley Bell, "Collective Bargaining," 12/21/45, RG 146, FPC Project Files, Box 48, P485–1 (cont.), Effective Relationships with Organized Employee Groups, 8/1/49, NARA.

99 NCSRL, "Employee Organizations in the Public Service," n.d. (circa 1946), NCSRL, Acc. 7947, Box 262, League Study of Employee Organizations, AHC.

100 On Beyer's philosophy and activities, see, for example: Beyer, "Labor Relations and the Public Service," n.d., Box 40, U.S. Government Labor Policy, 1946–47; "Employee Relations in Publicly-Owned Utilities," n.d., Box 40, U.S. Gov-

ernment Labor Policy, 1946–47; "Labor Relations Policy for the Interior Department's Agencies and Projects," Box 23, Labor Relations, Miscellaneous, ca.
1945–48, all in Beyer Papers, LC Mss.; *New York Times*, 5/24/46.

101 U.S. Department of Labor, *Collective Bargaining by Public Employees*, report
(Washington, D.C., 1948), copy in Civil Service Commission Historical Collection, OPML.

102 CSC memorandum, 1/10/47, RG 56, Office of Secretary, Box 95, Personnel—
Federal Personnel Policy, NARA; "Federal Personnel Policy," 1/4/48, RG 146,
FPC Project Files, Box 42, C-440, Federal Personnel Policy Statement Personnel
Committee, NARA. The 1941 circular is no. 251, 2/24/41, McReynolds Papers,
Box 3, C.S.C. Departmental Circulars, FDRL.

103 *The Hoover Commission Report on Organization of the Executive Branch of the
Government*, 127–28. Sanderson and Auvil to Davenport, 5/31/49, RG 146, FPC
Project Files, Box 47, P483-2, Employee Participation in Agency Management,
2/1/52 NARA.

104 Employee and Supervisory Participation Meeting, 9/23/49, RG 146, FPC Project
Files, Box 47, P483-2; Meeting Summary 1/26/50, dated 2/7/52, RG 146, FPC
Project Files, Box 45, C467, Council Consultation with Employee Groups,
NARA.

105 A copy of the plan is attached to Zappolo to Couch, 5/24/50, RG 146, Council Files, Box 14, 3 (14) Employee Relations, 1950; and in Committee Files,
Box 3, P584-B, Pamphlets on Participation and Communications, ERC, both
in NARA. For a discussion of the industrial democratic traditions represented
in these plans, see Harris, "Industrial Democracy and Liberal Capitalism," in
Lichtenstein and Harris, eds., *Industrial Democracy in America*.

106 Sanderson to Davenport, 3/12/52; Kean to Crosson, 3/7/52; Philadelphia FPC
Summary of 121st Meeting, 3/12/52; and Brown to Davenport, 3/17/52, all in
RG 146, Project Files, Box 47, P483-2.

107 Employee Relations Committee Meeting Minutes, 4/9/52, RG 146, Committee
Files, Box 3, Employee Relations Minutes, NARA; Walters to Adler, 4/10/52, RG
146, FPC Project Files, Box 47, P483-2.

108 Campbell to Davenport, 11/8/51, RG 146, FPC Project Files, Box 48, P485-
2, Effective Relationships with Organized Employee Groups, 8/1/49, NARA;
Shoemaker to Davenport, 9/21/51, RG 146, Committee Files, Box 4, Shoemaker
(CIO) letter to Davenport, NARA. For an early version of the guide see "Re-
port by Union-Management Subcommittee," attached to Couch to Davenport,
4/19/51, RG 146, FPC Project Files, Box 15, C156, Collective Bargaining, Labor
Unions 1944, NARA. For a final version see RG 146, Committee Files, Box 3,
P584-B.

109 "Grievances and Appeals," 3/15/51, RG 146, Committee Files, Box 5, ERC,
NARA; Lumer to Holloway, 3/7/46; Axtelle to Sayre, 3/11/46, both in RG 188,

OPA Management Offices, Box 55c, Entry 32, UFWA-CIO, NARA; Axtelle to Sayre, 3/13/46, RG 188, OPA Management Offices, Box 3, Entry 3, Employee Relations Branch Progress Report 1946, NARA.

110 AFGE Resolution, #185, n.d. (circa 10/23/52), RG 146, FPC Project Files, Box 48, P485–2, NARA.

111 Stahl to Watson, 12/31/52, RG 146, Council Files, Box 15, Council General, 1951–52, NARA.

5 Gender and the Civil Service

1 On the persistent discrimination against married women see Hartmann, *The Homefront and Beyond*, 82–85.

2 Ware, *Beyond Suffrage*, 116–26.

3 Significant works that examine occupational segregation by sex include Milkman, *Gender at Work*; Fine, *Souls of the Skyscraper*; Davies, *Woman's Place Is at the Typewriter*; and Strom, *Beyond the Typewriter*.

4 Margaret Barron, "The Emerging Role of Public Employee Counseling," *Public Personnel Review* 6 (Jan. 1945): 9–16, quotes from 9–10.

5 Council members discussed questions concerning marital status at the 133rd Council Meeting, 3/5/42, RG 146, FPC Meetings, Box 13, NARA.

6 See Women's Bureau, *Women in the Federal Service, 1923–1947, Part I*, 16, 19, 29, 35, and the same bureau's *Employment of Women in the Federal Government, 1923–1939*, 49–50.

7 Strom, *Beyond the Typewriter*, 11. On the way in which institutions and authority can be constructed around gender categories, see Baron, "Gender and Labor History: Learning from the Past, Looking to the Future," in Baron, ed., *Work Engendered*, 19, 25, 36–37, and Scott, *Gender and the Politics of History*, 15–50.

8 In 1939, female civil servants in Washington, D.C., represented 69.3% of the entire clerical, administrative, and fiscal service service. Of the 8,190 women appointed to federal jobs in 1939, 73% received clerical appointments. At the same time, 1.5% of the new female appointees received professional positions. See Women's Bureau, *Employment of Women in the Federal Government, 1923–1939*, 19. On women and war work, see for example: Campbell, *Women at War with America*, 103–37; Hartmann, *The Homefront and Beyond*, 21–24, 53–99; Anderson, *Wartime Women*, 23–74; Kessler-Harris, *Out to Work*, 273–99.

9 Employee Relations Committee Meeting, 9/24/41, RG 146, Council Files, Box 4, Council—Committees (14) Employee Relations, Prior to 1944, NARA.

10 Nelson, *Managers and Workers*, 118; Zunz, *Making America Corporate*, 117–18. Kwolek-Folland has labeled the construction of welfare departments in private business part of "corporate maternalism." She argued that firms used gender imagery as a means of enhancing their reputation with the public. Kwolek-

Folland, "Gender, Self and Work in the Life Insurance Industry, 1880–1930," in Baron, ed., *Work Engendered*, 170–73.

11 On efforts to "protect" working women and provide for their needs by building dormitories for them during World War I, see Sealander, *As Minority Becomes Majority*, 76–77; Meyerowitz, *Women Adrift*, 89.

12 Sarré to Davenport, 6/11/43, McReynolds Papers, Box 5, Council of Personnel Administration, FDRL.

13 143rd Council Meeting, 5/21/42, RG 146, FPC Meetings, Box 14, NARA.

14 Ibid.

15 Margaret Barron, "Employee Counseling in a Federal Agency," *Personnel Administration* 4 (Mar. 1942): 10. On the rejection of the paternal characterization, see, for example, Henry F. Hubbard, "The Elements of a Comprehensive Personnel Program," *Public Personnel Review* 1 (July 1940): 11–12; Zimmerman to Davenport, 6/24/43, RG 146, Council Files, Box 4, Council—Committees (14) Employee Relations Prior to 1944, NARA; Mitchell Dreese, "Guiding Principles in the Development of an Employee Counseling Program," *Public Personnel Review* 3 (July 1942): 200–4. Civil Service Commission classification specialists insisted that counselors not be titled "welfare" or "social service" workers. This may have been an effort to distance human relations programs from the stigma of welfare paternalism. U.S. Civil Service Commission, "Report of the Committee on Employee Counseling," n.d. (circa 7/10/42), McReynolds Papers, Box 3, Committee on Administrative Personnel II, FDRL.

16 On supervisory participation in welfare programs see Esman, "The Organization of Personnel Administration," 183.

17 Dreese, "Guiding Principles in the Development of an Employee Counseling Program," 200. On employee relations programs see Kammerer, *Impact of War*, 283–320.

18 Women's Bureau, Department of Labor, "Recreation and Housing for Women War Workers: A Summary of Standards, Policies, Procedures," February 1942, McReynolds Papers, Box 19, Labor Department: Executive and Judiciary Departments (Agencies) File, FDRL; *Washington Evening Star*, 7/13/42, 7/16/42.

19 Brinkley, *Washington Goes to War*, 243; *Washington Evening Star*, 2/8/42; Women's Bureau, "Recreation and Housing." Overcrowding in Washington, D.C., also overwhelmed the city's transportation infrastructure. As a consequence, Congress and the Council of Personnel Administration supported a plan to move agencies to outlying areas and in some cases to other cities. Most District of Columbia employees, however, had no means of traveling to Suitland, Maryland, for instance, to work at the Census Bureau. In essence, the move threatened to disrupt families and careers and, ironically, to damage the personal welfare of employees. See *Washington Evening Star*, 12/20/41, 12/24/41, 12/26/41, 12/28/41, 12/30/41, 12/31/41; 127th Council Meeting, 1/22/42, Box

112; 137th Council Meetings, 4/9/42, Box 113, both in RG 146, FPC Council Meetings, NARA; Brinkley, *Washington Goes to War*, 120–21; interview with Mary Lawlor, Washington, D.C., June 21, 1995.

20 *Washington Evening Star*, 8/31/41, 4/16/42.

21 See, for example, *Washington Evening Star*, 2/8/42, 4/16/42, 8/31/44.

22 *Washington Evening Star*, 1/30/42, 1/31/42, 2/1/42, 2/4/42.

23 *Washington Evening Star*, 10/8/44.

24 See, for example, *Washington Evening Star*, 10/11/44, 10/12/44, 10/14/44; *Washington Post*, 10/10/44, 10/11/44, 10/12/44, 10/13/44, 10/14/44.

25 *Washington Evening Star*, 10/14/44, 10/16/44.

26 *Washington Evening Star*, 10/19/44.

27 *Washington Post*, 10/14/44.

28 *Washington Evening Star*, 10/19/44, 10/16/44.

29 Employee Relations Committee Meeting Minutes, 2/7/45, RG 146, Council Files, Box 12, 3 (14) Council—Committees, Employee Relations 1948, NARA.

30 On the difficulties associated with federal day care legislation and centers, see U.S. Department of Labor, Children's Bureau, "Preliminary Report," 11/9/43, and articles in RG 146 Project Files, Box 11, C80 Child Care—Facilities, Welfare 1944, NARA; Anderson, *Wartime Women*, 122–53. Child care facilities were of particular interest to black women, who usually had no choice but to hold down jobs. They helped lobby Congress to keep child care centers open until 1947. *Pittsburgh Courier*, 4/27/46; see also Papers of Philelo Nash, Box 3, Child Day Care Centers, HSTL.

31 United Federal Workers of America Press Release, 7/7/44; War Manpower Commission—Working Mother's Club, 3/20/44, both in RG 146, FPC Project Files, Box 11, C80 Child Care—Facilities, Welfare, 1944, NARA.

32 U.S. Civil Service Commission, Minutes of Staff Conference, 3/12/43, Box 3; Examining and Personnel Utilization Division, Work Improvement Program, Minutes of Staff Conference, 5/20/43, Box 6, both in McReynolds Papers, FDRL; Herrell to Bureau Chiefs, 7/9/42, RG 16, Office of Secretary, Box 689, Personnel, Mar. 7–Aug. 31, NARA.

33 Milkman, *Gender at Work*, 49

34 162nd Council Meeting, 11/19/42, FPC Meetings, Box 16, NARA; Hendrickson to Lyle, n.d. (circa 1939), RG 16, Office of Secretary, Box 3059, Personnel, July–Oct., NARA; Helvering to Thompson, 6/3/42, RG 56, Office of Secretary, Box 103, Personnel, Women in Government, 1900–1952, NARA; *Bulletin* (National Association of Collectors of Internal Revenue) 1 (Aug. 15, 1942).

35 Edwards to Truman, 1/15/51; Mitchell to Dawson, 2/7/51; and Dawson to Edwards, 2/19/51, all in OF 120-A (1948–1953), HSTL.

36 U.S. Civil Service Commission, "Secretarial Practice," 1942, copy in McReynolds Papers, Box 3, Committee on Administrative Personnel—II, FDRL.

37 Ibid. Secretaries in the business world were described in very similar ways. See Davies's account of private business secretaries from the 1910s to the 1930s in *A Woman's Place Is at the Typewriter*, 129–62.

38 U.S. Civil Service Commission, "Secretarial Practice." On the relationship between "masculine" and "feminine" traits and occupations in the life insurance industry and unions, see Kwolek-Folland, *Engendering Business*, 71–73, 189–90; Elizabeth Faue, "Paths of Unionization: Community, Bureaucracy, and Gender in the Minneapolis Labor Movement of the 1930s," in Baron, ed., *Work Engendered*, 297–98.

39 Picketts to McHale, 10/14/47, Papers of India Edwards, Box 15, Correspondence, 1947–1977, HSTL.

40 Flemming to Kaplan, 10/16/43, NCSRL Papers, Acc. 7947, Box 147, 3200 Subversive Activities 1943, AHC.

41 Ibid. Flemming later observed that the war created opportunities for women but that traditional prejudices reasserted themselves after the war. Interview with Arthur Flemming, Washington, D.C., June 19, 1995.

42 Bradbury, Racial Discrimination in the Federal Service, 380–81.

43 Louise Snyder Johnson, "Are You Polishing Off Those Rough Spots?" *Independent Woman* (Jan. 1947): 28.

44 Ibid.

45 "Try a Democratic Attitudes Test," *Independent Woman* (June 1945): 165–66.

46 *Washington Times-Herald*, 6/24/50; *Washington Post*, 6/25/50. Copies in WHCF: Confidential File, Subject File—Sex Perversion (Investigations of Federal Employees), Box 32, HSTL.

47 Maletz to Spingarn, 7/3/50, WHCF: Confidential File.

48 Humelsine to Webb, n.d. (circa 1950), WHCF: Confidential File. On the use of psychiatrists to analyze homosexuals in the military during World War II, see Bérubé, *Coming Out under Fire*, 149–74.

49 Humelsine to Webb, n.d. (circa 1950), WHCF: Confidential File.

50 See, for example, *Federal Record* 4 (June 21, 1941; Nov. 7, 1941; June 17, 1943).

51 *Federal Record* 4 (June 20; July 18; Aug. 1, 1941); C. Renner to Perkins, received 5/1/42, RG 174, Office of Secretary, Box 112, Administration—Personnel 1942, NARA.

52 *Federal Record* 7 (June 6, 1945; May 1946).

53 *New York Times*, 11/18/48, 2/23/49, 3/19/49, 7/29/49, 3/23/50, 3/26/50, 5/1/51. *Washington Evening Star*, 3/27/49, 5/17/49. On the legal questions involved in the Bailey case, see Bontecou, *The Federal Loyalty-Security Program*, 64, 119, 133–35, 138–140, 226, 229–31, 233–34.

54 Strom has observed that women fought to move up in the labor hierarchy, not to restructure it. While feminists battled the marriage bar and sex discrimination,

they perceived their oppression in individualistic, not collective, terms. Strom, *Beyond the Typewriter*, 9.

55 Office of Personnel, USDA and Science Research Association, "Report of Employee Attitudes and Opinions," April 1953, RG 16, Office of Secretary, Box 2110, Employee Council Material, NARA.

56 Fritz to Edwards, 10/23/51; Edwards to Fritz, 11/9/51, both in Edwards Papers, Box 2, Subject File: General Correspondence 1951, HSTL.

6 Race and Merit

1 Alexander's employment history was reconstructed from "Statement of Union-Management Adjustment Committee on Employee Grievance in the Printing and Duplication Branch," n.d. (circa Jan. 1943), RG 188, OPA Management Offices, Box 20, Entry 13, A1, NARA; Bradbury, Racial Discrimination in the Federal Service, 32–36, 354.

2 "Statement of Union-Management Adjustment Committee on Employee Grievance," n.d. (circa Jan. 1943), Box 20, Entry 13, A1; Fact-Finding Committee to Rose, 3/16/43, Box 55c, Entry 32, Racial Relations, both in RG 188, OPA Management Offices, NARA; Bradbury, Racial Discrimination in the Federal Service, 354–56; interview with Arline Neal, Washington, D.C., July 18, 1991.

3 Looking back, Neal suggests that in part, many black employees were paid less than their white counterparts (young white women were earning between $1,420 and $1,600) because of the application process. On their applications, candidates were asked to list the lowest salary they would accept. Most blacks put down rather low wages, and administrators hired them at that amount, never bothering to increase their salary to reflect their job performance. Neal interview.

4 Neal interview; Fact-Finding Committee to Rose, 3/16/43, RG 188, OPA Management Offices, Box 55c, Entry 32, Racial Relations, NARA.

5 Fact-Finding Committee to Rose, 3/16/43.

6 *Federal Record* 4 (Feb. 19, 1943); Bradbury, Racial Discrimination in the Federal Service, 356.

7 For local studies of black employment during the 1930s and 1940s, see Trotter, *Black Milwaukee*, 147–95; Honey, *Southern Labor and Black Civil Rights*.

8 See, for example, Trotter, *Black Milwaukee*, 166–73; Ruchames, *Race, Jobs and Politics*, 100–20; 156–64.

9 King, *Separate and Unequal*, 45–46.

10 Gerrard to Hay, 6/19/43; Gerrard to Brown, 7/13/43, both in RG 188, OPA Management Offices, Box 1, Entry 1, Race Relations #2, Jacobsen File, NARA; *Federal Record* 4 (July 24, 1943).

11 "Report of Negro Housing," 4/18/44, RG 188, OPA Management Offices, Box 55c, Entry 32, Racial Relations, NARA; OPA, "Data on Total and Negro Employment—July 31, 194[4]," RG 188, OPA Management Offices, Box 55c, Entry 32, Racial Relations, NARA; Neal interview.

12 Bradbury, Racial Discrimination in the Federal Service, 293.

13 On race and the rise of "rights-based liberalism," see Brinkley, *End of Reform*, 138, 164–70.

14 With respect to employment discrimination, liberals focused on intent rather than effect, the latter of which is associated with institutional racism. See, for example, Haney and Hurtado, "The Jurisprudence of Race and Meritocracy," 224–28; Anderson, "Race, Meritocracy, and the American Academy," 151–52.

15 U.S. Civil Service Commission, *54th Annual Report*, June 30, 1937, and *57th Annual Report*, June 30, 1940, reprinted in 75th Congress, 2d sess., House Doc. No. 388 and 77th Congress, 1st sess., House Doc. No. 19, respectively.

16 White to Coy, 12/5/41; Coy to White, 12/17/41, both in RG 16, Office of Secretary, Box 355, Personnel 18 Negroes, NARA. Reid was appointed on December 1, 1941, and remained personnel director until 1951.

17 See, for example, Committee on Race Relations Memorandum, 2/13/41, RG 146, Council Files, Box 5, Council—Committees (31) Race Relations Prior to 1944, NARA; Bradbury, Racial Discrimination in the Federal Service, 124*n*.

18 Bradbury, Racial Discrimination in the Federal Service, 165; 101st Council Meeting, 5/15/41, RG 146, FPC Meetings, Box 10, NARA; Davenport to Belsely, 5/23/41, McReynolds Papers, Box 5, Council of Personnel Administration, FDRL; 106th Council Meeting, 6/19/41, RG 146, FPC Meetings, Box 11, NARA.

19 Appleby to Baldwin, 2/16/37, RG 16, Office of Secretary, Box 2606, Personnel [Jan.–July] [3 of 3], NARA. For statistical comparisons of African-American employment in 1939 and 1945, see Hendrickson to Alston, 8/5/40, Box 132, Personnel 18, Negroes and Reid to Anderson, 1/5/46, Box 1119, Personnel, both in RG 16, Office of Secretary, NARA.

20 Fact-Finding Committee to Rose, 3/16/43, RG 188, OPA Management Offices, Box 55c, Entry 32, Racial Relations, NARA. Steen to Cramer, 3/31/42, RG 228, Complaints against Government Agencies, Box 103, Fair Employment Practices, US CSC, Steen, Anna J, NARA; Bradbury, Racial Discrimination in the Federal Service, 127.

21 Many of these social scientists read and admired anthropologist Franz Boas, who questioned scientific racism in the early twentieth century. Otto Klineberg dedicated his book to Boas. Klineberg, *Race Differences*. See also Lee and Humphrey, *Race Riot*; Herskovitz, *The Negro and the Intelligence Tests*; Lowie, *Are We Civilized?*

22 Krislov, *The Negro in Federal Employment*, 32; King, *Separate and Unequal*, 64–65. I have been unable to uncover Ramspeck's motivation behind this move,

although one interview subject stipulated that Ramspeck was an "ardent supporter of liberal causes" and "way ahead of his time." Interview with Arthur Flemming, Washington, D.C., June 19, 1995.

23 Reed to Miller, 1/30/41, RG 228, Administrative Division, Entry 25, Box 103, Fair Employment Practice, 1–3 Department of Commerce, Census Bureau, NARA.

24 "Points Brought Out in Race Relations Discussion, Council Meeting," 2/13/41, RG 146, Council Files, Box 5, Council—Committees (31) Race Relations Prior to 1944, NARA.

25 Ibid.

26 Committee on Race Relations Memorandum, 2/13/41, RG 146, Council Files, Box 5, Council—Committees, (31) Race Relations Prior to 1944, NARA.

27 Krislov, *The Negro in Federal Employment*, 123.

28 "Andrew D. Wicketts, President, National Employees and Tenants Union Answer Dr. Scott's Letter," 5/12/41, and Wicketts to McReynolds, 9/6/41, both in Papers of William McReynolds, Box 17, Minority Groups—Robert Weaver, FDRL.

29 Committee on Race Relations Memorandum, 2/13/41.

30 "Race Relations Problems and Personnel Policy, Apr. 14, 1941," Appendix to Report of Committee on Problems of Minority Groups in Government Service, 6/26/41, RG 146, Council Files, Box 5, Council—Committees (31) Race Relations Prior to 1944, NARA; Brinkley, *Washington Goes to War*, 246.

31 98th Council Meeting, 4/24/41, RG 146, FPC Meetings, Box 10, NARA (hereafter cited as 98th Council Meeting, 4/24/41).

32 101st Council Meeting, 5/15/41, RG 146, FPC Meetings, Box 10, NARA (hereafter cited as 101st Council Meeting, 5/15/41); Davenport to Belsely, 5/23/41, McReynolds Papers, Box 5, Council of Personnel Administration, FDRL; phone interview with Kenneth Warner, May 22, 1995.

33 See, for example, Haney and Hurtado, "The Jurisprudence of Race and Meritocracy," quote from 239. By relying upon statistics, psychologists and sociologists presented their findings regarding merit as "fact." On this methodology see Brown, *Definition of a Profession*, and Ross, *The Origins of American Social Science*.

34 101st Council Meeting, 5/15/41.

35 106th Council Meeting, 6/19/41, RG 146, FPC Meetings, Box 11, NARA (hereafter cited as 106th Council Meeting, 6/19/41). See also Kirby, *Black Americans in the Roosevelt Era*, 28–35, 83–86.

36 Zimmerman to Davenport, 5/29/41, RG 146, Council Files, Box 5, Council—Committees (31) Race Relations Prior to 1944, NARA; Bradbury, Racial Discrimination in the Federal Service, 182.

37 98th Council Meeting, 4/24/41.

38 101st Council Meeting, 5/15/41; Warner to Cramer, 5/10/43, RG 188, OPA Man-

agement Offices, Box 55a, Entry 32, Fair Employment Practice Commission, NARA; 106th Council Meeting, 6/19/41.

39 106th Council Meeting, 6/19/41.

40 Ruchames, *Race, Jobs and Politics*, 13–21; Garfinkle, *When Negroes March*, 37–61.

41 McReynolds to FDR, 8/21/41, McReynolds Papers, Box 17, Minority Groups—Robert Weaver, FDRL; "Employment of Negroes by Federal Government," *Monthly Labor Review* 56 (May 1943): 889; *Washington Evening Star*, 9/7/41.

42 Steen to Cramer, 3/31/42, RG 228, Complaints against Government Agencies, Box 103, Fair Employment Practices, US CSC, Steen, Anna J, NARA.

43 Grant, *TVA and Black Americans*, 248; Ruchames, *Race, Jobs and Politics*, 26–27, 46, 53–57; Krislov, *The Negro in Federal Employment*, 33–34. See also Ross to Truman, 6/28/46, OF 40 (1946–1951), Box 265, HSTL.

44 Ruchames, *Race, Jobs and Politics*, 73–99.

45 Interview with Arthur Flemming, Washington, D.C., June 19, 1995.

46 FEPC, "Tables and Summary of Employment of Negroes in the Federal Government," December 1943, and "The Wartime Employment of Negroes in the Federal Government" (January 1945), both in RG 228, Office of Committee, George M. Johnson, Box 74, Entry 11, Employment of Negroes in the Federal Government, NARA; Sitkoff, *A New Deal for Blacks*, 44; Table no. 1, RG 16, Office of Sec., Box 694, Personnel 10–4 Discrimination—Preference, NARA; Reid to Anderson, 1/5/46, Office of Sec., Box 1119, Personnel, NARA; Hunter to Chickering, 6/7/42 and Oliver to Tumbleson, n.d., both in RG 188, OPA Management Offices, Box 55c, Entry 32, Racial Relations, NARA.

47 Bowles to Flemming, 12/3/45, RG 188, OPA Management Offices, Box 1, Entry 1, Civil Service Committee, NARA; Bradbury, Racial Discrimination in the Federal Service, 100*n*; Flemming to Zimmerman, 5/17/46, Papers of Raymond R. Zimmerman, Box 1, Civil Service Commission File: E.O 9691, Ending War Service Regulations, HSTL.

48 Krislov, *The Negro in Federal Employment*, 137–38; Bradbury, Racial Discrimination in the Federal Service,105–7, 110. For further information on wartime hiring of African Americans, see FEPC, "Tables and Summary of Employment of Negroes in the Federal Government," December 1943, and "The Wartime Employment of Negroes in the Federal Government," January 1945, both in RG 228, Office of Committee, George M. Johnson, Box 74, Entry 11, Employment of Negroes in the Federal Government, NARA; *Washington Evening Star*, 4/2/42; Kammerer, *Impact of War*, 53–56; Bowles, *Promises to Keep*, 64. On the TVA's often poor performance with regard to fair employment practices, see Grant, *TVA and Black Americans*, 21–24, 33–72, 137–46, and Fair Employment Statistical Appraisal, RG 146, Fair Employment Board Corresp. with Agencies, Box 5, Tennessee Valley Authority, NARA.

49 FEPC, "The Wartime Employment of Negroes in the Federal Government";
Cramer to Brown, 3/29/43, RG 188, OPA Management Offices, Box 55a, Entry
32, Fair Employment Practice Committee, NARA.

50 Bradbury, Racial Discrimination in the Federal Service, 305–308, 319–20.

51 FEPC, "The Wartime Employment of Negroes in the Federal Government";
Keddy to Houghteling, 11/27/51, RG 146, FEB, Box 5, Smithsonian Institution,
NARA.

52 Bradbury, Racial Discrimination in the Federal Service, 336–37, 380–81; *Richmond Planet*, 9/28/35, copy in NAACP Papers, Group I, Box C-273, Discrimination: Employment—Federal Service, 1934–35, LC Mss.

53 As quoted in Bradbury, Racial Discrimination in the Federal Service, 136.

54 Kirby, *Black Americans in the Roosevelt Era*, 59.

55 Bradbury, Racial Discrimination in the Federal Service, 135–36. Despite the
alleged lack of racial identity managers attributed to this professional, he eventually left Washington, D.C., and his government job, because he did not want
to raise his children in a Jim Crow city.

56 Some in the 1940s viewed racial identity as a "pathology." On perceptions of
race in the 1940s see Graebner, *Age of Doubt*, 91–95; Herman, *The Romance of
American Psychology*, 57–66, 174–95.

57 Bradbury, Racial Discrimination in the Federal Service, 135–36; Stromsen to
Baker, 10/20/39, Box 22, June–Aug. 1939; Reining to file, 11/17/39, Box 23, Nov.–
Dec. 1939, both in Davenport Papers, NIPA Correspondence, SUA; 98th council
Meeting, 4/24/41, RG 146, FPC Meetings, Box 10, NARA.

58 Bradbury, Racial Discrimination in the Federal Service, 379.

59 Anderson, "Race, Meritocracy, and the American Academy," 174. At TVA, appointment officers routinely stated that they knew of no blacks of "foremen
ability." Grant, *TVA and Black Americans*, 51.

60 Warner to Cramer, 5/10/43, RG 188, OPA Management Offices, Box 55a, Entry 32, Fair Employment Practice Commission, NARA; Wallace to Mitchell,
6/3/46, Zimmerman Papers, Box 2, Civil Service Commission File, Civil Service
Commission—1946, HSTL.

61 "Hearing on Appeal of Winston H. Luck," 12/19 and 12/20/51, RG 146 FEB,
Box 10, Winston H. Luck, NARA.

62 Francis and Hall to Henderson, 4/16/43, RG 228, Box 107, Entry 25, Fair Employment Practices, Treasury Dept., 1–3, NARA.

63 Appendix to Report of Committee on Problems of Minority Groups in Government Service, 6/26/41, RG 146, Council Files, Box 5, Council—Committees
(31) Race Relations Prior to 1944, NARA. See also 101st Council Meeting,
5/15/41, and on Alexander's visit see 98th Council Meeting, 4/24/41, both in
RG 146, FPC Meetings, Box 10, NARA. The canvassing of union opinion is
discussed in Bradbury, Racial Discrimination in the Federal Service, 363–71.

64 Henderson to deputy administrators, division heads, branch heads, 10/14/42; draft of Administrative Order, n.d.; UFWA Local 203 Adjustment Committee to Felker, 12/28/42; Felker to Warner, 1/1/43, all in RG 188, OPA Management Offices, Box 55c, Entry 32, Racial Relations, NARA.

65 Bradbury, Racial Discrimination in the Federal Service, 342.

66 Benson to Hamm, 11/5/42, RG 188, OPA Management Offices, Box 55c, Entry 32, Racial Relations, NARA; Bowles, *Promises to Keep*, 64; Bradbury, Racial Discrimination in the Federal Service, 341–45.

67 105th Council Meeting, 6/12/41, RG 146, FPC Meetings, Box 11, NARA.

68 Kirby, *Black Americans in the Roosevelt Era*, 151; Bradbury, Racial Discrimination in the Federal Service, 133.

69 Stafford to Sayre, 8/10/45; Sayre to Stafford, 8/20/45; and "Position of UFWA Local 203 on Employee Discrimination, OPA," 7/1/42, all in RG 188, OPA Management Offices, Box 55c, Entry 32, Racial Relations, NARA; Gody to Perkins, 5/15/43, RG 174, Office of Secretary, Box 113, Administrative—Personnel 1943, NARA; *Federal Record* 4 (Sept. 5, 1941) and 7 (Oct. 24, 1945).

70 *Federal Record* 7 (April 1946). On the UFWA/UPWA's efforts to end race discrimination see Bradbury, Racial Discrimination in the Federal Service, 168–72, 358–71. On the Congress of Industrial Organizations efforts in this area, see, for example, Honey, *Southern Labor and Black Civil Rights*, 117–41.

71 Bradbury, Racial Discrimination in the Federal Service, 159.

72 Ibid., 168–72, quotes from 170.

73 Ruchames, *Race, Jobs and Politics*, 121–36; Green, *Secret City*, 277; Secretary of Agriculture, Memorandum No. 1141, 1/5/46, Box 25, Executive and Judiciary, Agriculture 1; Zimmerman to Beane, 4/16/46, Box 1, Civil Service Commission File: E.O. 9691—Ending War Service Regulations, both in Zimmerman Papers, HSTL.

74 Mitchell to Richardson, 1/30/47, Papers of Philleo Nash, Box 4, Civil Service Commission—Non Discrimination, HSTL.

75 Dawson to Clifford, 3/8/48, OF 596, 1947–Mar. 1949, HSTL.

76 Nash to Dawson, 9/15/48, Nash Papers, Box 6, FEP Board–CSC Personnel Board, HSTL; *Washington Evening Star*, 7/28/48

77 Under the executive order, failure to act was also defined as a personnel action. Moffett to CSC, 9/30/49, OF 2-F, Fair Employment Board, HSTL. On liberalism and rights, see Brinkley, *End of Reform*, 164–70; Nelson Lichtenstein, "Epilogue: Toward a New Century," in Lichtenstein and Harris, eds., *Industrial Democracy in America*, 275–83.

78 Van Riper, *History of the United States Civil Service*, 438; Executive Order 9980, 7/28/48.

79 McCune to Houghteling, 8/10/51, RG 16, Office of Secretary, Box 2013, Personnel 10–2, Discriminations—Preference, NARA; FEB, "Fair Employment Board

Informational Bulletin No. 5," 6/8/51, OF 2-F, Fair Employment Board, HSTL; "Basic Guides for Appraisal of Personnel Actions Under Section 3(a) of Executive Order 9980," n.d.; "Instructions for Carrying Out the Fair Employment Program under Executive Order No. 9980," n.d., both in Nash Papers, FEP Board–CSC—Fair Employment Board vs. Veterans Administration, Box 6, HSTL.

80 Houghteling to Commission, 11/6/50, OF 2-F, Fair Employment Board, HSTL; *Washington Evening Star*, 5/11/49.

81 Donaldson to Houghteling, 3/13/51, Box 4, Post Office Department; Lawhorn to McCune, 8/12/49, Box 1, Agriculture Department; McCune to Lawhorn, 11/14/49, Box 1, Agriculture Department; and McCune to Houghteling, 1/3/50, Box 1, Agriculture Department, all in RG 146, FEB, Corresp. with Agencies, NARA. The FEB also canvassed groups such as the American Council on Race Relations and the National Association for the Advancement of Colored People for their views. *Washington Evening Star*, 12/30/48.

82 See, for example, *Washington Evening Star*, 10/5/49.

83 *New York Times*, 5/16/46; "The Federal Diary," n.d., article in RG 146, FPC Project Files, Box 15, C156, Collective Bargaining, Labor Unions 1944.

84 On the Truman loyalty program, see Bontecou, *The Federal Loyalty-Security Program*, 26–39, 52–72.

85 OPA Investigation Report, 1/29/47, RG 188, OPA Management Offices, Box 12, Entry 11, Sol Rabkin, NARA; *New York Times*, 4/18/50. Of the three general unions in the federal government—the NFFE, the AFGE, and the UPWA—only the UPWA objected to the loyalty program as an infringement upon the rights of employees. *New York Times*, 9/16/50; Nevin and Nevin, *AFGE Federal Union*, 47.

86 Flaxer to Truman, 11/24/48; Barnes to Truman, 12/2/48, both in OF 252-K, 1948, HSTL; *Public Record* (United Public Workers of America) 3 (Aug. 1948); Bontecou, *The Federal Loyalty-Security Program*, 138–40.

87 Murphy to Truman, 4/10/50; Richardson to Mitchell, 5/23/50; Mitchell to Dawson, 5/25/50; and Dawson to Murphy, 6/7/50, all in OF 93, Miscellaneous—1950, HSTL. On the damage done to the cause of integration by cold warriors, see Horne, *Black and Red*, 201–21, 226–53.

88 The Bureau of Engraving and Printing continued to be a focal point for charges of discrimination throughout the 1950s. Burk, *The Eisenhower Administration and Black Civil Rights*, 71.

89 Council Meeting Summary, 8/11/49, RG 146, FPC Project Files, Box 42, C-440, Federal Personnel Policy Statement, Personnel Staffing Committee, NARA; *New York Times*, 5/20/48, 5/28/50; *New York Herald Tribune*, 3/17/52.

90 Bradbury, Racial Discrimination in the Federal Service, 133, 140. On the use of national security issues to promote and stall efforts on behalf of civil rights,

see Sherry, *In the Shadow of War*, 49–50, 100–2, 108–9, 147–49. For a general review of fair employment during the Eisenhower era, see Burk, *The Eisenhower Administration and Black Civil Rights*, 68–88.

91 The National Alliance of Postal Workers was a prominent exception to the civil rights void among federal service unions, though clearly its concerns were focused on the Post Office.

92 Burk, *The Eisenhower Administration and Black Civil Rights*, 71–74.

Conclusion

1 Census Bureau, *Historical Statistics of the United States*, 1102.

2 Ibid.; U.S. Civil Service Commission, *70th Annual Report*, June 30, 1953, reprinted in 83rd Cong., 2d sess., House Doc. no. 260, 78–79.

3 King, *Separate and Unequal*; Krislov, *The Negro in Federal Employment*; Hayes, *The Negro Federal Government Worker*. For an early-twentieth-century exposition of this viewpoint, see *Washington Bee*, 9/3/04, and for a mid-twentieth-century reiteration, see White to FDR, 9/12/41, General Office File: Civil Service—Statement by NAACP to President Franklin D. Roosevelt, 1941, and letter to NAACP, n.a., 1/20/42, General Office File: Civil Service, General, 1940–55, both in NAACP Papers, Group II, Box A194, LC Mss.

4 Van Riper, *History of the United States Civil Service*, 534–39, 545–49.

5 Ross, *The Origins of American Social Science*, 451.

6 *Congressional Quarterly Almanac*, vol. 6, *1950* (Washington, D.C.: Congressional Quarterly News Features, 1950), 134, 137.

7 "Reform" was dropped from the name of the league in 1945, although many continued to include this word in the title into the 1950s.

8 Heclo, *A Government of Strangers*, 72; Nevin and Nevin, *AFGE Federal Union*, 71, 75, 81–82; *Government Standard*, 7/17/59, copy in NCSRL, Acc. 7947, Box 318, Federal (Misc.) Newspaper Clippings, AHC.

9 See, for example, two bills introduced by Representative George M. Rhodes (D-Pa.): H.R. 6, 1/3/57 (85th Cong., 1st sess., copy in RG 233, House Committee on Post Office and Civil Service, 85th Congress Committee Papers, Box 3810, NARA) was similar to H.R. 10237, 3/27/56 (84th Cong., 2d sess., copy in RG 233, Box 2737). At least one bill was specifically modeled after the National Labor Relations Act. See Representative Thomas J. Lane's (D-Mass.) bill, H.R. 8889, 7/24/57 (85th Cong., 1st sess., RG 233, Box 3816).

10 Council Meeting Summary 2/26/53; Council Meeting Summary 3/12/53, both in RG 146, FPC Meetings, Box 7, NARA; "Civil Service Policy on Unions Examined," 7/2/56, NCSRL, Acc. 7947, Box 329, Unions, AHC. For background and a general overview of the content of the bills, see Civil Service Commission, "Union Management Relations in the Federal Service, Background Papers," June

1961, RG 60, Office of the Attorney General, Box 41, NARA. In September 1952, the Navy Department became the first department to give official recognition to employee unions. Several government entities, including the Tennessee Valley Authority, Bonneville Power Administration, and Inland Waterways had established collective bargaining rights for unions in the 1930s and 1940s, but these were generally agencies that paid their employees through wage boards. Nesbitt, *Labor Relations*, 295–314.

11 *Washington Post*, 5/25/56; Cabinet Meeting Minutes, 6/6/58, and Siciliano to Heads of Executive Departments and Agencies, 6/3/58, both in Cabinet Meetings, Ann Whitman Files (microfilm), Dwight D. Eisenhower Library; U.S. Civil Service Commission, "Minutes of Meeting of Commission Staff and Employee Organization Representatives," 9/16/58, Civil Service Commission Historical Collection, OPML.

12 In undertaking a study of the union issue, league officials excluded representatives from AFGE and NFFE because they were certain that they could not get "any original or clear thinking from either of them." Goode to Pincus, 7/6/59, Box 259, Organization of Committee; NCSL, "Employee Organizations in Government Report," 1960, Box 263; Goode to Gladieux, 9/30/59, Box 266, Employee Organizations Project Prospective, all in NCSRL, Acc. 7947, AHC.

13 *Civil Service Leader*, 9/26/61, copy in Box 260, League Study of Employee Organizations in Public Service, Background Papers; Watson, memorandum, 8/9/61, Box 259, Organization of Committee; Watson to Paul, 8/28/61, Box 273, Chron File for Aug. 1961, all in NCSRL, Acc. 7947, AHC; *Washington Star*, 7/14/61.

14 President's Task Force on Employee-Management Relations in the Federal Service, "A Policy for Employee-Management Cooperation in the Federal Service," 11/30/61, copy in Civil Service Commission Historical Collection, OPML.

15 Ibid. "Appropriate units" were to be determined by special arbitration panels whose members would be nominated by the secretary of labor. Levine and Hagburg, *Public Sector Labor Relations*, 15–22.

16 Levine and Hagburg, *Public Sector Labor Relations*, 20.

17 Council members even perceived their own style of deliberation in these terms. On the wall of the council office, staff members posted a statement comparing their meetings to those of the Quakers: "by a combination of free discussion and quiet thinking, [Quakers] try to develop a group willingness to accept unanimously what appears to be the balanced judgment of the majority or of the best-informed." Niles and Niles, "On the Wall of the Council of Personnel Administration," n.d., Papers of Raymond R. Zimmerman, Box 5, Civil Service Commission File, Council of Personnel Administration—II, HSTL.

18 Davenport, "The Human Element in Personnel Management," 9/23/42, Papers of Frederick Davenport, Writings, Speeches, D–E, Box 40, SUA.

19 Personnel Management Subcommittee on Employee Motivation, 1/7/47, Zimmerman Papers, C.S.C. file, CPA III, Box 5, HSTL.

20 Davenport was apparently successful in receiving funds for this research. Davenport to Dawson, 1/5/50; Dawson to Davenport, 1/9/50, both in OF 2 (1950), Box 11, HSTL. See also Mitchell et al. to Truman 6/7/48; Pace to Dawson, 7/14/48; Dawson to Mitchell, 7/22/48, all in OF 2 (July–Dec. 1948), Box 10, HSTL.

21 Jacoby, *Modern Manners*, 227–28.

22 Harry Levinson, "Emotional First Aid on the Job" (1957); Brassor, "Problem No. 2," n.d. (circa 1950s), both in Papers of Francis Brassor, Subject File—Human Relations, Box 8, HSTL.

23 Arthur L. Rautman, "Employee Morale," *Personnel Administration* 13 (Nov. 1953): 5.

24 Rautman, "Employee Morale," 4–5.

25 Rautman, "Employee Morale," 7.

26 Brassor, "Problem No. 2," n.d. (circa 1950s), Brassor Papers, Subject File: Human Relations, Box 8, HSTL.

27 Rautman, "Employee Morale," 6.

28 On rights-based liberalism and unions see, for instance, Lichtenstein, "Epilogue: Toward a New Century" in Lichtenstein and Harris, eds., *Industrial Democracy in America*, 277–78.

29 Baron, Dobbin, and Jennings, "War and Peace."

BIBLIOGRAPHY

The bibliography contains a list of primary manuscript collections and significant periodicals cited in the notes. In addition, it provides a list of scholarly works used as secondary sources. Full citations to individual articles from a wide variety of trade journals and other periodicals occur within the notes rather than among the other secondary literature in the bibliography because I consider them primary sources.

Manuscript Collections

American Heritage Center, Laramie, Wyoming: Papers of the National Civil Service Reform League, Acc. 7947; Papers of Samuel Ordway Jr., Acc. 5003.

Brookings Institution Archives, Washington, D.C: Papers on the Institute for Government Research.

Dwight D. Eisenhower Library, Abilene, Kansas: Ann Whitman Files (available on microfilm).

Franklin D. Roosevelt Library, Hyde Park, New York: President's Official Files; President's Personal Files; Papers of William McReynolds; Papers of President's Committee on Administrative Management; Papers of President's Committee on Civil Service Improvement.

George Meany Labor Archives, Silver Spring, Md: Papers of the National Federation of Federal Employees, and American Federation of Government Employees (on microfilm).

Harry S. Truman Library, Independence, Missouri: White House Official Files; White House President's Personal Files; White House Central File; Papers of Francis Brassor; Papers of India Edwards; Papers of Philleo Nash; Papers of Raymond R. Zimmerman.

Library of Congress Manuscript Division, Washington, D.C: Papers of Otto Beyer; Papers of the National Association for the Advancement of Colored People.

National Archives and Records Administration, Washington, D.C.: Record Group (RG) 146, Federal Civil Service Agencies; RG 16, Department of Agriculture, Office of Secretary; RG 25, National Labor Relations Board; RG 56, Department of Treasury, Office of Secretary; RG 86, Women's Bureau; RG 174, Department of Labor, Office of Secretary; RG 188, Office of Price Administration, Administration Management Offices; RG 228, Fair Employment Practices Committee; RG 233,

Legislative Records, House Committee on Civil Service; RG 280, Federal Mediation and Conciliation Service.
Office of Personnel Management Library, Washington, D.C: Civil Service Commission Historical Collection.
Syracuse University Archives, Syracuse, New York: Papers of Frederick Davenport.

Periodicals

Federal Employee. National Federation of Federal Employees.
Federal Record. United Federal Workers of America.
Government Standard. American Federation of Government Employees.
Personnel Administration. Society for Personnel Administration.
Public Personnel Review. Civil Service Assembly of the United States and Canada.
Public Personnel Studies. Bureau of Public Personnel Administration.

Oral Histories

Davenport, Frederick M. "Reminiscences of Frederick Davenport," Columbia Oral History Project, Columbia University, New York City.
Flemming, Arthur. Interview with author, Washington, D.C., June 19, 1995.
Gichner, Isabelle. Interview by Suzanne Helfand, Jewish Historical Society of Greater Washington Oral History Project, July 30, 1980. Transcript in Martin Luther King Library, Washington, D.C.
Lawlor, Mary. Interview with author, Washington, D.C., June 21, 1995.
McNamara, Martin. Interview with author, Washington, D.C., June 14, 1995.
Neal, Arline. Interview with author, Washington, D.C., July 18, 1991.
Norby, Marian. Telephone interview with author, June 5, 1995.
Staats, Elmer. Interview with author, Washington, D.C., June 13, 1995.
Warner, Kenneth. Telephone interview with author, May 22, 1995.

Scholarly Works

Abbott, Andrew. *The System of Professions: An Essay on the Division of Expert Labor*. Chicago: Chicago University Press, 1988.
Adler, Les K., and Thomas G. Paterson. "Red Fascism: The Merger of Nazi Germany and Soviet Russia in the American Image of Totalitarianism." *American Historical Review* 75 (April 1970): 1046–64.
Aiken, Hugh G. J. *Taylorism at Watertown Arsenal: Scientific Management in Action, 1908–1915*. Cambridge: Harvard University Press, 1960.
Alchon, Guy. *The Invisible Hand of Planning: Capitalism, Social Science, and the State in the 1920s*. Princeton: Princeton University Press, 1985.

————. "Mary Van Kleeck and Social-Economic Planning." *Journal of Policy History* 3, no. 1 (1991): 1–23.

Anderson, James. "Race, Meritocracy, and the American Academy during the Immediate Post–World War II Era." *History of Education Quarterly* 33 (summer 1993): 151–75.

Anderson, Karen. *Wartime Women: Sex Roles, Family Relations, and the Status of Women During World War Two.* Westport, Conn.: Greenwood Press, 1981.

Arnold, Peri. *Making the Managerial Presidency: Comprehensive Reorganization Planning, 1905–1980.* Princeton: Princeton University Press, 1986.

Aron, Cindy Sondik. *Ladies and Gentlemen of the Civil Service: Middle-Class Workers in Victorian America.* New York: Oxford University Press, 1987.

Baker, Paula. "The Domestication of Politics: Women and American Political Society, 1780–1920." *American Historical Review* 89 (June 1984): 620–45.

Baritz, Loren. *The Servants of Power: A History of the Use of Social Science in American Industry.* New York: Science Editions, 1960.

Barkan, Elazar. *The Retreat of Scientific Racism: Changing Concepts of Race in Britain and the United States between the World Wars.* Cambridge: Cambridge University Press, 1992.

Baron, Ava, ed. *Work Engendered: Toward a New History of American Labor.* Ithaca: Cornell University Press, 1991.

Baron, James N., Frank R. Dobbin, and P. Devereaux Jennings. "War and Peace: The Evolution of Modern Personnel Administration in U.S. Industry." *Journal of American Sociology* 92 (September 1986): 350–82.

Bederman, Gail. *Manliness and Civilization: A Cultural History of Gender and Race in the United States, 1880–1917.* Chicago: University of Chicago Press, 1995.

Bernstein, Carl. *Loyalties: A Son's Memoirs.* New York: Simon and Schuster, 1989.

Bernstein, Irving. *The Lean Years: A History of the American Worker, 1920–1933.* Boston: Houghton Mifflin, 1960.

Berry, Mary Frances, and John W. Blassingame. *Long Memory: The Black Experience in America.* New York: Oxford University Press, 1982.

Bérubé, Allan. *Coming Out under Fire: The History of Gay Men and Women in World War Two.* New York: Free Press, 1990.

Best, Gary Dean. *Pride, Prejudice, and Politics: Roosevelt versus Recovery, 1933–1938.* New York: Praeger, 1991.

Bontecou, Eleanor. *The Federal Loyalty-Security Program.* Ithaca: Cornell University Press, 1953.

Borchert, James. *Alley Life in Washington: Family, Community, Religion and Folklife in the City, 1850–1970.* Urbana: University of Illinois Press, 1980.

Bowles, Chester. *Promises to Keep: My Years in Public Life, 1941–1969.* New York: Harper and Row, 1971.

Bradbury, William Chapman, Jr. Racial Discrimination in the Federal Service: A Study in the Sociology of Administration. Ph.D. diss., Columbia University, 1952.

Brandes, Stuart D. *American Welfare Capitalism, 1880–1940*. Chicago: University of Chicago Press, 1976.

Brinkley, Alan. *The End of Reform: New Deal Liberalism in Recession and War*. New York: Random House, 1995.

Brinkley, David. *Washington Goes to War*. New York: Alfred A. Knopf, 1988.

Brown, JoAnne. *The Definition of a Profession: The Authority of Metaphor in the History of Intelligence Testing, 1890–1930*. Princeton: Princeton University Press, 1992.

Burk, Robert Frederick. *The Eisenhower Administration and Black Civil Rights*. Knoxville: University of Tennessee Press, 1984.

Campbell, D'Ann. *Women at War with America: Private Lives in a Patriotic Era*. Cambridge: Harvard University Press, 1984.

Census Bureau, Department of Commerce. *Historical Statistics of the United States: Colonial Times to 1970*. Part 2. Washington, D.C.: Government Printing Office, 1975.

Chafe, William. *The Paradox of Change: American Women in the Twentieth Century*. New York: Oxford University Press, 1991.

Chandler, Alfred D. *The Visible Hand: The Managerial Revolution in American Business*. Cambridge: Harvard University Press, 1977.

Chester, Sir Norman. *The English Administrative System, 1780–1870*. Oxford: Clarendon Press, 1981.

Clark, Harold Glen. An Occupational Study of Personnel Workers in Selected Agencies of the Federal Government. Ph.D. diss., George Washington University, 1942.

Cohen, Lizabeth. *Making a New Deal: Industrial Workers in Chicago, 1919–1939*. Cambridge: Cambridge University Press, 1990.

Complete Presidential Press Conferences of Franklin D. Roosevelt. Vol. 10: 1937. New York: DeCapo Press, 1972.

Critchlow, Donald. *The Brookings Institution, 1916–1952: Expertise and the Public Interest in a Democratic Society*. DeKalb: Northern Illinois University Press, 1985.

Dahlberg, Jane S. *The New York Bureau of Municipal Research: Pioneer in Government Administration*. New York: New York University Press, 1966.

Dalby, Michael, and Michael Werthman, eds. *Bureaucracy in Historical Perspective*. Glenview, Ill: Scott Foresman and Company, 1971.

Davies, Margery W. *A Woman's Place Is at the Typewriter: Office Work and Office Workers, 1870–1930*. Philadelphia: Temple University Press, 1982.

Davis, Kenneth C. *FDR: Into the Storm, 1937–1940. A History*. New York: Random House, 1993.

Diggens, John P. "Flirtation with Fascism: American Pragmatic Liberals and Mussolini's Italy." *American Historical Review* 71 (January 1966): 487–506.

Dodd, Lawrence C., and Richard L. Schott, *Congress and the Administrative State.* New York: John Wiley and Sons, 1979.

Douglass, Frederick. *Frederick Douglass: Selected Speeches and Writings.* Ed. Philip Foner. Abridged and adopted by Yuval Taylor. Chicago: Lawrence Hill Books, 1999.

Drury, James Westbrook. Separations of Federal Employees, 1937–1947. Ph.D. diss., Princeton University, 1948.

Dyer, Thomas. *Theodore Roosevelt and the Idea of Race.* Baton Rouge: Louisiana State University Press, 1980.

Edsforth, Ronald. *Class Conflict and Cultural Consensus: The Making of a Mass Consumer Society in Flint, Michigan.* New Brunswick: Rutgers University Press, 1987.

Edwards, Richard C. *Contested Terrain: The Transformation of the Workplace in the Twentieth Century.* New York: Basic Books, 1979.

Emerson, Ralph Waldo. "Aristocracy." In *The Complete Writings of Ralph Waldo Emerson: Containing All of His Inspiring Essays, Lectures, Poems, Addresses, Studies, Biographical Sketches and Miscellaneous Works.* Vol. 2. New York: William H. Wise and Company, 1929.

Faue, Elizabeth. *Community of Suffering and Struggle: Women, Men and the Labor Movement in Minneapolis, 1915–1945.* Chapel Hill: University of North Carolina Press, 1991.

Ferguson, Kathy E. *The Feminist Case against Bureaucracy.* Philadelphia: Temple University Press, 1984.

Fine, Lisa Michelle. *Souls of the Skyscraper: Female Clerical Workers in Chicago, 1870–1930.* Philadelphia: Temple University Press, 1990.

Fish, Carl Russell. *The Civil Service and Patronage.* New York: Longmans, Green and Company, 1905.

Fones-Wolf, Elizabeth. *Selling Free Enterprise: The Business Assault on Labor and Liberalism, 1945–1960.* Urbana: University of Illinois Press, 1994.

Fried, Richard. *Nightmare in Red: The McCarthy Era in Perspective.* New York: Oxford University Press, 1990.

Friedrich, Carl Joachim. "Introduction: The Problem and Its Setting." In *Problems in the American Public Service: Five Monographs on Specific Aspects of Personnel Administration.* Commission of Inquiry on Public Service Personnel Monographs 7 to 11. New York: McGraw Hill, 1935.

Furner, Mary O. *Advocacy and Objectivity: A Crisis in the Professionalization of American Social Science, 1865–1905.* Lexington: University Press of Kentucky, 1975.

Garfinkle, Herbert. *When Negroes March: The March on Washington Movement in the Organizational Politics for FEPC.* Glencoe, Ill.: Free Press, 1959.

Gatewood, Willard. *Aristocrats of Color: The Black Elite, 1880–1920.* Bloomington: Indiana University Press, 1990.

Gillespie, Richard. *Manufacturing Knowledge: A History of the Hawthorne Experiments*. Cambridge: Cambridge University Press, 1991.

Goodnow, Frank J. *Politics and Administration: A Study in Government*. New York: Macmillan, 1900.

Graebner, William. *The Age of Doubt: American Thought and Culture in the 1940s*. Boston: Twayne Publishers, 1991.

————. *The Engineering of Consent: Democracy and Authority in Twentieth-Century America*. Madison: University of Wisconsin Press, 1987.

Grant, Nancy L. *TVA and Black Americans: Planning for the Status Quo*. Philadelphia: Temple University Press, 1990.

Green, Constance McLaughlin. *The Secret City: A History of Race Relations in the Nation's Capital*. Princeton: Princeton University Press, 1967.

Greene, John Robert. "Frederick Morgan Davenport: Portrait of a Progressive." *Theodore Roosevelt Journal* 12 (spring–summer 1986): 12–21.

Greenwald, Maurine Weiner. *Women, War and Work: The Impact of World War I on Women Workers in the United States*. Westport, Conn.: Greenwood Press, 1980.

Haney, Craig, and Aida Hurtado. "The Jurisprudence of Race and Meritocracy: Standardized Testing and 'Race Neutral' Racism in the Workplace." *Law and Human Behavior* 18, no. 3 (1994): 223–48.

Harris, Howell John. *The Right to Manage: Industrial Relations Policies of American Business in the 1940s*. Madison: University of Wisconsin Press, 1982.

Hartmann, Susan. *The Homefront and Beyond: American Women in the 1940s*. Boston: Twayne Publishers, 1982.

Hayes, Laurence J. W. *The Negro Federal Government Worker: A Study of His Classification and Status in the District of Columbia, 1883–1938*. Howard University Studies in the Social Sciences, vol. 3, no. 1. Washington, D.C.: Howard University Graduate School, 1941.

Heclo, Hugh. *A Government of Strangers: Executive Politics in Washington*. Washington, D.C.: Brookings Institution, 1977.

Henry, Nicholas. "The Emergence of Public Administration as a Field of Study." In *A Centennial History of the American Administrative State*, ed. Ralph Clark Chandler. New York: Free Press, 1987.

Herman, Ellen. *The Romance of American Psychology: Political Culture in the Age of Experts*. Berkeley: University of California Press, 1995.

Herskovitz, Melville. *The Negro and the Intelligence Tests*. Putnam, Conn.: Patriot Publishing Company, 1927.

Higham, John. *Strangers in the Land: Patterns of American Nativism, 1860–1925*. 2nd ed. New Brunswick: Rutgers University Press, 1988.

Hobbs, Margaret. "Rethinking Antifeminism of the 1930s: Gender Crisis or Workplace Justice? A Response to Alice Kessler-Harris." *Gender and History* 5 (spring 1993): 4–15.

Honey, Michael. *Southern Labor and Black Civil Rights: Organizing Memphis Workers.* Urbana: University of Illinois Press, 1994.

Hoopes, Roy, ed. *Washington at War.* New York: Hawthorne Books, 1977.

The Hoover Commission Report on Organization of the Executive Branch of the Government. New York: McGraw Hill, 1949.

Horne, Gerald. *Black and Red: W. E. B. DuBois and the Afro-American Response to the Cold War.* Albany: State University of New York Press, 1986.

————. "Reversing Discrimination: The Case for Affirmative Action." *Political Affairs* 71 (February–March 1992): 7–14.

Humphreys, B. V. *Clerical Unions in the Civil Service.* Oxford: Blackwell and Mott, 1958.

Ingraham, Patricia W. *The Foundation of Merit: Public Service in American Democracy.* Baltimore: Johns Hopkins University Press, 1995.

Jacoby, Sanford M. *Employing Bureaucracy: Managers, Unions, and the Transformation of Work in American Industry, 1900–1945.* New York: Columbia University Press, 1985.

————. *Modern Manners: Welfare Capitalism since the New Deal.* Princeton: Princeton University Press, 1997.

————, ed. *Masters to Managers: Historical and Comparative Perspectives on American Employers.* New York: Columbia University Press, 1991.

Johnson, Eldon. "The Administrative Career of Dr. W. W. Stockberger." *Public Administration Review* 1 (autumn 1940): 50–64.

————. "General Unions in the Federal Civil Service." *Journal of Politics* 2 (February 1940): 23–56.

Kahn, Jonathan. *Budgeting Democracy: State Building and Citizenship in America, 1880–1928.* Ithaca: Cornell University Press, 1997.

Kammerer, Gladys M. *Impact of War on Federal Personnel Administration, 1939–1945.* Lexington: University of Kentucky Press, 1951.

Kanter, Rosabeth Moss. *Men and Women of the Corporation.* New York: Basic Books, 1977.

Kaufman, Herbert. *The Administrative Behavior of Federal Bureau Chiefs.* Washington, D.C.: Brookings Institution, 1981.

Kessler-Harris, Alice. "Gender and Ideology in Historical Reconstruction: A Case Study from the 1930s." *Gender and History* 1 (spring 1989): 31–49.

————. *Out to Work: A History of Wage-Earning Women in the United States.* Oxford: Oxford University Press, 1982.

————. "Reply to Hobbs." *Gender and History* 5 (spring 1993): 16–19.

King, Desmond. *Separate and Unequal: Black Americans and the U.S. Federal Government.* Oxford: Clarendon Press, 1995.

Kirby, John B. *Black Americans in the Roosevelt Era: Liberalism and Race.* Knoxville: University of Tennessee Press, 1980.

Klineberg, Otto. *Race Differences*. New York: Harper and Brothers, 1935.

Krislov, Samuel. *The Negro in Federal Employment: The Quest for Equal Opportunity*. Minneapolis: University of Minnesota Press, 1967.

Kwolek-Folland, Angel. *Engendering Business: Men and Women in the Corporate Office, 1870–1930*. Baltimore: Johns Hopkins University Press, 1994.

Ladd-Taylor, Molly. *Mother Work: Women, Child Welfare and the State*. Urbana: University of Illinois Press, 1994.

Latham, Earl. *The Communist Controversy in Washington: From the New Deal to McCarthy*. Cambridge: Harvard University Press, 1966.

Lee, Alfred McClung, and Norman Daymond Humphrey. *Race Riot*. New York: Dryden Press, 1943.

Lemann, Nicholas. *The Big Test: The Secret History of the American Meritocracy*. New York: Farrar, Straus and Giroux, 1999.

Lemons, J. Stanley. *The Woman Citizen: Social Feminism in the 1920s*. Urbana: University of Illinois Press, 1973.

Lescohier, Don D., and Elizabeth Brandeis, *History of Labour in the United States, 1896–1932: Working Conditions and Labor Legislation*. Vol. 3 of *History of Labour in the United States*, ed. John R. Commons. New York: Macmillan, 1935.

Leuchtenburg, William E. *Franklin D. Roosevelt and the New Deal, 1932–1940*. New York: Harper and Row, 1963.

Leupp, Francis E. *How to Prepare for a Civil Service Examination with Recent Questions and Answers*. New York: Hinds, Noble and Eldredge, 1898–99.

Levenstein, Harvey A. *Communism, Anticommunism, and the CIO*. Westport, Conn.: Greenwood Press, 1981.

Levine, Marvin, and Eugene G. Hagburg. *Public Sector Labor Relations*. St. Paul, Minn.: West Publishing Company, 1979.

Lichtenstein, Nelson, and Howell John Harris, eds. *Industrial Democracy in America: The Ambiguous Promise*. Cambridge: Cambridge University Press and Woodrow Wilson Center Press, 1993.

Lockwood, David. *The Blackcoated Worker: A Study in Class Consciousness*. London: George Allen and Unwin, 1958.

Lowie, Robert. *Are We Civilized? Human Culture in Perspective*. New York: Harcourt, Brace, 1927.

Lunbeck, Elizabeth. *The Psychiatric Persuasion: Knowledge, Gender and Power in Modern America*. Princeton: Princeton University Press, 1994.

Lynch, Edmund C. "Walter Dill Scott: Pioneer Industrial Psychologist." *Business History Review* 42 (summer 1968): 149–70.

Lynch, John R. *The Facts of Reconstruction*. William C. Harris, ed. Indianapolis: Bobbs-Merrill Company, 1970.

Lynn, Laurence E., Jr. *Managing the Public's Business: The Job of the Government Executive*. New York: Basic Books, 1981.

MacMahon, Arthur W., and John D. Millett. *Federal Administrators: A Biographical Approach to the Problem of Departmental Management.* New York: Columbia University Press, 1939.

Mansfield, Harvey C. "Reorganizing the Federal Executive Branch: The Limits of Institutionalization." *Law and Contemporary Problems* 35 (summer 1970): 461–95.

Mayers, Lewis. *The Federal Service: A Study of the System of Personnel Administration of the United States Government.* New York: D. Appleton and Company, 1922.

Mayo, Elton. *The Human Problems of an Industrial Civilization.* New York: Macmillan, 1933.

Meyerowitz, Jo Anne J. *Women Adrift: Independent Wage Earners in Chicago, 1880–1930.* Chicago: University of Chicago Press, 1988.

Milkis, Sidney. "The New Deal, Administrative Reform and the Transcendence of Partisan Politics." *Administration and Society* 18 (February 1987): 433–72.

———. *The President and the Parties: The Transformation of the American Party System since the New Deal.* New York: Oxford University Press, 1993.

Milkman, Ruth. *Gender at Work: The Dynamics of Job Segregation by Sex During World War II.* Urbana: University of Illinois Press, 1987.

Miller, Herbert, and Robert Ezra Park. *Old World Traits Transplanted.* New York: Harper and Brothers, 1921.

Miyazaki, Ichisada. *China's Examination Hell: The Civil Service Examinations of Imperial China.* Trans. Conrad Schirokauer. New York: Weatherhill, 1976.

Montgomery, David. *The Fall of the House of Labor: The Workplace, the State, and American Labor Activism, 1865–1925.* Cambridge: Cambridge University Press, 1987.

Mosher, Frederick C. *Democracy and the Public Service.* New York: Oxford University Press, 1968.

Mumby, Dennis K. *Communication and Power in Organizations: Discourse, Ideology and Domination.* Norwood, N.J.: Ablex Publishing Corporation, 1988.

Murphy, Karen Lin. Reconstructing the Nation: Race, Gender and Restoration, The Progressive Era. Ph.D. diss., University of Minnesota, 1996.

National Civil Service Reform League. *The Civil Service in Modern Government: A Study of the Merit System.* New York: National Civil Service Reform League, 1937.

Nelson, Daniel. *Managers and Workers: Origins of the New Factory System in the United States, 1880–1920.* Madison: University of Wisconsin Press, 1975.

Nesbitt, Murray. *Labor Relations in the Federal Government Service.* Washington, D.C.: Bureau of National Affairs, 1976.

Nevin, Jack, and Lorna Nevin. *AFGE Federal Union: The Story of the American Federation of Government Employees.* Washington, D.C.: AFGE, 1976.

Noble, David. *America by Design: Science, Technology, and the Rise of Corporate Capitalism.* Oxford: Oxford University Press, 1977.

O'Malley, L. S. S. *The Indian Civil Service, 1601–1930.* London: John Murray, 1931.

Park, Robert Ezra. *Collected Papers of Robert Ezra Park*. Vol. 1, *Race and Culture*. Ed. Everett C. Hughes. Glencoe, Ill.: Free Press, 1950.

―――. "The Nature of Race Relations." In *Race Relations and the Race Problem: A Definition and Analysis*, ed. Edgar T. Thompson, 3–45. Durham, N.C.: Duke University Press, 1939.

―――. "Race Psychology: Standpoint and Questionnaire, with Particular Reference to the Immigrant and the Negro," *American Journal of Sociology* 17 (May 1912): 725–75.

Persons, Stow. *Ethnic Studies at Chicago, 1905–45*. Urbana: University of Illinois Press, 1987.

President's Committee on Administrative Management. *Report of the Committee with Studies of Administrative Management in the Federal Government*. Washington, D.C.: Government Printing Office, 1937.

President's Committee on Civil Rights. *To Secure These Rights: The Report of the President's Committee on Civil Rights*. New York: Simon and Schuster, 1947.

Purcell, Edward A., Jr. *The Crisis of Democratic Theory: Scientific Naturalism and the Problem of Value*. Lexington: University of Kentucky, 1973.

Roethlisberger, Fritz J. *Management and Morale*. Cambridge: Harvard University Press, 1941.

Ross, Dorothy. "The Development of the Social Sciences." In *The Organization of Knowledge in Modern America, 1860–1920*, ed. Alexandra Oleson and John Voss. Baltimore: Johns Hopkins University Press, 1979.

―――. *The Origins of American Social Science*. Cambridge: Cambridge University Press, 1991.

Ruchames, Louis. *Race, Jobs and Politics: The Story of the FEPC*. New York: Columbia University Press, 1953.

Scharf, Lois. *To Work and to Wed: Female Employment, Feminism and the Great Depression*. Westport, Conn.: Greenwood Press, 1980.

Schinagl, Mary S. *History of Efficiency Ratings in the Federal Government*. New York: Bookman Associates, 1966.

Scott, Anne Firor. "One Woman's Experience of World War II." *Journal of American History* 77 (September 1990): 556–62.

Scott, Joan Wallach. *Gender and the Politics of History*. New York: Columbia University Press, 1988.

Sealander, Judith. *As Minority Becomes Majority: Federal Reaction to the Phenomenon of Women in the Work Force, 1920–1963*. Westport, Conn.: Greenwood Press, 1983.

Sherry, Michael. *In the Shadow of War: The United States since the 1930s*. New Haven: Yale University Press, 1995.

Silberman, Bernard S. *Cages of Reason: The Rise of the Rational State in France, Japan, the United States and Great Britain*. Chicago: University of Chicago Press, 1993.

Sitkoff, Harvard. *A New Deal for Blacks: The Emergence of Civil Rights as a National Issue,* vol. 1, *The Depression Decade.* New York: Oxford University Press, 1978.

Sitkoff, Harvard, ed. *Fifty Years Later: The New Deal Evaluated.* New York: McGraw Hill, 1985.

Skowronek, Stephen. *Building a New American State: The Expansion of Administrative Capacities, 1877–1920.* Cambridge: Cambridge University Press, 1982.

Smith, Jay M. *The Culture of Merit: Nobility, Royal Service and the Absolute Monarchy in France, 1600–1789.* Ann Arbor: University of Michigan Press, 1996.

Smith, Rogers. *Civic Ideals: Conflicting Visions of Citizenship in U.S. History.* New Haven: Yale University Press, 1997.

Spero, Sterling D. *Government as Employer.* New York: Remsen Press, 1948.

———. *The Labor Movement in a Government Industry: A Study of Employee Organization in the Postal Service.* New York: George H. Doran Company, 1924.

Stewart, Frank Mann. *The National Civil Service Reform League: History, Activities, and Problems.* Austin: University of Texas, 1929.

Stivers, Camilla. *Gender Images in Public Administration: Legitimacy and the Administrative State.* Newbury Park: Sage Publications, 1993.

Stockberger, Warner W. *Personnel Administration Development in the United States Department of Agriculture: The First Fifty Years.* Washington, D.C.: U.S. Department of Agriculture, Office of Personnel. October 1947.

Strom, Sharon Hartman. *Beyond the Typewriter: Gender, Class, and the Origins of Modern Office Work, 1900–1930.* Urbana: University of Illinois Press, 1992.

Sullivan, Patricia. *Days of Hope: Race and Democracy in the New Deal Era.* Chapel Hill: University of North Carolina Press, 1996.

Susman, Warren. *Culture as History: The Transformation of American Society in the Twentieth Century.* New York: Pantheon Books, 1984.

Sutherland, Gillian, in collaboration with Stephen Sharp. *Ability, Merit and Measurement: Mental Testing and English Education, 1880–1940.* Oxford: Clarendon Press, 1984.

Thomas, William I. "The Mind of Woman and Lower Races." *American Journal of Sociology* 12 (January 1907): 435–69.

Tichi, Cecelia. *Shifting Gears: Technology, Literature, Culture in Modernist America.* Chapel Hill: University of North Carolina Press, 1987.

Titlow, Richard. *Americans Import Merit: The Origins of the United States Civil Service and the Influence of the British Model.* Washington, D.C.: University Press of America, 1979.

Trachtenberg, Alan. *The Incorporation of America: Culture and Society in the Gilded Age.* New York: Hill and Wang, 1982.

Trotter, Joe William, Jr. *Black Milwaukee: The Making of an Industrial Proletariat, 1915–45.* Urbana: University of Illinois Press, 1985.

UFWA. *The History and Structure of the United Federal Workers of America CIO.* Washington, D.C.: UFWA, 1946.

Van Riper, Paul P. *History of the United States Civil Service.* Evanston, Ill.: Row, Peterson and Company, 1958.

Vaughan, Michalina. "The Grandes Écoles." In *Governing Elites: Studies in Training and Selection*, ed. Rupert Wilkinson. New York: Oxford University Press, 1969.

Wacker, Roland. *Race and Ethnicity in American Social Science, 1900–1950.* Ph.D. diss., University of Michigan, 1975.

Ware, Susan. *Beyond Suffrage: Women in the New Deal.* Cambridge: Harvard University Press, 1981.

Waring, Stephen P. *Taylorism Transformed: Scientific Management Theory since 1945.* Chapel Hill: University of North Carolina Press, 1991.

Weber, Max. *Economy and Society: An Outline of Interpretive Sociology.* 2 vols. Trans. Ephraim Fischoff, Hans Gerth, A. M. Henderson, et al. Ed. Guenther Roth and Claus Wittich. Berkeley: University of California Press, 1978.

———. *The Theory of Social and Economic Organization.* Trans. A. M. Henderson and Talcott Parsons. Ed. Talcott Parsons. New York: Free Press, 1947.

Weiner, Lynn Y. *From Working Girl to Working Mother: The Female Labor Force in the United States, 1820–1980.* Chapel Hill: University of North Carolina Press, 1985.

White, Leonard. *Trends in Public Administration.* New York: McGraw-Hill, 1933.

Wilson, Woodrow. "The Study of Administration." *Political Science Quarterly* 56 (December 1941): 481–506.

Witz, Anne, and Mike Savage, eds. *Gender and Bureaucracy.* Oxford: Blackwell Publishers–Sociological Review, 1992.

Women's Bureau, Department of Labor. *Employment of Women in the Federal Government, 1923–1939.* Bulletin no. 182. Washington, D.C.: Government Printing Office, 1941.

———. *Women in the Federal Service, 1923–1947, Part I: Trends in Employment.* Bulletin no. 230-I. Washington, D.C.: Government Printing Office, 1949.

———*Women in the Federal Service, Part II: Occupational Information.* Bulletin no. 230-II. Washington, D.C.: Government Printing Office, 1950.

Yinger, J. Milton. *Ethnicity: Source of Strength? Source of Conflict?* Albany: State University Press of New York, 1994.

Young, Michael. *The Rise of Meritocracy, 1877–2033: An Essay on Education and Equality.* 2nd ed. London: Thames and Hudson, 1961.

Zieger, Robert H. *American Workers, American Unions, 1920–1985.* Baltimore: Johns Hopkins University Press, 1986.

Ziskund, David. *One Thousand Strikes of Government Employees.* New York: Columbia University Press, 1940.

Zunz, Olivier. *Making America Corporate, 1870–1920.* Chicago: University of Chicago Press, 1990.

INDEX

Addams, Jane, 25, 26

Affirmative action, 12, 22

African Americans, 123–24; attitude toward merit, 15, 159, 165; and character investigations, 90; civil rights of, 55, 69–75, 100, 179–82, 184; civil service opportunities for, 1–4, 14–16, 37, 38, 41–44, 46, 69–70, 73–75, 97–99, 101–2, 157–60, 162, 169–70, 171, 176–77, 194–95, 206 (n. 62), 207 (n. 80); and fair employment policies, 101, 158–71, 173–83, 195, 221–22 (n. 98); and federal unions, 61–62, 97, 111; and housing, 99–100; and human relations, 94, 97–102; loyalty of, 180, 181; and merit (*see* Merit: and African Americans); perceived abilities of, 10–11, 27, 41–43, 48, 70–72, 162–63, 171–73, 186; postwar employment of, 176–83; promotions and, 46–47, 53, 123, 157–59, 235 (n.3); and race conservatives, 160–62, 182; and race liberals, 159, 160, 163, 165–67, 172–73, 182, 236 (n. 14); racial division of labor, 3, 13, 21, 27, 33, 43, 73, 74, 98–99, 153, 162–64, 168, 169, 171, 172, 179, 182, 183, 193; and "rule of three," 16, 42, 74; segregation of, 15–16, 41–43, 97–99, 100, 117, 162, 164–65, 176, 182, 183, 184; status of, in Progressive era, 25–26, 27; wartime employment of, 157–60, 163–76,

183, 194; and white women, 98–99, 157

Agriculture Adjustment Agency (AAA), 68

Agriculture Department, United States, ix, xi, 1, 2, 20, 113, 203 (n. 26); and federal labor-management committee, 128; female employees in, 38, 146, 147, 155; Graduate School, 52; human relations in, 80, 84–85; loyalty concerns in, 87; personnel administration in, 34, 113, 121, 209–10 (n. 35); and race, 20–21, 161, 162, 169–70, 178–79; unions in, 59, 60, 61, 105, 113, 124–25, 126

Alexander, John, 157–58, 159, 176

Alexander, Will, 70, 172, 174

Alger, Horatio, 10

American Council on Race Relations, 241 (n. 80)

American Federation of Government Employees (AFGE), 122, 128, 243 (n. 12); and African Americans, 61–62, 117; and collective bargaining, 130, 134; conservative leadership of, 59–63; criticism of federal labor policies, 135, 187; and efficiency rating reviews, 121; establishment of, 54, 209 (n. 22); and grievance procedures, 116, 134–135; Lodge 31, 61; Lodge 91 conflict with NRA, 56–59, 210 (n. 41); Lodge 421, 117, 122; militant lodges in, 60–61, 62, 111, 210 (n. 42);

American Federation of Government
  Employees (*continued*)
  opposition to economy measures,
  55, 56, 60; opposition to right to
  strike, 124; opposition to section 213,
  66; in State Department, 120; and
  subversives, 219 (n. 59), 241 (n. 85);
  supports open employee files, 122; in
  Treasury Department, 112
American Federation of Labor (AFL),
  39; and African Americans, 61–62,
  117, 123; and federal unions, 61, 110;
  NFFE split with, 54, 208–9 (n. 22)
American Management Association, 84
Anderson, James, 172, 173
Anderson, Marian, 175
Anderson, Mary, 40, 205 (n. 55)
Appleby, Paul, 105–6, 162, 209–10
  (n. 35)
Arlington Farms, 142, 143, 145. *See also*
  Women: housing for
Army, United States, 32
Aron, Cindy Sondik, 11, 28, 38
Assimilation, 6, 16, 17, 26, 71–72, 165,
  169, 213 (n. 83); and racial identity,
  70–71, 172, 239 (nn. 55, 56)

Babcock, E. Claude, 55; and Donovan
  case, 57, 59–60; and section 213, 65;
  supports open files, 122
Bailey, Dorothy, 95, 153–54, 180
Baker, Jacob, 109
Balaban, Adassa, 129
Ballinger, Edwin C., 84
Barnett, Robert, 115, 161
Barron, Margaret, 76–77
Baruch, Ismar, 92, 114
Beitscher, Henry, 129
Bell, Daniel W., 74
Bellamy, Edward, 25, 48
Berrum, Dorothy, 143–44

Bethune, Mary McCleod, 70, 88
Beyer, Otto, 106, 118, 126, 129–32
Bilbo, Theodore, 99
Birth of a Nation, 25, 43
Black cabinet, 69–70
Blackerby, E. Buckner, 129
Blacks. *See* African Americans
Boas, Franz, 236 (n. 21)
Bonneville Power Administration, 132,
  243 (n. 10)
Bowen, William, 120
Bowles, Chester, 170, 174
Bradbury, William, 160
Brassor, Francis, 191, 193
Brookings Institution. *See* Institute for
  Government Research (IGR)
Brown, Edgar, 70
Brown, JoAnne, 32, 42, 48
Brownlow, Louis, 83, 208 (n. 16), 216
  (n. 27)
Budget and Accounting Act (1921), 44
Budget, Bureau of, x, 74, 77, 126, 128,
  177, 187, 190
Bureaucracy, 4, 16, 17; characteristics
  of, 19–21, 28; construction of, 3; and
  culture, 12–14, 79; and patriarchy, 13,
  14, 63–69, 137, 155, 211 (n. 55). *See
  also* Civil service, United States
Burleson, Albert, 43
Burns, James, 128
Busbey, Fred, 89

Cain, Joseph, 36
Camp, Mae Wilson, 65
Campbell, James, 134
Carlson, Dick, 113
Carroll, Molly Ray, 121
Census Bureau, 41, 43, 123, 164, 212
  (n. 60), 232 (n. 19)
Chambers, Justice, 161, 163
Children's Bureau, 39, 40

China, 190, 200–201 (nn. 16, 18)

Civil Aeronautics Authority, 113

Civil servants: accountability of, 19, 106, 110, 111, 130, 136, 188; behavior of, 104; character investigations of, 90–92, 151; efficiency of, 31; employee programs for, 99, 138; loyalty of, 19, 86–94, 130, 151, 153, 179–81; morality of, 152; participation plans for, 132–34; recruitment of, 49–50, 144; rights of, 92, 106, 108, 110; sexual identity of, 151–52. *See also* African Americans; Civil service, United States; Men; Women

Civil service, United States: business principles in, 18–19, 24, 27–29, 35, 37, 82–83, 103, 106–7; class relations in, 18, 27, 35–36, 49–63, 117, 185, 186, 187; classification of positions in, 44–45, 140; classified, ix, 64, 106, 119, 126–27, 129, 132; collective bargaining in, 19, 61, 62–63, 105–6, 108–9, 110, 111, 125–36, 138, 183, 185, 187–90, 196, 243 (n. 10); definition of, ix–xi; departmental service, ix, 119 (*see also* Washington, D.C.); efficiency ratings in (*see* Personnel administration: efficiency ratings); exam system in, 8, 23, 30–31, 40, 169, 185, 186; expenditures cut in, 55; field service, ix, 119; functions of, 184; grievance procedures in (*see* Personnel administration: grievance procedures); influence of personnel practices by, 2–3, 195; merit system in (*see* Merit: system in civil service); numbers of employees in, 4, 184, 216 (n. 20); personnel policies of, 21, 34; professionals in, 19, 51; right to strike in, 19, 106, 108–10, 118, 138, 179, 225 (n. 44); "rule of three" in, 16, 34, 42, 74, 123; segregation in (*see* Jim Crow: in civil service); social justice mission of, 194; unclassified, ix; unions, 19, 22, 26, 53–63, 208 (n. 19) (*see also entries for specific unions*); veterans preference in, 12, 146, 188; wage boards in, 106, 108, 126, 243 (n. 10)

Civil Service Act. *See* Pendleton Civil Service Act (1883)

Civil Service Assembly of the United States and Canada, 47, 106, 131

Civil Service Commission (CSC), United States, x, 20, 24, 27, 57, 59, 77, 82, 114, 128, 147, 173; and character investigations, 90–93, 149; conciliation committee in, 113; discrimination against blacks in, 98, 165; duties of, 28, 34; and efficiency rating reviews, 119, 120, 121, 190; employees of, 33, 47, 95; and exams, 31; and federal labor relations, 107, 108, 115, 126, 130–32, 134, 187, 188, 225 (n. 44); and female civil servants, 143, 144–45; gender regulations of, 40, 147; and grievance procedures, 116, 118; and human relations, 191; and labor management committees, 81, 127–28; links to unions, 54; and loyalty issues, 87, 88–91, 149, 218 (n. 56); and position classification, 44–45, 232 (n. 15); proposal to abolish, 83; proposal to reorganize, 204 (n. 31); and race, 41, 73, 123, 161–62, 167, 168, 176, 177, 214 (n. 87); and recruitment of federal employees, 51; survey on employee file access, 122

Civilian Conservation Corps, 50, 70

Clapp, Gordon, 126

Classification Act (1923), 40, 44, 119

Cleveland, Frederick, 33, 35, 44

Cleveland, Grover, 15, 41

Cold War, 15; and defense expansion, 132; domestic conformity stressed during, 152; gender roles during, 155; and human relations, 102, 196; and loyalty concerns, 93–94; and racial equality, 183

Colored National Democratic League, 2

Columbia University, 27, 56

Commerce Department, United States, xi, 57, 70, 120

Committee for Economic Advancement of Messengers, 123

Committee on Administrative Management, 77, 208 (n. 16); and federal labor relations, 107–8, 223 (n. 7); views of, 82–83, 110

Committee on Civil Rights, 100

Committee on Civil Service Improvement, 51

Committee on the Classification of Personnel, 32

Communism: fears of, 86–87, 152–53, 183; and feminism, 151, 154; hostility toward, 22, 89, 102, 103–4, 135, 138, 176, 179–81, 184, 218 (n. 56), 218 (n. 59)

Communist Party, 89, 149, 182

Congress of Industrial Organizations (CIO): challenges race and sex discrimination, 185; creation of UFWA in, 59, 108; emergence of, 106; and feminism, 154; opposition to participation plans, 134; rejects CPA policies, 134; and UPWA, 130, 181. *See also* United Federal Workers of America (UFWA)

Congress, United States, ix, x, 28, 232 (n. 19); authority over civil service, 21, 34–35, 36, 54, 61, 86, 87, 104, 111, 115, 127, 129, 134, 184, 188; control of civil service salaries, 33, 35, 38, 40, 108, 130; cuts CPA appropriations, 129; and employee arbitration, 116, 119; and federal unions, 36–37, 54, 59, 60, 62, 105, 110, 135, 179, 180, 187; and patronage, 20, 107, 196; and racial equality, 163, 166, 168; and segregation, 43; southerners in, 83, 166, 168

Constitution, United States, 9, 66

Cook, Russell, 113

Cooke, Morris, 31

Coolidge, Calvin, 124

Couch, Virgil, 132

Council of Economic Advisers, x

Council of Personnel Administration (CPA): considers grievance procedures, 113–16, 135; considers participation plans, 128, 132–35; deliberation style of, 243 (n. 17); demise of, 191; and efficiency rating reviews, 119–22, 127; establishment of, 63; and human relations, 80–81, 83, 190; and labor relations, 112, 113, 120–22, 196; and race, 160–62, 163–67, 174, 175; supports removal of agencies from Washington, D.C., 232 (n. 19); training seminars for women by, 146; and union rights, 106, 124, 125–26, 127, 129–32, 187–88; women on, 95, 96

Coy, Wayne, 161

Croly, Herbert, 31

Crozier, William, 36

Cummings, Homer, 70

Curtis, William, 23

Customs Bureau, 123

Daniels, Josephus, 43

Darwin, Charles, 72

Darwinism, 25

Daughters of the American Revolution, 176

Davenport, Frederick, 45, 127, 134, 195, 196; background of, 77; and efficiency rating reviews, 119; and grievance procedures, 115; and human relations, 80, 83, 85, 102, 190–91; and NIPA, 51; and race, 165, 172, 175; and unions, 106, 112

Dawson, Donald, 147

Democratic National Committee (DNC), 147, 149, 155

Democratic Party, 5, 89; and African Americans, 75, 99; southerners in, 21, 73, 83

Dewson, Molly, 212 (n. 58)

Dies, Martin, 86–87, 90, 219 (n. 59). *See also* House Committee to Investigate Un-American Activities

Diversity. *See* African Americans; Pluralism; Women

Doherty, William, 128

Donaldson, Jesse, 128

Donovan, John: controversy over firing of, 56–60, 209 (nn. 31, 34), 210 (n. 37)

Douglass, Frederick, 10, 15

Drayton, Evelyn, 144

Durkheim, Emile, 78

Economy Act (1933), 55, 59, 60; section 213 of, 64–69

Economy and Efficiency Commission, 29, 33–34

Edson, Howard, 121

Edwards, India, 147, 155–56

Efficiency, Bureau of (Division of Efficiency), 31, 33, 34, 119, 204 (n. 31)

Efficiency ratings. *See under* Personnel administration

Eisenhower, Dwight D., 22, 183, 184, 187

Ellis, Frank, 114, 124

Ely, Richard, 30

Emerson, Ralph Waldo, 9–10

Engraving and Printing, Bureau of, 15, 39, 66, 180, 241 (n. 88)

Enlightenment, 7

Eugenics, 26, 32

Executive Order 7916 (1938), 51, 63, 111, 113, 126, 132

Executive Order 8802 (1941), 158–59, 167–68, 174, 181

Executive Order 9252 (1942), 121

Executive Order 9830 (1947), 132

Executive Order 9835 (1947), 87, 181

Executive Order 10988 (1962), 189

Fair Employment Board (FEB): abolition of, 183; establishment of, 177; operation of, 177–79, 241 (n. 81); race discrimination by member of, 99; views of discrimination, 173

Fair Employment Practices Committee (FEPC), 4, 99, 173, 185; operation of, 117, 167–168, 177, 178, 181–82, 214 (n. 87), 221 (n. 84)

Farm Credit Administration (FCA), 70, 85, 116, 147–48, 157

Farm Security Administration (FSA), 67, 70

Fascism, 66; fears of, 82–83, 86, 185; opposition to, 89, 102, 103, 152

Federal Bureau of Investigation (FBI), 88, 100, 218 (n. 56), 219 (n. 60)

Federal bureaucracy. *See* Bureaucracy; Civil service, United States; *and entries for specific departments*

Federal Communications Commission, 88

Federal Conciliation Service, 210 (n. 42)
Federal Council on Negro Affairs. *See* Black cabinet
Federal Deposit Insurance Agency (FDIC), x
Federal Emergency Relief Administration, 70
Federal Farm Loan Bureau, 157
Federal Home Loan Bank Board, 116
Federal Housing Administration, 2
Federal Loyalty-Security Program: and civil rights, 153, 179–81; establishment of, 87, 153
Federal Personnel Association, 122
Federal Personnel Council. *See* Council of Personnel Administration (CPA)
Federal Power Commission (FPC), 117, 122
Federal Security Agency (FSA), 88, 115, 117–18, 138, 170
Federal Service Personnel Relations Board, 108
Federal Trade Commission, 57, 170
Federal Works Agency, 161, 165, 174
Feldman, Herman, 46
Felix, Robert, 151
Feminism, 17, 234–35 (n. 54); opposition to, 151–54; trends in, 137; and women's right to work, 65, 66–67
Ferguson, Kathy E., 13
Fillo, Nicholas, 210 (n. 42)
Flaxer, Abram, 180, 181
Flemming, Arthur, 128; background of, 77–78; and female civil servants, 149–50, 234 (n. 41); and loyalty investigations, 89, 90, 92, 219 (n.62); and race, 170
Foreman, Clark, 6, 69
France: civil service in, 7–8, 9, 49, 208 (n. 16); postal workers in, 35, 204 (n. 40)

Franklin, Benjamin, 10
Fried, Richard, 86

Gainer, Edward, 55
Garfield, James, 23
Gender. *See* Men; Women
General Accounting Office, 60, 187
Germany, 152, 190, 208 (n. 16)
Gilded Age, 18, 31
Gilman, Charlotte Perkins, 25
Ginsberg, David, 88
Goddard, Henry H., 32
Godkin, E. L., 23
Goldberg, Arthur, 188
Gompers, Samuel, 224 (n. 26)
Good Government movement. *See* Merit: reform movement
Goodnow, Frederick, 27–28, 30, 35
Government Printing Office (GPO), 2, 16, 17, 39, 74
Government Standard, 59
Graebner, William, 78
Graves, Harold, 33
Great Britain, 10, 190; civil service in, 8, 20, 30–31, 49, 52, 208 (n. 16)
Great Depression: gender discrimination during, 53, 63–69, 137–38, 155; race discrimination during, 53, 69–75; rights during, 185; undermines faith in democracy, 50–51, 83
Green, William, 61, 110
Grievance procedures. *See under* Personnel administration
Griffith, D. W., 25
Guggenheim Foundation, 190

Hard, James, 180
Harding, Warren, 124
Hargrove, James, 158
Harris, Alphonzo, 213 (n. 74)
Harrison, Benjamin, 15

Hart, Scott, 52
Hastie, William, 70, 165, 174
Hatch Act, 87, 92, 118, 137
Hay, Edward, 158
Haywood, Allan, 128
Heffner, Bernice, 66
Henderson, Leon, 174, 175
Hendrickson, Roy: loyalty concerns of, 87; management views of, 84–85, 113, 114–15, 127; and unions, 120, 124–25, 126; views on women, 147
Herskovitz, Melville, 162
Hill, T. Arnold, 174–75
Hillman, Sidney, 167
Home Missionary Movement, 26
Homosexuals, 151–52, 184
Hoover Commission on Organization of the Executive Branch of the Government, 83–84, 132
Hoover, Herbert, 55, 64, 124
Houghteling, James T., 173
House Civil Service Committee, 126, 163
House Committee on Civil Service Reform, 43
House Committee to Investigate Un-American Activities: targets federal employees, 86–87, 88, 153, 218 (n. 56)
Houston, Charles, 73
Howard University, 75, 100
Howe, Louis, 65
Hubbard, Henry, 120, 163
Human relations, 17; attacks on, 153–54; background of, 78–80; counseling programs of, 138, 141; and democracy, 18, 82–86, 102, 103–4, 140, 190; and gender, 12, 13, 94–97, 103, 137–46, 148, 151, 153–55, 156, 191–93; and housing, 99–100, 141–42, 154; introduction of, into civil service, 69, 76–78, 80–81, 106, 138, 185; and

loyalty to state, 86–94; maternalism of, 96–97; participatory features of, 18, 132, 174; paternalism of, 78, 137–46, 154–56, 232 (n. 15); and perceived needs of men, 145; and pluralism, 197; in postwar era, 190–93, 195; and race, 12, 13, 94, 97–102, 103, 162–63, 169, 182, 193; and recreation associations, 99, 138, 141–42, 154; relationship of, to unions, 97, 114, 135, 190; and social sciences, 20, 69, 77, 78–80, 97–98, 142, 153, 195
Humphrey, Norman D., 162
Hunt, Harry, 70

Ickes, Harold, 6, 69, 70, 91
Iler, Henry, 62–63
Indian Civil Service (Great Britain), 8
Inland Waterways Corporation, 210 (n. 42), 243 (n. 10)
Institute for Government Research (IGR), 26, 29, 44, 47, 203 (n. 16), 204 (n.31)
Interdepartmental Committee on Investigations, 218 (n. 56)
Interior Department, United States, x, xi, 15, 70, 95, 96, 120, 132, 161, 166, 203 (n. 26)
Internal Revenue, Bureau of, 55, 124, 147
International Association of Machinists, 125
Interstate Commerce Act (1887), xi, 24
Interstate Commerce Commission (ICC), xi, 60, 113, 115

Jackson, Andrew, 184
Jacobsen, Walter, 158, 159, 160, 162
Japan, 152, 190
Jefferson, Thomas: and natural aristocracy, 9–10, 12, 49

Jim Crow, 41; in civil service, 15–16, 43–44, 97–99, 123, 165; in Washington, D.C., 42, 75, 99–100, 239 (n. 55). *See also* African Americans: segregation of

Johnson, Hugh, 56–59, 210 (n. 37)

Joint Congressional Commission on Reclassification, 39

Jones, Eugene Kindle, 70

Justice Department, United States, ix, 68

Kaplan, Henry, 130

Kennedy, John F., 188, 189

Kerlin, Malcolm, 33

King, Desmond, 16, 184

Kirby, John, 70

Klineberg, Otto, 162, 236 (n. 21)

Korean War, 187

Krislov, Samuel, 41

Labor Department, United States, ix, xi, 30, 180, 188, 205 (n. 55), 219 (n. 60); and collective bargaining rights, 132; conciliation committee in, 113, 114, 116; efficiency rating reviews in, 122; and employee recruitment, 52; unions in, 60, 97, 112, 113, 117, 126, 153

Labor relations, federal, 3; at agency level, 110–25, 196; compared to private sector, 4–5, 55, 59–63, 105–10, 116, 125–26, 130, 132, 135, 136, 140–42, 183, 188–89, 195–96; and gender, 137–38, 151–52; during New Deal, 53–63; prior to New Deal, 34–37, 54; paternalism in, 58, 107; policy, 105–6, 107–110, 125–36, 186–87, 229 (n. 97); and scientific management, 26–27. *See also* Personnel administration; *entries for specific agencies; entries for specific unions*

LaFollette, Robert, 105, 106

LaGuardia, Fiorello, 167

LaSalle Extension University, 123

Lathrop, Julia, 39, 40

League of Women Voters, 45, 66, 212 (n. 60)

Lee, Alfred McClung, 162

Leffingwell, Russell, 49

Leighton, Alexander, 93, 190

Leiserson, William, 126, 128, 129

Lewis, Denny, 60

Lewis, John, 60

Liberalism, 88, 140, 185; rights-based, 177, 193, 194–95, 196. *See also* New Deal: liberalism

Library of Congress, 128, 217 (n. 41)

Lloyd-LaFollette Act (1912), 36, 54, 225 (n. 44)

Lowie, Robert, 162

Loyalty. *See* Civil servants: loyalty of; Federal Loyalty-Security Program

Luke, Nancy, 56–57, 67–68

Lynch, John, 15

McAdoo, William, 43

Macaulay, Lord Thomas, 8

McBride, Isaac, 166

McCarran, Pat, 181

McCarthy, Joseph, 152

McCartney (doctor), 81

McCarty, Helen, 66

MacLeish, Archibald, 128

McNally, Gertrude, 39, 62, 66, 128

McNamara, Thomas, 52

McReynolds, William, 33, 56, 129, 167, 225 (n. 44)

Madurga, Henry, 91

March, Caso, 117

Maritime Commission, 161

"Married person's clause." *See* Economy Act (1933): section 213; Women: and section 213

Matasoff, Louis, 105
Matthews, Annabel, 99
Maulding, Julia Atwood, 95, 96, 120, 166
Mayo, Elton, 78–80, 93, 103, 191, 215 (n. 9)
Men: and bureaucracy, 13; in civil service, 14, 17, 24, 26; perceived needs of, 145; perceived traits of, 10, 16, 139, 145, 150, 151–52
Meriam, Lewis, 44, 204 (n. 31)
Merit, 6; and African Americans, 10–11, 38, 42–43, 73–75, 99, 156, 159–61, 163, 164–66, 169, 171–73, 177, 178, 181–83, 185–86, 193–94, 237 (n. 33); among American businessmen, 10; in China, 200–201 (n. 16), 201 (n. 18); conflicts with closed shop, 107, 131; in France, 7; historical definition of, 6–13, 30, 200–201 (n. 16); reform movement, 6, 12, 23–27, 37, 73, 185; system in civil service, 2, 6, 12, 20, 21, 23–24, 50–53, 116, 123–24, 159, 184, 193–95, 196; and women, 10–11, 38, 46, 66–68, 75, 148, 185–86, 194
Meritocracy: in federal bureaucracy, 4, 185; and gender, 66, 67; introduction of term, 6; and race, 73, 160
Metropolitan Life Insurance Company, 32
Milkman, Ruth, 146
Miller, Helen, 51–52, 53, 153, 154
Miller, Kelly, 74
Mines, Bureau of, 65
Mint, Bureau of, 112
Mitchell, Harry, 51, 108, 126
Moffett, Guy, 177–78
Morgenthau, Henry, 49, 73
Moynihan, Daniel Patrick, 188
Mugwumps, 23, 30. *See also* Merit: reform movement

Municipal Research, Bureau of, 24, 29, 47

National Alliance of Postal Employees, 62, 123, 180, 242 (n. 91)
National Archives, 166
National Association for the Advancement of Colored People (NAACP), 62, 161, 180, 241 (n. 81); supports merit system, 73, 123
National Association of Letter Carriers (NALC), 55, 62, 128; opposition to participation plans, 133–34
National Association of Women Lawyers, 66
National Civil Service League. *See* National Civil Service Reform League
National Civil Service Reform League (NCSRL), 24, 54, 204 (n. 10), 206 (n.62); promotion of merit system, 47, 49, 131, 187; and unions, 26, 36–37, 106, 126, 130, 135, 188–89
National Employees and Tenants Union (NETU), 123
National Federation of Federal Employees (NFFE), 128, 132, 243 (n. 12); and African Americans, 61, 117; break with AFL, 54, 208–9 (n. 22); and efficiency rating reviews, 121; establishment of, 35, 39; and federal employee rights, 54, 61, 62–63, 108–9, 124, 135, 136, 241 (n. 85); and grievance boards, 116; opposition to Economy Act, 55; opposition to section 213, 66; in State Department, 120; view of scientific administration, 45
National Industrial Recovery Act (1933): section 7 (a) of, 54, 55, 57, 59
National Institute of Mental Health, 151

National Institute of Public Affairs (NIPA), 5, 51, 53, 172, 203 (n. 16)

National Labor Board (NLB), 57–58, 209 (n. 34). *See also* National Labor Relations Board

National Labor Relations Act (1935): and federal labor unions, 4, 54, 61, 63, 106, 130, 242 (n. 9); passage of, 107

National Labor Relations Board (NLRB), x, 108, 126, 130, 218 (n. 56); relationship to federal employees, 58, 60, 106, 209 (n. 34), 210 (n. 37). *See also* National Labor Board

National League of Government Employment, 36

National League of Women Voters, 45, 66, 212 (n. 60)

National Negro Council, 70

National Recovery Administration (NRA), 55, 56–59, 88, 210 (n. 41)

National Research Council, 32

National Rural Letter Carriers Association, 62

National Security Council, x

National Urban League, 177

National Women's Party, 65

National Youth Administration, 70, 88, 167

Navy Department, 52, 162; labor relations in, 36, 108, 112, 125–26; loyalty of employees in 87; segregation in, 44, 165; unions in, 35, 243 (n. 10)

Nazis, 88, 219 (n. 59)

Neal, Arline, 102, 158, 159, 235 (n. 3)

Nelson, Daniel, 140

Nelson, Eleanor, 128

New Deal, x, 5, 19, 22, 108, 186; and African Americans, 70–71, 72, 159, 169; anticommunism under, 86; attacks on, 88, 178; expansion of federal bureaucracy under, 65; federal

employees under, 50, 77–78, 210 (n. 42); and liberalism, 4, 21, 69, 75, 165, 184; policy toward federal unions under, 53–63, 105, 126, 135; principles of, 119; and women, 137

New Freedom, 43

New Left, 195

Newport Torpedo Station, 125

Nicol, Eric, 127, 129

Northwestern University, 123

Office of Education, 190

Office of Price Administration (OPA), x, 144, 150, 166; African American employees of, 97, 99, 102, 160, 170, 175; attacks on, 168; loyalty of employees in, 88, 180; personnel administration in, 77, 103, 145, 155; race discrimination in, 122, 157–60, 162, 171, 173, 176; race related policies of, 99–102, 167, 174–75; unions in, 97, 125, 128–29; women employed by, 138–39

Office of Production Management (OPM), 69, 168, 174

Oklahoma City, 4

100 percent Americanism, 25–26

Onthank, Heath, 56, 165

Ordnance Department, 31

Ordway, Samuel, Jr., 82, 85, 98, 115, 126, 165

Pallister, Helen, 95

Palmer, Clive

Park, Robert, 71–72, 78, 164, 213 (n. 83)

Parmelee, Maurice, 91–92

Patriarchy. *See* Bureaucracy: and patriarchy

Patronage, 6, 11, 12, 19, 67; academic, 74, 186; advent of, 184; and labor relations, 107, 136; under New Deal,

50; opposition to, 23, 45, 54; and race, 73, 74; role of politics and, 89; shift from, 20, 196

Pearl Harbor, 127

Peck, Gustav, 57, 58, 209 (n. 31)

Pendleton Civil Service Act (1883), ix, 8, 11, 20, 39, 47; and African American federal employment, 41, 159; operation of, 28, 30–31; passage and provisions of, 23–24, 211 (n. 55)

Perkins, Frances, 90–91, 92, 114, 210 (n. 37), 219 (n. 62)

Personnel administration: desire for harmony in, 103; efficiency ratings, 12, 15, 114, 119–22, 125, 142, 171, 174, 186, 190–91, 225 (n. 45); and flow of information, 121–22; and gender, 94–97, 103, 138–41, 205 (n. 55), 220 (n. 76); grievance procedures, 106–7, 110, 113–19, 121, 122, 125, 134, 168, 175; maternalism of, 96–97, 231 (n. 10); participatory plans, 132–134; paternalism in, 18, 107, 111, 115, 136, 145, 154; "psychological paternalism" (*see* Human relations: and "psychological paternalism"); and psychology, 3, 12, 32, 68, 137, 138, 142, 144, 147, 151, 152, 155; and race, 97, 100–101, 103, 166–67, 169, 170–76, 178–79, 182; role in federal agencies, 84–85; and "school for scandal," 152; and sociology, 3, 68, 100, 142, 147, 169; specialists in public, 17–19, 21–22, 26, 29, 31–34, 44–48, 63, 80–81; and unions, 104, 106–7, 110, 111, 115–16, 117, 124–25. *See also* Human relations; *entries for specific agencies*

Phalanx Club, 123

Piozet, Charles, 52, 112, 117, 120–121, 162, 163, 165, 208 (n. 15)

Pluralism: in America, 185; in civil service, 11, 12, 16–18, 21–22, 75, 184, 196–97; and cultural hierarchy, 72, 172; discrimination and, 2; efforts to control, 84, 85, 104; in labor relations, 102–103, 110; and New Deal, 5–6, 75. *See also* African Americans; Women

Post Office, United States, ix, 5, 128, 203 (n. 26); employees in, 5; personnel practices in, 34, 114, 179; racial discrimination in, 73; unions in, 35, 36, 54, 112–13, 124, 180

President's Committee on Administrative Management. *See* Committee on Administrative Management

President's Committee on Government Employment Policy, 183

Progressive Era, 17, 18, 49; gender and race in the, 24–26, 48, 63; influence on management practices, 77, 78–80, 85; and state expansion, 184

Progressive Party, 55

Psychology. *See* Human relations; Personnel administration: and psychology

Psychometrics, 32–33, 42, 185, 215 (n. 10)

Public Administration: early conceptions of, 27–34; and gender, 24, 37–38; and loyalty to state, 86; in 1930s and 1940s, 77–78, 82–84; support for merit system, 131, 186. *See also* Personnel administration

Public Servants. *See* Civil servants

Public Service. *See* Civil service, United States

Race. *See* African Americans

Railroad Retirement Board (RRB), 52, 91–92, 120

Railway Mail Association, 62

Ramspeck Act (1940), 119
Ramspeck, Robert, 126, 127, 163, 236–37 (n. 22)
Randolph, A. Philip, 73, 123, 167
Rautman, Arthur, 191, 192, 193
Red Cross, 180
Red Scare. *See* Communism: hostility toward
Reed, Stanley, 51
Reid, T. Roy, 161, 236 (n. 16)
Reilly, Gerard, 130, 131, 223 (n. 11), 229 (n. 90)
Republican National Committee, 187
Republican Party, 15, 89, 178; criticism of Franklin D. Roosevelt, 124; members of, 78
Resettlement Administration, 60, 105
Rhine, Henry, 56, 57
Rockefeller Foundation, 29, 51, 203 (n. 16)
Roethlisberger, Fritz J., 80, 93
Roosevelt, Eleanor, 6, 70–71, 144
Roosevelt, Franklin Delano, x, 2, 5, 19, 21, 212 (n. 58); brain trust and, 49; and Committee on Administrative Management, 77, 107–8; and communism, 218 (n. 56); federal labor relations policy of, 59, 63, 107–10, 113, 125, 126, 132, 223 (nn. 12, 13); and race, 69, 73, 75, 123, 124, 158, 161, 163, 167–68, 181, 213–14 (n. 85); recruitment of civil servants, 49–51; reorganization efforts of, 110, 217 (n. 34); support for balanced budget, 55; supports closed employee files, 122
Roosevelt, Theodore, 15, 31, 36; African American appointments by, 41–42; and federal labor relations, 35; and New Nationalism, 18, 19; racial views of, 25, 26, 42

Rose, Durant, 158
Ross, Dorothy, 72
Ruskin, Gertrude Magill, 149–50

Sarré, A. J., 161–62
Sayre, Wallace, 77, 103
Schurz, Carl, 23
Scientific management, 1, 17, 18, 79, 222–23 (n. 5); and gender, 94–95; introduction into civil service, 27–36, 68–69; among merit reformers, 24, 26–27, 36–38, 44–47. *See also* Personnel administration
Scientific racism, 17; in Progressive era, 25–26, 27, 42, 185–86; refutation of, 71–72, 162–63, 193; and social sciences, 71–72, 169, 236 (n. 21)
Scott, Hazel, 176
Scott, Walter Dill, 32, 33, 78, 79
Sears, Roebuck and Company, 180
Section 213. *See* Economy Act: section 213; Women: and section 213
Securities and Exchange Commission, x
Segregation. *See* African Americans: segregation of; Jim Crow
Selective Service, 139
Shea, Catherine, 84
Sherman Anti-trust Act (1890), 24
Shoemaker, Richard, 134
Short, Oliver, 120
Siciliano, Rocco, 188
Smith Committee, 168
Smith, Jay M., 7
Smith, Robert, 112, 113, 122
Smithsonian, 171
Social Gospel, 78, 165
Social Science Research Council, 49
Social Security Board, 88, 98, 161
Socialism, 138, 151, 154
Society for Personnel Management, 153, 154

Society for the Advancement of
    Management, 153, 154
Sociology. *See* Human relations:
    and social sciences; Personnel
    administration: and sociology
Soil Conservation Service, 67
Somers, Lee, 61, 62
Soviet Union, 89, 102, 152
Spanish Civil War, 124
Spoils system. *See* Patronage
Staats, Elmer, 77–78
Stabler, Margaret, 58
State Department, United States,
    ix, 113, 152; African American
    employment in, 41–42; human
    relations in, 84; unions in 120
Stengle, Charles, 60
Steward, Luther, 128; and government
    labor policy, 108–9; opposition to
    Economy Act, 55; opposition to union
    militancy 62; priorities of, 54
Stivers, Camilla, 37
Stockberger, Warner W., 1, 4, 5, 11, 18,
    20
Strom, Sharon, 66, 96
Strong, Clarence, 117
Students for a Democratic Society, 195
Sullivan, Patricia, 70
Supreme Court, United States, 68, 153
Susman, Warren, 30
Sweet, George Henderson, 162, 163, 164
Switzer, John, 113–16

Taft Commission, 29, 33–34
Taft, William Howard, 29; and federal
    labor relations, 35, 36; and race, 42,
    43, 124. *See also* Taft Commission
Taft-Hartley Act (1947), 179
Taylor, Frederick, 79, 94
Taylor, Molly Ladd, 96
Taylor Society, 31, 47

Taylorism. *See* Scientific management
Tead, Ordway, 81, 93
Tennessee Valley Authority (TVA), ix,
    x, 130; discrimination of blacks by,
    98, 170, 214 (n. 87), 239 (n. 59);
    unions in, 62–63, 126, 223 (n. 13),
    229 (n. 90), 243 (n. 10)
Tepping, Morris, 88
Thomas, William, 72
Thorndike, Edward L., 32
Thurman, Lewis, 32
Thurstone, L. L., 32
Tichi, Cecelia, 48
Treasury Department, United States,
    ix, 2, 15, 203 (n. 26), 213 (n. 74);
    discrimination against African
    Americans in, 73, 170, 174, 180;
    discrimination against women in, 64;
    labor relations in, 112, 113, 124
Trent, William, 165, 174
Truman, Harry S.: and civil rights, 100;
    federal labor relations policies of, 131,
    132; and FEPC, 177; loyalty program
    of, 179–80, 181
Tugwell, Rexford, 6

Unions. *See* Civil service, United States:
    unions; Labor relations, federal;
    entries for specific unions
United Federal Workers of America
    (UFWA), 2, 56, 130; and African
    Americans, 61–62, 97, 100, 111, 117,
    123, 158, 160, 174, 175–76, 182; in
    Agriculture Department, 105; attacks
    on, 86–87, 112, 152–53; collective
    bargaining supported by, 61, 62–63,
    126, 129, 130, 134, 135, 136; criticizes
    employee investigations, 92; and
    efficiency ratings, 119; establishment
    of, 59, 60–61, 108; and federal labor
    policy, 109, 223 (n. 12); and labor

United Federal Workers of America
(*continued*)
management advisory committee,
127–28; Local 1, 97; Local 12, 51,
153; Local 203, 97, 128–29, 134, 158;
and loyalty program, 88, 89–90, 241
(n. 85); militancy of, 111; negotiations
with OPA, 128–29; recruiting practices
of, 124; in State Department, 120;
supports open employee files, 122;
and "victory committees," 81, 128;
and women, 68, 146, 153; Working
Mothers' Clubs of, 146
United Government Employees Union,
70, 123
United Public Workers of America
(UPWA), 153; attacks on, 179–81;
and right to strike, 92, 130–31, 179;
supports fair employment, 177, 179,
181; supports Soviet Union, 92, 131.
See also United Federal Workers of
America (UFWA)
United States Employment Service
(USES), 153, 176
United States Housing Authority, 69,
113
United States Rubber Company, 32
University of Chicago, 71, 78
Urban League, 177

Van Kleeck, Mary, 31, 40, 205 (n. 55)
Van Riper, Paul, 184
Vann, Robert, 70
Veterans Administration, 98–99, 162,
164
Veterans Preference Act (1944), 146

Wagner Act. *See* National Labor
Relations Act (1935)
Wagner, Robert, 107
Walker, Irene, 68

Wallace, Henry, 61, 169
War Department, 70, 165, 174; labor
relations in, 36; loyalty of employees
in, 87; unions in, 35
War Finance Corporation, 46
War Production Board (WPB), xi, 88,
127
Ware, Susan, 137
Waring, Stephen, 17
Warner, Kenneth: management
philosophy of, 77–78, 190; and race,
166, 167, 173; and union rights,
128–29
Washington Bee, 41
Washington, Booker T., 41, 71
Washington, D.C., 23, 43, 65, 168, 178;
African American civil servants in,
14, 16, 41, 44, 123, 160, 166, 206
(n. 62); African American housing in,
99–100; civil rights demonstrations
in, 75; civil service establishment in,
ix; employees of, 64; federal agencies
removed from, 157, 232 (n. 19);
federal employees in, 35, 54, 56,
81; federal unions, 59; female civil
servants in, 39, 138, 142–45; housing
shortage in, 142; night schools in,
52; planned march on, 73, 167;
segregation in, 42, 75, 99–100, 239
(n. 55)
Washington Evening Star, 131, 144
Washington, Forrester B., 70
Washington, George, 9
Washington Post, 52
Weaver, Robert, 6, 69, 172, 174
Weber, Max, 13, 19–20, 21, 136
Welfare capitalism, 17, 84, 141, 142
Western Electric, 78
White, Leonard, 33
White, Walter, 161
Whitley Councils, 116, 127

Whitten Amendment (1950), 187
Wicketts, Andrew, 123–24, 165
Wilkins, Roy, 123
Williams, Aubrey, 167
Willis, Charles, 187
Willoughby, William F., 30
Wilson, Earl, 143
Wilson, James, 34
Wilson, Theodore, 116
Wilson, Woodrow, 16, 49; administrative
  essay, 27; and race discrimination, 43,
  73
Winchester Repeating Arms Company,
  32
Wolman, Leo, 209 (n. 31)
Women: and child care, 81, 145–46, 233
  (n. 30); civil service opportunities for,
  1–4, 14, 37–40, 138–40, 146–47, 154,
  184, 194–96, 205 (n. 50); civil service
  salaries of, 38, 40, 146; counseling for,
  138–39, 140, 141; discrimination of,
  during Great Depression, 53, 63–69;
  housing for, 81, 99, 140, 141, 142;
  and human relations (*see* Human
  relations: and gender); and loyalty,
  154, 155; and merit (*see* Merit:
  and women); morality of, 142–45;
  orientation programs for, 138, 139;
  perceived abilities of, 10–11, 16, 27,
  45–46, 48, 72, 137–48, 186; perceived
  needs of, 140–41, 142, 143; perceived
  traits of, 138, 139, 147–50, 152,
  154–55, 184–85; and promotions,
  39, 53, 148, 150–51, 153, 155, 194,
  196, 234–35 (n. 54); and section
  213, 64–67, 137, 211–12 (n. 57), 212
  (nn. 58, 60); and sexual division of

labor, 3, 13, 17, 21, 27, 33, 45,
  137, 139, 140, 146–47, 151, 155,
  156, 183, 193, 231 (n. 8); social
  lives of, 143, 153; status in the
  Progressive era, 24–25, 63; support
  for scientific administration, 45; and
  unions, 55, 138, 152–53; wartime
  employment of, 137–51, 155, 184,
  194
Women's Bureau, 40; studies of female
  civil servants, 45, 53, 65
Works Progress Administration (WPA),
  50, 60, 108
World War I, 26, 31, 66, 95; federal
  employment during, 43; labor
  shortage during, 39, 40
World War II, x, 3, 4, 22, 95; African
  American employment during,
  157–60, 163–76, 183, 194; federal
  labor relations during, 110, 127–30;
  feminism during, 151; government
  personnel practices during, 76–78,
  80–94, 96, 141, 169–72; labor shortage
  during, 53, 138, 140, 145–46, 155,
  171, 172, 185; state expansion during,
  184; unity during, 172; women's
  employment during, 137–51, 155,
  184, 194

Yardley, Edward, 113, 120
Yerkes, Robert, 32, 33
Yinger, J. Milton, 16
Young, Michael, 6
Young, Phillip, 188
Youngman, Emma, 68–69

Zimmerman, Raymond, 76, 77, 131